Open access edition supported by the National Endowment for the Humanities /
Andrew W. Mellon Foundation Humanities Open Book Program.

© 2019 Johns Hopkins University Press
Published 2019

Johns Hopkins University Press
2715 North Charles Street
Baltimore, Maryland 21218-4363
www.press.jhu.edu

The text of this book is licensed under a Creative Commons
Attribution-NonCommercial-NoDerivatives 4.0 International License:
https://creativecommons.org/licenses/by-nc-nd/4.0/.
CC BY-NC-ND

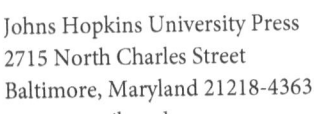

ISBN-13: 978-1-4214-2993-9 (open access)
ISBN-10: 1-4214-2993-4 (open access)

ISBN-13: 978-1-4214-3033-1 (pbk. : alk. paper)
ISBN-10: 1-4214-3033-9 (pbk. : alk. paper)

ISBN-13: 978-1-4214-3075-1 (electronic)
ISBN-10: 1-4214-3075-4 (electronic)

This page supersedes the copyright page included in the original publication of this work.

FLORENCE IN TRANSITION
VOLUME TWO
STUDIES IN THE RISE OF THE TERRITORIAL STATE

FLORENCE IN TRANSITION

VOLUME TWO
STUDIES IN THE RISE OF THE TERRITORIAL STATE

MARVIN B. BECKER

THE JOHNS HOPKINS PRESS, BALTIMORE

Copyright © 1968 by The Johns Hopkins Press, Baltimore, Md. 21218
All rights reserved
Manufactured in the United States of America
Library of Congress Catalog Card Number 66–28027

Again to Betty

ACKNOWLEDGMENTS

Dottore Guido Pampaloni, of the Archivio di Stato in Florence, has been a friend and guide to the wondrous riches of the archives. Without his generous assistance important runs of documents would have gone unnoticed. Miss Marianna Hassol, my editor at The Johns Hopkins Press, has been more helpful with her *buon senso* than any sequence of documents. Much gratitude for her good counsel. Last, thanks to my friend Jack P. Greene who made our stay at The Johns Hopkins University so pleasurable while this book was being written.

Marvin B. Becker

University of Rochester

CONTENTS

INTRODUCTION
3

I.
FLORENTINE POLIS AND CULTURE AT THE ADVENT
OF CIVIC HUMANISM
25

II.
THE "NOVI CIVES" IN FLORENTINE POLITICS FROM
1343 TO THE END OF THE CENTURY
93

III.
THE *MONTE* FROM ITS FOUNDING (1343–45) UNTIL
THE LATE FOURTEENTH CENTURY
151

IV.
THE RENAISSANCE TERRITORIAL STATE AND CIVIC
PERSPECTIVE
201

EPILOGUE
251

BIBLIOGRAPHY
257

INDEX
269

FLORENCE IN TRANSITION
VOLUME TWO
STUDIES IN THE RISE OF THE TERRITORIAL STATE

INTRODUCTION

Remembering Henry James's admonition that if there is no theory, then the subject is not "discutable," it will be necessary to venture certain hypotheses.

Although Florence was very much a part of late medieval Europe and shared amply in its spiritual and intellectual problems, yet there was a marked difference between the Arno city and other cities of Europe. The crisis in medieval theology and the development of radical nominalism were abundantly evident in Arno culture as were the penchant for the arcane and the endless allegorizing. Traditional political ideology still furnished hierarchical scaffolding to some—certainly not the least influential—but tensions between old and new were discernible in the lives of individuals as well as in the actions of political blocs. A foreigner coming into Florence would have been much at home within certain segments of the political milieu. Yet with it all, there were changes in process alien to him.

J. Huizinga in *The Waning of the Middle Ages* convincingly portrays "the violent tenor of life" and the "high-strung personality" of North and Northerner. Lucien Febvre extends these insights in his *Le Problème de l'Incroyance au XVIe Siècle: La Religion de Rabelais* (Paris, 1947), showing the high degree of "fluidity of a world where nothing is strictly delimited." Mystical in their faith, with preference for vivid color and jarring sound, the sixteenth-century Frenchman was in close contact with the sources of emotional life. The *trecento* Florentine, too, was attracted by the lure of the "fluidité d'un monde où rien n'est strictement délimité, où les êtres eux-mêmes, perdant leur frontières, changent en un clin d'oeil, sans provoquer autrement d'objection de forme, d'aspect, de dimension, voire de règne."[1] During the second half of the *trecento*, however, a new paideia emerged to repress this colorful world. What was unmistakable to the visitor in Florence was the stern geometric pattern of

---

[1] Z. Barbu, in his *Problems of Historical Psychology* (London, 1960), pp. 21–26, presents a useful summary of the theme "History and Perception."

the new polis as well as its buildings. Contemporary paintings of the city, town plans, and even oratorical descriptions reveal the transition from a *civitas* in disarray to the well-ordered, carefully structured polis of early *quattrocento*.[2] A regularized public world had coalesced, and around it emerged the first great profusion of civic statuary since antiquity. Oratory, the study of ancient history, moral philosophy, and politics became the capstones of a new education, the values of which became increasingly civic. Herein lay something of the distinction between Florence and other European cities: the force of law, the coercive power of the state, citizen involvement in bureaucracy—each had done its work to fortify the reality of the Florentine *civitas*.

Hegel propounds a great analogy when he speaks of the construction of a house wherein the very elements utilized to prepare the building materials, such as fire to melt the iron, wind to blow the fire, water to set wheels in motion to cut wood, are finally shut out by the completed dwelling. In the same manner do human passions "produce the edifice of human society" and, having finished it, discover a structure of law and order directed against themselves.[3] Without subscribing to Hegel's pessimism, we can still understand the repressive political structure erected in Florence during the two generations following the early 1340s.

If the bonds of state were to be strengthened and the scope of law extended, then emphasis had to be lent to repression and its handmaiden, sublimation. Jacob Burckhardt's medieval Florentine, emerging from the womb of illusion and fantasy, might indeed discover the unique powers of his persona or ego, but he was compelled to shape them to the imperatives of a public world. Moreover, the effects of these compulsions were not infrequently felicitous, artistically and literarily. Recently it has been suggested that Burckhardt's favorite Renaissance man, Leon Battista Alberti, benefited even psychically by his first prolonged contact with the Arno polis; nor was it fortuitous that his best period of humanistic productivity coincided with his Florentine sojourn.[4] Burckhardt's prize Renaissance thinker was Machiavelli, who would surely speak for the new autonomous political morality, yet his passion for justice and order was abiding. In a world bereft of traditional modes of legitimation, the Flor-

---

[2] Compare the mural in the Loggia del Bigallo (*ca.* 1352) with the woodcut copy of the Florentine engraving of *ca.* 1480, reproduced in H. Baron's *The Crisis of the Early Italian Renaissance* (Princeton, 1955), 1, 162–63. For parallel developments in the field of oratory, see A. Galletti, *L'eloquenza (dalle origini al XVI secolo)*, (Milan, 1938), pp. 511 ff. For an example of an oration that is a bizarre mixture of old and new, see G. Villani, *Cronica*, ed. F. Dragomanni (Florence, 1844–45), 12, 110. Later definitions of good preaching should of course include the one proclaimed by S. Bernardino in Florence in 1425, when he equated it with the "science of eloquence." Cf. his *Prediche volgare*, ed. C. Cannarozzi (Pistoia, 1940), 3, 260–70.

[3] G. Hegel, *Reason in History*, trans. R. Hartman (Indianapolis, 1953), p. 35.

[4] C. Grayson, "The Humanism of Alberti," *Italian Studies*, 12 (1957), 49–50.

INTRODUCTION

entine dedicated his intellect to a quest for knowledge to secure public order.

A few years ago, in his Reith Lectures, the art historian Edgar Wind considered Rousseau, Schiller, Hegel, and Burckhardt in introducing *Art and Anarchy* (London, 1963). He pointed out that the splendid liberation of artistic energies during the Italian Renaissance was accompanied by baleful political disintegration. Burckhardt's chapters "Der Staat als Kunstwerk" in *The Civilization of the Renaissance in Italy* were painfully ironic and probably derived from Hegel's discussion of the magnificent spirit of Athens, so "amiable and serene in the face of tragedy." Gaiety and recklessness were inappropriate mourners at the tomb of civic morality. However we translate the title of Burckhardt's chapters, it does not fit the experience we shall review. Postponing social and economic arguments until later in this book, we should note nonetheless that the artistic revolution in Florence during the early Renaissance was inspired in large measure by needs of the public world. It might be better to forge a nexus between art and civic consciousness instead of between "art and anarchy."

One problem besetting historians of Renaissance politics and art has been to seek to telescope diverse and protracted experiences. For example, sixteenth-century developments indicating a dichotomy between public and private worlds cannot be read back into an earlier time. Indeed, the recent writings of Felix Gilbert and Nicolai Rubinstein suggest the persistence of a vigorous public world throughout most of the history of the Florentine republic. Respect for law and constitutionalism endured even under adverse conditions. Civic humanism and devotion to republican forms was not undone until the first half of the *cinquecento*. The vitality of these ideals was displayed in the stirring defense of Florence against foreign soldiery at a time when the Italian despots themselves were capitulating.[5]

In banishing chronology from his work on Renaissance civilization and in seeking to define the period in terms of an inner ideal of unity of personality, Burckhardt does not make cautious distinctions between different forms of interaction between individual and polis over the centuries. His casual approach is taken even by leading art historians, who mix evidence from the sixteenth century with that of the fourteenth until the

---

[5] N. Rubinstein's painstaking work discloses the exquisite concern for legality among *quattrocento* political men of Florence. The myth of a crumbling republican ethos is scientifically challenged. Cf. *The Government of Florence under the Medici (1434 to 1494)* (Oxford, 1966). F. Gilbert shows the vitality of the republican commitment in the time of Machiavelli in *Machiavelli and Guicciardini; Politics and History in Sixteenth-Century Florence* (Princeton, 1965). For a model review article treating crucial matters in Machiavelli scholarship, see J. Pocock's "'The Onely Politician': Machiavelli, Harrington and Felix Raab," *Historical Studies:* Australia, New Zealand, 12 (1966), 265-99.

resulting concoction is as bizarre as it is unpalatable. More serious, however, is the recent confusion propounded by economic historians who assert that the Florentine Renaissance is a thing of quantity rather than of quality. Professor C. Violante has indicated the mischief at bottom of this simplistic analysis by affectionately criticizing the teachings of Armando Sapori. The latter has spoken of "the *renaissance of the economy* rather than the *economy of the Renaissance.*" That increase and expansion were hallmarks of the economy in late medieval Florence does not justify the use of the term "renaissance" in a serious way.[6] First, as Violante has suggested, distinctions between medieval and Renaissance economic systems are not quantitative. Second, to use such grasping, insecure merchants as Francesco Datini to typify the triumph of a niggling, cowardly business ethic in Tuscany at late *trecento* is to refuse to examine the civic, patriotic, and imperialist milieu emerging under burgher guidance and business control.

Again, to quote Henry James, "Life is monstrous and infinite." One can only listen to its irregular heartbeat. In this paradise of loose ends, the advice of the master historian Federico Chabod should be entertained: The questions are, to what minor fraction of life can an age consciously react, and how abbreviated a version of knowledge and feeling will their reaction be? Chabod gives a telling example of what he believes to be an essential difference between the medieval north and the Renaissance south by contrasting the piteous lament of Eustache Deschamps (*ca.* 1345–1404-5) and the tract *De dignitate et excellentia hominis* (1396–1459) by the Florentine Gianozzo Manetti. Deschamps can only succumb to the adversity of everyday life whereas Manetti seeks to employ public values to elevate it into a creed or program: "Everything which surrounds us is our work, the work of man: houses, castles, cities, magnificent buildings over all the earth. They resemble the work of angels more than man; notwithstanding they are the work of men. There are pictures, sculpture, science and doctrine. There are inventions and literary works in many languages and finally machines. And when we see these marvels, we realize that we are able to make better things, more beautiful, more adorned, more perfect than those that we have made until now."

Indeed, Chabod's admonition that we must not confuse practical life with the life of the mind, or the day-to-day activities of man with his rational consciousness of these activities, is worth respect. Such a clear statement disposes of the naïve disclaimer of the historian who argues in the name of "common sense" that medieval practices differed not at all,

---

[6] See C. Violante's remarks in *Il rinascimento significato e limiti* (Atti del III Convegno Internazionale sul Rinascimento), (Florence, 1953), pp. 134–36. For A. Sapori's comments, see pages 126–32 of the same volume.

INTRODUCTION

at least on the conscious level, from those of the Renaissance.[7] When we periodize, our concern is not with certain instinctual and fundamental passions but rather with their elevation from this primary condition to the status of a consciously articulated program of life. These political, cultural, and moral ideals, and the institutions in which they find expression, serve to fix the character of the Renaissance terrain.

I

It is also important to emphasize consciousness as a positive force, as a partial awareness of the possible and not simply a mechanical reflection of events.[8] In underscoring the possible as it pertains to Florentine awareness we must return to the realization that the Arno city belonged to the late medieval world in crisis. Radical nominalism had worked to undermine the optimistic connection between man and God. The power of the Deity was absolute and unintelligible; He could act to abrogate all ordained norms of morality. Furthermore, church and clergy were losing occult and metaphysical powers in this terrible experience of "demystification" (as Hegel might have termed it).[9] Although Florentines felt the

---

[7] G. Post, *Studies in Medieval Legal Thought* (Princeton, 1964), p. 252. For Chabod, see his *Machiavelli and the Renaissance*, trans. D. More (London, 1958), p. 162, and his *Scritti su Machiavelli* (Turin, 1964). Manetti's tract is published in E. Garin's *Prosatori latini del Quattrocento* (Milan–Naples, 1952), pp. 422–87. For presentations of the Crocean position (Chabod being its principal historical spokesman), see *Rivista di Studi Crociani*, a newly founded journal edited by A. Parente.

[8] See the helpful comments of G. Lukács in his *Realism in Our Time* (New York, 1962), p. 8. In treating consciousness in this volume it should be underscored that the figures and ideas discussed are those most amenable to the emerging polis of the early Renaissance. In my third volume persistent challenges to the new culture will be examined in some detail. Likewise literati occupying a halfway house between new and old will be considered. For present purposes, types are selected because they possess those human and social determinants essential for responding to and even activating this nascent public world. By definition, then, they are *types* since they possess these qualities in their highest state of development.

[9] We observe in Petrarch, Salutati, Sacchetti, Bruni, and others that reference is seldom made to the saving role of priest; nor is sacramentalism central to their prose discourse. On the contrary, extreme voluntarism leads them to stress the individual and his spiritual and ethical responsibility: "The object of the will is to be good; that of the intellect truth. It is better to will the good than to know the truth" (F. Petrarch, "De sui ipsius et multorum ignorantia," trans. H. Nachod in *The Renaissance Philosophy of Man*, ed. E. Cassirer [Chicago, 1948], p. 105). From the scholastic Aristotelians one can acquire massive learning, but not the keen appetite for virtue. Cf. F. Petrarch, *ibid.*, p. 103.

H. A. Oberman in his *The Harvest of Medieval Theology* (Cambridge, Mass., 1963) and his triumphal article, "Some Note of the Theology of Nominalism with Attention to its Relation to the Renaissance," *Harvard Theological Review*, LII (1960), 47–76, demonstrates how modern scholarship has rescued the term "crisis" from the realm of the trivial. Cf. also the valuable studies of M. Seidlmayer, *Currents of Medieval Thought*, trans. D. Barker (Oxford, 1960), pp. 154 ff., and G. Leff, *Gregory of Rimini* (Manchester, 1961), pp. 18–28. On the status of the church, see C. Perrin's review article, "L'histoire de l'église de 1378 à 1449," *Revue Historique*, 236 (1966), 317–46.

full measure of loss, they were coming to appreciate an alternative: feelings and fulfilled aspirations could be transferred in part to the polis itself; the public world and the instruction of civic humanists might compensate to some degree for this fact of loss.

Dante's employment of the formal Thomistic system as a mode for guaranteeing the intelligibility of a personal vision was rendered dubious. Primacy of the intellect and a confident epistemology were in question. By the time of Petrarch the lyric is accompanied by a dissipation of philosophical conviction. Suffering and misadventure need have no ultimate significance; indeed, if they do, how can man, whose intellect is so imperfect, ever discover it in a cosmos that belongs to God? A favorite phrase of Petrarch's and of his humanist followers ran to the inability of man to know the "secret counsels of God." The lyric stance was predicated upon the belief that man's history, private and public, is one of loss of youth, beauty, and friends.[10]

> But is there any comfort to be found?
> Man is in love and loves what vanishes,
> What more is there to say?

Yeats's lines could serve well as an introduction to Petrarch and to so many other humanists. The awareness of the unintelligibility of cosmos and the failure of ritual bonds between phenomenal and noumenal led the latter to say much more. Reason was not directed at reason in order to demonstrate for all time the impossibility of achieving knowledge. Nor was a mysticism stressing relics, saints, and the Holy Virgin's corporality in vogue as in the North. Instead, man's strength was felt to derive from his use of reason to discover his limits. Fideism and Christian skepticism became the basis of robust faith rather than of spiritual despair. Although man was ensconced in no cosmos and his individuality was detached from a transcendent order, enduring models of virtue did exist. History and the secular hero were well worth "imitatio." It might be true that theologians, scientists, and dialecticians could disclose nothing of the mind of God, but this failure only intensified Petrarch's belief in the role of poet. In his coronation oration of 1341 Petrarch celebrates the role of poet and historian, for they incite men to seek true virtue and glory. "The poet's office," however, "is loftier than the historian's or the philosopher's in that he can stretch this truth without breaking the link with

---

[10] I wish to thank R. J. Kaufmann for allowing me to read some of his illuminating comments on the lyric style. My comments on Petrarch have been guided in important particulars by the many issues of the annual *Studi Petrarcheschi*, ed. by Umberto Bosco for the *Accademia Petrarca di Lettere Arti e Scienze di Arezzo*.

the human."[11] In the hands of his foremost Florentine disciples, Giovanni Boccaccio and Coluccio Salutati, this high notion of the "officium poetae" was solemnized until the literary man was transformed into a kind of priest performing a sacred act. Boccaccio placed poetry on the same plane as Holy Scripture, affirming that there was no opposition between poetry, philosophy, and theology. The sacred task of the poet was to penetrate the veils of seeming. Pagans had intimations of this single truth, never completely disguised, but hidden from the many. Our Lord himself spoke in parables, and Scripture would lose much of its glorious meaning if the poetry were stripped away.[12]

In a time of separation between the logical and ontological order of things, when it was becoming increasingly difficult to reason backward from His creation to His being, this confidence in the poet was striking. The philosophical luminaries of late medieval Europe, Duns Scotus (1265/70–1308) and William of Ockham (d. 1349), contributed to an environment where intense study of logic led to skepticism, where speculation gave way to criticism, where metaphysical truth arrived at through deduction could be only tentative, and where the absolute power of God made deductive theology difficult if not impossible.[13] God's *potentia absoluta* had always been an element of theological discussion, but for the most part quite marginal. Now, in the first half of the fourteenth century, the radical nominalists focused upon it to the exclusion of all else. Man's powers of perception and expression did not extend as far as earlier scholastics had believed. Thus metaphysical and theological realms were sealed off from the questing human intellect. No longer were theologians of the fourteenth century so convinced of a pre-established harmony between universe and teleology.

Much as St. Augustine had adored Virgil, he censured poets for their numerous lies and poetry for its blasphemies. More serious was his con-

---

[11] A. Bernardo, *Petrarch, Scipio and the "Africa"* (Baltimore, 1962), p. 7; E. Wilkins, *Studies in the Life and Works of Petrarch* (Cambridge, Mass., 1955), p. 307. For the use of Cicero's *Pro Archia* as "a sacred text," wherein letters offer the best surety for immortality, see H. Gray, "Renaissance Humanism," *Journal of the History of Ideas*, 24 (1963), 503–4. Cf. also G. Boccaccio, *The Fates of Illustrious Men*, trans. L. Hall (New York, 1965), p. 106: "In reality poetry is a celebrated body of knowledge, elevated and beautiful, requiring skill. Only by the aid of poetry is it possible, within the limits of human weakness, to follow in the footsteps of Holy Writ. For as Scripture reveals the secrets of the Divine Spirit and the prophecies of things to come under the guise of speech, so poetry tries to relate its lofty concepts under the veil of fiction." For Salutati, see his celebrated letter of 1405, trans. E. Emerton, in *Humanism and Tyranny* (Cambridge, Mass., 1925), pp. 312–77. The debt of these writers to Petrarch is apparent. Cf. his *Le Familiari*, 6, 2: "We are all to read philosophy, poetry or history in such a fashion that an echo of Christ's gospel, by which alone we are wise and happy, may be ever sounding in our hearts...."
[12] C. Osgood, *Boccaccio on Poetry* (Princeton, 1930), p. xvi.
[13] See footnote 9 and P. Vignaux, *Nominalisme au XIVe siècle* (Paris, 1948); R. Guelluy, *Philosphie et théologie chez Guillaume di Ockham* (Paris, 1947).

demnation of poet and poetry as the theologians and theology of paganism.[14] St. Thomas' intense rationalism led him to distrust the figurative language of the poet, and his scientific scrupulousness caused him to call them inveterate liars. At best he would concede that these users of metaphor painted pretty pictures which were pleasing to men.[15] Petrarch's Augustine, who speaks in the *Secretum*, gladly acknowledges that truth abides in the fictions of poets, "and one perceives it shining out through the crevices of thought." Petrarch made a startling connection, concluding that poets well trained in rhetoric, grammar, literature, history, as well as in ways of understanding and describing nature in metaphorical terms, were best qualified to govern their fellow men. If Cicero was so eminent a statesman, why could not poets, who ground their art in his teachings, achieve this position? From the foregoing one can infer, first, that the term "poetry" came to encompass all branches of secular learning while at the same time retaining its older theological aura, and second, that the emphasis placed on poetry and hence secular studies was strikingly political. If we turn to Petrarch's Florentine literary heirs we see that this latter aspect became increasingly exaggerated.

Both Boccaccio and Salutati emphasized the social role of poetry and the political function of poets. The latter were the earliest educators of mankind and in their poetic fables sought for means whereby men might be brought together to form a *humanitas*. The deities they invented were but poetic devices to educate and shape man's moral sense. A combination of religious concern and social responsibility encouraged the Florentine literary man to view his role as that of priest-politician. Both the crisis in theology and the imperatives of the Florentine public world prompted him to assume this dual identity.[16]

A telling difference between Petrarch and his Florentine followers rests in their attitudes toward the present. The master saw the contemporary world as worthy of ridicule and scorn and the deeds of his own day suitable for satire, not history. His literary heirs in Florence felt a growing

[14] *Confessions*, 1, 13; *The City of God*, 18, 13; 7, 13; 2, 14.
[15] *Summa Theologiae*, 1, q. 1. a. 9 ad 1; II Sent. d. 13 q. 1. a. 2. E. Panofsky's early work, *Idea*, trans. E. Cione (Florence, 1952), still remains basic.
[16] See Boccaccio's proem to *De casibus virorum illustrium*, in which the author seeks to recall the rulers of the world from careers of vice and debauchery, using literature and history for examples to place them on the "straight road." Salutati argued that if the Holy Scripture were deprived of history it would be barren and not bring fruit (cf. *Epistolario*, ed. F. Novati [Rome, 1891–1911], 2, 289–95). This is the remarkable letter of 1392 written to Juan Fernandez de Heredia on the nature and uses of history, in which history is employed to furnish the guidance and direction once provided by sacred studies. The implication is that Christian truth itself would be less compelling were it not for the historical dimension. Conversely, the law has for Salutati a profoundly religious aura not adequately commented upon by scholars. Cf. *De nobilitate legum et medicinae*, ed. E. Garin (Florence, 1947), pp. 1–272. His most intense religious celebration of poet and poetry is to be found in his cumbersome, unfinished last work, whose excesses embarrassed even latter-day fellow humanists. Cf. *De laboribus Herculis*, ed. B. Ullman (2 vols.; Zurich, 1951).

INTRODUCTION

respect for the dignity of contemporary life. Petrarch addressed himself to Roman antiquity or to an uncertain posterity; civic humanists, chroniclers, and poets spoke to the present.[17] Traditions of intellectual obligation to the citizenry had been strong since before Dante, and while these did not confer dignity upon contemporary history, they did condition thought and attitude. Dante understood well in his *Convivio* "la cura familiare e civile, la quale convenevolmente a sé tiene de li uomini lo maggior numero, si ché in ozio di speculazione esser non possono." Petrarch, growing up in exile, living near the court at Avignon, stood outside society. His program focuses upon cultivation of self (of the "gentile spirito") with the new poetic ideal of "la solitudine elegiaca." The poet is a meditative man, a confessor of the soul who seeks a religious solitude, never relinquishing, however, strong literary tastes. Petrarch would baptize monastic solitude in the waters of humane letters. His Christian fixes his thoughts on eternity, but a literary rather than a theological eternity. Whereas Dante reproved a monarch whose devotion to literature led to neglect of country, Petrarch called this his finest hour ("omnium eius de rebus altissimus sermo erat").[18]

The Florentine humanists' view of the role of poetry (profane knowledge) was inextricably connected with mounting awareness of a civic matrix. The history of this milieu is worthy of sympathy, if not laudation. Like Petrarch, these intellectuals were increasingly unresponsive to the political ideologies of Guelf and Ghibelline, the heroic paradigms of chivalry, and the noble tests of tourney. Unlike their master, they had the alternative of identification with polis.[19]

II

In *Florence in Transition, Volume One: The Decline of the Commune* (Baltimore: The Johns Hopkins Press, 1967) we observed the recession of those cohesive ideals at the base of Florentine politics and education which had indicated a confidence on the part of the patriciate that the process of socialization could be achieved through gentle persuasion rather than legal coercion. A cluster of trusting sentiments had provided

---

[17] Fundamental to any consideration of Petrarch is Umberto Bosco's monograph, *Petrarca* (Turin, 1946).
[18] For an illuminating comparison of these two poets, see L. Russo's "La poetica del Petrarca," *Belfagor*, 3 (1948), 541–68, but especially 546–47.
[19] In his *Trionfo d'Amore*, Tristan and Lancelot barely rate a mention, whereas the heroes of antiquity are magisterially rendered. Chivalric loves are *insani amores*, and the "duelli cavallereschi" are "miranda vulgo praedia." (*Metrica* I, 5, 72–77.) In the *Trionfo della Fama* there is only a single verse to Charlemagne and his paladins, and only a glance at "Lancilotto, Tristano e gli altri erranti." Nothing of the Dantean lament for the decline of courtesy and valor in the lands of the Adige and Po; instead the observation that neither a Scipio nor a Caesar entered the lists. L. Russo, "La poetica del Petrarca," pp. 551–52.

material for the "gentle paideia." Firm had been the belief in the educability of men through the promptings of chivalry and courtesy. Ideals of this society had been placed in a secure frame wherein continuity between the secular world and the realm of the transcendent was no mere allegory. The stuff of political exposition had its origins in a Christian belief in the possibility of individual spiritual rebirth (*renovatio*). The extension of this hopeful view had been made explicit by popular Joachite prophecies of collective *renovatio*, whereby all "true" Christians would soon enter the Age of the Holy Spirit. The message of the Calabrian Joachim as well as of the Umbrian St. Francis pointed toward the moment when men would be free of the compulsions and bonds of society and might live under a higher dispensation guided by overflowing feelings of *carità* and *amore*.

The religious ideals of the Italian prophetic movement in the late Middle Ages suggest something of a disbelief in the permanence of a public world. That such teachings found much favor with north Italian townsmen indicates this incredulity was shared. The constraints of politics and society were costly and highly displeasing to a patriciate whose ideals were resolutely accented in a work like the *Decameron*, where the sympathies of the audience coalesce around the individual and the claims of nature rather than the harsh imperatives of the legalistic polis.

Secure and always worthy of tender regard are private feelings and impulses. Blood feud and vendetta, personal vows of poverty and chastity, private loyalties or dedication to promptings of courtly love, are seldom in doubt. Were we to examine such a celebrated work of autobiography as Dante's *Vita Nuova*, we would see that the exquisitely personal, not the grossly public, furnished the threads for this interiorized narrative. Almost by definition the term "allegory" came to mean a spiritual journey. This did not imply contempt for or indifference to the public world. Dante's youthful contemporary, Giovanni Villani, was profoundly conversant with its workings, but it always receded, like the fabled Camelot, when the stain of human sin became visible. There is a monotonous and inevitable conflict between human sinfulness and divine judgment almost Augustinian in its polarity.[20] Despite his vivid interest in economic life, he could not furnish Florentine capitalism with any theoretical justification or formulate what the Italians called "la sua ragion d'essere."

The onset of crisis in the late 1330s and early 1340s accentuated the fissures in the late medieval world. Neither capitalist enterprise nor political action possessed those enduring, self-justifying values that would have buttressed a disintegrating patrician public world. In the eyes of

---

[20] See F. Chabod's review of E. Mehl's *Die Weltanschauung des Giovanni Villani* (Leipzig, 1927), entitled "La 'concezione del mondo' di Giovanni Villani," in *Nuova Rivista Storica*, 13 (1929), 335 ff. Still very helpful on the topic of Italian historiography in general and Giovanni Villani in particular is G. Lisio's *La storiografia* in the series *Storia dei Generi Letterarii Italiani* (Milan, n.d.), pp. 435 ff.

INTRODUCTION

Giovanni Villani, despairing now, the medieval orders and classes had failed. Solid accomplishments in literature and art were put in jeopardy as poet, chronicler, and painter became less confident that the ordering values of the burgher could be harmoniously blended with the ideals of the knight or that concord between the profane and sacred could be demonstrated.

The present volume considers the onset of the decline of traditional principles whereby cultivated men had expressed their commitments. The work of the foremost literary men of the generation after Giovanni Villani reveals the extent to which structure broke down. Knowledge was not infrequently disjointed and encyclopedic; unity of style and content was rare in poetry and history. In painting it was not surprising to see abstract and realistic elements side by side. In the 1380s and 1390s, for example, we observe artists like Agnolo Gaddi, in his *Legend of the Holy Girdle,* achieving unified composition. In other works he employs a semicircular plan intimately connected with his concept of a spatial continuum while at the same time introducing systematic focus perspective.[21] His contemporary, Spinello Aretino, democratizes the world depicted by Giotto; his point of view is vernacular, so that he dilutes some of the aristocratic seriousness of Giotto. His vivacity, however, is not uncontrolled or random. In the frescoes of San Miniato, for example, the figures are conceived in powerful line and simple volume and are often placed within a limited and well-defined space.

The organizing principles introduced into Florentine literature by Giovanni Boccaccio and Coluccio Salutati need not detain us here, since our purpose is merely to indicate a movement toward order self-consciously pursued in the generation after Giovanni Villani. Nor is it necessary to dwell upon the fact that crisis in the late fourteenth century did not provoke despair with regard to the values of the public world. The field of sculpture, for instance, was virtually usurped by reverence for civic experience. And the political iconography of Masaccio's frescoes in the Brancacci Chapel relate to the fiscal program of the polis as well as its successful military policies.[22]

Although no attempt will be made to analyze such hard-won formulas

[21] John White, *Art and Architecture in Italy (1250–1400),* (Baltimore, 1966), pp. 373–76; R. Salvini, *L'arte di Agnolo Gaddi* (Florence, 1936).
[22] P. Meller, "La Cappella Brancacci," *Acropoli: Riviste d'Arte* (1960–61), 3, 186–227. (I wish to thank Professor Anthony Molho for this reference.) At the outset stress must be placed upon the close ties between humanist programs and the new civic art. Art historians of recent years have made significant discoveries and valuable suggestions in this critical area. Cf. H. Janson's "The Image of Man in Renaissance Art: From Donatello to Michelangelo," in *The Renaissance Image of Man and the World* (Columbus, 1966), pp. 87–103; C. Eisler, "The Athlete of Virtue," *Essays in Honor of Erwin Panofsky* (New York, 1961), p. 86; C. Guasti, *S. Maria del Fiore, la construzione della chiesa* (Florence, 1887), p. 293, and *La cupola di S. Maria del Fiore* (Florence, 1857), p. 230; J. Pope-Hennessy, *Italian Renaissance Sculpture* (London and New York, 1958), pp. 297 ff.

for integrating on esthetic or scientific grounds, as the emergence of ocular perspective, an effort shall be made to suggest a substantive change which, though it proffered no unity of form, did furnish possibilities for both primary and secondary kinds of order. The literary critic Richard Blackmur observes that the first involves notions of sequence and development which aid "things and affairs" to be seen as declaring themselves and becoming "realizable in the mind as if they were just themselves."[23] Secondary kinds of order are "bound up with the notions of the moral, the prophetic, the ideal." What I should like to emphasize is the fact that the polis itself became a bridge capable of spanning these two kinds of order. The first grew more evident in the nature and character of historical observation and comment. As early as the mid-fourteenth century we note Matteo Villani referring to the polis as the heir and trustee of "Romana libertà" and attributing to adverse circumstance the weakening of the Empire and the increased sway of the tyrant (*Cronica*, 3, 1). Florence alone, according to Villani, maintained "*la franchigia e la libertà* borne in them from the ancient Roman people." The durable public world of the *civitas* will not recede in the night of Augustinian dualism. In the hands of the Florentine chancellor and man of letters Coluccio Salutati, this world developed dignity. Even at his most ascetic, Salutati found space in *De saeculo et religione* (1381) for a lovely poetic quotation honoring the beautiful city.[24] The leading chronicler, Marchionne di Coppo Stefani, was eager to accept the world as he found it; he shunned apocalyptic meaning and ignored theories of historical transcendence.

A mounting involvement in the historical and public does not of course preclude a deliberate concern with the prophetic. Just as for key literary men the polis stood as an embodiment and proof of the concepts of sequence and development, so, too, for others it came to be a repository for prophecy. As Donald Weinstein has ably shown, the civic began to engage the religious fervor and moral expectation of a populace frequently convinced that the polis was the sacred object of divine election.[25] Here the possibilities for secondary kinds of order were intense, since believers in the polis were able to make moral judgments that placed a good public world against the forces of evil.

The experience of the foremost prose writer of Italian after Boccaccio furnishes a more concrete illustration. At the time when Franco Sacchetti was composing his *Trecentonovelle*, he was filled with nostalgia for the

[23] See his *The Lion and the Honeycomb* (New York, 1955), pp. 149–51.
[24] *De saeculo et religione*, ed. B. Ullman (Florence, 1957), p. 60, "hanc regiam urbem, gloriosam patriam tuam atque meam, que, ni fallor, 'tantum inter alias caput extulit urbes/Quantum lenta solent inter viburna cupressi.'" From Virgil, *Ecl.*, I, 24–25.
[25] D. Weinstein, "Millenarianism in a Civic Setting: The Savonarola Movement in Florence," in S. Thrupp (ed.), *Millennial Dreams in Action: Comparative Studies in Society and History*, Supplement II (The Hague, 1962). Cf. also his "Savonarola, Florence, and the Millenarian Tradition," *Church History*, 27 (1958), 3–17.

INTRODUCTION

"bel tempo"—those easier days when a gentle paideia prevailed and a relaxed aristocracy ruled. Paying tribute to illustrious men no longer alive, his heart fills with grief when he thinks of all the "populi e famiglie" who are reduced to a "poor and miserable condition." Writing in 1392 he observes that many have been felled by civil war, but he blames human nature which contains "the germs of evil," not the polis or politics. What is strongest in Sacchetti's last prose, final poems, and letters is his commitment to the public world and dedication to civic career. Democratic, firmly upholding the virtues of law, he is spokesman for a sterner paideia though he knows well the price. Even as a young man in the throes of composing a poem to his beloved, he had slipped off the lyric pedestal to compare his lady fair with the Sainted City. In old age and personal suffering, the public world served him well by stabilizing his emotions and sustaining his ideals.[26]

By the 1360s, Petrarch's repeated use of secular models of virtue had already taken hold in Florence. Ideals concerning human individuality had been detached from the cosmic order. Virtue, however defined, was no longer explicitly or implicitly derived from divinity; nor did human choice lie between salvation and damnation. Petrarch's lifelong hero was Scipio, and he exalted him to the ranks of great Biblical figures. Man's ultimate goal is "to live virtuously in the sight of God and act virtuously among men,"[27] according to Petrarch, and events and experiences are recorded so that moral deductions can be made; their relevance is not ultimate or final and therefore lacks the figural quality so essential for Dante's view of history. If man would learn to be human and not a god, then he had to look to the public world and its history.

Petrarch's commitments did not eradicate doubt and despair, but nowhere did his insights win firmer support than in Florence; it was there that the new historicism and secularized moral philosophy were to flourish. Upon Petrarch's death, Salutati celebrated him as the godlike knower whose holy work had been to create and defend a literature capable of edifying the soul. How different from the teachings of the windy, contemporary Sophists of the Schools was Petrarch's radiant invitation to virtue! Writing to Luigi Marsili, an Augustinian priest and friend of Florence who best epitomized piety and civic concern, Salutati lamented bitterly the recent deaths of Petrarch and Boccaccio. As champion of letters in Florence, Salutati hoped for divine assistance so that "honorem patrie" would continue to be served. Salutati, like Sacchetti, Boccaccio, Matteo Villani, and so many other literary men, lived no tranquil life. The very

---

[26] V. Pernicone, *Fra rime e novelle del Sacchetti* (Florence, 1942), pp. 188 ff.; E. Li Gotti, *Franco Sacchetti uomo "discolo e grosso"* (Florence, 1940), pp. 71 ff.
[27] *Familiari*, 11, 3. Especially useful among recent work on Petrarch is A. Bernardo's *Petrarch, Scipio and the "Africa."*

education of a Florentine of this period impelled him to think and write in self-consciously articulated antitheses. Arguments were deduced in favor of the contemplative life to be put against those urging the active life. Orations in favor of and against the very practice of oratory and exercises for or against rhetoric were commonplace, as were tracts composed by the same individual alternatively espousing both sides of a political question. This was a restless, intellectual milieu, and the general philosophic disquiet throughout late *trecento* Europe continually intruded in intellectual circles. Not surprisingly, Salutati was skeptical of epistemological certainty and of the possibility of creating truly fine literature in this atmosphere. These doubts diminish when he defines the social ends of knowledge and literature: It is not in any absolute sense that we fail or succeed to understand and create, but only relatively. Thus he does not descend into nihilism or Christian despair, because social and political imperatives justify the activity of the mind. Following Petrarch, he wrote a tract, *De nobilitate legum et medicinae*, in which he exalts the bonds of the public world. His experience was much richer than that of his master. He argues that nature never divulges her purposes and ends to mortals, while "with the laws this end is the conservation of society, the common good and political felicity."[28] Fideism replaced the cosmic faith in intelligible ties between creator and creation, and out of this stemmed a skepticism as to the possibilities of natural and physical scientific knowledge. Paradoxically, what remained most certain, valuable, and worthy of being taught in Salutati's eyes was knowledge about the public world.

When Salutati vilified Scholastics and Aristotelians, he sought to discredit neither medieval voluntarism nor the logic of Aristotle. It is the valuation he places on literary and personal experience rather than new knowledge or new classical texts which serves to explain what is novel in his approach. His is an orientation towards historical research, philological inquiry, and politico-juridical study. As Ernst Cassirer indicated a few years ago, Salutati opted for the secular and phenomenal, for the *studia humanitatis*—not because it is superior to the transcendental but because it is "intelligible." Whether we take Eugenio Garin's position or that of Bruno Nardi as to the philosophical origins of the dilemma posed by the Avveroists who would devalue man and his history or the Ockhamists stressing singularity and thereby undermining unitary and hierarchical conceptions of the world, the fact remains that Salutati preferred to conduct his search for intelligibility and structure in a world that was his-

---

[28] See E. Garin's introduction to Salutati's *De nobilitate* and chapters 14–16. Cf. also Garin's *I trattati morali di Coluccio Salutati* (Florence, 1943), pp. 29–32.

INTRODUCTION

torical. The transcendent is never insignificant for him, only unknowable.[29]

Although man can understand only *res mutabilia*, not *res eternae*, this unhappy realization paralyzed neither Salutati nor his generation. Intellectual engagement with history and critical attitudes toward the past were much in evidence during the last decades of the *trecento*. Benvenuto Rambaldi, author of an excellent commentary on Dante, questioned the legends pertaining to the foundation of Florence by Julius Caesar. In the 1370s he asked how the great Caesar could find time to found a city when so immersed in Roman civic life.[30] Giovanni Villani's nephew Filippo in his *De origine civitatis Florentie* (1381–82) likewise displayed a critical stance towards traditional legend, suspecting that the impulse of aggrandizing the *patria* was at work. The same position was adopted by the humanist Luigi Marsili, according to latter-day reports of his conversations.[31] Domenico Bandini in his *Fons memorabilium* was also skeptical about mythic origins, since he found no confirmation for them in the "annalibus romanorum." In later writings of Coluccio Salutati, especially his *Invectiva*, and in the early works of his disciple, Leonardo Bruni Aretino (particularly the *Laudatio Florentinae urbis*), involvement with classical *topoi* relating to the life of the polis became more intense. The public world came to be a primary cause setting into motion subsidiary cultural effects. Salutati defended vigorously the dignity of contemporary civic affairs; the polis became an arena where man proved his spiritual mettle. For Bruni it conferred the only durable identity man could achieve; thus the quest for fame was legitimized and served as a substitute for the medieval ego props that had been overturned. Finally, both master and pupil refined that critical historical sense that accompanies awareness of the existence of a polis detached from cosmic orientation or eschatological expectancy. According to Bruni cultural health and the virtue of the citizen flow from the well-ordered polis whose *libertas* is

---

[29] I wish to thank Professor Nancy Struever for allowing me to read her penetrating dissertation on Florentine rhetoric and politics, where she demonstrates the relevance of Cassirer's insights for an understanding of Salutati and other leading orators. Cf. E. Cassirer, *The Individual and the Cosmos in Renaissance Philosophy*, trans. Mario Domandi (New York, 1964), pp. 42 ff. Cf. also E. Garin, *Dal medioevo al Rinascimento* (Florence, 1950), pp. 37–42; B. Nardi, *Saggi sull'aristotelismo padovano del secolo XIV al XVI* (Florence, 1958); *Studi di filosofia medievale* (Rome, 1950).

[30] For a detailed and telling discussion of the rise of doubts and the new historicism, see N. Rubinstein, "Il Poliziano e la questione delle origini di Firenze," in *Il Poliziano e il suo tempo* (Florence, 1957), 101–4, and also his "The Beginnings of Political Thought in Florence," *Journal of the Warburg and Courtauld Institutes*, 5 (1942), 198 ff. Cf. also A. Hankey, "Domenico di Bandino of Arezzo," *Italian Studies*, 12 (1957), 110–28.

[31] H. Baron, *Humanistic and Political Literature in Florence and Venice at the Beginning of the Quattrocento* (Cambridge, Mass., 1955), pp. 13–37. See especially p. 27 and N. Rubinstein's comments on the source for Luigi Marsili's remarks in "Il Poliziano," p. 102.

assured. It was no accident that the Golden Age of Rome coincided with the virtuous times of the republic.

Too frequently it has been argued that the intellectual trends evidenced by literary men from the later Boccaccio, with his interest in biography, history, and scholarship, through the last writings of Salutati, where the anthropomorphic human notions of the divine are stressed to the exclusion of all others, did not have their analogue in the world of the *volgare*. One of the principal contributions of Professor Hans Baron is his effective disclosure that in fact the imperatives of the public world loomed even larger in certain vernacular writings. Two figures, neither professional literary men nor humanists, responded faster to the transformation of the polis than Salutati or Bruni. As early as 1397, in his spirited defense of the dignity of contemporary economic and political life in the polis,[32] Cino Rinuccini testified to a civic frame of mind by stressing the role of the merchant. Replying as a private citizen to serious charges against the integrity of republican Florence by Antonio Loschi, the Milanese chancellor of the Visconti rulers, he asserts that the grandeur of the free polis is enhanced not only by artists, soldiers, and literary men, but also by the business community. His own kinsmen were important members of this last group. New to politics, they were leading creditors of the republic, having invested substantial portions of their patrimony in government stock (*Monte* shares). Cited among "the more liberal elements in communal politics" by a recent historian, two of them suffered political disfranchisement at the hands of the aristocratic captains of the propapal *Parte Guelfa*.[33] Cino's brother was honored not long after in recognition for service to the polis and the popular cause.

More germane to the general development of Renaissance political thought and more pertinent as an example of the intimate relationship

---

[32] I have followed Hans Baron's exposition of Rinuccini's thought and recommend his chapter "Florentine Humanism and the *Volgare* in the Quattrocento" in *The Crisis of the Early Italian Renaissance*, rev. ed. (Princeton, 1966), pp. 332–53; cf. also pp. 75–78, 291–95. Too frequently critics have concentrated on Baron's dating of texts and failed to credit the valuable insights he supplies on the nexus between vernacular culture and the classical revival in Tuscany. His researches indicate that Italian scholars of the late nineteenth and early twentieth centuries were prone to overestimate the retrograde effects of Renaissance humanism upon vernacular literature. Influenced by the causes of Italian unification, they tended to see chiefly the elitist qualities in a humanism allied with tyrant and court in an abiding opposition to democraic traditions of the medieval commune and its *volgare* culture. Baron has directed our attention to the question of the extent to which Renaissance *quattrocento* culture did have strong, popular characteristics.

[33] G. Brucker, *Florentine Politics and Society 1343–1378* (Princeton, 1962), p. 427; L. Martines, *The Social World of the Florentine Humanists* (Princeton, 1963), pp. 263–66. Cino's father had 4,500 florins in the *Monte*. At mid-fourteenth century Cino held close to 30,000, and at early *quattrocento* his heirs owned shares in excess of 33,000 florins. Cf. *ibid.*, pp. 110–11, and G. Brucker, "The Medici in the Fourteenth Century," *Speculum*, 23 (1957), 6.

between this thought and the vernacular mentality is that part of Rinuccini's *Response to the Invective of Antonio Loschi* in which he associates Florence, daughter of Rome, with the Tiber republic and not, as was traditional, with the Empire. Visconti spokesmen praised monarchical rule; Cino showed "how Rome grew but little under the king, acquired the empire over the world within a short time under the senate, and was again reduced to nothing under the emperors." He diatribes, too, against Julius Caesar, his nephew, and the Empire itself. The seeds of dissolution were planted by Caesar, who in his lust for power overturned the right order of "all things human and divine"[34] and caused Rome to forego her hegemony: "For one ruler in the affairs of mankind cannot be perfect"; although Augustus was talented, Nero would succeed him. If Rome had preserved her constitution, she would have remained alive through the radiant glory gained under republicanism. "You [Loschi] should, therefore, understand, you slave, how great the fruits of happy liberty may be; of liberty, for which Cato the Younger did not hesitate to die, that choice mind, whom Lucanus rightly places on a level with the Gods by saying 'the conquering cause was pleasing to the Gods, but the conquered one to Cato.' "[35]

This merchant, so active in guild and business life, concluded his *Response* by telling Loschi that nothing brings more pleasure and is more heartening to him than seeing "how during my lifetime in my city a *brigata* of young men of eminent talents is growing up, which would be fit for Athens, most cultured of all cities." Soon, however, he felt impelled to castigate that same *brigata* in his robust defense of Tuscan vernacular culture. In his *Invective Against Certain Slanderers of Dante, Petrarch and Boccaccio (ca. 1400)*, he writes of this cultured youth:

> They ridicule the books of Petrarch, the laurelled poet, saying that his work *On Illustrious Men* is a medley, fit to be a text for Lenten sermons; they do not say how universal he was as a poet in Latin as well as Volgare.... They say that the famous Dante Alighieri, most glorious of poets, was a poet for cobblers; they do not say that the diction of poetry soars like an eagle above all others.... Dante, the illustrious poet, prefers to depict the deeds of men in Volgare in order to be of greater use to his fellow-citizens than he would have been by writing Latin. And those detractors ought not to break out into blatant laughter because ... Dante with marvellous brevity and grace puts two or three similes into one rhythm in Volgare, such as Virgil does not set forth in twenty hexameters.... Therefore, I hold that poetry in Volgare is a thing of much greater difficulty, and demands greater excellency, than poetry in Latin.[36]

---

[34] H. Baron, *Humanistic and Political Literature*, p. 76.
[35] *Ibid.*, p. 77.
[36] *Ibid.*, p. 287.

Satire abounds in the work, but so too does earnestness when he mocks "the vain and foolish disputations" of those who,

> ... in order to appear most erudite to the man in the street, cry out in the public square, arguing how many diphthongs existed in the language of the ancients, and why today only two of them are used; which grammar is the better one, that of the time of Terence the comedy-writer, or the refined one of Virgil the epic poet; and how many metres were used by the ancients in their poetry, and why today the anapest with four short metrical feet is no longer used. And with such fantastic speculations they waste all their time.[37]

It is civic duty and public responsibility that serve as organizing metaphors, bestowing form upon values. This is the substance of Cino's critique against the *brigata*:

> Of housekeeping and family they have no high opinion, but with contempt of holy matrimony live an inordinate and dissolute life, and do not care for a father's dignity and the benefit of having children. They are such as to deserve the sentence of the Roman censors, Camillus and Postumius, who ordered the fortunes of two men, who had remained chaste (and would not marry) unto old age, to be confiscated for the community; threatening them with double punishment if they should dare complain in any way of so just a ruling.
>
> As to politics, they do not know which government is better, monarchy or republic, the rule of many or that of a few elect. They shun hard work (for the common weal), affirming that he who serves the community serves nobody; neither do they give advice to the Republic in the (councillor's) robe, nor do they defend her, arms in hand. Nor do they remember that the more common a good is, the more divine it becomes.[38]

How like the civic perspective of early *quattrocento* portrait painters is Cino's stance! Florentine artists depict their subjects in formal public dress identifying them with communal roles.[39] An understanding of the subject's private world and any sense of intimacy are forestalled by the profile view; the social rather than the personal tone pervades early Florentine Renaissance portraiture. Recently, an art historian has called attention to the imperative expressed in this genre: the values lending dignity to the individual are those of the public world.

Over the last half of the fourteenth century we witnessed at least partial and in certain respects total installation of the values of this polis. During those years a silk merchant, perennial officeholder and man of the vernacular, composed the first work of European history in which *lo*

---
[37] *Ibid.*, p. 293.
[38] *Ibid.*, p. 315.
[39] R. Hatfield, "Five Early Renaissance Portraits," *The Art Bulletin*, 47 (1965), 315–34.

stato (the state) possessed an energy, a drive, a life of its own.[40] Gregorio Dati, author of the remarkable *L'Istoria di Firenze dal 1380 al 1405,* was no man of classical letters and had no close connections with its latter-day proponents, the civic humanists. His reflections on politics remain a tribute to the possibilities open to less formally tutored but politically experienced Florentines. No one appreciates better than Dati the operation of impersonal forces in government and society. For him, absolute obedience to the laws of the polis was so ingrained that he could not easily imagine dissent on any grounds. He characterized the realm of the polis by its systematization, with the rational explicit in plan and action. At the base of his argument as to why Florence must triumph over her despotic adversary is the historian's appreciation of socioeconomic change. Wiser and more insightful than his more literary contemporary, Bruni, Dati suggested that citizen wealth and durable political forms, not the fortunate demise of Duke Giangaleazzo, were responsible for the Arno republic's triumph over the Visconti.

Literary and artistic perspectives on the public world altered so that the polis assumed geometric proportions. No longer did the unique and individual loom large: in Dati's history, factions and contending political opinions were regarded unworthy of inclusion. the principle operating was regularity, and the resultant was scientific. The polis displayed a life of its own and was by definition capable of rational description. A public world was projected whose secrets were no mystery to those with eyes to see the underlying order. Explanations of the Florentine constitution paralleled the geometric descriptions of the polis and its site. Not only did contemporary life possess dignity, but the very stage on which it was played possessed a beauty defined as "the harmony of its parts." There was a new veneration of the Euclidian world of proportion on the part of historian, teacher of rhetoric, artist, and architect alike.[41] The polis itself became the educator of men. Formerly it was believed that virtue could be truly achieved only in solitude. The civic humanists argued to the contrary the most repressive of doctrines: Man is virtuous only in the public sphere, under constraint of law and the scrutiny of his fellows. In mid-*quattrocento* the humanist Poggio Bracciolini, sensing the oppressiveness of civic restraints, argued that law and polis were so overwhelming that

---

[40] I wish to thank Professor A. Molho for allowing me to read his unpublished study on Dati. Dati, in his *L'Istoria di Firenze dal 1380 al 1405,* ed. L. Pratesi (Norcia, 1904), p. 153, places "gli uficiali del monte" (officials over the funded public debt) at the very center of government administration, for they had "grande balìa e autorità, e quasi tutte l'entrate del Comune vengono nelle loro mani: il quale è un numero infinito e costoso rendono gli interesi ai loro cittadini e forestieri i quali hanno credito scritto al detto Monte...." Cf. also H. Baron's chapter, "Dati's *Istoria* of Florence," pp. 167–88.

[41] See the inspired study of G. Argan, "The Architecture of Brunelleschi and the Origins of Perspective Theory in the Fifteenth Century," *Journal of the Warburg and Courtauld Institutes,* 9 (1946), 96–121.

great deeds could only be performed by men willing to break the chains of legality.[42] At the beginning of the next century, Machiavelli furnished a most sportive defense of the imperatives of this public order, for the landscape of the interior world was no concern of his. In general, problems of conscience and religion were banished from historical treatment as involvement with statal forces intensified.

The argument of the present volume centers upon the emergence of that mechanism indispensable to the architect Brunelleschi as well as to the political theorist Machiavelli—the Florentine territorial state. We shall seek to delineate the social and economic forces prompting its rise—specifically law, public finance, and social mobility.

Finally, a cautionary note: we shall observe that the emergence of the early Renaissance polis provided new psychic as well as material possibilities. Citizen loyalty and historical insight furnished politician, investor in state loans, and humanist with a more secure public identity. The new classicism, the new ocular perspective, and the new rhetoric conferred dignity upon the public world. Both men of education and of business were anxious to believe in the durability of the polis; the former looked to the bureaucracy for employment, and the latter to the treasury for payment of interest on government shares. Both appreciated the greater security inherent in strict enforcement of public law. A stern paideia boded especially well for the intellectuals of the late *trecento* and early *quattrocento*. Unlike the generation of Dante, which suffered the ravages of internecine war, the humanists remained safe and prosperous in the sinecures of a grateful republic. Devotion to the state and cultivation of a civic persona were sure recipes for achieving public fame. As the cartography of the public world grew more exact and more legible, the individual was confronted with easier choices. Conflict and hence disorder lessened; the polis was the one viable bridge between Richard Blackmur's two types of order mentioned previously. In late-fifteenth-century Florence, when foreign invasion undermined this bridge, the disarray was apparent everywhere, from the nervous line of Botticelli to the failure of measured political discourse in the council halls.

My argument is not intended to suggest that the human psyche ever opts for black or white—much less to indicate individual political choices. Instead, we are interested in the rise of this novel force, the Renaissance territorial state, and its magnetic pull upon lives in the aggregate. Though diminished, other pulls and lures persisted. Single lives conformed or deviated. Some were well aware that the price of lov-

---

[42] E. Walser, *Poggio Florentinus Leben und Werke* (Berlin, 1914), pp. 218 ff., contrasts Salutati's earlier unequivocal support of supremacy of law with Poggio's guarded commitment that ("sola plebecula et inferiores urbis tenentur") it was binding only on inferiors.

INTRODUCTION

ing their country might be loss of salvation of their souls. There was drama enough and tension aplenty. Side by side with the austere classicism of the public world was late Gothic style. But things are born quantitatively; that is, there comes to be more and more of them. In the same way the polis grew, and so, too, did its intrusion into men's private worlds. This process found its ideal expression in the radically different theories of civic education propounded by various civic humanists in the early *quattrocento*. But this is the stuff of a subsequent volume.

ARCHIVAL SOURCES

All documents cited are to be found in the Archivio di Stato, Florence, Italy, unless stated otherwise.

Abbreviations are given for several of the sources.

Archivio Notarile
Archivio dei Sindaci
Atti del Capitano
Atti del Esecutore
Atti del Podestà
Balie
Cambio
Camera del Comune, Entrata (CCE)
Campioni del Catasto dei cittadini
Capitoli
Capitoli Protocoli (CapP)
Consulte e Pratiche (CP)
Diplomatico
Duplicati Provvisioni (DP)
Estimo
Giudice degli Appelli

Lana
Libri Fabarum (LF)
Missive della Prima Cancelleria
Monte
Parte Guelfa
Prestanze
Proveditore di Camera (PC)
Provvisioni (P)
Scrivano
Scrivano piccolo
Sindacato del Capitano e Podestà
Statuti de Capitano
Statuti del Podestà
Tratte
Ufficiali del Biado

ABBREVIATIONS FOR PUBLISHED WORKS

Archivio Storico Italiano (ASI)   *Rerum Italicarum Scriptores (RIS)*

FLORENTINE POLIS AND CULTURE AT THE ADVENT OF CIVIC HUMANISM

I

At least in the case of Florence, Jacob Burckhardt would have been better advised to characterize the state not as a "work of art" but rather as a work of public indebtedness and social mobility. There is much to distinguish the republic of the later *trecento* from its medieval counterpart. However, the distinction cannot be clarified by comparing the bold nature of medieval venture capitalism with the niggardly and timorous quality of the early Renaissance economy. Not even the brilliant economic historian Armando Sapori could justify his use of the unheroic figure of Francesco Datini to epitomize the character of capitalism after the 1350s.[1] Even a brief visit to Florence reveals a profusion of civic art that dates precisely from a period supposedly bereft of courage and energy. Datini, merchant from neighboring Prato, is hardly representative of an ethos whose only precedents were ancient Greece and Rome. Although there had always been insecure and grasping businessmen, their behavior was not a hallmark of the mid-fourteenth century. Furthermore, the numerous economic documents of the period disclose robustness and durability, not fatigue and senescence.

Indeed, a cursory survey of economic data pertaining to Florentine recovery after the holocaust of the Black Death (1348) suggests the startling capacity of the polis for rejuvenation. The customs toll, one of the best indicators for assessing the economic energies of this trading and banking city, displayed remarkable recuperative powers. In 1353, the first year for which we have complete returns in the post-Black Death

---

[1] For Sapori's treatment of the rich, *nouveau* merchant of Prato as a type of cowardly late fourteenth-century antihero, see *Studi di storia economica (secoli XIII–XIV–XV)* (Florence, 1955), pp. 155–79. G. Brucker (*Florentine Politics and Society*, p. 45) makes the plausible observation that Datini's *Angst* was more the expression of a parvenu's "rootlessness and isolation" than characteristic of the timorous late *trecento* capitalism. Very recently D. Herlihy in his *Medieval and Renaissance Pistoia* (New Haven, 1967), p. 249, stresses the civic nature of Datini's bequest of his fortune on his death in 1410. I. Origo has done a biography of Datini, *The Merchant of Prato* (New York, 1957).

period, the customs toll topped 24,300 florins.[2] The following year only a slight gain was registered so that the total rose only to 25,000 florins. There is a lacuna in the records of 1355, but for the interim May, 1357, to April, 1358, returns from this vital source registered 47,021 florins. In 1358–59 they capped the respectable if not generous sum of 58,384 florins; four years later the amount was up by a little over 8,000 florins. Although there were numerous troughs, the impetus was clearly upward. The impetus may have been induced in part by increases in the tax rate but they would not account for the persistent and energetic climb of this index of prosperity.[3] By the 1380s receipts averaged over 100,000 florins annually, exceeding the figure recorded during the halcyon period of Florentine well-being—the biennium 1336–38—celebrated by Giovanni Villani in the eleventh book of his renowned chronicle. If this were only an isolated phenomenon, economic historians would hardly be persuaded of the onset of Florentine prosperity in the post-Black Death period. Other indicators do exist, however, such as returns from the tax on salt, wine, cattle, and even business transactions that serve to support statistical inferences drawn from the *gabella portarum*.[4] But my purpose at this juncture is not to argue for startling recovery. I wish only to suggest that just as Florentine economic vigor was not extinguished after 1348, nei-

---

[2] A more ample discussion of the statistical evidence can be found in M. Becker, "Economic Change and the Emerging Florentine Territorial State," *Renaissance Studies*, 13 (1966), 7–39. For additional materials pertaining to the resurgence of urban revenues after the Black Death, see D. Herlihy, "Direct and Indirect Taxation in Tuscan Urban Finance, ca. 1200–1400," in *Finances et comptabilité urbaines du XIIIe au XVIe siècle*, pp. 404–5. Extensive bibliography on the effect of plague upon Tuscany is to be found in W. Bowsky, "The Impact of the Black Death upon Sienese Government and Society," *Speculum*, 39 (1964), 1–34. Cf. also E. Carpentier, *Une Ville devant la peste. Orvieto et la peste noire de 1348* (Paris, 1962).
[3] Between 1364 and 1367 it averaged 85,320 florins—only 4,000 florins less than the top yield achieved in 1336–38, considered to be the peak of Florentine economic prosperity. Economic historians are sorely divided on the theme of depression and recovery in fourteenth-century Europe. Cf. *Cambridge Economic History* (Cambridge, 1952), 2, 129–354; *ibid.* (1963), 3, 411 ff.
[4] Perhaps the most telling of all economic indicators for communal well-being is the customs toll, and it continued to hold up even during the 1390s, with the Visconti war in progress. The low was only 82,000 florins, but soon after peace was made (1394) it topped the very respectable figure of 115,000 florins, sustaining it for the balance of the century (*PC*, 1–14). For a study stressing continuity of economic development, see P. J. Jones, "Florentine Families and Florentine Diaries in the Fourteenth Century," *Papers of the British School at Rome*, 24 (1956), 183–205. The latest date for the onset of Florentine recovery from the Black Death is 1360. Cf. Y. Renouard, *Recherches sur les compagnies commerciales et bancaires utilisées par les papes d'Avignon avant le Grand Schisme* (Paris, 1942). For a more extensive review of the literature, see G. Brucker, *Florentine Politics and Society*, pp. 14–18; M. Becker, *Florence in Transition* (Baltimore, 1967), 1, 194–200. Gino Luzzatto, dean of Italian economic historians, enters his cautionary note on alleged economic deterioration in Renaissance Italy. Cf. his *An Economic History of Italy from the Fall of the Roman Empire until the Beginning of the Sixteenth Century*, trans. P. J. Jones (New York, 1961), pp. 141 ff.

ther can the Angst-ridden figure of a single merchant be employed as an example of the regressive character of late *trecento* life. Again, without attempting any positive characterization of the era and its culture, it should be noted that a strong deprecation of its economic style would find little statistical support. Simplistic assertions suggesting viable correlations between economic decline and emerging cultural tone can be viewed only with extreme caution.

The two commanding scholars of Florentine literary and philosophical culture of this period are Eugenio Garin and Hans Baron. Neither would stress economic depression as a causal factor. The former assumes the existence of a solid connection between politics and thought, always emphasizing continuity of development. For Garin, early *quattrocento* culture is an immediate outgrowth of late medieval *trecento* experience. Baron, while concurring as to the substantive nature of emerging civic humanism in the early *quattrocento*, would underscore discontinuity. He maintains that a particular set of circumstances—the protracted wars with the despotic Visconti of Milan which began in the late fourteenth century—served to galvanize a new intellectual world.

Let me suggest that it may be possible to enlarge our understanding of the polis and its intellectual life, briefly described by Garin, as well as to dissent from Baron's thesis of discontinuity if we treat certain social, economic, and political changes after the 1340s. A depiction of these changes may disclose that many of the elements quintessential for the rise of civic philosophy, art, and literature were already abundantly evident long before the early *quattrocento*. If this hypothesis is tenable, Garin's observations on historical continuity would be more attractive. Although Baron's claims for the catalytic role of the Visconti war would then be scaled down, his valuable insights into the character of civic humanism would remain firm. If the later years of the Florentine *trecento* prove to be ones of creative development and evolutionary change rather than of deterioration and fatigue, Armando Sapori's economic interpretation should be modified. My angle of vision reveals the strained and unmistakable birth pangs of the Renaissance polis along with the decay of the late medieval world. Social, economic, and political data appear to justify a study whose perspective is paternalistic, that is, more concerned with the rise of the new than the senescence of the old.[5] The

---

[5] Ample evidence does support H. Baron's confidence in the vitality of the late *trecento* republic. See his exchange with R. Lopez in *The American Historical Review*, 61 (1956), 1087–89. Similarly, the insights of E. Garin concerning the vibrancy of civic humanism have a strong socioeconomic base. In addition to the previously cited works of Baron, see "Das Erwachen des Historischen Denkens im Humanismus des Quattrocento," *Historische Zeitschrift*, 147 (1952), 5–20. Among Garin's numerous works on Renaissance thought in general, and Florentine thought in particular, see *Der italienische Humanismus* (Bern, 1947) or *L'umanesimo italiano Filosofia e vita civile nel rinasci-*

organizing metaphor of the present volume is the public world, and we shall search out those persistent factors that caused its obtrusion into art and literature as well as its intrusion into citizen life.

I

In considering sharp differences between the polis of the late fourteenth century and its earlier medieval counterpart, much emphasis should be given the inordinate flow of capital into the public sector of the economy. It is no oversimplification to observe that the earlier city was characterized by a thriving private economy and a most modest public sector. After the 1340s the balance shifted radically, and public spending and state consumption of capital became the hallmarks of a novel type of economy. Elsewhere I have tried to elaborate my description of this emerging system, which I classify as an early form of state capitalism, and to explore the possibility of a nexus between this new economic system and particular cultural developments.[6] We observe that sizable increases in the budget of the polis were provoked by expensive wars chronic during the second half of the *trecento*. A program of deficit financing was installed and the public debt vastly expanded. Simultaneously two related developments occurred: first, a pervasive democratization of the Florentine guild world, and second, a strengthening of the bonds of public law. As we shall see, both of these changes owed much to the rise of the new citizens (*novi cives*). (This crucial group is identified by virtue of a membership stemming from families called to high communal office for the first time after 1343.) We shall also notice increasing demands for more efficient and effective government originating from the nagging need to meet interest obligations on the mounting funded debt or *Monte*. By the mid-1340s scrupulous legality and constitutionalism loomed as needed remedies. Exactly then, *novi cives* entered the arena of politics in great numbers, and the mounting public debt became a matter of pressing civic concern.

Of course bitter patrician resistance ensued, and at first efficient government was displaced by a more lax oligarchical rule. Gradually the power of the polis was augmented so that oligarchical reaction was less

---

mento (Bari, 1952). Both scholars would agree that neither the late *trecento* nor the early *quattrocento* were characterized by *Angst*, nor were epitomized by the grasping merchant. Although Garin would proffer no explanation, since his intent is to analyze the philosophy of the period, Baron would contend that the alteration in thought came as a response to Florentine defense of republican *libertas* against Milan, denying that the transformation was rooted in socioeconomic life. It is this base for early Renaissance culture that the present study is eager to describe.

[6] Such a suggestion is made by M. Becker in "Problemi della finanza pubblica fiorentina," *Archivio Storico Italiano* (hereafter *ASI*), 123 (1965), 433–66.

intense, with the result that public law intruded into that preserve once the exclusive and uncontested domain of the old patriciate. No longer could a few families manage the government as if it were personal property; nor could the signory remain relaxed and permissive. Unlike the easier, pre-1340 period, the fiscal needs of the new polis had multiplied while political mobility took its toll among the old ruling order.[7]

Perhaps the most telling aspect of this transformation, from a casual government dominated by a handful of great clans operating with modest budgets, to a stricter regime, was the dramatic rise of the Florentine bureaucracy at mid-*trecento*. This increase in the numbers of state functionaries was an outgrowth of the quest for greater efficiency so that the polis might meet its burdensome public debt. Finally, the tightening of administration was a consequence of mounting pressure from *novi cives* for a stricter rule of public law to contain an overprivileged and lawless patriciate. A reading of the records of the advisory councils to the signory (*Consulte e Pratiche*) demonstrates the resiliency and durability of civic spirit among those called upon to counsel the rulers of the republic. Rarely during the numerous meetings held by the signory over the last half of the *trecento* were political sentiments less than confident. Considering the tragic events of those times—attacks by marauding companies, failure of harvests, chronic warfare and pestilence—this is a remarkable tribute to the stability of civic conscience. Unlike the nervous debaters of the next period of intense crisis over a century later, who intoned glittering generalities and spoke in fragile abstractions, the earlier councilors were calm, even phlegmatic, in time of stress. Fourteenth-century governmental advisers did not piteously and tearfully invoke the name of God or humbly sue for His protection and the assistance of His saints. While other areas of culture betrayed tension and insecurity, the world of *trecento* political discourse stood firm. Although public orators and the republic's councilors certainly recognized the dangers besetting the polis, they continued to act politically with courage. Whatever misgivings were apparent in the private world, the outlines of the public order stood fast. Between the 1350s and the early *quattrocento* an assured polis forged the links of state as well as the expanding chains of empire.[8] These creations were among the most notable triumphs in an age of

---

[7] Cf. M. Becker, *Florence in Transition*, 1, 88–121.
[8] Of paramount importance is the emergence and accentuation of the theme of imperialism in Florentine poetry and art. Cf. P. Meller, "La Cappella Brancacci," 200–1; W. Welliver, *L'impero fiorentino* (Florence, 1957), pp. 14 ff.; J. Wilde, "The Hall of the Great Council of Florence," *Journal of the Warburg and Courtauld Institutes*, 7 (1944), 65 ff. On the surge of patriotic poetry, see F. Flamini's valuable study, *La lirica toscana del rinascimento* (Pisa, 1891), pp. 35–147. On the vast question of exploitation of *contado* by polis, see P. J. Jones, "Per la storia agraria italiana nel Medio Evo: lineamenti e problemi," *Rivista Storica Italiana*, 76 (1964), 347–48.

widespread patriotism, flamboyant imperialism, and brimming civic energy.

During this half century the polis also acted to undermine the hegemony of the Tuscan church and humble the once-arrogant magnates of the city. There was further and drastic curtailment of the authority of the aristocratic Guelf party after 1378. Similarly, the jurisdiction of the august Court Merchant and the autonomy of the once-proud guilds were limited. Feudal privileges and even ancient treaties conceding fiscal immunity were readily violated so that the obstreperous Ubaldini and the fierce Counts Guidi became loyal, albeit reluctant, subjects of the vastly stronger territorial state. Soon the polis dominated the courts of the inquisition demanding that Rome select the inquisitor from a list of Florentine citizens declared eligible by the signory. Worse yet, the republic tolerated the presence of Fraticelli (arch enemies of the Holy See) within the city walls. By the 1360s and 1370s Florence asserted hegemony over the Tuscan church, with the signory pressing for an end to benefit of clergy, the right of sanctuary, and clerical immunity from public imposts.[9]

Erosion of ancient privilege and the dissipation of prerogative in the various orders in medieval society increased the power of the polis until one system of law prevailed and a unitary fiscal structure emerged. It was hoped that reform in the interest of more efficient rule would make management and funding of the public debt simpler and more effective. Still these changes did not alter the problem: in the 1370s and 1380s carrying charges on indebtedness increased until they equaled total annual state income from ordinary revenue sources. Only once did the yearly average for public borrowing fall below 100,000 florins, and then it still totaled above 90,000 florins. Soon the figures became intimidating: by 1390 it was a half million florins, then 670,000 florins, and by 1393 it topped 1,300,000 florins.[10]

---

[9] A. Panella, "La guerra degli Otto Santi e le vicende della legge contro i vescovi," *ASI*, 99 (1941), 36–49. It should be remembered that the Fraticelli and other sects were officially ousted from Florence only after 1382. Earlier, their attacks against the papacy and clerical riches were not discouraged by the signory. The heretical current in Florence during the decade of the seventies cast the polis in the role of savior of a corrupt Italy and fallen ecclesia. Only after their doctrines created disquiet among the workers did the regime banish the Fraticelli. Cf. M. Becker, "Florentine Politics and the Diffusion of Heresy in the Trecento," *Speculum*, 34 (1959), 60–75; N. Rodolico, *I Ciompi* (Florence, 1945), pp. 67 ff.

[10] *PC*, 6–10. On the origins of the *Monte*, see B. Barbadoro, *Le finanze della repubblica fiorentina imposta diretta e debito pubblico fino all'istituzione del monte* (Florence, 1929), pp. 629–87. By the *quattrocento* the solvency of this debt, as well as the fiscal potency it conferred upon a signory who could continue to borrow seemingly unlimited sums from a citizenry, was celebrated in an elaborate poem wherein the author announced that the viability of the *Monte* was the primary reason for Florence's successful defense of her liberty against Milan. Cf. F. Flamini, *La lirica toscana*, p. 74.

There was no surcease from pressure to garner additional state revenue. Meanwhile, from the 1340s to the coming of Cosimo de' Medici in 1434, the expanded creditor class of the polis tended to be identical with the administrative and ruling cadre of the city. Starting in 1343–45 we observe political power devolving upon that large group of citizens able to make generous loans to the treasury. The implications for the democratization of the signory and its colleges were of course substantial. These political bodies came to include leading members of the creditor class notwithstanding their new status. Although family connections were still useful and ancestry seldom a deterrent, political influence could be won through purchase of negotiable government credits. The numerous *novi cives* in the signory lent their support to legislation calculated to curtail patrician privilege as well as to administrative reform for revenue to finance the debt.[11]

From the foregoing we might infer the existence of a hardy amalgam of new and old citizens qualified to conduct the business of state. By comparing this coalition of merchants and affluent artisans who acquired rich political experience over the middle years of the *trecento* with their ruling forebears of the late Middle Ages, we discover significant differences. Commencing in the 1280s with the foundation of the priorate and continuing through the 1330s, we observe that control over finances and foreign policy usually rested with a few of the city's great business houses. The Acciaiuoli, Bardi, Cerchi, Peruzzi, Scali, and others who financed key public ventures tended to acquire political power. The utilization of limited sums of private capital was effective as long as costs of war and carrying charges on the debt were minimal. During the 1340s many of these firms lost political influence because they went bankrupt and their resources dissipated. Further, astronomical sums were required to finance wars too expensive to be underwritten by a coterie of patricians. Many citizens both new and old were invited to invest larger shares of their patrimony in the state's burgeoning public debt. Treasury records reveal the names of 4,500 to 5,000 citizens from a total of 13,000 to 14,000 rate payers who were considered creditors of the republic. A status formerly the prerogative of a few score of the republic's first families was now conferred upon the affluent Florentine middle class. Of paramount importance is the fact that from 1,000 to 1,500 of these men were summoned biannually to staff the numerous public posts. Thus the growth of communal bureaucracy exactly paralleled the emergence of the new, expanded creditor class.[12] Bureaucrat, creditor, and citizen politician fur-

---

[11] M. Becker, *Florence in Transition*, 1, 177–230.
[12] Not only can an equation be suggested between officeholder and creditor class, but also between the guild masters of the city and those enjoying full citizen rights. In 1343 the number of Florentines included in the scrutiny (*squittino*) of qualified citizens

nished the civic humanists of the early Renaissance with an audience; the last half of the fourteenth century witnessed the simultaneous coming of the publicists and their public.[13]

II

The shape of the public world became more definite after the 1340s as the citizen derived his political identity from participation in the polis rather than from ties with private groups and medieval corporate bodies. That bedazzling array of conflicting loyalties and allegiances characteristic of the earlier world included tower society, *consorteria*, Guelf party, Angevin cause, philopapalism, religious confraternity, and so forth. The middle years of the fourteenth century saw a firmer identity conferred on

---

for communal office was 3,446. The final sortation or *tratta* from the leather bags containing the names was performed after this large number had been winnowed down. Only 10 per cent were declared eligible for posts in the signory. On the intricate procedures involved, see N. Rubinstein, *Government of Florence*, pp. 4–5. In effect, then, 90 per cent of those declared eligible were to occupy lesser posts in government administration. Cf. G. Villani, 12, 22. Over the next years the demand for additional personnel to serve in internal offices as well as territorial administrators increased. By the 1380s, 5,000 Florentines were included in the scrutiny. (If we adjust this figure to take into account losses due to the Black Death, then the number of qualified citizens has almost doubled, and this jump is approximately equal to the growth of communal bureaucracy over those years.) Cf. *Delizie degli eruditi Toscani*, ed. Fr. I. di San Luigi (Florence, 1770–89), 16, 125 ff. Indicative of the problem of staffing this bureaucracy was the opening to lesser guildsmen of many offices once reserved for magnates and *haute bourgeoisie*. Cf. *CP*, 8, f. 33 (Jan. 18, 1367), where discussion before the signory centered on extracting lesser guildsmen for the posts of *podestà* and castellan in rural districts. Indeed, this was merely a belated recognition of what had been commonplace for over a decade. As I hope to suggest in a subsequent volume, the government's need for administrators transcended the limits of social prejudice. Magnates and *haute bourgeoisie* alike were reluctant to serve in remote and inhospitable places.

[13] Not all were so advantaged. The lament of the finest late *trecento* Florentine composer, Francesco Landini, in which he personifies the figure of Music weeping because "intelligent people desert her sweetness," may be more than artful. He bewails the demand for popular songs, contending that ignorance and vice abound, whereas in times past his "sweetness was prized by knights, barons and great lords." Of considerable interest is the fact that the musician was also one of the firmest defenders of the logician William of Ockham and medieval scholasticism against such civic humanists as Coluccio Salutati. Cf. L. Ellinwood, *The Works of Francesco Landini* (Cambridge, Mass., 1939). Representative of the civic humanists, so many of whom were *novi cives*, was Domenico Bandino of Arezzo. Like Bruni and Salutati, he identified himself completely with the interests of his adopted *patria*. In the 1380s, when Florence began rule over his native city, he exhorted the Aretines to submit humbly. Cf. A. Hankey, "Domenico di Bandino of Arezzo," *Italian Studies*, 12, 127. He, along with Salutati, received the coveted status of Florentine citizen. Yet another civic humanist, Buonaccorso da Montemagno of Pistoia, argued vigorously for nobility of deed over birth and revealed much of his own respect for the Florentine public world when he wrote, "For when I understood that human skills are so much the more glorious when placed at the service of the Republic, I gave myself entirely to my fatherland. Never thereafter did I cease to think of its safety and prosperity, fearing no labor and no danger, which might bring it glory and security." Cf. D. Herlihy, *Medieval and Renaissance Pistoia* (New Haven, 1967), p. 260.

citizen by a more highly articulated public world. Matteo Villani, continuator of his brother Giovanni's chronicle and the most perceptive analyst of Florentine political life, wrote during these painful years when the demands of polis were voiced to the detriment of earlier loyalties. Time-honored allegiances to the house of Naples were severed because they were too burdensome for the republic's treasury. At first the chronicler was deeply troubled as indeed are the advisers to the signory who proudly recall the ancient and glorious alliances with the kingdom to the south.[14] Matteo was further outraged when young princes, descendants of the republic's old allies, were refused entry into the city. Like so many of his countrymen he was appalled at this brutal rejection when, simultaneously and for strategic reasons, Florentine interests were fulfilled by an alliance with tyrannous north Italian lords, once the city's dread enemies. Equally disturbing were the crafty dealings with the Visconti despots of Milan, notorious heretics and treasonous Ghibellines, yet soon to become respected signatories of a nonaggression treaty with Florence (Sarzana, 1353). The shabby treatment the signory accorded the progeny of venerable, heroic Florentine families as well as the devious decrees promulgated against the ancient liberties of the church distressed him, and the treacherous rapprochement of Florence with Holy Roman Emperor reinforced his pessimism. Only a few years later, however, dramatic alteration was discernible in chronicle and chronicler. The very form of his history changed: local events took precedence. Concentration upon minute details of life in the polis replaced extensive treatment of pope, emperor, and medieval monarch. Thus the structure and content of his work departed from the frame erected by his famous brother who had composed the most persuasive of all Italian medieval chronicles, fixing the fate of Florence in the amplitude of the world of the Middle Ages.

Matteo divested consideration of the earthly polis from the sacramental, political mentality prevalent in the thirteenth and fourteenth centuries. This provoked the painful realization that the principal threat to the well-being of this polis was posed by the very social orders and institutions charged with the sacred trust of maintaining the structure of that world inviolate. No longer were the greedy and over-ambitious *novi cives* of Dante's day, who would not remain in their assigned position within the social hierarchy, portrayed as villains. Nor were the heretical Ghibelline nobles of Giovanni Villani's time identified as the prime menace to the republic and its laws. Instead, the high prelates and princes of the Christian world and the status-worthy members of the Florentine patriciate were considered the relentless enemies of *buon governo* and willing betrayers of Florentine *libertas*.

[14] G. Brucker, "The Ghibelline Trial of Matteo Villani (1362)," *Medievalia et Humanistica*, 13 (1960), 48–55.

Matteo and his young contemporary, the chronicler Marchionne di Coppo Stefani, singled out many of the city's ancient clans for castigation. That very bastion of aristocratic influence and center of orthodoxy, the venerable Guelf party, once seen as savior of a beleaguered polis, was cast in a treasonous role—diabolical and brutal pawn of a corrupt clergy bent upon subverting the republic. The *Parte* stood as a doctrinaire opponent of a pragmatic foreign policy as well as of an internal program framed to meet the needs of the great and middling guildsmen of the city. Dominated by ideologues who would foment civil war in the service of a shopworn and archaic philopapalism, this once-proud organization emerged as the principal subverter of the republic's *libertas*.[15]

In the middle years of the *trecento* a new paideia much sterner and more egalitarian came to consciousness. The stress upon the rule of law coincided with the creation of an expanded and more effective bureaucracy. Though earlier political thinkers like Brunetto Latini, Giovanni Villani, or even Dante would have supported the need for such a rule in theory, they displayed little sympathy for practical problems of courts and judges seeking law enforcement. Instead, they alternated between an abiding passion for justice and a defamation of those officials of the republic who performed routine legal tasks. Until the 1340s Florentines concerned with problems of law and its enforcement expressed interest either through the traditional form of invective against public magistrates or through handbooks replete with bland and virtuous political nostrums. A decade later we observe a deeper understanding of the difficult role of the magistrate and a keener appreciation of practical details of administration. Two centuries later, the greatest of all Florentine historians, Niccolò Machiavelli, concluded that this legal transformation, whereby greater citizen equality was achieved, was the most splendid accomplishment of this age. His sense of irony made him well aware of the price of this sterner rule, which suppressed the martial qualities and passion for violence of the overmighty denizens of the polis.[16]

Gradually, Matteo Villani recognized that the civic health of the republic depended upon the loyalty and patriotic involvement of its businessmen, industrialists, and even tradespeople. He understood what was to become a *topos* of latter-day humanism: a flourishing republic must win the affection and solicitude of its citizenry both new and old. The first of the humanist chancellors of Florence, foremost literary man of his generation, Coluccio Salutati, maintained in the late 1370s that the *mercatores* and *artifices* were the true architects and defenders of the

---

[15] U. Dorini, *Notizie Storiche sull'Università di Parte Guelfa in Firenze* (Florence, 1902), p. 39.
[16] *History of Florence and of the Affairs of Italy*, ed. F. Gilbert (New York, 1960), p. 111.

polis. The enemies of the well-ordered republic were none other than the *milites* of medieval renown. Further, humble trade and industry were the sinews of the vigorous body politic. Such humanist Florentine chancellors of the next generation as Leonardo Bruni Aretino and Poggio Bracciolini embellished the metaphor to expose important philosophical implications when they declaimed against stoic contempt for wealth, the outstanding ingredient in many a manual of medieval moral recipes. The wealth of the citizenry would provide lifeblood for the republic, they claimed, and from the 1370s on, civic humanist, chronicler, and patriotic cleric joined to make the citizen more mindful of his civic responsibility. All the while there was the nagging question as to whether the desire for wealth in itself might not be a good, just as citizen ambition might redound to the advantage of the polis. All this was far removed from the organic hierarchical view of a more conservative past.[17]

Matteo's chronicle was the first to confer dignity and value upon contemporary history. The last books close with the republic as buffer and resolute champion for an industrious business community. The socioeconomic character of this polis is not subject to invidious comparison with a perfect, past mythic world. Unlike those earlier writers of Dante's time, Matteo achieved an unswerving socioeconomic perspective—a disjunction, a distancing. Therefore neither the memory of lost innocence nor the awareness of contemporary evil darkens or obscures the dimensions, qualities, and achievements of the present. A generation ago chronicler and poet willingly charged their times with the damning vice of cupidity; thus the locus and cause of decadence were the boundless reaches of man's depraved appetites. To them even the growth and expansion of Florence induced a sense of sinfulness. This was no real progress since its roots were in man's corrupt nature. For Dante the present times could be stable and peaceful only when factiousness and cupidity ended. Only a *renovatio* within the human heart could restore the innocence required to herald the advent of a law-abiding world. Such a world would of course be governed in part by pure-blooded, ancient Florentines unmoved by ambition; in a word, by the ancestors of Dante himself. Lacking this, the rule of a single man—the emperor—unstained by *cupiditas* must prevail.[18]

With Matteo, the chronicler Stefani, and the civic humanists from Salutati to Bruni, the old prejudices against the *novi cives* abated as they did against trade and the expansion of the polis. Again the willingness to accept present experience implied a popular critique of medieval stoic

---

[17] M. Villani, *Cronica*, ed. F. Dragomanni (Florence, 1846), 11, 1; E. Garin, "I cancellieri umanisti della repubblica," *Rivista Storica Italiana*, 71 (1959), 199 ff.
[18] M. Becker, "Dante and His Literary Contemporaries As Political Men," *Speculum*, 41 (1966), 665–80.

moralizing. Ambition, wealth, and energy were no longer so generally regarded as obstacles to virtue. Qualities damning to social commentators in the era of Dante were thought worthy of praise. Just as writers were more willing to accept the rough-hewn qualities of men (Petrarch's admission in the *Secretum* that he desired to be not a god but only a man), so the chronicler no longer was as eager to hypothecate the existence of a medieval golden age and suggest that the return to this arcadia could only be through the path of spiritual regeneration. The consequences of this altered perspective can only be alluded to here, but one, the growing dignity of a contemporary public world, was not insignificant.[19]

Another change in mid-*trecento* Florentine society relevant for the men of Matteo's generation and the civic humanists of the next was the transvaluation of the ideals of chivalry. The noble ends of knighthood were not modified; rather, they came to be associated with a public world stressing citizen service to the polis. Beginning with these years the polis itself came to be the largest single purveyor of the dignity of knighthood. Where once monarch, emperor, or pope conferred patents of nobility, now it was the *civitas* who dispensed the high honor. Most esteemed of course were those who had done honorable service for the city. Kinfolk of prominent Florentines regularly made payment into the treasury of the republic to ensure that gaudy funerals replete with state ceremonial would honor the deceased. Also there was an increase in the incidence of civic bequests by notables. Public funeral orations became more elaborate, and outstanding political figures were promised eternal fame and untarnished luster. The passion for a fusion of public renown and religious reward found expression in the poetry of Petrarch as well as in the life of the most remarkable of late *trecento* political leaders, Guido del Palagio. The ideals of militia service and military obligation also underwent revivification—at least on a theoretical level. As the precepts of chivalry lost much of their private meaning, they came to be invested with a public significance.[20]

A work such as Boccaccio's *Decameron* illustrates an earlier stage before this transformation. The most persuasive of modern scholars of this

---

[19] As has been suggested earlier, Petrarch was unable to find *virtù* among contemporary rulers. Their lives are material only for "satyre materiam," not "historie materiam." Originally, he had decided to include contemporaries in his *De viris illustribus*, but later apologized that he could not guide his pen through such darkness. Cf. *Rerum memorandum libri*, ed. G. Billanovich (Florence, 1945), pp. cxxiv–cxxx; *Le Familiari*, ed. V. Rossi (Florence, 1942), 4, 24; 8. Unlike the civic humanists of Florence, Petrarch disvalued the history of his own times. At the end of his epic poem, *Africa*, he expresses his hopes for a better future. His historical schematization but not his contempt for the times, in all their political manifestations, was acceptable to his Florentine peers. Cf. T. Mommsen, "Petrarch's Conception of the Dark Ages," *Speculum*, 17 (1943), 226–49.
[20] C. C. Bayley, *War and Society in Renaissance Florence* (Toronto, 1961).

masterpiece, V. Branca, has shown that the temporal locus of the work is in the late thirteenth and early fourteenth centuries. The commitment of characters and author is to the educative value of private passions and personal codes.[21] The ethos of so many of the stories is intensely individualistic, and Boccaccio's sympathies are with the single person against the harsh claims of society. Further, the youthful Boccaccio is devoted to a social rather than to a political ideal; it is the virtuous orders of society acting without harsh restraint who can achieve a happy blend of chivalric daring and bourgeois respect for personality. Through the refined, ennobling, personal experience of love, the low and corrupt can be redeemed; the harsh compulsions of law and government stand as an impediment.

Soon after the 1350s, however, Boccaccio could not sustain this hopeful vision of a harmony between the two interpenetrating cultures. Indeed, as has been suggested in the first volume of my study, the world of the *Decameron* reflected the hortatory tone of early *trecento* political life. In those easier times the individual patrician (noble or commoner) could satisfy private claims by outwitting the demands of the public world. This gentle, permissive aristocratic culture receded, however, as law enforcement at mid-*trecento* was strengthened. The legalistic triumph of new citizen and patrician-adherent undermined aristocratic optimism and casual life style. Again Machiavelli's *History of Florence* furnishes valuable insight: at mid-*trecento* the rule of law commenced to level the upper reaches of society so that prowess at arms and magnanimity were stifled within the ranks of the nobility. Private sources of prestige and honor dwindled so that men were more dependent upon the public order for ennoblement. All too eagerly did once-proud magnates clumsily imitate prudent and parsimonious burghers. The documents of the time lend support to Machiavelli's contentions: petitions from magnates to the signory requesting commoner status were abundant, with petitioner agreeing to renounce his *consorteria*, relinquish his title and coat of arms, and even assume a new family name. The public courts imposed severe penalties against the old magnates, with leniency only occasionally being exhibited to those who would abandon the code of honor. Magistrates extended pardon to some who foreswore vendetta, disowned their lawless kinsmen, moved to another quarter of the city, and finally agreed to post substantial bond for continued good behavior. Little opportunity existed for expressing the old chivalric spirit; the last public tournament was held in 1343. Later, when the next knightly contest was announced, it was in answer to strengthened civic imperatives: the tourney was staged

---

[21] V. Branca, *Boccaccio Medievale* (Florence, 1956).

in honor of the corporate symbol of the polis, that ideal fusion of secular and spiritual—the *Madonna Libertà*.[22]

Dedicated spokesman for conformity of the individual to the sterner paideia was the next leading Florentine poet and novelist. Writing in the second half of the *trecento*, Franco Sacchetti could only ridicule the once-precious, personal ideals of chivalry. Since he never seriously entertained this lyric and overwrought code, he made it the butt for bitter jibes. The refining qualities of the world of courtesy were considered so ineffectual that even their anachronistic charm had dissipated. Along with contemporary civic humanists such as Coluccio Salutati, Sacchetti transvalued the older ideals of *amore* and *carità* until they lost much of their individuality. Instead he defined them as love of country, devotion to neighbor, and dedication to civic well-being. The less heroic virtues of the politically conditioned man replaced more abstract forms of commitment to *la Donna Angelica*, Dame Philosophy, or Holy Mother Church. Gone was the originality of the poets of the Sweet New Style; no large collection of this verse was to come forth. The last generation of poets (Francesco da Barberino, Ser Ventura Monachi, Zanobi da Strada) had been that of the thirties and forties. Since literature no longer gained energy from the ideal of *renovatio* through love, the result was pallid imitation.

Interior renewal through subtle education of the gentle heart, which arose from pure devotion to *la Donna Angelica*, no longer was central to the literary mentality. Omnipresent instead was the relentless moralizing tone of a Sacchetti, relying on blatant precepts rather than on the delicate promptings of a knowing heart. Intelligence must be attuned to the imperatives of society: wit may be too dangerous an instrument for the individual to employ for achieving his ends since it can only irritate the collectivity. For Sacchetti the public world was so formidable that he advised extreme self-control, despite unbearable provocation. Wit and love, prime ingredients of an earlier literature, could no longer be encouraged as forces for preserving identity or maintaining integrity.

Other Tuscan writers tried to utilize the same forms as Boccaccio to create the illusion of magic grace implicit in the carefree, hopeful world of the *Decameron*. The consequence was esthetic failure; they were too fearful of society and lacked confidence that individuals could satisfy the claims of nature and yet maintain the good will of the public world. The tales of Giovanni Sercambi, for example, composed at the close of the fourteenth century, are fixed in a rigid frame. Even the narrator is a part of a formal organization. Speakers go so far as to elect a treasurer and other officials, while the tales themselves always conclude with the in-

---

[22] E. Li Gotti, *Franco Sacchetti*, p. 39.

evitable punishment of the evildoer. The *novelle* of Ser Giovanni Fiorentino have little that is "gentili e poetici" and reveal an awesome consciousness of the atrocious revenge society can visit upon the unwary.[23]

III

Painting after the death of Giotto expressed nostalgia for the recession of the older ideals of a medieval world once capable of transmuting the cruel realities of daily life. Dissipated was that abundant confidence in the possibility of capturing the moment at which a transcendent ideal ennobles some familiar happening in the phenomenal world. In the frescoes by the master painter of the mid-*trecento*, Orcagna, in the Santa Croce cycle of the *Last Judgment* and the *Torments of Hell*, the Florentine artist is concerned with the reality of death and the certainty of suffering in this world. No one, not noble or great cleric, can conform to a superior code at a moment of adversity. So, too, at the Camposanto of Pisa we see splendid courtly horsemen who can only hold their noses at the stench of death. The new realistic psychology had its day when Orcagna saw fit to depict the poor welcoming deliverance by the Reaper. Paralleling this are the portrayals by Francesco Traini evincing intense feeling for human suffering and all the ills that flesh is heir to. There is more to pinpoint than the onset of plague and pestilence in 1348. As early as 1342 the figure of Job entered Tuscan art to counsel the faithful and set an example. The influence of the puritanical Fra Simone Fidati brings mystical interpretation to favorite Biblical stories much before the coming of the Black Death.

Evidence for the dissolution of the unitary synthesis achieved in the age of Giotto is abundant. The balance between sacred and profane, the comfortable fusion of humanity with divinity, had been disturbed since the late thirties. We move into a world where the possibility of subsuming every contingency under the rule of a universal became ever more remote.

---

[23] E. Li Gotti, "Storia e poesia del 'Pecorone'," *Belfagor*, 1 (1946), 103–10; *Il Pecorone di Ser Giovanni Fiorentino, e due racconti anonimi del trecento*, ed. Salvatore Battaglia (Milan, 1944). Compare the delicacy of treatment accorded the wise Jew Abraham in *Decameron* 1, 2, with the crude handling of the theme in *Il Pecorone*, 6, 1. Cf. also *Il Pecorone*, 2, 2; 3, 1. On Giovanni Sercambi, see A. Chiari, "La fortuna del Boccaccio," *Questioni e correnti di storia letteraria*, ed. A. Momigliano (Florence, 1949), 297–98. E. Fusco opines in his *La lirica* (Milan, 1950), p. 128, that Sacchetti's best poetry is civil or ethicoreligious. For a pertinent statement by Sacchetti revealing the extent to which he has broken in this democratized era with the language of the chivalric courts and the schools, see his *Il Libro delle trecentonovelle*, ed. V. Pernicone (Florence, 1946), nov. 80. The citation from nov. 71 is worth recording: "E però veramente al dicitore, che ha a dire bene alcuna cosa, non gli conviene avere l'animo ne 'I pensiero, se non solo a quello che de' dire, perocchè ogni piccola cosa, che viene alla mente fuori della sua diceria, lo impedisce per forma, che spesse volte rimane in su le secche; ed è incontrato già a perfetti dicitori."

In one of the most celebrated art works of the time—the Baroncelli Chapel in Santa Croce—we are aware that the profusion of descriptive detail serves to heighten the emotionality of the work.[24]

The most influential artist of this period, Taddeo Gaddi, active in the city from 1330 to 1363, distanced himself from that unitary synthesis, which partook of so high an order of spirituality, to pursue more limited objectives. Instead of being effectively contained under the canopy of chivalry and hagiolatry, piety, probity, and the burgher virtues dominated. Emotive expression prevailed when pathos could be heightened by new effects with light. Well before 1348 Bernardo Daddi popularized the world of Giotto and in so doing weakened the formal ordering elements of his art. He ministered to religious feelings fixed not to a hierarchical pattern but rooted in personal devotion. Soon the earlier equilibrium between form and space, solid and void, so hard won, was supplanted by prevalent tensions. With Orcagna, figures of "dramatic desperateness" move in a nonrational universe. Interestingly enough, although this world is constructed from the naturalistic elements of a Giotto, the effect is nonnaturalistic. His people are solemn and obsessive, not contemplative or tranquil.[25]

The *Decameron* looks both ways. It attempts to take us back to aristocratic-burgher ideals and to recall the medieval comic schema wherein the reader is led from the gross to the sublime. In discussing this classic, the formidable literary critic of our time, Erich Auerbach, dwells upon the inability of this work to confront in any meaningful way the fact of human suffering. If it is true that the ideas undergirding certain of the arts during the first part of the *trecento* failed to sustain men in later trials, we will perhaps feel greater sympathy for the heroic and terrible confrontation artists were summoned to make in the following generation. Among Florentine literary men as different as the humanist Coluccio Salutati and the religious mystic Giovanni dalle Celle, there existed a remarkable level of awareness concerning the inadequacies of the medieval stoic stance in the face of tragedy. More celebrated still are Petrarch's

---

[24] John White, *Art and Architecture in Italy: 1250 to 1400* (Baltimore, 1966), pp. 370 ff.; R. Salvini, *L'arte di Agnolo Gaddi* (Florence, 1936), pp. 1–6.

[25] M. Meiss, *Painting in Florence and Siena after the Black Death* (Princeton, 1951), pp. 6–23. A modest disclaimer should be entered against this masterful study to which the present volume is so beholden: the onset of tension and anxiety observed by Meiss does antedate the Black Death by seven or eight years. Some of the major cases of restitution of usury by Florentine patricians occur in the late thirties and early forties. Cf. my "Some Economic Implications of the Conflict between Church and State in Trecento Florence," *Mediæval Studies*, 21 (1959), 1–16.

The dramatic contrast characteristic of Taddeo Gaddi is evident in the juxtaposition of figures animated by bourgeois piety and those agitated by intense religious fervor. Orcagna's Strozzi altarpiece indicates that the artist recognizes tension as a positive value. Cf. R. Salvini, "La Pala Strozzi in Santa Maria Novella," *L'arte*, 8 (1937), 37–41.

dialogues in which medieval prescriptions and formulas for conquering suffering are viewed from the vantage point of a realistic psychology shown to be wanting. In Petrarch's case, the aim is not to elevate the real to the ideal but to deny that man, given his nature, can ever achieve the ideal.[26]

Self-analysis such as Dante and his mentor St. Thomas practiced was predicated upon metaphysical not empirical concepts and derived from theories concerning the nature and inherent qualities of the human psyche. The more empirically oriented psychology of Petrarch or his Florentine disciple Coluccio Salutati emphasized the laws by which the mind operated—laws essentially lawless in that they stressed the instability of the mind. This instability served as a limit so that the individual could present as axiomatic against the injunctions of theologians and metaphysicians the mind's incapacity to obey instruction. Therefore in the *Secretum*, when Augustine admonishes Petrarch to keep the fear of death always before him, the poet counters by arguing this is impossible, for the human psyche is simply too mobile: new passions and preoccupations are always intruding and in turn being replaced by others. The same realistic psychology is espoused by Salutati but with greater anguish. In his justly celebrated letter, composed upon the death of his beloved son, the humanist sees the helplessness of wisdom in confronting the isolation resulting from tragedy. Philosophy, even as taught by the sublime Cicero, is impotent before insupportable burdens. Christ Himself sweated blood when dying on the cross.[27]

In the 1340s no major artist duplicated the accomplishments of Giotto and his school by attempting an equilibrium between form and space. No longer do we discern "supple figures moving freely in a measured, easily traversable world." In the Spanish Chapel of Sta. Maria Novella,

---

[26] E. Auerbach's *Mimesis* and his *Dante Poet of the Secular World*, trans. R. Manheim (Chicago, 1961). The ambiguity of the humanist stance in general merits analysis. On the one hand there was an abhorrence of the formulas for withstanding pain and loss; on the other there was admiration for the heroic virtues and furies of Senecan tragedy. Again, over the long run, the exigencies of the public world appear to act as a filter, allowing passions and instincts valuable to the polis to be legitimatized and even ennobled. The term "realistic psychology," as applied to Petrarch, is intended to indicate that the humanist is convinced that the mind has its own laws, which must be obeyed. Therefore one can be persistently admonished by a St. Augustine to meditate always on the imperatives of salvation. Against this the humanist will project the mobility of the human soul wherein passions and preoccupations continually displace each other. For an excellent analysis of this theme, see A. Tenenti, *Il senso della morte e l'amore della vita nel rinascimento* (Turin, 1957).

[27] C. Salutati, *Epistolario*, 3, 393–94, 416–21. For a sensitive appraisal of this attitude, see E. Garin, *Italian Humanism, Philosophy and Civic Life in the Renaissance*, trans. Peter Munz (Oxford, 1965), pp. 28–29. Through his careful reading of ancient poets such as Propertius and Tibullus, Petrarch came to appreciate an art bound to deep suffering. It was no longer sufficient for literature to demonstrate technical competence and ingenuity at allegorizing; it had to be proof of high conscience as well.

where the greatest frescoes of the sixties were painted, we observe that continuity was achieved only with the suspension of the laws of diminution. The people of Giovanni del Biondo stand "wrapt and non-communicative," while Giovanni da Milano (who had probably lived in Florence since 1350, becoming a citizen in 1366) portrays one of Giotto's favorite themes with very different spirit. His meeting of Joachim and Anna at the Golden Gate depicts Anna, head bowed, humbly contemplating the mystical conception while Joachim stares gravely into the beyond. The couple avoid a familiar embrace; isolation and withdrawal are evident.[28]

Rather than term this art decadent and thereby suggest a sharp decline in creativity, we can emphasize the positive contribution of the post-Giotto generation. The extensive use of foreshortening and recession enabled them to attain a high order of subjectivity, just as their novel use of light permitted an increase of pathetic accents. Emotional intensity of design matched the psychological tension in the figures. Contrast existed between architectural setting and subject, and even between two scenes placed side by side.

The introduction of these strongly subjective elements does involve a loss of that hard-won equilibrium between the transcendental and the sensible which existed a generation earlier. The work of such commanding artists as Orcagna and his brother Nardo were no longer so likely to present the human figure well integrated into space. There was frequently a contrast between chromatic and plastic elements or between perfectly frontal and perfectly profile figure arrangements. Often psychological penetration was achieved through the unceasing spiritual struggle between human and divine. If awkwardness was sometimes the consequence of overinvolvement, it was the price of increasing uncertainty on the part of the artists that their creations walked in an ambiance where the divine and human converge.

IV

Without straining the quest for analogies in art and literature, it would seem that a dramatic mutation was in process. Heightened interest in subjective awareness and a tendency to cultivate one's nuances of feeling were surely the living message of the foremost of contemporary poets—Petrarch. The sense of personality became more complex and burdensome as it lost the support of the medieval frame of ritual. Florentine literature at the close of the Middle Ages was characterized by an intense, albeit receding, millenarianism. A sizable corpus of poetry expressed the

---

[28] M. Meiss, *Painting in Florence and Siena*, pp. 43 ff.

hopeful ideal of *renovatio mundi*, and leading chroniclers were still committed to structuring the past in terms of charismatic figure and messianic expectation. Both Dante and Giovanni Villani responded initially to this lively tradition of mythos, although they found it increasingly difficult to accommodate historical experience within this religio-political framework.[29]

The middle years of the *trecento* were the locale of a formidable critique of traditional medieval eschatology. Instead of riveting their gaze on the imminence of the Second Coming and the finitude of time, observers fixed their attention on problems of individual salvation. For the first time, an entire generation of chroniclers failed to structure historical writing in accord with traditional medieval formulas. Likewise, their contemporaries, the poets, were comparatively indifferent to religio-political *renovatio*. Boccaccio failed completely to understand the messianic vision and millennial doctrine of the recent past; his highly personal religious orientation was divested of apocalyptic elements over the last decade of his life. Reading from his beloved Dante before leading citizens in Florence in 1373, he displayed a monumental insensitivity toward the political symbolism and allegory of the early cantos of the *Inferno*.[30]

A few years after, when Coluccio Salutati pre-empted the role of literary arbiter, he also proved a resolute opponent of the mythic tradition that once served so well to structure political experience. The humanist went a step further when he lampooned the *lymphatice prophetantes* who pretended to possess a knowledge no mortal could hope to acquire.[31] History was no longer seen as a linear progression toward the advent of the Antichrist or the Second Coming; nor could it be made meaningful in terms of the charisma of pope or emperor. Clearly, too, historical fulfillment cannot be induced through those forces of spiritual regeneration, the religious orders. The prophecies of the more fervent among them seemed even farther from realization than when they had been proclaimed in the time of St. Francis and St. Dominic. Certainly the failure

---

[29] For the later attitudes of Villani, see M. Becker, *Florence in Transition*, 1, 142–44. On the susceptibility of the youthful chronicler to the vision of "un mondo nuovo," see A. Frugoni, "Il Giubileo di Bonifacio VIII," *Bullettino dell'Istituto Storico Italiano per il Medioevo*, 62 (1950), 105–6.
[30] G. Padoan, *L'ultima opera di Giovanni Boccaccio* (Padua, 1959), pp. 82–83. (That the Florentine signory should propose a public reading on a vernacular text by a layman, and that this should be overwhelmingly approved by the communal council, is dramatic evidence of the transvaluation of sensibilities toward contemporary culture. As far as I know, northern European analogues for such a step are not to be found. Medieval commentaries were of course reserved for sacred, Biblical, and legal writings. Contemporary profane poetry could be accorded comparable treatment only by the blasphemous.)
[31] *Epistolario*, 1, 299; 2, p. 332. (I wish to thank my former student, Father Bonnell, for his valuable insights into Salutati's views of the active and contemplative life.)

of such sacramental concepts of history did much to prepare a Salutati for reviving classical ideals of imitation and example. If the ritual and ceremonial bond existing between individual and God is broken in the world of time, then man must learn through imitation and example. History and moral philosophy took precedence over metaphysics, the natural sciences, and even theology.[32]

With Matteo Villani, the chronicler Stefani, and Franco Sacchetti the medieval emperor became at best an ineffectual figure and at worst an absurdity.[33] Again, in the most imposing work of art of the period, the Spanish Chapel of the Dominican Friary of Sta. Maria Novella, pope and emperor are portrayed in ordinary scale while Knowledge and Order and Christ are enthroned. Indeed, those two charismatic figures of the Middle Ages are all but lost in the milling crowd. The emperor holds in his hand an orb of dominion, which upon closer inspection seems to be a skull. The irony is almost too complete.[34]

The frescoes in the Chapel display surprising juxtapositions of the naturalistic and abstract. Generally, traditional medieval schema failed to provide durable frames for experience. Literary men of backgrounds as varied as that of the plebeian Antonio Pucci and patrician Franco Sacchetti possessed a culture that is "encyclopedic and disorganized."[35] This was not true of the youthful Boccaccio and his generation; only with mid-*trecento* do we observe ample evidence of features and interests leading to disarray. Dissipated was the fine and balanced artistic perspective achieved by the delicately wrought frames of earlier writings, which had depended upon young Boccaccio's artistic confidence in the esthetic validity of medieval schema, especially the comic view of man's capacity for spiritual progress.[36] From the *Corbaccio* on, his didacticism became

---

[32] Again, the contrast between Salutati and Petrarch is worth considering. The latter's stress upon historical example and model is fundamental; not so his commitment to the belief that his age was unfavorable to learning and his penchant for comparing the degenerate present with the radiant classical past. As for Salutati, his willingness to defend contemporary civic culture against its detractors has been insufficiently emphasized. He assimilates Petrarch's ideal of the *studia humanitatis*, but would include the best creations of the men of the Florentine polis. His *De Tyranno* is not so much a defense of monarchy as of the worth and dignity of civic culture. This theme will be treated in a subsequent volume.

[33] See the valuable study of F. Magri-Leone, "La Politica di Giovanni Boccaccio," *Giornale Storico della Letteratura Italiana*, 15 (1890), 104 ff.

[34] J. Wood Brown, *The Dominican Church of Santa Maria Novella* (Edinburgh, 1902), p. 139.

[35] N. Sapegno, *Il Trecento* (Milan, 1934), pp. 423 ff.; E. Li Gotti, *Franco Sacchetti*, pp. 34–46.

[36] G. Getto, *Vita di forme di vita nel Decameron* (Turin, 1956); V. Branca, *Boccaccio, passim*. Roberto Palmarocchi in his *I Villani* (Turin, 1937), pp. 90–91, compares the contorted prose of Matteo with the precise and limpid style of his older brother. More relevant perhaps as evidence of this disjunction is the absence of an organic fusion between the younger chronicler's narrative and his explanation.

more explicit, his learning more encyclopedic, and so the noumenal glow receded in a profusion of classical scholarship, with its veneration for past history and the ancestral Latin tongue.[37] Weakened were those medieval ordering principles that drew strength from a commitment to a superior world of courtesy, magnanimity, and nobility. Old virtues with roots in the private world were not so magnetic. No longer do we observe with frequency that inexorable logic of the exemplum that can effectively command the subordination of workaday reality to some fixed aristocratic ideal.[38]

From his earliest poetry in the middle years of the *trecento*, Franco Sacchetti displayed a heavily coercive moralism. His sympathies were blatantly on the side of a regulated polis and an energetic conscience. For him ethical judgment was a means of dominating this mobile world. The individual must always live with a consciousness of conflict and contrast; always there is tension between the intellect, will, and memory. Sacchetti's organizing metaphor is that of warfare (*guerra*). Although his language is not so overly intellectual and baroque as Catherine of Siena's, still it is redolent with conflict. Her symbols were bellicose, too, bespeaking war and conquest, blood and battle, and suffering. The simile is *vita* like a tourney, with the believer in the lists fully armed and even wearing spurs.[39] This is a language mighty and yet "assurdo," becoming more stereotyped, abstract, and symbolic. The images tumble forth from a fecund imagination little responsive to nature. Unlike the popular preacher Cavalca of an earlier time, St. Catherine is not in possession of a firm ordering principle. Sacramental tie and hierarchical gradation do not operate as effectively to structure her experience.[40]

Only to review the titles of Antonio Pucci's sonnets is to gain a feeling for the poet's robust irritability. His art conveys a sense of a crowded, abrasive, always impinging world, with sonnets composed "against" (*contro*) everything from women to false friends, and if this be not sufficient provocation, there is always the general theme of human ingratitude. One of his most memorable compositions begins each verse with an

[37] M. Stocchi, *Tradizione medievale e gusto umanistico nel "De montibus" del Boccaccio* (Padua, 1963).
[38] For one of the last effective poetic spokesmen of the first part of the *trecento*, who maintained that the burgher could readily assimilate the noble lessons of the chivalric code, see G. Garavaggi's study of *Folgore da San Gimignano* (Milan, 1960), pp. 189 ff. The last great codifier of "cortesia e gentilezza," Francesco da Barberino, praised and despised as an instructor of the *gente nuova*, died in 1348. See especially Part XVIII of his *Reggimento e costumi di donna* (Bologna, 1875).
[39] G. Getto, *Saggio letterario su S. Caterina da Siena* (Florence, 1939), pp. 93–132. On the failure of Sacchetti's early work stemming from older traditions, which by the 1350s seemed irreconcilable, see V. Pernicone, *Fra rime e novelle del Sacchetti* (Florence, 1942).
[40] E. Theseider, "L'attesa escatologiea durante il periodo avignonese," *L'attesa dell'età nuova nella spiritualità della fine del medioevo* (Todi, 1962), 118–22.

apostrophe to irritability: "A noia m' e quando. . . ."⁴¹ Bonds of ritual, ceremonial, or pageant, which at an earlier time might have helped assuage his spiritual isolation, are no longer evident, so that we observe in him, as in the painting of the period or in the writings of Sacchetti, that life is subject to "every evil" (*ogni male*).

If we return to Andrea da Firenze's fresco of Paradise in the Spanish Chapel, painted *ca.* 1366–68, we note that even the saved Christians are neither happy nor carefree. The very saints appear "rigid" while gazing "transfixed upon the Saviour. . . ."⁴² Proems to novels of the period regularly included moral and religious promptings, and the tales themselves frequently closed on a note of punishment or repentance—especially significant since the *novella* probably derived from earlier exempla in which the culprit was permitted to escape and the reader made to smile at human frailty. Again we are reminded of the formal and aloof figures in the painting of Giovanni del Biondo standing "wrapt and noncommunicative," with deeply stirred feelings smoldering behind their religious masks.⁴³

Interiorization of religious feelings prompted two developments of considerable import for the study of late *trecento*–early *quattrocento* civic humanism. First, a decreasing emphasis upon ritual and sacrament was evident in the Latin writings of a Coluccio Salutati as well as in the more popular vernacular works of Franco Sacchetti. Indeed, the latter attended to ethical problems and was not particularly responsive to dogmatic or theological questions. For him neither the symbolic nor the allegorical nor the abstract, but the materials of everyday life, rough-shaped in accord with the insights of *buon senso*, were the indispensable ingredients of religious dialogue. Faith is an undeniable fact of human existence which when coupled with good will ("la buona volontà fa salvo ogni uomo") brings some surcease to struggle. The exterior forms, whether they be sacramental or ritualistic, seldom are invoked.⁴⁴ Salutati would also endorse this, stressing the sanctity of practical conscience as the true guide for Christians; the sacraments played a very secondary role. Throughout his writings the civic humanist seldom mentioned any but two of the seven—baptism and matrimony. Since he usually considers grace a direct gift from God to man, priest and church play only a negligible part in his deliberately unsystematic discourses.⁴⁵

---

⁴¹ See his "Sonetti diversi" in *Delizie degli eruditi toscani*, 5, 286–96.
⁴² E. Borsook, *The Mural Painters of Tuscany from Cimabue to Andrea del Sarto* (London, 1960), p. 140.
⁴³ M. Meiss, *Painting in Florence and Siena*, p. 43.
⁴⁴ F. Sacchetti, *Opere*, ed. A. Chiari (Bari, 1938), 2, "Sposizioni di Vangelli," nos. XIII and XIV.
⁴⁵ We observe in as early a work as the *Decameron* that the traditional, medieval exemplum is employed to demonstrate not the operation of God's love or grace, but instead

THE ADVENT OF CIVIC HUMANISM

A second development, also related to the interiorization of religious feeling, concerned celebration of man's earthly role. Sacchetti feared greatly the possible separation of social from religious life; consequently he sought to elevate practical life to the level of religious serenity. His concept of work has almost a modern Protestant tone. Work is the means furnished the individual, and if he employs it virtuously—that is, in accord with the precepts of conscience, he may find release from the anxiety flesh is heir to. Especially useful in this quest for serenity are the many good civic works available to the citizen.[46] In one of his sermons, the lay preacher Sacchetti served up a stronger brew by advising Florentines who would gain glory to loan money to the republic without seeking interest.[47] As we shall see, he moved far beyond this modest imperative in an effort to justify the more extensive claims "Holy Florence" could rightfully make upon her sons. Salutati would concur, this time laying even more stress on the "bonum comune." The humanist stripped the antique virtue of *caritas* of its theological character so that it became the generative impulse relating man to man and citizen to country. Human fulfilment comes when man is helpful to his neighbor and useful to his polis. Did not even Christ weep over Lazarus and Jerusalem? Did not Socrates teach philosophy in the piazza, soldier for his city, and even marry and beget children? Surely this was no ascetic sage preaching withdrawal. Did not St. Jerome as well as St. Augustine do battle against the heretics? Did God love Abraham and Jacob less because they tended their flocks, treasured their wives, and fathered numerous progeny? For Salutati, as for Sacchetti, demands of the contemporary world had compelling dignity. They are the objects of the will, and it is the very primacy of this will that renders man so admirable, for acquired, not innate, virtue is worthy of esteem. Whoever allows himself to become so absorbed in contemplation that he ignores the imperatives of *caritas* is as a stick of wood or a piece of stone. Through sacrifice and work the citizen must find civic immortality.[48]

---

the workings of nature and human intelligence. Cf. E. de' Negri, "The Legendary Style of the *Decameron,*" *The Romanic Review,* 43 (1952), 166 ff. In Petrarch the notion of *caritas* as a moving force is singularly lacking; so is personal concern for working toward the salvation of others. Perhaps B. Smalley, in her *English Friars and Antiquity* (Oxford, 1960), p. 298, was a bit extreme in her judgment that Petrarch bequeathed his loathing of humanity to humanistic thought. Her comments do, however, point up the diminished force of *amore* and *caritas* as cosmic, regenerative forces. While Petrarch and Salutati move toward a fideism, we see on the popular level a substantial increase in use of portable altar pieces. Both this phenomenon and the possible connection between spiritual crisis in the North and fideism in Italy merit further analysis.

[46] F. Sacchetti, *Opere,* Vol. 49.
[47] *Ibid.,* 35, and R. Roedel, "Poggio Bracciolini nel quinto centenario della morte," *Rinascimento,* 11 (1960), 51–67.
[48] C. Salutati, *Epistolario,* 1, 21. In this youthful and ebullient letter to a fellow notary

With Salutati, Sacchetti, Stefani, Matteo Villani, and even the older Boccaccio, one sees the polis asserting its primacy over the individual. Law contributed manifoldly toward human perfection. No longer was the relation between citizen and polis relaxed; the public world was commanding and its outlines steady. Not many citizens escaped the rigors of prevailing civic morality and the force of law. To illustrate: until the late 1330s the signory regularly appointed special commissions that performed the ritual pardoning of those who collected interest from loans to the treasury. Hopefully this forgiveness liberated the sinner from the temporal onus of usury. Similarly, the signory was exceedingly reluctant to enact a formal decree licensing manifest usurers. In both instances this exquisite sensibility represented the tribute that form rendered to uneasy conscience.[49] With the 1340s a very different ethos appeared in the public world. The enforcement of the Christian antimonopoly legislation before this date revealed the formal homage rulers paid to sacrosanct norms, but to turn to the problem of enforcement of these laws by the courts was to recognize the gap between theory and practice. Antimonopoly legislation before the 1340s was enforced largely against petty artisans and food vendors, while the great guildsmen escaped unscathed and unchallenged.[50]

---

he writes, "nulla enim caritas est que sit cum caritate patriae. . . ." Later, he combined injunctions from the Bible with definitions from Aristotle to indicate that man is not "alone as the divine voice of God announces [Eccl. 4, 10] and "homo sit animal politicum et sociale, bone sunt hominum congregationes et ipsa natura necessarie, sine quibus vivere politice non valemus." Even monks and those dedicated to the solitary and contemplative life are dependent on society and law: "Cum ergo necessaria societas hominum sit, necessarie sint oportet leges que societates tuentur atque conservant. Quid autem hoc efficacius operatur et manifestius facit quam lex humanitas promulgata que, sicuti Cicero diffinivit, improbos suppliciis afficit, bonos autem tuetur atque defendit?" Cf. *De nobilitate*, p. 162.

[49] Only after the 1330s did an enacted law appear in the *provvisioni* authorizing *feneratores ad pignus* to ply their trade. Before that time only a record of the vote taken by the communal councils is recorded in the *Libri Fabarum*. This is done in large measure in deference to the Bishop's Constitution and reflects something of the character of the "gentle paideia," considered in the first volume of *Florence in Transition*. For an example of this earlier practice, see *LF*, 16, 1, f. 5r (May 5, 1333). Cf. also folios 153–57, 189, of the same volume. It can also be noted that until the 1340s the commune employed two clergymen as treasury officials expressly charged to act as syndics "ad remictendum et pardonandum," all receiving interest payments from the commune. Cf. *ibid.*, 17, f. 122r (May 7, 1339). At the same time consuls of leading guilds, such as the *Lana*, appointed syndics to see that wool merchants and manufacturers extended mutual pardons for usurious loans. Cf. *Lana*, 41, f. 42 (March 12, 1341). With the recession of the gentle paideia, this formalism dissipated and the polis assumed greater jurisdictional prerogatives. On the complex question of usury, see M. Becker, "Three Cases Concerning the Restitution of Usury in Florence," *Journal of Economic History*, 17 (1957), 445–50, for additional bibliography.

[50] M. Becker, "La esecuzione della legislazione contro le pratiche monopolistiche," *ASI*, 117 (1959), 8–28.

THE ADVENT OF CIVIC HUMANISM

After 1343 this separation between theory and practice gradually narrowed, with all guilds liable for prosecution. Comparable changes occurred in the enforcement of communal sumptuary laws. With the second half of the *trecento* and the attendant democratization of the polis, these were enforced impersonally against all. The life of the polis was influenced by a puritanism asserting the need for a single standard over public and private life. Older, more patrician regimes had been tolerant and easygoing, thus inconsistent in the punishment of human frailty. Later, strict enforcement and a high degree of democratization occurred side by side. Meaningful for latter-day Florentine experience was not the success or failure of the enforcement of statutes against prostitution or sodomy, but that the signory was seen as an agency for implementing moral codes and effecting spiritual rejuvenation. It has been commonplace for historians of art, literature, and music of this period to observe that in these forms of expression democratization was pervasive. Not so appreciated is the emergence of a democratized government as a force for achieving a *renovatio* of man and society.[51]

V

Certainly the *trecento* literary argument that "scientific subtlety as well as philosophy are vain and useless" is all too familiar a motif. It is a theme of writers as diverse as the humanistic Petrarch on the one hand and Passavanti, the great, fiery Dominican preacher of Florence's Sta. Maria Novella, on the other. The 1350s were the locale of a protracted onslaught against the metaphysical foundations of the grand cathedrals of ideas—those expansive logico-theological systematizations from the world of the scholastics. Scholasticism, which relied upon logic and dialectic to delimit possibilities and place them within a pre-established frame, no longer seemed an attractive alternative.[52] Doggedly, Franco Sacchetti denied that version of medieval Aristotelianism which contended that knowledge and science are "il sommo bene" and "la somma

---

[51] D. Weinstein, "The Myth of Florence in Sermon and Prophecy." This article is soon to be published in *Italian Renaissance Studies*, Vol. 2.

[52] On Passavanti, see M. Aurigemma, *Saggio sul Passavanti* (Florence, 1957), p. 19. Petrarch's comments in *De otio religioso*, bk. 2, are aptly treated by C. Calcaterra, *Nella del Petrarca* (Bologna, 1942), p. 281. For Petrarch, "pietas est sapientia."

Philosophi autem vestri, huius sententiae contemptores aut ignari, ut de Theologis nunc dicebam, ad verbosam nudamque dialecticam sunt redacti. Itaque de Deo Illi, hi autem de natura temerarie fabulantes, illi omnipotentissimam maiestatem ventosis sophismatibus circumscribunt, et subsannanti ridentique Deo suae insolentis inscitiae leges ponunt; isti vero de naturae arcanis ita disputant, quasi e coelo veniant, consilioque Dei omnipotentis interfuerint; obliti quod scriptum est: Sensum domini quis novit? Aut quis consiliarus eus fuit? Neque nostrum audientes Ambrosium qui saepe id multis ac validis argumentis, eo autem libro, in quo fratris obitum luget, praecise admodum breviterque: Philosophi, inquit, de coelo disputantes, quid loquantur, ignorant.

felicità." For Coluccio Salutati the language of politics had lost much of its traditional meaning; thus only in this world which man creates and orders by his own acts could he be fully himself.[53]

To Petrarch, most favored instructor of that generation, the choices men make are not between damnation and salvation or even between good and evil. Rather, they are between *virtus* and *voluptas*. Moreover, he raises human glory, "a temporal good," to the realm of the divine. In his work of history, *De viris illustribus*, he does not derive *virtus* from God and thus leaves the reader to draw the inference that man is capable of shaping his own destiny.[54] Indeed, he is the maker of his own history. The *Vita Scipionis*, a tribute to Petrarch's lifelong idol, avers that the greatness of Rome was achieved and sustained by the actions of its individual heroes. Livy's history had made Petrarch aware of how lasting the remembrance of heroic deeds and works could be. To him there was nothing shameful about the quest for temporal fame: in this life it befitted mortals to concern themselves with human things.[55]

In his *Secretum vel de contemptu mundi*, written in the early 1340s, St. Augustine, who has been preaching the vanity of earthly things that can only bring "the distresses of this mortal life," asks his balking but loving disciple Petrarch "to practice meditation on death and on man's misery. . . ." The saint persists in this solemn, if not morbid, tone through two lengthy dialogues until Petrarch induces him to make a damaging compromise. The poet inquires as to whether Augustine genuinely wishes him to renounce every earthly ambition. A strangely prudent Augustine replies:

> I will never advise you to live without ambition; but I would always urge you to put virtue before glory. You know that glory is in a sense the shadow of virtue. And therefore, just as it is impossible that your body should not cast a shadow if the sun is shining, so it is impossible also in the light of God Himself that virtues should exist and not make their glory to appear. Whoever,

---

[53] R. Bonnell, "An Early Humanistic View of the Active and Contemplative Life," *Italica*, 48 (1966), 225–29; C. Vasoli, "Le 'Dialectical Disputationes' del Valla e la critica umanistica della logica aristotelica," *Rivista Critica di Storia della Filosofia*, 12 (1957), 412–34.

[54] A. Bernardo's *Petrarch, Scipio and the "Africa"* (Baltimore, 1962), pp. 100 ff., is a balanced analysis and summary of Petrarchan texts and scholarship. Cf. also T. Mommsen, "Petrarch and the Story of the Choice of Hercules," *Journal of the Warburg and Courtauld Institutes*, 16 (1953), 189–90; also his "Petrarch and the Decoration of the Sala Virorum Illustrium in Padua," *Art Bulletin*, 34 (1952), 95–116.

[55] *La vita di Scipione l'Africano*, ed. G. Martellotti (Milan–Naples, 1954), pp. 150 ff., and *De viris illustribus*, ed. G. Martellotti (Florence, 1964), pp. 156–313. In Salutati's *De fato et casu* (1396–97), he compares the heroic morality of a Seneca with Aristotle's doctrine of the mean, extolling the superheroic sublimity of the tragedian. Cf. L. Gasperetti, "Il 'De fato, fortuna et casu' di Coluccio Salutati," *La Rinascita*, 4 (1941), 555–82.

> then, would take true glory away must of necessity take away virtue also; and when that is gone man's life is left bare, and only resembles that of the brute beasts that follow headlong their appetite, which to them is their only law.... What then? Let a man march steadily to the goal set before him, his shadow will follow him step by step: let him so act that he shall make virtue his prize, and lo! glory also shall be found at his side. I speak of that glory which is virtue's true companion; as for that which comes by other means, whether from bodily grace or mere cleverness, in the countless ways men have invented, it does not seem to me worthy of the name.[56]

What a curious Augustinian definition of virtue! Still more novel is Petrarch's enthusiasm for separating temporal and heavenly felicity. When one considers the anguish with which Dante in his political tract, the *Monarchia*, approached the terrible possibility of this dread schism, then Petrarch's light tone becomes even more startling:

> My principle is that, as concerning the glory which we may hope for here below, it is right for us to seek while we are here below. One may expect to enjoy that other more radiant glory in heaven, when we shall have there arrived, and when one will have no more care or wish for the glory of earth. Therefore, as I think, it is in the true order that mortal men should first care for mortal things; and that to things transitory things eternal should succeed; because to pass from those to these is to go forward in most certain accordance with what is ordained for us, although no way is open for us to pass back again from eternity to time.

The growth and popularity of Petrarchan lyrical poetry disclose a dramatic weakening of the philosophical conviction that the sufferings and mischances of this life possess an ultimate significance knowable to man. The surge of this poetic mode is rooted in the deep conviction that man's history, both private and public, is one of loss of youth, beauty, and friends. Unlike an earlier epic which compensated for individual impermanence by stressing the persistence of some durable ideal such as continuity of church and empire, or the existence of a noumenal essence embodied in courtly love, the lyric cannot subordinate tragedy to an overarching principle.[57] We see the same appreciation for the singular and discontinuous in Petrarch's justly celebrated view of history, in which he dissents sharply from the medieval chronicler who regularly commenced his work with a notice of the creation of the world and would, if the Deity allowed, have concluded with a florid description of the Last Judgment. For the medieval, history evinced a continuous, linear devel-

---

[56] *Petrarch's Secret*, trans. W. Draper (London, 1911), pp. 189, 192.
[57] See the comments of C. Calcaterra in his edition of *I Trionfi* (Turin, 1927), pp. xxi–xxxv.

opment, so that he was confident of steady progress from the times of heathen darkness to the age of light accompanying the Divine mission of God's son. No such certainty for Petrarch: at the very moment the name of Jesus Christ began to be venerated in Rome and to be worshiped by the Roman emperors, a "dark" age of obscurantism and decay also set in. The humanist was painfully conscious of the separation between himself and the days of pristine Christianity.[58]

Neither the temporal church of his times nor the empire had continuing ties with the "two swords" of antiquity. As faith in poetic-allegorical, historical interpretation proved less durable, other particular criteria for rendering judgment appeared more tenable. The arcane and mythic receded, and contemporary Florentine literature moved from the timeless world of the fable to that of verisimilitude. Popular art forms like the *novella*, always "exemplary or demonstrative," were cast by a master of the stature of Boccaccio as "history rather than fable."[59] A progressive decline of those elements in the traditional medieval romance once guaranteed to ennoble and universalize the particular passions is apparent in Boccaccio's writings.[60] Exquisite attention is given to time and place, so that historical sensitivity replaces the sublimity of a transcendent personage.

The aristocratic schema of the earlier *Filocolo* and *Ameto* gave way, as did the young author's penchant for intellectual analysis. Two commitments are evident in the writings of the mature Boccaccio: his extensive involvement with history and his zealous pursuit of scholarship. One has but to read his biography of the late but unlamented despot of the city— Walter of Brienne—to appreciate the author's quest for the specific and precise in human personality. Whatever is exemplary in man's behavior invariably exists within the temporal dwelling place of the historical. Again he reveals himself to be a great respecter, even venerator, of time and place, who relied upon contemporary chronicles and past histories for effective materials. Relevant, too, was his use of Saba Malaspina's writings for *De claris mulieribus* and of Giovanni Villani's chronicle as a source for important details in *De casibus virorum illustrium*. More drastic and pleasing was the telling combination of history and scholarship evinced in *Decameron* III, 2; relying upon the history of Paul the Deacon, he penetrates the dry husk of antiquarianism to fix the historical

---

[58] T. Mommsen, "Petrarch's Conception of the Dark Ages," *Speculum*, 17 (1943), 226–49. See also E. Panofsky's enlightening discussion of the consequences of achieving this "distance historique" for the arts as well as literature; *Renaissance and Renascences in Western Art* (Upsala, 1960), pp. 10–11. A. Buck's general paper is brief but useful, *Das Geschichtsdenken der Renaissance* (Cologne, 1957).
[59] M. Becker, *Florence in Transition*, 1, 244.
[60] L. Russo, "La dissoluzione del mondo cavalleresco 'il Morgante' di Luigi Pulci," *Belfagor*, 7 (1952), 36–54.

position of King Agilufo. He provides an appropriate temporal setting wherein the barbaric and violent tenor of those days is recaptured, thus furnishing verisimilitude. The ritualistic, ceremonial, and sacramental no longer sufficed.[61]

Earlier commitments essential for the continued vigor of the poetry of the *dolce stil nuovo* were not nourished. The philosophic contest in the human soul, so attractive to Dante or Guido Cavalcanti, or to lesser poets like Guittone d'Arezzo and Panuccio del Bagno, were neglected. The generation of poets still committed to the "sweet new style"—Sennuccio del Bene, Ventura Monachi, Franceschino degli Albizzi, and Dino Frescobaldi—was passing.[62] Writers of Boccaccio and Sacchetti's stripe saw character shaped by man's contest with *fortuna*. This battle served as the anvil on which the moral qualities of men were forged. Yet, because there was less faith in a priori principles—experience being all important—we notice the familiar tendency toward the encyclopedic and disorganized in the late works of Boccaccio. Many of the ideals advanced in the *Decameron* were abandoned a few years later in the *Corbaccio*. In the latter the author pronounces his concern for "gli accidenti del carnale amore" and the "oltraggio e ingiuria" he had suffered at the hands of the female.[63]

Stylized confessions of extensive suffering and increasing awareness of the "bestiality and insolent cruelty" practiced by the female were of course more than a resort to a literary *topos*.[64] Still, the discouragements and disintegration of traditional postures concerning human possibilities

---

[61] V. Branca, *Boccaccio*; G. Getto, "La pesta del 'Decameron' e il problema della fonte lucreziana," *Giornale Storico della Letteratura Italiana*, 75 (1958), 507–23.

[62] For a recent treatment of this poetic genre, see M. Musa, *The Poetry of Panuccio del Bagno* (Bloomington, 1965), pp. 219–32.

[63] In the proem to the *Corbaccio*, he tells us he was seated in his room when these thoughts seized him, and he realized that the indignities and injuries he had suffered were no fault of his own (*senza alcuna mia colpa*) and that he had never deserved them. For a sensitive appraisal of this prose work, valuable even if the author's thesis on the dating is not entirely convincing, see G. Padoan, "Sulla datazione del 'Corbaccio,'" *Lettere Italiani*, 15 (1963), 1–27.

[64] Reluctance to stress the educative power of love suggests the failure of an important element of the gentle paideia. Cf. *Florence in Transition*, Vol. 1, Chapter 1. For a succinct presentation of earlier views, see M. Musa, *Panuccio del Bagno*, pp. 220–23. Although nourishment derived from ideals of *amore* and *cortesia* no longer sustains the Boccaccio of the post-*Decameron* period, not so history. Weight should be placed upon Boccaccio's contribution as the founder of the art of writing biographies of women. His *De claris mulieribus* became inordinately popular throughout Europe, and perhaps it would not be untoward to praise him as the first to place women systematically in the public world by giving them a history. It might also be noted that Florence became a center for this important new mode of conceptualizing. Northern European works such as Christine de Pisan's *Cite des Dames* (ca. 1404–5) or Martin le Franc's *Champion des Dames* (ca. 1430–40) have been described as compilations of medieval arguments. Cf. C. Fahy, "Early Renaissance Treatises on Women," *Italian Studies*, 11 (1956), 30–35, especially page 31.

should not obscure the fact that Boccaccio continued to respond to the imperatives of the public world. Nor were these responses negative, for he contributed heroically to the founding of the Renaissance art of biography—an art which almost by definition focused entirely upon man in the public world.[65]

Just as Boccaccio failed to understand the messianic vision and millennial doctrine of that earlier generation, so, too, in his *Trattatello in Laude di Dante* he proves incapable of appreciating the inner nature of his subject's passion for Beatrice.[66] He externalized the materials of literature to such a degree that he felt called upon to comment on the heavy strain of lechery in Dante's personality. Boccaccio's eloquent letters written at about this time indicate his debt to the celebrated rhetoricians of antiquity, as does his shining polemic in defense of poetry. He and the other outstanding contemporary commentator on the *Divine Comedy*, Benvenuto da Imola, little appreciate the metaphysical content of the poetry. Their comments are rich in details of recent history but insensitive to the Dantesque commitment to the *renovatio* of Christian society through *carità* and *amore*.[67] Indeed, it is a hallmark of this later age that the interior thrust of Christianity could not generate a durable public philosophy. Only when Christian purpose blended with the patri-

---

[65] Cf. preceding footnote. In *Defensione delle donne*, written subsequently and attributed to Agostino Strozzi, the author observes that much of the misogynistic character of his times is a consequence of the overemphasis by male historians of the roles played by men in the polis. Cf. C. Fahy, "Treatises on Women," p. 46. Apropos of Salutati, yet another question on which he differed from Petrarch was that of marriage. He defends this useful institution against the harsh judgments of his literary mentor, encouraged to this re-evaluation by his involvement in the public world. V. Rossi, *Il Quattrocento* (Milan, 1933), p. 131. Vehemently he protests against the practice of compelling young girls to enter the convent against their wishes: "Thus when I consider this woman and see the sacred bands and vestments of nuns hiding furtive love, I cannot help laughing at the madness of some. . . . They say that they have dedicated those virgins to God so that with their prayers their own affairs will prosper more, and after death they will gain eternal life. This is ridiculous and foolish. They do not know that an idle woman serves Venus." Cf. *ibid*. Later Salutati was to answer his own rhetorical question that only *libertas* is sweeter than a wife and children. Cf. *Invectiva in Antonium Luschum Vicentinum* in E. Garin's *Prosatori Latini del Quattrocento* (Milan-Naples, 1952), p. 30.

[66] Writing about the fifth canto of the *Inferno* on the tragedy of Paolo and Francesca, he confides, "it is possible it happened like that. I believe it, however, to be a probable fiction rather than anything known to the author." G. Boccaccio, *Il commento alla Divina Comedia*, ed. D. Guerri (Bari, 1918), 2, 137–38.

[67] E. Cavallari, *La fortuna di Dante nel Trecento* (Florence, 1921), pp. 216–17. Compare Benvenuto's apt treatment of factionalism in Pistoia or his narration of the intervention of Boniface VIII, with his failure to comprehend problems so central to Dante's intellectual concern as salvation of the virtuous pagan or punishment of the simoniacs. Likewise, Benvenuto cannot appreciate the subtlety of Dante's political allegory; he judges Pier della Vigna innocent and finds the root cause of difficulties in avarice. Cf. his *Commentum super Dantis Aldigherii Comoediam* (Florence, 1887), 2, 304.

otic enthusiasm for the expanding polis was there to be confidence in a new engine capable of achieving a *renovatio* of society.

VI

Aptly the writings and sermons of such leading clergymen as the Augustinian Luigi Marsili and the Vallombrosan Giovanni dalle Celle have been termed exercises in "communal theology."[68] Early in the 1360s the first Italian translation of Marsiglio of Padua's *Defensor Pacis* was completed by a Florentine. Polemical and anticlerical writings proceeded to cast the Arno republic in the heroic role of defender of *libertas* against the machinations of the "carnal church." Avignon became synonymous with iniquitous Babylon, and cultural leaders like Marsili assembled under the banner of Florentine *libertas*. When the civic-minded cleric met Petrarch in Padua, the great humanist designated him his literary executor. When the polis warred against Mother Church in the mid-seventies, Marsili counseled a leading Florentine politician, Guido del Palagio, to still his scruples: Petrarch himself would have upheld the Arno republic's cause. Then he dispatched three celebrated sonnets of his master in which the humanist poet upbraids the curia. The war was portrayed as a crusade against a corrupt clergy and avaricious church; the struggle, said Marsili, was a "blessed enterprise."

The Augustinian who had been instructed by his master to lay the groundwork for a "pious philosophy" was in regular conversation with a politically influential group of Florentines. Together they sought to reconcile the precious Christian heritage with the civic culture of the humanists. In his correspondence with Del Palagio he had acknowledged that a man unwilling to battle for his country must destroy the better part of his nature, for such individuals are little more than beasts. The core of human identity derives from an individual's participation in the concerns of his day; thus the good man and the good citizen are synonymous. The teacher discoursing with disciples extolled the virtues of poetry and history as well as furnishing justification for an active life. At the convent of S. Spirito (a center for religious patriots) he spoke for the

[68] H. Baron, *Humanistic and Political Literature in Florence and Venice at the Beginning of the Quattrocento* (Cambridge, Mass., 1955), p. 32. Marsili, a native-born Florentine (*ca.* 1342), remained a loyal son of the polis continuing to advise the signory on crucial public questions and performing delicate diplomatic missions. Beloved by the civic humanists from Salutati and Bruni to Poggio, he was regarded as the most effective champion of the Tuscan vernacular, historical and poetic studies, and finally, the dignity of contemporary culture as it was personified in the works of genius written by a Dante, a Petrarch, and a Boccaccio. It was to his convent of S. Spirito that Boccaccio bequeathed his library. For bibliography and details of the particulars, see U. Mariani, *Il Petrarca e gli Agostiniani* (Rome, 1946), pp. 74 ff.

idea of a national Italian church, reminding listeners of the evils of schism and the price paid for the dissoluteness of Avignon. Fear of the election of a foreign pope induced him to hope that the polis might serve as the vehicle of God to help restore His fallen house. Again, writing to the politician Del Palagio, Marsili opined that an unjust excommunication launched by the pontiff was not binding upon those supporting the war to purify His church.

That other influential holy man of those years was Dalle Celle, and being little given to impractical excess, although he rejected the millenarianism of such heretical sects as the Fraticelli, he did announce one of his visions foretelling the fall of the Church of Rome.[69] Further, he resorted to the pseudo-Joachite *Book of the Popes*, favorite of religious nonconformists, to buttress his prophecies. Conservative and hardly antipapal by the flexible standards of his age, he still resisted St. Catherine of Siena's summons to abandon the polis when Florence warred on the Holy See.

Like Marsili, he corresponded with Del Palagio, displaying empathy and understanding for the demanding activities of "uomini secolari." To his friend, sorely troubled by his recently gained wealth, the holy man advised a reading of the Scripture; many Testament figures were wealthy and yet achieved sainthood. In a letter to the Fraticelli, the Vallambrosan conjectured that a rich man knowing how to use wealth could be more holy than a pauper never called on to resist temptation.

Dalle Celle saw that wealth and love of country were not incompatible with true Christian piety. Well aware of ties binding men to the polis, he wrote to Del Palagio that a citizen's first obligation is to honor God; next comes the "buono stato della città." He considered the duty to defend one's country, serve in the signory, and pay taxes especially binding at the moment. Florence was battling corrupt papal lieutenants in the War of the Eight Saints, truly a "santa" undertaking. In the "blessed enterprise" of Marsili or the "holy undertaking" of Dalle Celle, those contributing were to be honored. Unsubtle political allegories were murmured throughout the city revealing that the republic's coat of arms—the red lily—would emit so pleasant a fragrance that even the putrescence of the corrupt church would be dispelled.[70]

By the 1370s a circle of clerics and politically influential Florentines

---

[69] B. Sorio, *Le lettere di Beato Don Giovanni dalle Celle monaco vallombrosano e d'altri* (Rome, 1845); P. Cividali, "Il Beato Giovanni dalle Celle," *Atti della R. Accademia dei Lincei*, Memorie, 12 (1906), 354–477.

[70] Decima Douie, *The Nature and the Effect of the Heresy of the Fraticelli* (Manchester, 1932), p. 217. Looking back a quarter of a century later, Salutati saw this period of war with the church as the real beginning of the struggle of the polis for *libertas*. *Invectiva*, p. 28. For a thorough account of the events of those years, see G. Brucker, *Florentine Politics and Society*, pp. 297–335.

conversed and wrote on a major theme of the time: What role should the polis assume in the *renovatio* of God's own church?[71] Since the topic was uncharted territory, plans would be numerous and tensions high. Tortured souls sought quick release from anxiety by embracing extreme positions. For years the signory had attempted little to discourage diffusion of heresy throughout the city. Now the regime tried to control the nomination of the Inquisitor; when that failed the activities of the Holy Office were suppressed. Sects like the Fraticelli, fervent advocates of the ideal of evangelical poverty, despised the materialistic church. Readily, they identified the cause of Florence with the old prophecies of Joachim of Flora and the inspired message of St. Francis of Assisi: the republic had been elected by God to perform the holy task of cleansing "the Babylonian and carnal church." The Fraticelli were not alone when announcing this stirring news; others also named the Florentines "veri cristiani eletti da Dio" and blessed their mission. A spate of prophecies stemmed from Tuscan lands, with the Arno polis the allegorical hub of civic hagiography. Religious nonconformity contributed toward strengthening citizen bonds of allegiance to the public order.

These were the early years of Coluccio Salutati's chancellorship over the republic. He began his celebrated literary campaign to identify Florence's aspirations with the reflowering of antique Roman virtue. The superiority of the polis stems from the uniqueness of her political system, which has its analogue only in ancient Rome. Like the Eternal City, the Arno republic is more than justified in extending her hegemony, since hers is a *libertas* superior to anything on the *trecento* horizon. A few years earlier the writer Franco Sacchetti had enumerated the twelve labors of "Holy Florence." These were monumental tasks akin to those of Hercules, with the first labor involving the prosecution of successful war against Pisa in 1362–64. This glorious triumph was but the initial step on the republic's odyssey toward immortality. The poet Antonio Pucci in his patriotic verse saw Florence as paternalistically concerned with the well-being of neighboring states.[72] Early in the 1360s an ingrate Pisa failed to appreciate the altruistic motives animating Florence in her contest for rule. Pucci asked the beleaguered Pisans if they understood that his city was but "brother and neighbor," wishing them only "to live

---

[71] F. Tocco, "I Fraticelli," *ASI*, 35 (1905), 349–50. E. Theseider believes that Marsili held to the idea of a national Italian church at this time. Marsili's comments on Petrarch's "Italia Mia" and "Lettera contra i vizi della corte del papa" go far to support this observation. Cf. Theseider's "La duplice esperienza di S. Caterina da Siena," *Rivista Storica Italiana*, 62 (1950), 551–60. Another Augustinian of similar persuasion was Martino da Signa. Friend to Boccaccio and fellow poet, he was executor of Giovanni's bequest to S. Spirito. Likewise, he was regularly consulted by the signory on state affairs. Cf. U. Mariani, *Petrarca*, pp. 70–72.
[72] Ferruccio Ferri, *La poesia popolare in Antonio Pucci* (Bologna, 1909), pp. 75–77.

well" (*ben vivere*). In what must surely pass as a unique tribute by piety to imperialism he called upon the Pisans to recall the words of the Gospel: "Whoever shall be humiliated will be exalted." (*Chi si aumilierà sara esaltato.*) Did not the Judas-like Pisa recognize this simple holy truth? Such blindness was hardly surprising, for the Holy Father himself did not appreciate Florence's noble intent. His lieutenants held Tuscan towns in "Babylonian captivity"; the polis sought but to restore peoples to liberty, never to tyrannize over "fortress or city."

Again he and Franco Sacchetti elevated the role of the polis in her conflict with the church: God had placed a sacred trust on the city so that she must strip the church of her "worldly goods" (*gli ben tempori*). Deprived of these ill-acquired incumbrances ("il male acquisto"), church and clergy would again follow the path of purity trod by our Sacred Redeemer.[73] In Dante's day the poets decried that moment when the largess of Constantine involved the Holy Church in mundane matters. At the time of the Donation, voices sounded in the sky uttering black prophecies. Few Florentines of that period, however, would have believed the machinery of the republic sufficient to correct the damage wrought by Constantine and Pope Sylvester. For Dante, at least, the intervention of the Holy Roman Emperor himself was essential.

The tone of a Pucci or Sacchetti was mild compared to that of the Florentine chancellory under Coluccio Salutati. Luigi Marsili launched his invective against the French clerics he accused of corrupting Italian ecclesiastical life. His praise was reserved for those nations—especially the Germans—who made certain that foreign-born clergy never meddled in the workings of their church. Salutati went further when he hoped God might lend the polis and her allies sufficient strength to eject the barbarians of the Gallic church from the sacred lands of the Latins. The theme of his letters was *libertas Italiae* and Florence's sacred mission in the holy war against a Francophile pope, his barbarian soldiery, and French lieutenants.[74]

---

[73] F. Sacchetti, *Il libro delle rime*, ed. A. Chiari (Bari, 1936), p. 210. In sessions of the advisory councils held at this time, one speaker referred to the apostolic nuncios as "wolves" (*vulpini*), while another called the Holy Father "durus." Prelates who did not side with Florence in her war with the church were prosecuted as "rebelles" against the republic, for they were "hostes." Franco Sacchetti's brother Jacopo made one of the fiercest speeches against clerics ever to be recorded in the minutes of the councils. Clergy obeying the interdict and refusing to celebrate mass were deprived of citizenship, and large tracts of church lands were confiscated. *CP*, 15, fols. 29–47.

[74] *Epistolario*, 1, 194–216. Of considerable interest is the fact that Salutati was a "new man," having been born outside Florence near Pistoia. He stood in the company of so many other civic humanists, from Leonardo Bruni Aretino to Poggio Bracciolini, who were both *novi cives* and firm champions of Florentine *libertas*. Domenico Bandino of Arezzo was another spokesman for the polis during the 1380s who described Florence as a "italice libertatis mater." Cf. N. Rubinstein, "Florence and the Despots: Some Aspects of Florentine Diplomacy in the Fourteenth Century," *Transactions of the Royal Histori-*

This language was not exceptional or the ideas idiosyncratic. To quote from a long letter written in November, 1375, by Gherardino di Niccolò Gherardini Gianni, a typical greater guildsman, to his friend Tommaso de' Bardi relating that the commune

> ... is prepared to impose a loan every day, if this proves necessary to defend our liberty against those treasonous pastors of the Holy Church. Their rule is a monstrous tyranny, and everyone in this city should be prepared to sacrifice his property and his person to maintain his freedom and to avoid falling into their hands! You are well aware that in those lands where they rule they do not leave any woman alone but vituperate her person and her family. The Florentines think of this, those who have mothers, sisters, wives or daughters, who might fall into the hands of these clerical traitors, or those who supply them or their soldiers or their Englishmen, who have become too arrogant in the church dominions and think that all these women belong to them. The Florentines are not disposed to suffer these indignities.[75]

Although anxiety may have multiplied in the private world of the Florentines, hopefully the arguments of a Giovanni dalle Celle or a Luigi Marsili eased the path for public men. Their solicitude for the devout and politically involved touched deeply the lives of Guido del Palagio, Donato Coreggio (of the Acciaiuoli), Giorgio di Guccio Gucci (vigorous participant in public life), and Ser Lapo Mazzei (in the chancellory under Salutati). Other great religious figures in Tuscany had the opposite effect. St. Catherine of Siena, for example, instructed her Florentine disciples on the evils of warfare with the church.[76] Yet whatever guilt was generated, debate in the council halls over these years showed a confident tone. The durability of civic conscience and strength of public

---

cal Society, 5th series, 2 (1952), 21–45. Such statements became commonplace with Florentine counselors who spoke of the polis as protector of the region and indicated the need for discussion with neighbors "de pace et statu libertate Provincie Tuscie." *CP* 16, f. 128; *ibid.*, 15, fols. 33, 108r, 111. Such leading figures as Salvestro de' Medici were much concerned with preventing outside powers from gaining a foothold in Tuscany. The influential political man Filippo di Cionetto Bastari had a clear understanding of the need for regional arrangements with neighboring states so that "status civitatis" might be "sicura." In this instance negotiations with marauding companies were under discussion. *CP*, 17, f. 138r; 19, f. 143r.

[75] G. Brucker, "Un documento fiorentino sulla guerra sulla finanza e sulla amministrazione pubblica (1375)," *ASI*, 115 (1957), 172–73.

[76] G. Brucker, *Florentine Politics and Society*, pp. 332–34. E. Theseider, "S. Caterina," pp. 548–49, observes that although there were many humble folk among Catherine's disciples and correspondents, her actions in Siena in 1377 did appear to tie her to the aristocratic Salimbene family. The same interpretation could be placed upon her disastrous intervention into Florentine politics when appearances served to support the popular judgment that she was linked to the patriciate of the *Parte Guelfa*. The revolutionary nature of the times will be discussed in a subsequent volume. Within the context of these socially volatile times, her letter (121) to the heads of the Sienese republic can be read with great profit: "Ognuno deve esser sollecito dell'arte sua: l'arte che Dio ci ha posta e questa."

commitment were impressive. Seldom was a wavering voice raised or note of political uncertainty struck. Opponents of governmental policy stood remarkably sure in their dissent, and protagonists were equally firm in advocacy. For the most part, political figures appeared convinced that the polis would endure and prosper. Only one public document, promulgated when the city was struck by plague, displayed a sense of human inadequacy in the struggle against the unseen.[77] Florence was warring for "pax et libertas Italiae," advisers to the government had said. Later it was against the forces of the pope; a few years before it had been the emperor and his minions who threatened Tuscan liberty. Like Gianni in his letter, speakers concurred that no expense be spared to preserve "libertas populi." The pull of the public world centered around *libertas*, which was "of inestimable worth."[78]

Although by the seventies and eighties *libertas* signified different things, all were related to the needs and valuable qualities of a polis worthy of ample respect and much devotion. It denoted freedom from arbitrary rule by a despot—a meaning owing much to the unfortunate experience of the city with Walter of Brienne in 1342-43.[79] Second, it encompassed the idea of freedom from domination by a foreign state or prince—that is, the notion of sovereignty. Third, the free city must not be controlled or its citizenry intimidated by a few of the *potentes*. In this last respect the experience of the early seventies was crucial: the leaders of the two vying factions, Albizzi and Ricci, were declared ineligible for high public trust because they wielded inordinate influence. The curtailment of the power of the *Parte Guelfa* also stemmed from identical provocation.

Most significant for later developments was the belief that *libertas* im-

---

[77] *P*, 38, f. 77 (June 21, 1350). In this provision the need of that "multitudenum peccatorum" for *caritas* is noted.

[78] One speaker assured the signory that if the citizenry aided the commune with money, liberty would be assured and "Deus dabit pacem bonam." *CP*, 15, f. 33 (Sept. 7, 1377).

[79] See a model speech in praise of liberty written at the time of the overthrow of Brienne: God permitted you to recover your "santissima liberta," which is to be treasured above all things. Cf. N. Rubinstein, "Florence and the Despots," p. 21. Bocccacio's "De Gualterio, Athenarum Duce" is illuminating on several counts:

> After much debate, this power, limited by the law, was given to Walter, as if to a friend of proven faith.
> . . . .
> For a long time it brought hope to certain citizens, whom our ancestors call "magnates" to have a man in the city accustomed to and desirous of power and one who would take over the administration of the war. They were inclined to put this plan in operation. Foolishly they preferred the tyranny of a foreigner whom they did not know to the yoke of the law of the city to which they were accustomed.

G. Boccaccio, *The Fates of Illustrious Men*, trans. L. B. Hall (New York, 1961), p. 229. Franco Sacchetti's observations in *novella*, 181, that war and eternal strife have caused many cities once "libere" to submit to a despot were familiar at the close of the *trecento*. So, too, was his moral notation that today they are "triste ville."

plied equality of citizenry under the rule of law. To appreciate the degree to which these definitions were internalized and became the scaffolding of Florentine political conscience, it should be noted that the very misgivings of thoughtful men concerning the validity of civic commitment did not lead to dramatic questioning of the value of *libertas* itself. Nor did they induce reflective citizens to postulate alternative political systems or ideologies. Discourse assumed shape and achieved credibility within a paradigm of *libertas* whose perimeter was the varied definitions of that unquestioned good. Sympathetic religious figures like Giovanni dalle Celle understood that "this earthly pilgrimage" was but a preparation for the decisive "heavenly passage." True, the "patria corporale" was less than our "true home," but man's affection for this *patria corporale* was not lessened by this knowledge. On occasion, that firm spokesman for *libertas*, Salutati, made similar acknowledgments. Still, like the Vallambrosan, he appreciated the joys of the Earthly City and believed that without *libertas* such pleasures would indeed be hollow. Much engaged in the old argument of free will and Divine Providence, he extended the meaning of *libertas* into the realm of philosophy. Of course, resolution was not simple, but this did not detract from the worth of human freedom and free will. His extreme voluntaristic cast of mind was a tribute to his solemn dedication.

If there was a model citizen in those years it was unquestionably Guido del Palagio. The chronicler and political activist, Buonaccorso Pitti, praised him as "the best and most trusted man in Florence," while at his death Salutati delivered a funeral eulogy voicing reasons for veneration: Guido had achieved the harmonious reconciliation of love for polis with love of God. Those who knew him became aware that his character demonstrated an ideal blend of the two dearest things in life—politics and religion. The poem attributed to him expresses his passion for both when he summons the Lord of Love to assist him in speaking of that most beautiful of all ladies—"Fiorenza."[80] This devotion to polis and God is coupled with suspicion of the worldly church and its wealthy prelates who have wandered far from the pristine paths: Avignon becomes the "rapacious wolf" (*lupo rapace*), while the pope's lieutenants are "fierce tyrants."

---

[80] Giovanni da Gherardo, *Il Paradiso degli Alberti*, ed. A. Wesselofsky (Bologna, 1867), 1, 95–96; *Rime di M. Cino da Pistoia e d'altri del secolo XIV*, ed. G. Carducci (Florence, 1862), pp. 439–41. In Salutati's funeral oration for Guido del Palagio it is the hero's patriotism and piety that are eulogized. The chronicler Buonaccorso Pitti spoke of him as "il magiore e il più creduto huomo di Firenze," and Ser Lapo Mazzei referred to him in a letter as "il santo e l'amico di Dio." Cf. Salutati, *Epistolario*, 3, pp. 345–55; Pitti, *Cronica*, ed. B. Della Lega (Bologna, 1905), p. 76; L. Mazzei, *Lettere di un notaro a un mercante*, ed. C. Guasti (Florence, 1880), 1, 63. For another contemporary example of the same type of political personification, see G. Zaccagnini, "Jacopo da Montepulciano," *Giornale Storico della Letteratura*, 96 (1925), 225–88.

VII

Citizen patriots, sympathetic clergy, early humanists, and vernacular poets responded to the tarnishing of a universalist political ethic. At mid-*trecento*, ardent Ghibelline poets like Fazio degli Uberti abandoned the empire to find solace in the new imperialism of Florence. The leading *trecento* Italian jurist, Bartolus, doubted the authenticity of the Donation of Constantine to the papacy. Moreover, the words "Guelf" and "Ghibelline" were vain, without substantial meaning: "As these words are used today a man may be a Guelf in one place and a Ghibelline in another because allegiances of this type refer to a variety of issues."[81] Once-sacred ties of the medieval world were loosened and civic bonds became primary. Contemporary affairs possessed new dignity; no longer was it necessary to justify allegiances and civic careers in terms of a hierarchy of transcendent values which placed the polis at the lower end of a long chain of political beings. The language of politics reflected this transformation. Metaphors of a sacramental character grew less prevalent; nor did political writers employ spatial metaphor to fix the polis in an elaborate hierarchy of political bodies. The most revered Tuscan clerics of the early *quattrocento* separated the earthly city and the active life from *patria* everlasting in heaven. Time enough for contemplation in the next world, asserted the practical San Bernardino of Siena: In this world "one must stand in line," for we are here to work and love. The Ciceronian accents were unmistakable, as was the tender regard for human society and government. The Dominican, Fra Giovanni Dominici, mentor of St. Antonino, wrote a detailed work on family life for an aristocratic Florentine *signora*. Here he denies millennial expectation, contending men are locked in the present and cannot hope to live as "our fathers in the evangelical days of the church." Since the time when the Apostles trod the earth will not occur again, we must educate our children for the civic obligations of an inexorable present.[82]

The thirteenth and early fourteenth centuries produced much creative political theory, with St. Thomas, Dante, Ptolemy of Lucca, and a host of others adapting the Aristotelian frame to fit the political experience of their contemporaries. The tradition of medieval concern with ideal orders and final ends made this structure seem most hospitable. St. Thomas, Dante, and the rest started their inquiries with the postulation of an ideal political form; from this secure and lofty vantage they proceeded to examine institutions and practices. Even those not concurring

---

[81] See Bartolus' treatise "De Guelfis," trans. E. Emerton, in his *Humanism and Tyranny* (Cambridge, Mass., 1925), pp. 273–84.
[82] Giovanni Dominici, *Regola del governo di cura familiare*, ed. D. Salvi (Florence, 1860), p. 136.

in the judgment that the hierarchy and universality of the temporal order was predicated on the *plenitudo potestatis* of the pope, and who attempted to introduce greater variety into the systematization, still entertained theological issues and continued to conceptualize in terms of ideal forms.

Surely by Dante's time the inadequacy of these approaches was obvious. First, the singular and therefore unique historical event incessantly obtruded. No amount of commitment to theory could reduce the cluttered landscape of Dante's political poetry. Indeed, the *Divine Comedy* stands as a stunning tribute to the failure of medieval political theory to subordinate the particular to some general rule. Finally, the tendency, in a tract such as the *Monarchia*, to separate the beatitude of this life from that of eternity is apparent. Essentially, throughout Dante's career the intellectual ordering frame remained intact, but less and less historical detail could be successfully integrated within its symmetrical confines. With heretics blissfully joining the exalted company of Christian saints and popes shunted off to the *Inferno*, it is not surprising that this great religious poet reached a philosophical impasse.

Early Florentine civic humanists were suspicious of systematic thought in general and the philosophy of the schools in particular; therefore their contribution to theoretical studies, ethical or political, was limited. With the advent of the second half of the *trecento*, the fruitful union between metaphysics and politics dissolved. Political analysis was stripped of its scholastic architecture and commitment to theory. In return for this sacrifice, greater involvement in the practical workings of the public world was achieved. The transformation was heralded by the shift from a magisterial, political work like the *Monarchia* (the last Florentine opus on political theory), to Marsiglio's *Defensor Pacis* (a treatise redolent with everyday interests of the Italian citizen).[83]

By the sixties and seventies Florentines were using the *Defensor Pacis* to justify the anticlerical, antipapal policies of the polis. The teachings of this radical treatise were immediately accessible to citizen experience. Marsiglio began with the notion that noble ends do not furnish the polis with a *raison d'être*. Whereas the older tradition postulated primacy of ideal orders and final goals, Marsiglio advanced the axiom that the origins of the state do not stem from the need to realize a perfected end, but rather from the necessity to modify and control human appetites. If by the close of the *trecento* the *Monarchia* was remote from Florentine political thinking and the messianic cast of Dante's mind unintelligible, not so Marsiglio's assessment that the role of government was to coerce its membership into a "due proportion."

[83] M. Reeves, "Marsiglio of Padua and Dante Alighieri," *Trends in Medieval Political Thought*, ed. B. Smalley (Oxford, 1965), 92-93.

This stern, repressive judgment also involved drastic modification of prevailing theories about relations between *regnum* and *ecclesia*. The most enduring purpose of government is not promotion of the blessed or even "good" life; rather, it is coercion of its members, especially the clergy, into a "due proportion." When Professor Charles McIlwain in *The Growth of Political Thought in the West* concludes that Marsiglio "regards the church as a department of state in all matters of earthly concern," he is aptly summarizing the Paduan's judgment. The clergy lose their temporal punitive powers, and what remains is the threat of penalties to be exacted in the world to come. This stark solution was too novel to be embraced at once, but it was within the orbit of the teachings of *trecento* political writers and glossators, whose vision of the role of commune in the affairs of men was much expanded.[84]

At mid-*trecento* the polis began to circumvent the authority of the church with a chain of restrictions. Taxation of clergy was regularized, and there were frequent attacks on ecclesiastical immunities and the right of sanctuary. Jurisdiction of church courts was sharply curtailed; as early as 1345 the signory requested that the curia consider appointing a native-born Florentine to the commanding position of Tuscan inquisitor. Less dramatic but more telling in the long run was the intrusion of public courts into petty concerns once regarded under the purview of church tribunals. Few crimes existed for which the commune did not disclose a legal interest. Public courts assumed jurisdiction over cases of blasphemy involving a ten-lire fine as well as over offenses from abortion to witchcraft. The polis stood as the great engine for enforcement of statutes against usury, monopoly, and heresy. (The word "enforcement" implied also the passage of laws designed solely to remove particular questions from the purview of church courts; communal tribunals could never initiate action. These laws were effective in cases involving charges of usury under secular jurisdiction where damages were difficult to collect because of obstacles against bringing suit.) The later books of Matteo Villani's chronicle disclose an appreciation of the new orientation in communal politics. Sympathy intensified for the role of the signory as defender of the polis against the prerogatives of an overzealous clergy and nobility. The strengthened polis had to be supported against the machinations of the many semiautonomous, quasi-political bodies which were vestiges of the medieval commune.[85]

---

[84] Charles McIlwain, *The Growth of Political Thought in the West* (New York, 1932), p. 313.
[85] On the origins of the Commune, see L. Chiappelli, "Formazione storica del Comme," *ASI*, 84 (1926), 3–24. For incisive definition of the term, see D. Herlihy, *Pisa in the Early Renaissance* (New Haven, 1958). On difficulties of bringing suit in cases involving a charge of usury, see M. Becker, "Nota dei processi riguardanti prestatori di denaro del 1343 al 1379," *ASI*, 114 (1956), 93–104.

THE ADVENT OF CIVIC HUMANISM

The polis became a greater bulwark for the individual and a mightier legal shield for the collectivity. Tragically for Matteo, protection proved illusory, for he suffered disfranchisement in 1362 at the hands of the foremost quasi-political organization—the *Parte Guelfa*. In his distress he could be comforted in the knowledge that so many other literary men, beginning with the first eminent Florentine chancellor of almost a century ago, Brunetto Latini, had been visited with more terrible fates. Latini's exile was followed by that of his illustrious disciple, Dante, and, later, by that of Dante's dear friend, the poet Guido Cavalcanti. Disfranchisement was directed against the chronicler Dino Compagni, and the fathers of Petrarch and Coluccio Salutati were exiled. In 1343 Giovanni Villani also fell in partisan strife when Walter of Brienne relieved him of his official post. Florentine intellectual life became more stable when the polis was able to protect poet, chronicler, and humanist from internecine political war. Not surprisingly, in late *trecento* and early *quattrocento*, when the man of letters could feel greater security, allegiance to the polis was strengthened.

The role of "political independent" (the *bonus civis* who attempted to maintain a neutrality and devotion to *il bene comune* by resisting the blandishments and threats of factions) was all too vulnerable. To relinquish the protection of political cliques was to welcome persecution. Moreover, if the "good citizen" sought to transcend faction, he rendered himself politically ineffectual. In describing the political fate of his beloved Dante, Boccaccio relates that when the poet understood "that he could not all alone support a third faction, which in its perfect justice should cast down the injustice of the other two and reduce them to unity, he consorted with the one [of the two factions] which in his judgment had the greater measure of reason and justice, ever working for that which he recognized as wholesome for his country and her citizens."[86]

Equally vulnerable was the burgeoning administrative cadre staffing the numerous offices of the republic. Bartolus labeled this large neutral block "homines communes"; they were expected to enforce public law, collect delinquent taxes, and recover property and rights of the polis, as well as to distribute equitably fiscal burdens and political obligations.[87] Responsibility for reprisal against the lawless and overmighty in an age when vendetta and blood feud were matters of honor was particularly exacting. To the patrician the compulsions of public law were degrading; compensating for this humiliation, they might strike out at lowly minions charged with enforcement. That the *homines communes* were subject to political harassment and even violence is no mystery.

[86] *Trattatello in laude di Dante*, ed. P. Wicksteed (London, 1904), p. 3.
[87] P. J. Jones, "Communes and Despots: The City State in Late Medieval Italy," *Transactions of the Royal Historical Society*, 15 (1965), 77.

Although the polis of the mid-*trecento* could not effectively safeguard the political person of Matteo Villani or others serving in the bureaucracy, the trend toward factiousness was soon reversed. Matteo's generation of chancellory officers, commissioners over the public debt, and treasury officials was the last of an honorable line of victims of civic strife. Beginning with the 1380s the authority of the signory was extended so that neither church nor quasi-political body nor overmighty aristocrat could easily play the accustomed role of spoiler. Civil servants in all varieties of posts, from minor treasury official to exalted chancellor, were freed from the menace of proscription by the captains of the Guelf party or excommunication by a high prelate. Great feudatories of the countryside were brought to heel under public law; ancient jurisdictions were limited, rendering the power of vying factions less disruptive.

Contests for hegemony continued at the highest levels of communal society, but they left the bureaucracy relatively undisturbed. Exile usually involved only a few men at the top. A single body of public law, already in process of formation, had effected greater citizen equality. Since the 1340s the *novi cives* and their patrician supporters had used the law to subdue the intransigent who insisted on being bound only by an earlier code. The last years of the *trecento* witnessed the harvest of this greater egalitarianism. The solidification of bureaucratic structure lent stability so that contests for power, while dramatic, did not menace the civil servant and citizen patriot.

Arno society during the generation after the thirties was in process of democratization; the prose of Sacchetti, the poetry of Pucci, and even the music expressed egalitarianism.[88] Individuals could identify more easily with the public world. If a Salutati respected the dignity of the merchant calling, great guildsmen were more solicitous toward public careerists. The justification of a public world and the extension of law and equality meant disruption of chivalric ideals, mystical expectations, and an enthusiasm for the political act prompted by metaphysical impulse. Individual anxieties and insecurities could no longer be assuaged by affirmations of ceremonial identity or ritual ties.[89] Acts of fealty and homage were gratuitous and only emblematic. In the painting of mid-*trecento* we ob-

---

[88] Nino Pirrotta, "Lirica monodica trecentesca." *La Rassegna Musicale*, 9 (1939), 324–25. Cf. also G. Tigri, *Canti popolari toscani* (Florence, 1869); A. D. Ancona, *Saggi di letteratura popolare* (Livorno, 1913).

[89] On Sacchetti, see the observations of L. Russo, "La dissoluzione del mondo cavalleresco 'Il Morgante' di Luigi Pulci," *Belfagor*, 7 (1952) 41. Here we see that Sacchetti has re-evaluated the world of nature so that "per la prima volta" distinctions between man and animal have been blurred; both are compelled to make their way through life "per le stesse strade." No hierarchical view of society, with its commitment to the great chain of being, would be buttressed by such an ultimate in democratization.

serve the deterioration of the lyric grace and elegance of a receding aristocratic world. Crowding, cluttering, and subjectivity displaced the restrained and objective rational order precious to the men of Giotto's time, with its easily traversable and readily measurable space.

Neither the noble nor his code continued to exert the fatal fascination of a former age. The hero of the late *trecento* was not a gallant Corso Donati or an imprudent Giano della Bella; instead, pious and civic-minded Guido del Palagio and the shrewd, patriotic Niccolò Uzzano came to the fore. Soon the greatest diplomat-merchant of the Renaissance basked in the affection of the populace; Cosimo de' Medici won the title "Father of his Country."[90]

A polis embracing the ideal of law and speaking in the unaccustomed accents of a "rotto parlar" could not be expected to be tranquil. The subduing of hubris and medieval commitment to blood and honor entailed distress, upheaval, and rebellion. In the past, there were interludes when democratization and the rule of law seemed meaningful alternatives; but soon they receded, engulfed in a sea of oligarchical reaction. Impersonal government yielded to the customary rule of patricians who were responsive to the claims of leading families for recognition of privileged status. After the forties, as we have noted, law was extended and regularization of administrative procedure intensified. The number of civil servants increased by 25 per cent at a time when the Black Death had reduced the city's population by at least one-third. A generation later, the bureaucracy employed over 1,500 workers; this represented an increment of better than 25 per cent.[91]

This mass of officeholders, little affected by political maneuvering at the top, transferred from one minor post to another during protracted and tranquil careers. A *cursus honorum* had been programed for lesser

---

[90] On the charisma exerted by these "grandi uomini" over the medieval chronicler, see F. Chabod, "La 'concezione del mondo,'" 335–38. The process of repression, wherein expectations transcending everyday experience are coupled with interiorization of restraints dictated by society, is reflected in the portraiture of the early Renaissance. Cf. R. Hatfield, "Five Early Renaissance Portraits," The Art Bulletin, 47 (1965), 315–34. The mid-*trecento* manner book of Paolo da Certaldo (*Libro di buoni costumi*, ed. A. Schiaffini [Florence, 1945] n. 82) contains a definition worth quoting: "Cortesia non è altro de non misura, e 'misura dura': e non è altro misura se non aver ordine ne' fatti tuoi." For an illuminating discussion of the above quotation, as well as a consideration of the rhetorical injunction of *suavitas*, see B. Terracini, "L' 'aureo Trecento' e lo spirito della lingua italiana," Giornale Storico della Letteratura Italiana, 134 (1957), 1–36. One aspect of early Renaissance civic life worthy of extensive analysis is the ready entry of oratorical concepts into books of etiquette. Such a development indicates the need for a more self-consciously constructed persona.

[91] In the next volume the careers of certain bureaucrats will be examined in detail. On the decline of great medieval magistracies, see A. Sorbelli, "I Teorici del Reggimento," Bullettino Istituto Storico Italiano, 59 (1944), 30–136.

officials so that they passed from minor posts in the countryside, through administrative office in subject towns, until they reached the numerous positions of civil responsibility in the polis. By the end of the *trecento* few alterations in the legal and fiscal organization of the republic were in process. The problems of government were seldom ideological but mainly administrative and bureaucratic. Solidification of law, certainty of procedure, and security of personnel were hallmarks of the emerging public world. Problems centered on the funding of the communal debt, interest rates on public loans, costs of mercenaries, efficient administration of the *contado*, and techniques for assessment and distribution of taxes. The needs of the polis and its burgeoning empire were for an army of civil servants trained in techniques of governing.

VIII

An analysis of the discussions by various advisory councils to the signory reveals that two problems held the attention of all governments between the 1370s and the 1430s. Making distinctions between policies advocated by the Albizzi faction after 1393 or Cosimo de' Medici after 1434 is a delicate undertaking. It would seem that one might utilize the tenure of a radically democratized signory (1378–82) as a point of comparison, since the earlier period would presumably give evidence that a new fiscal regimen was installed. Instead, the fact of this new regimen was that much of the novelty was limited to empty statements of intent seldom translated into practice. The gap between the character of recorded legislation (an expression of intention) and the daily operation of administrative agencies served to discourage any who looked for a logical nexus. Important differences in political ethos and style can be discerned between regimes, but persistent pressures and chronic problems remained constant. Governments soon lost their gloss, and neither program nor ideology could deter the moment of confrontation, remarkably similar in each political instance. Moreover, the extension of law, the proliferation of bureaucracy, and veneration for precedent encouraged conformity.

The rule of law and the creation of political machinery to effect the safe passage of a damaged polis engaged politicians during the mid-*trecento*. This involvement in the public world increasingly impinged on diaries and family memorials. Pragmatic in tone, they displayed more concern with the price of government stock than with remoter questions. Activities of a pope or a prelate were most meaningful in terms of the effect upon the public debt, just as seditious movements by workers were judged in terms of possible influence on public credit rates. Private correspondence displayed similar interest in the workings of the public world; experience and the concrete problem displaced theory and ideology.[92]

The suggestion has been made that the Renaissance state can be treated as the creation of economic change and mounting indebtedness (the former being handmaiden to the other). The metaphor, not so esthetic as Burckhardt's "The State as a Work of Art," may yet illuminate a greater segment of late *trecento* Florentine life. To present such a metaphor is not to suggest the absence of social and political imperatives. Individuals and social orders were affected by the economic transformation; they in turn acted or failed to act in relevant ways. Creative social and political struggle accompanied the change, so that to fill out the metaphor, the social and political forces acting to shape the public world should be delineated. Democratization of the polis in the early forties and sustained participation of *novi cives* prompted the growth of law and bureaucratic machinery. With the partial displacement of an older patriciate, the easier style of favoritism and personal government receded. The laissez-faire regime, permissive toward the urban patriciate, generated a political structure capable of being managed by a small clique and financed with slight citizen sacrifice. Records of the communal councils in the 1320s and 1330s show influential bankers, corporate guilds, or the *Parte Guelfa* lending sizable sums. Only modest demands were made on the citizenry; even these were frequently resisted by the communal councils. A timid, uncoercive system of this type could flourish only when budgets were limited and public debt meager. At mid-*trecento* both these preconditions were altered to the accompaniment of extensive political democratization.

The fourth decade of the century witnessed the start of the climb of public indebtedness until it came to dominate communal debate and treasury operations. To meet the minimal interest payments on this indebtedness or *Monte* would require almost half of the republic's total tax revenue. So unwieldy and inflated had the *Monte* become that amortization could only remain a pious hope. In 1387 carrying charges on the *Monte* stood higher than 150,000 florins, and this was just a harbinger of things to come. By 1394 the total had reached almost 190,000 florins. Ten years later, just after the outbreak of the second Pisan war, it had expanded to approximately 250,000 florins.[93] To this were added many of the forced loans, regularly exacted. Although it is not always possible to obtain a precise estimate of these *prestanze*, since the communal system of treasury bookkeeping was exceedingly complex, we can judge that by

---

[92] See E. Bonora's review of Giovanni di Pagolo Morelli's *Ricordi*, in *Giornale Storico della Letteratura Italiana*, 74 (1957), 602–9.
[93] *PC*, 4. For the total just after the Pisan war (1407), see *PC*, 21.

the early *quattrocento* the sum total of these *prestanze* stood at over seven times the total of all commercial wealth in the city. By any standards, the amount of citizen capital being absorbed by the state was enormous.

Again we see how different the situation in the late *trecento* was from that of an earlier time, when a Bardi or a Strozzi might have advanced the *camera* 30,000 florins or so in order that the polis weather a crisis. The city could finance its activities from indirect taxes; in 1345, therefore, less than one hundred families had large-scale holdings in the public debt. By the 1370s the number had increased tenfold, and by 1427 it stood at twentyfold. Further, the amounts involved were thirty and forty times as great as investments in the original *Monte* of 1345. The *Catasto* of 1427 demonstrates compellingly that virtually every Florentine whose patrimony exceeded 3,000 florins was a shareholder in the republic's funded debt. No longer, then, could any one of these thousands of investors in government public securities (the political elite of the city) disregard operation of the public sector of the economy.[94]

Gradually the Arno republic moved away from a private economy in which government intake and outlay were negligible causal forces toward the formation of an economic system in which public credit and spending were to play a crucial role. During the middle years of the *trecento*, successive regimes had enforced the law with unaccustomed rigor. The implications were that medieval immunities, privileges, and liberties tended to dissolve. This process could only enhance the Florentine treasury, since when the Tuscan church was heavily taxed or the ancient guilds lost many of their prerogatives there would be more funds for the creditors of the republic. We must recall that the creditor class had come to be synonymous with that substantial number of Florentine citizens participating in public life, either as elected officials or bureaucrats. Meanwhile, the need to acquire revenue also led the republic to a persistently harsh regimen over its *contado* and domains. The difference between this stern program and its medieval antecedent rested in its continuous operation. Earlier, governmental decisions were generally *ad hoc*; if the treasury required funds, loans would be forthcoming and gabelles to secure them pledged. As soon as public money was more plentiful or warfare abated, the *camera* reverted to its habitual relaxed policies. In this respect, too, the distinction between early and later *trecento* Florence was apparent:

---

[94] This statement is based upon a survey of rate payers listed in *Campioni del Catasto dei cittadini*, Vols. 64 to 72. We observe that elsewhere in north Italy, particularly in Venice, as private banks proved unable to cope with persistent credit problems there was an increasing call over the second half of the *trecento* for government to create a state bank. Cf. R. Cessi, "Il problema bancaria a Venezia nel secolo XIV," *Atti della R. Accademia di Torino*, 52 (1917), 789–93. The creation of the Casa di San Giorgio at Genoa in 1408 is another case in point.

after the forties the need for revenue was chronic so that monetary policies were more uniform. Without radical shifts, and given the persistent need for revenue, there would be no withering away or relaxation of communal authority. Not that Florentines were not anxious to trim the overweening demands of the *camera*; rather, the mounting debt and pressure for more impersonal government made it extremely difficult to do so. The consequence was that the polis assumed a fixed form. The monied classes of the republic committed a large portion of their wealth to the ministrations of the polis. As communal creditors, they were unlikely to opt for the easy rule of the past, since such a regimen would also be casual about restitution.

The search for revenue led to the integration of Florentine territory and the rise of empire, but the treasury's fiscal dilemma persisted. In the late sixties the customs toll and returns from other major imposts declined alarmingly at the very moment when Florence embarked upon a series of wars, each of which proved more costly than its predecessor. The War of the Eight Saints against the papacy occasioned expenditures of over 2,500,000 florins, outlays soon dwarfed when hostilities erupted with Milan. By the early *quattrocento* approximately 500,000 florins were being expended annually for the hire of mercenaries; moreover, when the tempo of warfare heightened, the outlay increased by as much as 50 per cent. At best, communal levies could be expected to cover only a fraction of this expenditure. Although the yield from gabelles remained steady, it was barely sufficient to meet the commonplace demands of government.[95] In the late 1360s a new practice was initiated which was to continue for the balance of the century: the treasurer of the *Monte* was authorized to lend on the average of 200,000 florins per year to the treasury. This practice, coupled with ever-more-frequent recourse to the interest-bearing forced loan, caused the public debt to soar into the millions. Soon this system of deficit financing raised public indebtedness until it stood at five times the total commercial wealth of the citizenry, and within less than a generation it registered over ten times that amount. In the year of the imposition of the *Catasto* (1427), the accumulated debt of the polis equaled the grand total of all citizen patrimony, of fixed or of movable goods.[96]

This redeployment of capital into the hands of the state was further in-

---

[95] Income from indirect taxes and accustomed sources remained steady at approximately 250,000 florins per annum, while the costs of the various *Monti* (carrying charges and administrative expenses) ran to almost 390,000 florins. A balance of October, 1470, anticipates the former at 256,500 florins (from taxes) with the latter at 386,800 florins (carrying charges). *P*, 161, f. 171.

[96] P. J. Jones, "Florentine Families," pp. 196–97, presents the most recent estimate of the total capital of the Florentine citizenry as being between eight and nine million florins.

tensified in 1425 when the *Monte delle Doti* was founded. This credit institution served as a type of insurance bank in which deposits were made by families so that their daughters might be guaranteed a dowry and they might be assured progeny. In an age when a girl without a dowry had virtually no opportunity to marry, this ingenious plan would appear to have been a boon to the unfortunate. It was possible to make arrangements with the officials of this *Monte* whereby one could deposit a fixed sum over a specified number of years and thus obtain a suitable dowry. The term of a normal contract ran from seven to fifteen years; if one selected the shorter term, one made a larger annual payment. If the daughter died or went into a convent before the term expired, part of the deposit went to the commune; if, however, she had marriageable sisters, the capital could be transferred and a new contract drawn up under slightly less favorable conditions. This particular *Monte* added substantially to the obligations of the republic, for Florence was committed to pay $3\frac{3}{8}$ per cent on all deposits. By 1470 the liability of the republic for the *Monte delle Doti* was 196,000 florins yearly, well over half the annual revenue of the city.[97] Not only was the republic responsible for the defense of the Florentines but even for the proper marriage of their children. As much as any other single fiscal stratagem, the foundation of this *Monte* induced the citizenry to look toward the state for its well-being. When Cosimo de' Medici postponed making payments on the *Monte delle Doti*, the chronicler Giovanni Cavalcanti averred that he had broken the bond which tied "la grandezza della Repubblica colla libertà del Monte."[98] So tight was the nexus between the grandeur of the state and the integrity of the *Monte* that in the mind of this chronicler they had become inseparable.

By the 1350s a rugged program was already well in evidence whereby the Florentine treasury could garner an ever-increasing share of rural and dominion wealth. Public policy was, then, chronically dictated by budgetary deficits and the pressing need to underwrite the inflated state credit structure. If sufficient revenue could be collected from the territories, the customs toll and other gabelles could be placed at the disposal

---

[97] L. Marks, "The Financial Oligarchy in Florence under Lorenzo," *Italian Renaissance Studies* (New York, 1960), 127–29. The particular *Monte* in question, called *Monte delle Doti*, was founded in 1425 at the time of the wars against Filippo Maria Visconti to alleviate pressure on the public debt. Within a generation, the annual obligation of the state to those who had invested in this *Monte* was 199,000 florins. Added to the republic's other liabilities to *Monte* shareholders, it amounts to 347,000 florins, required simply to meet the annual interest payments. This figure is in excess of annual revenues by some 129,300 florins. Cf. G. Canestrini, *La scienza e l'arte di stato* (Florence, 1862), 1, 163 ff.

[98] *Istorie fiorentine* (Florence, 1839), 2, 203. For a description of the nexus between public confidence and the reliability of the management of the state debt, see G. Luzzatto, *Il debito della pubblico della Repubblica di Venezia* (Milan, 1963), pp. 241 ff.

of the *Monte* treasurer for restitution to communal creditors or later for payment of dowries. Before the 1350s the general rule had been that subject cities ought to maintain garrisons of knights and foot soldiers. Almost at the same time as the *camera* extracted money in lieu of rustic military duty, the obligation of castle-guard was converted into a cash subsidy. These assessments were steadily augmented until the 1370s, when subject cities had come to be virtually incorporated into the Florentine fisc. The treasurers of San Miniato were now Florentine citizens who paid receipts directly into the *camera* of the republic. Revenue from customs tolls, gabelles on wine, and levies on contracts were transferred to Florence. Over the next years the rate of taxation doubled and sometimes tripled. Many subject cities could not hope to meet their crushing responsibilities to Florence, and soon their treasuries began to run sizable deficits.[99] New taxes, new debts, and a stern program of Florentine mercantilism did little to encourage the economic growth of these towns.[100] Out of the ever-widening claims of the Florentine treasury were forged the links of empire, and the pattern of exploitation of the *contado* hastened this transition.

This Spartan regime in its search for money was acting to integrate rural territories into a political complex that can perhaps be best described as a Renaissance state. So different was this type of regime from its medieval predecessor of the thirteenth and early fourteenth centuries that although terms like "republic" or "commune" might continue to be employed to describe the Florentine political configuration by men from the thirteenth through the fifteenth century, the fact was that the entity described in the later period differed markedly from that of the earlier.

[99] Soon after the thwarting of the rebellion of San Miniato, Florentine officials were empowered to collect all the important gabelles and to supervise the fiscal administration of this subject town. By 1371 revenues from courts of San Miniato were being paid directly into the Florentine treasury. Cf. *CCE*, 135–40 (1370–71). The communities under Florentine dominion were consistently incurring debts by their steady borrowing from the *camera* of the republic. For San Gimignano, see E. Fiumi, *Storia economica e sociale di San Gimignano* (Florence, 1961), pp. 185 ff. For the disarray of the *camera* and the administration of yet another subject territory, see D. Herlihy, *Medieval and Renaissance Pistoia*, pp. 159–60. The statutes of rural communes reveal the same impulse toward regulation of an ever-increasing spectrum of human activity. This problem will be treated in detail in my next volume.

[100] On mercantilism, see R. Davidsohn, "Blüte und Niedergang der fiorentinischen Tuchindustrie," *Zeitschrift für die gesamte Staatswissenschaft*, 85 (1928), 225–55. For additional bibliography, see M. Becker, "The Republican City State in Florence," *Speculum*, 25 (1960), 39–50. By the end of the *trecento*, a tax was placed on each piece of imported cloth. Even inexpensive varieties were being excluded from the Florentine market. E. Fiumi has graphically described the impact of Florentine legislation that imposed gabelles on goods exported by citizens of San Gimignano to any other town than the Arno republic. Cf. E. Fiumi, *Storia economica e sociale di San Gimignano*. For exercise of control of the Pisan guilds by their Florentine counterparts, see M. Gentile, "Le corporazione delle arti a Pisa nel secolo XV," *Annali della Scuola Normale*, 60 (1940), 198–99.

The lax and easy government of the Middle Ages had receded and in its stead emerged a strict, almost exploitive, regime. By the fifteenth century the term "commune" no longer signified a government characterized by a relaxed rule over its rural domains. Instead, the government was anxious to garner substantial tribute from the countryside. In time of peace this revenue could be disbursed to the republic's creditors, while in time of war it could be utilized for the hire of mercenaries. The laissez-faire rule of a medieval commune was replaced by the strict rule of a Renaissance territorial state, and this change was dictated, at least in part, by the pressing economic exigencies of the public world of the late *trecento* and early *quattrocento*.

We have seen that the stringent control of subject cities began in the second half of the *trecento* and that this development paralleled the emergence of the republic's sterner policy for the *contado*. Florentine officials were being appointed by the signory to oversee the collection of gabelles in certain districts. By the 1360s and 1370s payment of taxes collected by subject cities was not made into the local *camera* but directly into the Florentine treasury. Almost at once these returns were expended either for the hire of mercenaries or payment of interest to communal creditors.[101]

IX

The later career of Giovanni Boccaccio offers an opportunity to appreciate the healing the world of the polis might minister to the distraught psyche of a sensitive citizen. The year 1362 saw the author of the *Decameron* seized with guilt; a monk visited him bearing news of a dreadful prophecy uttered a short time ago by a Carthusian visionary of Siena on his deathbed. Famed for his sanctity, the holy man instructed his emissary to warn Boccaccio of his imminent eternal damnation if he did not renounce at once his poetic and profane studies. Panicked, Boccaccio wrote to his literary counselor that he was on the threshold of abandoning the world to dedicate himself to the life of the spirit. His mentor's celebrated reply served to assuage his friend's anxiety. Petrarch explained that the study of literature had never been judged irreconcilable with

---

[101] *CCE*, 149 (July–August, 1372). One of the effects of Florentine actions was to encourage the formation of regional economies in certain of her dominions. Communes such as Pistoia did acquire advantages. To begin with, however, the conditions under which Florence gained custody of the town in 1351 were exceptional. The chronicler Stefani, in telling of this acquisition, opined that the freedom retained by the Pistoiese by treaty was too great and "meant liberty for them and expense for us." This quotation is noted in N. Rubinstein's "Florence and the Despots," p. 35. Cf. also D. Herlihy, *Medieval and Renaissance Pistoia*. For a description of the damaging effects of Florentine policy, see P. Silva, "Intorno all'industria e al commercio della lana in Pisa," *Studi Storici*, 19 (1910), 329–400.

the practice of a religious life. Did not the dogged devotion to scholarship of a St. Jerome or St. Augustine amply demonstrate this? "The vision was indeed astounding," noted Petrarch ironically, "if only it be true. For it is an old and much used device to drape one's own lying inventions with the veil of religion and sanctity, in order to give the appearance of divine sanction to human fraud." Resolutely, Petrarch went on to demonstrate that literature and study advanced morality and eloquence and even serve as a buffer for the Christian religion.[102]

Although we cannot be certain of particulars of Boccaccio's life at that time, yet the general pattern is visible. In 1366 he added the striking defense of poetry to his overly long work on the genealogy of the gods. In the last decade of his life, poetry continued to be a singular concern. It entailed the serious study of such civic disciplines as history and was inseparable from moral philosophy. Indeed, the tone of his civic orientation shifted from one of invective toward the civic milieu and its democratized governments, as expressed in his earlier *Consolatorio* to Pino de' Rossi, to that of polemic against the exclusivistic nobility. The law-abiding populace stood as a counter to the violent noble.[103] Not surprisingly, Boccaccio was restored to his honored career as ambassador for the polis, and discussions of the advisory councils demonstrated the respect such popular leaders as Uguccione de' Ricci felt for this poet and scholar. Leading spokesmen eagerly awaited his report on the situation at the papal curia.[104]

He became first state man of letters when he was appointed by the signory to comment publicly upon the poetry of his beloved Dante for the moral instruction of the citizenry. Although these were clouded years for Boccaccio and seldom lacking in pessimism, his writings display little affinity for the messianic and apocalyptic. Modern scholars have detected influence by the most civic-minded of the religious orders in Florence—

---

[102] E. Wilkins, *Petrarch's Later Years* (Cambridge, Mass., 1959), pp. 31-32; *Senili*, 1, 5.

[103] The invective against the regime in the *Consolatorio* to Pino is stylized and not characteristic of the later Boccaccio's civic concern. Cf. P.Ricci, "Studi sulle opere latine e volgari del Boccaccio," *Rinascimento*, 20 (1959), 23-26. For the expression of popular feeling, see *Il Corbaccio*, ed. N. Bruscoli (Bari, 1950), pp. 208 ff. It is the men of "alto legnaggio e del nobile" who are "rapaci lupi." Later he employs stronger language calling them "ladri" and "predoni." Cf. also M. Becker, "Notes from the Florentine Archives," *Renaissance News*, 17 (1964), 303-4.

[104] For Uguccione's statement, see *CP*, 9, f. 18r (Dec. 15, 1367) when speaking "pro gonfaloneriis consuluit quod revocetur de curia Dominus Iohannes Boccaccii." The adviser to the signory for the Twelve also counseled "revocetur Dominus Iohannes Boccaccii ut supra." A bit later the signory was urged to send a "litteratum" to our Lord Pope on the grounds that such an ambassador would be above faction and "quod habeat potius animum ad facta Communis quam propria; et de hoc domini et collegia provideant" (*ibid.*, f. 29r [Jan. 12, 1368]). It is possible that the literary man in question may have been Giovanni Boccaccio. For the Florentine wish to aggrandize the career of Boccaccio, see G. Billanovich, *Restauri Boccacceschi* (Rome, 1945), p. 27.

the Augustinians of S. Spirito. Boccaccio's second redaction of the *Genealogia* indicates he had renounced the doctrine of the Immaculate Conception in favor of a position close to that of the Augustinians.[105] Not only did he turn from the mariolatry of Franciscan mystical persuasion, but likewise, in his exposition of the *Divine Comedy* (1373), he departed radically from the commentary then in vogue which stressed the sacred and eschatological character of Dante's work. Courageously he reversed the earlier position of his *Trattatello* (Life of Dante), denying that his hero had the gift of prophecy. Respect for history intensified during the last decade of his life.

The sage Boccaccio exhibited an interiority of religious feeling, stressing the need for a contrite heart and God's boundless grace. Gone was his willingness to champion the cause of wit and ingenuity in the face of Christian moral imperatives. Instead, he expressed the puritanism of his times in a celebrated letter of 1373 to his dear friend Mainardo Cavalcanti, to whom he had dedicated his *De casibus virorum illustrium*. He wrote: "I am certainly not pleased that you have allowed the illustrious women in your house to read my trifles; indeed I beg you to give me your word that you will not permit it. You know how much in them is less than decent and opposed to modesty, how much stimulation to wanton love, how many things that drive to lust even those most fortified against it. . . . My feminine readers will judge me a filthy pimp and an incestuous old man, shameless, foul-mouthed and malignant, eager to spread tales of the dissoluteness of others. . . ."[106]

There was to be no defense of the moral prerogatives of the individual at the expense of society. The gentle paideia, so sympathetic to impulses of the private world, receded in the face of a puritanical ethos. Waning, too, was confidence in the capacity of man to achieve renewal through chivalric quest or mystical odyssey. Gone also was the abundant faith in the regenerative force of spiritualizing love. The tone was pessimistic and didactic, and Boccaccio explained that we came to this pass because "la fede venuta meno." Once this faith had been ample, uniting and binding mankind.[107] Boccaccio appreciated the force of law, recognizing that it alone served to order the public world. Quoting a long passage from the Roman, Vitruvius, describing how by daily use chance syllables were joined and given as names to the things men first used, Boccaccio added facetiously that one must remember that the Roman knew not the Bible, or he would have related how Adam named all things. In espous-

---

[105] G. Martellotti, *Le redazioni delle Genealogie del Boccaccio* (Rome, 1951), pp. 16 ff.
[106] Translation by M. Meiss, *Painting in Florence and Siena*, p. 161; G. Boccaccio, *Le lettere edite e inedite*, ed. F. Corazzini (Florence, 1877), p. 289.
[107] See the persuasive study of G. Padoan, *L'ultima opera di G. Boccaccio* (Padua, 1959). Also, Giovanni Boccaccio, *Il Commento alla Divina Commedia*, 3, 185.

ing a theory of evolution like that of Lucretius, Boccaccio observed wryly that the ancients were unaware that Cain constructed not only houses but an entire city.

Sensitive to the configuration of a public world, the much-praised Florentine ambassador defended the new education whereby profane and sacred studies co-operated to mold the good citizen. Again Petrarch showed the way; in Boccaccio's eyes his genius was not as a poet alone, but also as a historian. The last decades of the *trecento* saw the intense cultivation of a more exacting historical inquiry. Challenges were launched against legends once sacrosanct concerning the founding of the city. S. Spirito became the center for the *studia humanitatis* and its handmaiden, critical historical inquiry. Boccaccio associated himself with the work of the Augustinians of S. Spirito when he named one of their order, Martino da Signa, as executor of his will. This cleric, regularly consulted on state affairs by the rulers of the republic, was to effect the transfer of Boccaccio's library. His second bequest revealed a passion as intense as his love of scholarship and devotion to lay piety. Only a year earlier Petrarch had bequeathed his friend fifty florins; now the friend bequeathed half to his beloved natal city.

The other leading contemporary writer, Franco Sacchetti, also experienced a psychological crisis. *Trecento* language would term this crisis "natural and moral" and emanating from the contest between "intelletto, volontà, e memoria." Sacchetti's creations reflect this struggle; seldom are they integrated, and style is awkward.[108] The early poetry is violent and melancholy; neither he nor his generation seriously entertained chivalric ideals that might give unity to personality and fix the individual harmoniously in this world. Instead, the young Sacchetti was conscious that the rules and "ordinamenti" of society were decaying. So abundant was decadence that it provided Sacchetti an angle of vision as well as the most compelling metaphors. The very absence of discernible order in the world became for him an ordering principle. As we have observed, his art is didactic and his moralizing coercive. The world is an enemy and the customary condition obtaining between men warlike. Only through repression by the strengthened polis and exercise of iron human will can order emerge among men. For the individual the locus of morality must lie in his will. Like Salutati and others he disparaged the efficacy of intellect. Admonition and gentle persuasion gave way to stronger remedies. Appeals to reason were valuable only insofar as they operated to modify *volontà*; such beliefs contributed to the voluntaristic character of new oratorical styles. Eloquence had to be measured in terms of its ability to influence will and reconcile the individual to demands of the public

---

[108] F. Sacchetti, *Opere*, 2, 283; E. Li Gotti, *Franco Sacchetti*, pp. 34–46.

world. The orator by stressing public alternatives placed the citizen in history.

Sacchetti controlled the theme of tension by distancing himself from it. A story was bruited through Florence that Boccaccio, in a moment of spiritual crisis, when visiting the Certosa of S. Stefano in Calabria, decided to become a member of the order—a Certosino. Viewing the decision as the result of clerical propaganda and monastic wish fulfillment, Sacchetti dispatched a sonnet to his friend paying mock homage to the new *frate* of Certosa.[109] Sacchetti was surely one of those poets Goethe intended when speaking of bards "who do not bear a heavy burden of guilt." Stylized, self-dramatized religious conflict can be the stuff of humor. Directing his sharpest barbs against the hierarchical world of the church, Sacchetti also displayed little concern for sacrament and ritual. The cult of the saints filled him with disgust. Priests are but "pescatori religiosi" desiring to fish, but not as Christ and His disciples: Striving always for greater wealth and prestige, the latter-day Pharisees multiply saints and martyrs only to dupe the superstitious and poor. In the company of Salutati and Petrarch, he exhibited a fideism underscoring the fact that faith is an undeniable human experience. At the same time, he, like them, rejected the pronouncements of those who believed themselves to possess the secret counsels of God.[110]

A firm boundary and bulwark of his mind were religious faith of an inner nature; not the ceremonial, but piety, the will, penitence, and work were his stabilizing commitments. In equilibrium with this interiorized lay religiosity was an unswerving dedication to the public world. He felt the defenses of the psyche to be structured from a faith in the value of civic devotion and lay piety during that century when the exterior ideals of the chivalric world and medieval Christendom were less impelling.

---

[109] Giovanni Boccaccio, *Le lettere*, p. xliii: "Sonetto di Franco Sacchetti mandato a Messer Giovanni Boccaccio quando fama corse lui esser fatto frate di Certosa a Napoli."
[110] F. Sacchetti, *Opere*, Vols. 2, 14, 21, 34. In response to the assertion by some that man will not be saved unless baptized, he writes, "Io [Sacchetti] ti rispondo che la fede e la buona volontà fa salvo ogn'uomo." Men can't know each other's minds and hearts or the secrets of nature or God. The intellect may have "tutta la ragione e la scienza del mondo," but such knowledge is meaningless "se la volontà non si muove a amare e volere Dio." (On Petrarch, see footnote 52.) Like Sacchetti, Salutati espouses fideism and extreme voluntarism. Also, it is "la sua esperienza di uomo politico" that lends cohesion to his life. Cf. V. Pernicone, *Sacchetti*, p. 118. Cf. also *De nobilitate legum et medicine*, p. 180, where Salutati addresses a certain Bernardo thusly:

> Dic michi, Bernarde, sapientem ne dixeris, qui sic celestia illa divinaque cognoverit quod humanus intellectus ulterius altiusque nequeat progredi, si sibi non provideat, si non amicis, non familie, non coniunctis, non denique patrie consulere poterit et opitulari? Ego quidem, quo verum fatear, audacter dixerim ingenueque fatebor me tibi et speculationem in celum efferentibus omnes alias veritates sine invidia et sine contentione dimittere, si michi rerum humanarum veritas et ratio relinquatur. Tu speculatione vero plenus sis, sed ego redundem qua bonus efficiar bonitate.

We noted earlier that Sacchetti compared the many wars waged by "Holy Florence" to the labors of Hercules. He himself participated extensively in the politics of those years, serving the government during the War of the Eight Saints against the church, regularly attending deliberations of the extraordinary commission (*balìa* of Eight), going repeatedly on diplomatic missions for the republic, sitting in the signory, and, finally, as magistrate in territories and domains of Florence. In June, 1378, as war with the church was ending, Salvestro de' Medici, leading figure in the signory, offered radical proposals to curtail the authority of great magnates of the polis. Sacchetti warmly endorsed these measures, even composing a political poem little short of blasphemous in nature.[111] Since Salvestro desired to save the polis from the tyrannical aspirations of "grandi e possenti uomini," wrote Sacchetti, he should no longer be spoken of merely as Salvestro but as "Savior of the world" (*Salvator mundi*).

The claims of the public world were justified by Sacchetti: marriage, children, and family are solemn obligations to the good citizen. Wealth was not to be despised but seen as an aid to living virtuously. Asceticism and withdrawal were not to be championed, since they contribute little to *il bene comune*. For the few, these virtues are not negligible, but they cannot serve as ideals for the many. Too frequently they are only a screen for avaricious clerics.

The poet described in a sonnet the frescoes decorating the walls of the chambers of the treasury, moralizing thus: If a citizen abides by the law, he will be not a Midas or Crassus, but rather a Fabrizius or Mettulus. Patriotism is inherent in citizen responsibility for taxes. Sacchetti waxed reflective on the theme of the public debt (hardly a modern poetic *topos*): Is it licit to pay interest on shares in the *Monte*? This question was the subject of his thirty-fifth sermon, wherein he touched upon positions assumed by Dominicans and Franciscans on the matter. Because their conclusions were contradictory, with the former condemning while the latter permitted, Sacchetti moved the argument to a higher plane. If the citizen is truly virtuous he should make loans to the government without expecting interest. Further, it is the patriotic imperative born of the needs of the public world that permits the writer to resolve this dilemma of conscience. More noteworthy is the fact that such high-minded suggestions were not unique; repeatedly, speakers made similar proposals to the advisory councils meeting with the signory.[112]

For Sacchetti the commune assumed a separate, distinct identity so that

---

[111] F. Sacchetti, *Il libro delle rime*, 208. Cf. also G. Capponi, *Cronichette antiche di vari scrittori* (Florence, 1753), p. li, where the author tells Salvestro "che salva hai fatto con nobil savere la patria tua."
[112] F. Sacchetti, *Opere*, Vols. 2, 35. Cf. *CP*, 18, fols. 91 ff. (March 18, 1380) for statements advocating loans "sine fenore et interesse."

his sentences are replete with such phrases as "il comune fa cosi." Emotional involvement with polis made enemies of the republic the enemies of Sacchetti. Threats emanated from the tiny city of San Miniato al Tedesco to the awesome Visconti capital of Milan. A blanket condemnation of all obstreperous citizens could be placed upon the great Ubaldini feudatories as well as upon some impoverished rural house. Within the context of this identification there are characteristics lending variety and dimension. His observations on public life are explicit and untheoretical; his vantage point is that of a bureaucrat whose tenure has included high ambassadorships and lowly rustic magistracies. The organizing metaphors useful to the medieval in structuring experience are not his. Polis, not empire, papacy, Guelf, or Ghibelline, furnished him with political idiom and figure of speech. He was also capable through irony of distancing himself from his own political role. When speaking of his terms as public magistrate it is as if he wished to play the new world against the old, then he was "servus servorum diaboli," not "servus servorum Dei."[113]

Sacchetti, in describing himself as "discolo e grosso," acknowledged his lack of superior education. If we accept his evaluation, then this man without formal philosophical training illustrates the fact that an intelligent layman can argue and understand questions occupying the best scholars of his generation. He appreciated Petrarch's highly developed laic sense of death and, like the master whom he quotes, saw the good life, not ritual, as the best preparation for death. Like Salutati, this "uomo discolo e grosso" challenged certain teachings of the Stoics. Sacchetti believed them unrealistic in contending that honor is the highest good. All men have defects and must be permitted to respond to less lofty imperatives. Upholding the doctrine of primacy of the will, he felt it necessary to dissent from the Stoic position: reason and the will do often war. Although the former may not prompt the individual to eat gluttonously, if the will directs to the contrary, of what avail is reason?[114] The same voluntarism is evident in Salutati when he denies the Stoic maxim that the individual can achieve rational control. Such a doctrine may obtain for our Saviour and His apostles but cannot be valid for the citizen body of a polis. Both Sacchetti and Salutati concurred that learning can only take place when that virtue which moves the will to action is operative. Rhetoric and poetry assumed primacy, legitimizing civic concerns, while lay piety expressed tender regard for those whose earthly pilgrimage led

---

[113] *Opere*, 2, 106. Also it should be observed that the polis and society became more compelling and even menacing. Cf. *CP*, 16, f. 75 (January 9, 1379) for an early use of the verb "to sin" *contra statum*. An adviser to the signory counsels "qui enormiter peccaverunt, peccaverunt contra statum puniantur."
[114] *Opere*, Vols. 2, 15, 16.

them through the streets of the polis. Again it was preoccupation with the public world that conferred structure upon personality.[115]

To appreciate the extent to which the public world diminished private anxiety, we have but to note the reaction of certain prominent individuals when the commune called for devotion. Niccolò Sodorini, Carlo Strozzi, Piero degli Albizzi, Stoldo Altoviti, Ristorio di Piero Canigiani, and Sacchetti's own brother Giannozzo all responded negatively during a moment of crisis. Harboring misgivings, they finally repudiated the polis when it embarked on a clash course with the church and its lieutenants. Adherents of the aristocratic Guelf party, they believed that obligations transcending those of citizen to polis did indeed exist. They were, moreover, dedicated followers of St. Catherine of Siena, who had become a formidable Florentine adversary when she publicly denounced the political leadership for waging war against the church. Her sympathies allegedly ran toward the *Parte Guelfa,* at that time an intractable opponent of the government and its policies. Many believed that St. Catherine approved the numerous proscriptions visited on bureaucrats and *novi cives* by the *Parte* for their support of centralized and impersonal government.[116] So closely associated had she become with an obdurate patriciate that the populace set fire to her Florentine dwelling.

The political metaphors employed by Catherine originated in the world of chivalry. She and her disciples were knights, captained by Christ, doing battle. Their wounds were flowers which bore fruit. Like the perfect knight, Christ himself, her followers were to know ecstasy. As her images were grounded in the feudal romances of a generation past, so her theological constructs stemmed from a simplified version of earlier Thomism, wherein intellect, not will, was primary. Meditation and self-knowledge, not action, were the essentials; the intellect needed freeing in order to know "il bene vero." The voluntarism of civic humanism was scorned. Anachronistic was her political program with its insistent espousal of the crusade. The earthly city could be salvaged only if Christians renounced war against each other to unite against the infidel.

St. Catherine shared elements of the style and restless psychology of her literary contemporaries. Vivid language designed to achieve psychological particularization was her forte, but the stock of her ideas—the sub-

---

[115] In *De verecundia,* ed. E. Garin (Florence, 1947), pp. 304–6, Salutati says he meditated long before deciding that there were praiseworthy passions. In order for a passion to become a *virtus* it is necessary that it becomes a *habitus*—that is, the product of deep consideration or of repeated action. Only in this way can the will be perfected—through choices and acts. The scholastic principle *nihil in actu nisi prius in intellectu* is false. Contrary to the teachings of "the venerable Doctor Aquinas," it is the will that has "regalem dominatum" over the "appetitum sensitivum. . . . Nam cum virtus sit habitus electivus et electio non sit nisi voluntarius."

[116] The Saint's patrician followers will be considered in detail in a subsequent volume.

stance of her arguments—derived from a world already receding. Neither crusades nor *renovatio* nor even service in the cause of a united Christendom could galvanize the energies of men of the emerging polis. The most vibrant reforming forces had their base in the present; the engine of renewal was the city-state itself, and those anxious for change had to respect the newly acquired authority of the public order. To educate for responsibility in the polis was to instruct in the lessons of history and the moderate counsels of moral philosophy.

How different were the ingredients of political consciousness among the Florentine disciples of the Saint. Unreconciled to the contemporary world, they would not accept any limitations to religious aspiration. They swung instead from absolute reliance on ecclesiastical authority to self-annihilation in mystical rapture. Neither the imperatives of chivalry, the hierarchy of a feudal world, nor the act of crusading could reduce this extreme mobility of consciousness, for they were no longer secure anchors in the late *trecento* political world. Literary men like Canigiani in the Saint's *cenacolo* wrote poetry that was misogynous and other-worldly, while Giannozzo Sacchetti denounced the rulers of the earth in bitter verse and then composed lauds extolling the deity. The latter appropriately underwent conversion, renouncing his profession as gambler to be a penitent, then died on the scaffold as a martyr in a conspiracy against the popular government. This was a political consciousness that dramatized the polis as an arena for sin while holding out a mystical expectation that men might soon be released from the imperfect bonds of this earthly city. Unlike those who gathered around S. Spirito or corresponded with Luigi Marsili or Giovanni dalle Celle, they could not fuse lay piety with a civic vision that stressed the dignity and autonomy of the world of the polis.[117]

There was a deep bond of sympathy between Catherine and Giovanni dalle Celle. When envious clerics charged her with the sin of pride and, even worse, heretical beliefs, the Vallambrosan was quick to defend her. The existence of such sympathy rendered his differences with her more striking, for he was an admirer. Not only did they differ as to the rightness of defending country against church or in their interpretation of the validity of decrees of excommunication, but the import of their political teachings was separated by the experience of at least a generation. Catherine in her zeal for the crusades invited Tuscan women to join a "bella brigata" destined to spend their blood for Him at the Holy Sepulchre. When news reached Dalle Celle that Florentine women were preparing for this holy adventure, he wrote to one of his spiritual daughters, charg-

---

[117] G. Getto, *Saggio letterario su Santa Caterina* (Florence, 1939), 104–5; M. Meiss, *Painting in Florence and Siena*, p. 89; G. Brucker, *Florentine Politics and Society*, pp. 332–34.

ing her to read his letter to the assembled so they might be dissuaded: Go again to St. Catherine and ask how she achieved such perfection. She will tell you that it came through silence and prayers: she maintained the vow of silence for eight years. According to her own words she remained in her chamber and prayed all that time. Do this first and when you have achieved perfection, I shall certainly give my permission to betake yourselves overseas for crusading.[118] More a practical man than a mystic, he defended moderate counsels: If man keeps "the eye of the mind on the honor of God and the welfare of the commune and the needs of the poor," there will be nothing to fear in this world. Unlike Siena, Pisa, and many another Tuscan town, Florence sired "practical" mystics, compassionate toward the exigencies of the public world.

X

Numerous imperatives operating to focus citizen attention upon the public world already functioned in the 1370s and early 1380s. Mercantilistic policies resulted in greater dependence of merchant upon signory. Citizen investment in the funded public debt accentuated this economic interdependence. Meanwhile, the explosive brew of patriotism and imperialism became even more volatile. Florentine territorial aggression could not easily find justification in the matrix of traditional medieval ideology, Guelf or Ghibelline. For those seeking a reform of Christian practices, the regenerative political agency became the Florentine polis, abstracted from the context of a universal Christian society. Patriotism and piety fused so that the citizenry were "true Christians elected by God." This transvaluation can be described in the language of Max Weber as "the disenchantment of the cosmos" and the ensuing "enchantment of the polis."

Florence stood justified in the sight of God and man, for, said political prophets, she had been chosen to perform a holy mission. Sacrosanct she stood according to the new messianic tradition from late *trecento* to the time of Savonarola. During the *quattrocento* the tone of prophecy became more political. Earlier, in the second half of the *trecento*, it had been *il popolo minuto* who were harbingers of the new day; when they achieved power, the rule of law would be displaced and polis wither away. Now the republic became the sacred object and durable entity. The polis is depicted in popular verse as the "Ark of Paradise"; assuredly, if the Ark is wisely governed, *renovatio* will follow in the *civitas*. Next, the "perfected" community will assume leadership over a humanity devoutly hungering for peace. All the faithful of Christ are to be welcomed

---

[118] P. Cividali, "Giovanni dalle Celle," 354–471 and especially 366–68 and 417.

into the city so that the history of the "true Florentine empire" may begin.[119]

The new role of the arts in Florentine life was prefigured in 1378 when the painters, still affiliated with the guild of physicians and apothecaries, were authorized by the signory to form a branch independent of this guild. The enabling act affirmed that their metier "had consequences of great importance in the life of the state and appeared already advanced for the life of the state."[120] The tendency in architecture was to search for forms that would permit the interior world and public world to be harmoniously accommodated. The arts in general were receptive to that objective, and no one was more appreciative of the need for "harmony" than the civic rhetorician, or humanist. A new genre of literature and art responded by celebrating the obvious virtues of the polis. Quotations from the sessions of the advisory councils to the signory illustrate a new brand of oratory and emotion in tune with the sacredness of this public world: "Deus est respublica, et qui gubernat rempublicam gubernat Deum. Item Deus est iustitia, et qui facit iustitiam facit Deum."[121] Such respected political sages as Niccolò da Uzzano proclaimed that "Virtue reveals itself in adversity; when things go smoothly anybody can conduct himself well. Liberty is to be valued higher than life. The spirit cannot be broken

---

[119] E. Garin, "L'attesa dell'età nuova e la 'renovatio'," *L'attesa dell'età nuova nella spiritualità della fine del medioevo* (Todi, 1962), p. 27. Florence is depicted in popular verse as; "un'arra di paradiso/ questa città pareva/ sendo ciascuno unito/ gran pace si vedeva." Numerous other prophecies dated 1359, but obviously dealing with events of the late 1370s and thereafter, blend aspirations for political revitalization with the expectation of imminent religious reform. In both, the chosen instrument is to be the city of Florence. Cf. D. Weinstein, "The Savonarola Movement in Florence," p. 198.

[120] M. Meiss, *Painting in Florence and Siena*, p. 63, note 16. At about the same time, Recco di Guido Guazza, speaking for one of the colleges, advises the signory "super platea fori veteris" that provision should be made "ad utilitatem communis, pulcritudinem civitatis et contentam artificum." There was increasing involvement of civic humanists and literary men with the art of the times. Along with the instances cited in footnote 22 of the Introduction, mention should be made that Franco Sacchetti was responsible for the program of subjects for the ceiling of Orsanmichele, whereas Bruni was similarly occupied with the program for Ghiberti's second set of doors to the Baptistry. Cf. E. Borsook, *The Mural Painters of Tuscany from Cimabue to Andrea del Sarto* (London, 1960), p. 141.

[121] *CP*, 51, f. 169 (July 3, 1431). J. Hyde's recent study, *Padua in the Age of Dante* (Manchester, 1966), pp. 309–10, goes far to show an identity between the administrative class and the intellectuals. "The administrative class from which all the Paduan thinkers sprang, looked to the commune for their sustenance." This city, center of the most intense philosophical and literary activity in the early *trecento*, lost its primacy when the republic fell. The background to this "cultural emergence," the essential ingredient, was "a body of writings on current affairs, mainly local in interest, emanating from the milieu not of the schools or university, but of the administrative class of the Commune." To fall to the Carrara princes (1328) was to initiate a courtier culture: "A state where so much depended on the will of the ruler was hardly the place to encourage a sensitivity towards the significance of impersonal factors in the rise and fall of political systems which had been tentatively explored by the writers of the communal period."

unless one wills it so."¹²² Such a quotation suggests that this most influential Florentine had a need to articulate a postulate from his political psychology in a meeting of governmental advisers. A few years later, when he died and the Uzzano bust was made by Donatello from a death mask, it is probable that the mask was transformed by the sculptor into a likeness of Cicero. So the public man of Florence attained immortality in the image of antiquity and the world of shared public experience gained durability.[123]

The Trinity mural of Masaccio, in the third bay of the western aisle in the church of Sta. Maria Novella, shows a member of the Lenzi family commemorated in red robes—probably those of the highest elected official of the republic, the *Gonfaloniere di Giustizia*. This depiction of the donor of the Trinity seems to bring the earthly city so near to its heavenly counterpart that the just officeholder can easily cross the modest divide. In an earlier work, executed by Nanni di Banco and Donatello (possibly the first piece of sculpture to be influenced by a program dictated by a civic humanist), the figure of David on the *Porta della Mandorla* of the Cathedral stands as a symbol of both civic and theological fortitude.

The relief of Hercules on the jamb of the *Porta* exhibits the classical hero as the prefiguration of the Christian athlete. *Ascesis* has assumed a meaning and public relevance never before associated with the athletes of virtue so beloved of the Church Fathers. Even the Annunciate Mary has her unusually short hair bound by the fillet of an Olympic victor. A not inconsiderable interpretation of the famous reliefs entered by Ghiberti and Brunelleschi in the renowned competition of 1401 for the Baptistry doors might emphasize the fact that the crucial moment selected for the Biblical portrayal was the appearance of the angel just as the knife is to be plunged into Isaac's throat. That Florence was in mortal jeopardy from her dread enemy Giangaleazzo Visconti at exactly that time and therefore looked to the Lord for deliverance, may have been more than coincidental.[124]

A note of caution: signs of the extension of the claims of the public world are evident—by-products of social and economic changes in process for over half a century. Despite this, it would be simplistic to substitute the ordered and rational conceptualization of the public world found in

---

[122] H. Baron, *The Crisis of the Early Italian Renaissance* (Princeton, 1955), 1, 338. Striking is the intensification of patriotic poetry to which public response was enthusiastic and sustained. One of the functions for which the heralds of the signory were much lauded was the composing of verse "tanto mirabilmente et con tanta dolcieza, qual filomena in bosco. . . ." Contemporary accounts tell of how attentive and pleased *il popolo* was at these sessions. F. Flamini, *La lirica toscana*, pp. 6 ff.

[123] A. W. Janson, *The Sculpture of Donatello* (Princeton, 1957), 2, 236–40.

[124] C. Eisler, "The Athlete of Virtue," *Essays in Honor of Erwin Panofsky* (New York, 1961), p. 86; F. Hartt, "Art and Freedom in Quattrocento Florence," *Essays in Memory of Karl Lehmann* (New York, 1964), p. 124.

civic art for the welter of political emotions expressed by the citizen body. Civic art and civic doctrine did encourage the citizen to assume the persona of man of the polis. The attractions of the public world were projected, and the citizen might structure his personality in collective terms rather than by exclusively private imperatives. Patriotism and strict enforcement of law could serve as modes of repression, yet the Florentine seldom responded consistently to civic messages of artists or imperatives of law. The public world was no less real because its values were not completely internalized; the very ambiguity engendered into citizen life by the claims of polis lent vitality to civic thought and art. Had loyalty to the republic triumphed totally, what need would exist for a new public art and philosophy? Had men been persuaded completely of their civic duty, what need for rhetoricians and orators to convince the convinced?

At the core was an ambiguity capable of entrancing many. It was readily acknowledged that the active life was virtuous, yet there persisted a feeling that it was valueless and much inferior to the contemplative life. Public men regularly announced their intention of abstaining from the political world while continuing to engage in active careers until death. The favorite last words to one's heirs by political figures ran to paradox: Shun politics, but without political office a Florentine is nothing. The architect Leon Battista Alberti, anxious to fuse public and private worlds in his art and knowing the damage republican politics could wreak, was a party to the prudential counsel that citizens should shun public life. His birth in exile was a stunning tribute to the political menace lurking behind the patina of public spiritedness. During the life span of the republic, enthusiasm for political careers might wane, but few would deny that service to the polis was not the chief ingredient of true nobility. The same individual who regularly made payment into the treasury so that he might be relieved of the onerous responsibility of assuming a particular office was the first to laud careers of public service. Francesco Guicciardini, worldly, skeptical observer, wrote: "In Florence it would seem as if you were almost not a man if you have not served at least once in the signory." Banished from politics upon the return of the Medici, Machiavelli told his friend Vettori: "Fortune has decreed that knowing nothing of silk manufacturing nor the wool business, nor of profit or loss, I must talk politics and unless I take a vow of silence I must discuss them."[125]

---

[125] J. H. Whitfield, *Machiavelli* (Oxford, 1947), p. 61. Cf. also Guicciardini's comment in R. Ridolfi, *Vita di Francesco Guicciardini* (Rome, 1960), p. 8: "Crebbe sì, con un rispetto grandissimo per lo studio delle lettere che danno all'uomo la perfezione dei beni dello animo; rispettò anche i filosofi pur parendogli che, attendendo essi a scrutare le cose che non si veggono, dicessero mille pazzie; ma preferì di molto lo Stato."

Government tax policies were likely to provoke intense conflict in the Florentine political conscience. Precisely because the merchant was reluctant to renounce the norms of either world (private or public), he instructed his familiars at once in the delicate art of tax evasion or falsification of business ledgers in order to mislead communal revenue assessors while at the same time taking great pride in the contributions he and his fellow guildsmen made for defense of the polis. Decrying the cruel incidence of taxation of his patrimony, the businessman still upbraided the signory for not pursuing a costly war to its end.

If we turn to the art of the first part of the *quattrocento* and consider the two unique frescoes in the Brancacci Chapel, a high level of civic content is readily apparent. Recently, a commentator argued tellingly that Masaccio's *Tribute Money* as well as the *Death of Ananias* had a relevant message for men in the public world of the polis.[126] In exact equation to such exalted apostolic acts of Christ as the baptism, preaching, and healing is the collection of tax monies. Indeed, the doctrine of the divine approval of imposts for purposes of defense seems explicit in the *Tribute Money*. This, too, was the interpretation given by the Florentine bishop of the mid-*quattrocento*—St. Antonino—when he came to discuss the appropriate passage from St. Matthew upon which the scene is based. The *Death of Ananias* likewise treats the very special theme of taxation. We are witness to the terrible punishment dealt those refusing to contribute to the community in time of need, as well as to the benefits derived from the equitable distribution of taxation. There is no better sermon on the evils of tax evasion than that given in Acts 4. 34–35; 5. 1–6, the source of the painter's narrative: Peter and the Apostles are busily distributing alms to the men, women, and children, denizens in a Tuscan-like landscape, while in the foreground lies the body of Ananias, who has been struck down by the Lord because he selfishly withheld part of the profits from a farm.

The use of the term "identity" from *amerikanische Popularpsychologie* may not be altogether gratuitous. One of the central problems of the early *quattrocento* Florentine polis concerned the emergence of new bonds to replace the frayed medieval ties of ritual, ceremony, and pageant. Not that older traditions furnished no support for the citizen ego; rather, they nourished the private instead of the public world. Between the 1390s and 1420s the most vital artistic development was in civic sculpture, and this art form ministered to citizen identity in a novel, even revolutionary way. During that period thirty-two greater than life-size male figures by artists no less gifted than Ghiberti and Donatello were installed in the small area that is the business, religious, and governmental

[126] F. Hartt, "Art & Freedom," pp. 128–29; P. Meller, "La Cappella Brancacci," pp. 186–227.

heart of the polis. When politician, bureaucrat, administrator, and taxpayer strolled through the *agora* on one of many daily excursions, they would see this new host of freestanding figures. These public monuments depicted a new breed of saint and prophet, fully aware of the deadly opposition that can undo them. Sometimes they are brimming with confidence, occasionally they are alarmed, but always they know they must summon their resources in order to preserve their precious identity in the ceaseless struggle of every day.

These were figures dedicated to the benefaction of mankind. When Donatello's *David* was placed in the Palazzo Vecchio, home of the signory in 1416, the inscription at the base read: "To those who fight bravely for the fatherland the gods will lend aid." The figure wears the crown of amaranth, the purplish flower symbolic of the everlasting fame of the hero. Soon Masaccio began his revolutionary quest for the very roots of "the beginnings of man's awareness of himself as a moral being and of his place in history."[127] The preference turned to the depiction of the human situation "in its dormant, potential state" when it is germinating in the mind and the will, and being evaluated in the light of moral responsibility. These plastic forms, creations of Renaissance artists, exist on the dangerous plane of history, locked as they are in time and space, and subject to the blows of fortune and the adversities of duration. Unlike their Gothic counterparts, they cannot transcend the quest for the subtle and illusive. They have only their individual quality to enable them to prevail.

To shift from the world of painting and sculpture to that of the Florentine citizen in his business and family milieu is to appreciate the extent of the loosening of medieval ties. Ritual identity slackened with the decline of traditional ideals of chivalry, the code of vendetta, and Guelfic ideology: the very fabric of the family underwent modification. To compare the role of the family in Genoa or Venice with its *trecento* counterpart is to observe marked differences with consequences for the public world. First, Florentine society was characterized by a much higher degree of political mobility during the same period than either of its two republican neighbors.[128] Indeed, while the Arno city was the beneficiary, although sometimes very reluctantly, of social revolution in the second half of the *trecento*, Venice had already installed that legal machinery so ef-

---

[127] G. Argan, *From Van Eyck to Botticelli* (New York, 1964), pp. 90 ff.
[128] Cf. footnote 12. Very telling was a session of the advisory councils to the signory where it was suggested that inhabitants of the Florentine *contado* be declared eligible for certain key administrative positions in the territories. The session took place in January, 1379, and constituted formal recognition of practices already in vogue for nearly a generation. The fact was that capable personnel was in short supply, and this prompted extensive political mobility—prejudice against the parvenu notwithstanding. Cf. *CP*, 16, f. 85. Personnel of the administrative class will be considered in detail in my next volume.

fectively designed to make her the most appropriate example since antiquity of a closed republican society. Of course families rose and fell throughout north Italy, as they always had, but Florence went farther toward achieving that dread mobility than her more conservative and sensible peers. However, Arno politics did more than catapult the *novi cives* into positions of authority and places of command. By its very character it served to divide patrician houses so that we discover members of the same clan on opposite sides of a public issue. Interpretations of Florentine history based upon rigid notions of class division must take into consideration that one member of the house of the Medici, Strozzi, or Alberti might champion a popular cause, while a kinsman, at exactly that moment, was allied with the most intransigent political conservatives in the community. In the 1350s, there were divisions within families on foreign policy questions; in the next decade they deepened over the role of the philopapal Guelf party. Disagreements multiplied between 1372 and 1382. Families were confronted with cruel choices and frequently took opposing sides in the war with the papacy, in the workers' revolution, and on democratic reform in the four years after 1378. This was the crucial decade for the weakening of certain family bonds.[129]

The divisive character of Florentine politics was accompanied by a movement toward the stern regulation of the city's magnates. Particular regimes acted to undermine the hold of the noble *consorteria* upon its membership. By the 1360s dozens of the oldest magnate houses in the republic had dissolved their antique allegiances, even renouncing their coats-of-arms and assuming new family names in order to win coveted commoner status.[130] One of the most damaging distraints still laid upon magnates was collective responsibility for misdeeds of kinsmen. By separating themselves from a *consorteria*, individuals were no longer liable. In several instances those who did sever clan connection agreed to move to a new quarter of the city, far from upstart relatives.

Such scholars of Florentine business, society, politics, and intellectual life as R. de Roover, Philip J. Jones, Gene Brucker, Lauro Martines, and A. Sapori furnish abundant evidence of the pervasive strain exerted upon the *trecento* family. The individual was increasingly compelled to emerge as a public figure. In general we can observe that the harsh rule of father over son was much relaxed by Italian jurists of the late Middle Ages. The

---

[129] The divisive effect of politics will also be treated subsequently. For the predominance of family and persistence of the "fraterna," see J. C. Davis, *The Decline of the Venetian Nobility as a Ruling Class* (Baltimore, 1962), pp. 25-26, 66-69. For power of the "albergo," see J. Heers, *Gênes au XVe siècle. Activité économique et problèmes sociaux* (Paris, 1961). For the "paraiges" of Metz, see J. Schneider, *La ville de Metz au XIIIe et XIVe siècles* (Nancy, 1950), pp. 114 ff. For the *consorteria*, see E. Cristiani, *Nobiltà e Popolo nel Comune di Pisa* (Naples, 1962).
[130] *P*, 37, fols. 99 ff.; *Baile*, 5.

attitude toward illegitimate children became more generous. In Tuscany bastards were permitted to employ the arms and insignia of their family, and the tendency to vituperate women, chronic among the more ascetic of the past, was modified. Indeed, the use of the *fideicommissum* was not evident in Florence. This meant that inheritances could be sold or alienated and that the order of succession was not irrevocably fixed. When only the first-born son inherited the patrimony, he alone was in a position to marry. This of course was the ideal way to conserve the clan nucleus inviolate. In Florence such a heritage from Roman law held little attraction. Moreover, the family partnership in business or *fraterna,* dominant elsewhere in north Italy, became increasingly rare in the Arno polis.[181] Particularly telling is the fact that exactly at mid-*trecento* family business organization underwent damaging stress. Old partnerships broke down and blood ties lost strength. Common ancestry did not prevent contests for control of businesses between different branches of the same family. The crisis of those years was the crucible out of which more individualized business arrangements arose. Outsiders were recruited as partners.

Leon Battista Alberti's tract *Della famiglia* has been cited with monotonous regularity to demonstrate the continued hold of lineage. His was one of the principal clans to undergo fragmentation on social, economic, and political levels, so that the author, born in exile and writing in the first part of the *quattrocento,* strongly idealized the close-knit structure of the family. His was perhaps more a work of nostalgia than a commentary upon the qualities of the present. Differences in outlook and patrimony which set kinsmen against kinsmen were at work during the *trecento,* but the most commanding of all recent studies of medieval history, undertaken by Georges Duby, indicates the primary factor to influence family solidarity was the capability of the state to provide security. The more protection the government provided, the less need the individual had for close family links. If we can project the results of Duby's monumental studies to encompass the Florentine polis, we can note that as the commune guaranteed more ample protection to the individual, the latter could afford to slacken the reins of kinship.[182] The growth of rule of law and augmentation of authority of the polis over the second half of the *trecento* furnished the Arno citizen with just such an opportunity.

---

[181] A. Pertile, *Storia del diritto italiano,* 2nd edition (Turin, 1892-98), 3, 276-82; 4, 148-55; E. Besta, *La famiglia nella storia del diritto italiano* (Padua, 1933), pp. 192 ff.; F. Lane, "Family Partnerships and Joint Ventures in the Venetian Republic," *Journal of Economic History,* 4 (1944), 178-96.

[182] G. Duby, *La société aux XIe et XIIe siècles dans la region Mâconnaise* (Paris, 1953), pp. 136-37, 263-64, 279-82.

THE ADVENT OF CIVIC HUMANISM

XI

How to place the individual in the public world? That was the question. After the 1340s traditional modes of establishing identity grew less effective. All the while a civic definition of self became more attractive. Surely an art that projected harmony between public and private worlds proved reassuring to the citizen, just as a rhetoric sympathetic to the difficulties of political choice enhanced his ego. Yet a balance between the imperatives of polis and private life was hard-won. The civic humanists taught that private value judgments were not always applicable to the public world. Some leading citizens realized that states could not be governed according to Christian principles. Others understood that love of country might even place the immortal soul in jeopardy.

The robust connection between politics and philosophy was sustained only through two generations of civic humanists. After Salutati and Bruni, confidence in a balance between citizen ego and the exigencies of the public world grew precarious. To a Machiavelli, problems of private conscience were no longer of prime interest; it was the bonds of society instead that were fascinating and self-justifying. For Poggio, the community was seen as evanescent, and for Ficino it was enduring only to the extent that it was spiritual. No spokesman emerged convinced that equilibrium was a cogent possibility. Indeed, the harmony and order of the short-lived, classical interval in Florentine Renaissance painting was over; it had also coincided with the halcyon time of civic humanism. Subsequently painting was less geometric and more tense. The writhing figure against a restless landscape was not without analogy to Machiavelli's Prince in his overwrought setting.

To many citizens the rise of the state in the second half of the *trecento* offered new hope at a moment when the unifying threads of the late medieval world were visibly frayed. No longer was it as easy to subordinate everyday reality to the teachings of the schoolmen or to the confident theology of the Thomists. Nor did the study of logic and dialectic seem as certain of dispelling that lingering miasma of doubt besetting searchers for an understanding of God's ways. The brutalities of a warring age were difficult to subsume under the promptings of chivalry, with its fixed ideals of courtesy and nobility. There was, moreover, little in the operation of the late medieval Christian world to encourage trust in such traditional engines of spiritual regeneration as pope, emperor, or religious order. Likewise, artist and poet were less able to sustain belief in the sacramental ties between man and the noumenal world. Theologians stressed the inability of man to know God in any meaningful way; by the measure of human intelligence, His ways could appear only arbitrary and capricious.

Science, too, was futile, since His will is absolute and there is no reason for Him to obey natural law.

The harsh facts of the late medieval world might be compensated for through the citizen quest for fame, if not immortality, within the world of the Renaissance polis. Further, there was an intriguing possibility open to the idealist: the new political creation—the Renaissance polis—might itself be employed successfully to renovate the Christian order. The vitality of the bond between polis and *renovatio* in the age of Savonarola, as well as the honorable history of citizen sacrifice in defense of Tuscan republics in *cinquecento* wars for *libertas* against impossible odds, suggests that Florentines were not altogether misguided in their new hopes.[133]

---

[133] The late G. Mattingly of Columbia University was fond of dwelling upon the feebleness of Renaissance despotisms when confronted with invaders from the North in the late fifteenth and early sixteenth centuries; it was the supposedly effete and poorly organized republics that offered virile resistance.

THE "NOVI CIVES" IN FLORENTINE POLITICS FROM 1343 TO THE END OF THE CENTURY

II

One of the most striking features of Florentine *trecento* history was the progressive democratization of the city's political life through the entry of new citizens (*novi cives*) into the signory. During its earliest days, rule over the primitive urban commune had been the exclusive preserve of the Florentine aristocracy and the great rural proprietors of Tuscany. At that time, and throughout the twelfth century, the city was a signorial center and its organization a loose medieval configuration of lay and ecclesiastical liberties, immunities, prerogatives, and privileges. Over the course of the next two and a half centuries we witness the erosion of certain of these traditional rights and the emergence of novel forms, procedures, and practices that mirror the aspirations and interests of a changing urban society.

This society was the creation of successive waves of immigrants who flocked to the city in hope of increasing their patrimony and augmenting their status. This mass influx produced a quantitative change that is relatively easy to assess, for the phenomenal urban growth of the city is a fact of number.[1] Much more difficult to determine, however, is the qualitative effect of these migrations on the political character of Florentine life. Here perforce the question is that of the changing nature of the rapport between newcomer and established patrician, and this is not a

---

This is an expanded version of a paper published in *Mediaeval Studies*, 24 (1962), 35-82.
[1] For recent studies on Florentine demography, see E. Fiumi, "La demografia fiorentina nelle pagine di Giovanni Villani," *ASI*, 58 (1950), 78-158; P. Battara, *La popolazione di Firenze alla metà dei 500* (Florence, 1935) and "Le indagini congetturali sulla popolazione di Firenze fino al Trecento," *ASI*, 93 (1935), 226-27; B. Barbadoro, "Finanza e demografia nei ruoli fiorentini d'imposta del 1352," *Atti del Congresso Internazionale per gli Studi sulla Populazione* (Rome, 1931), 13-34. Few documents survive for the north Italian countryside before 1200. Cf. F. Schneider, *Die Entstehung von Burg und Landgemeinde in Italien* (Berlin, 1924). On the origins of the city, see M. Lopes Pegna, *L'origine di Firenze* (Poggibonsi, 1957). For a penetrating analysis of the heightened state of economic activity in the Florentine *contado* during the thirteenth century, see J. Plesner, "Una rivoluzione stradale nel dugento," *Acta Jutlandica*, 10 (1938), pp. 29 ff.

fact that can be expressed statistically. Alterations in the relationships between classes and the attendant modifications in social feeling and political sentiments lead the student to that land from which few who are committed to the teachings of rational psychology ever return. Even more rare is the devotee of irrational psychology who upon his return is able to communicate his experiences. If the history of ideas walks across time on dove's feet, as Nietzsche has suggested, how is one to follow the still more delicate traces created by the nuances of social change during the second half of the fourteenth century? The documentation is starkly public and frankly economic, with little evidence that might serve to illuminate the interior social world of the Florentines. The illusiveness of the quarry is no reason for abandoning the hunt, but the trial has been so little explored and so ill defined that one must forego more conventional and rigorous methodological approaches in favor of flexible and impressionistic techniques.

Over the thirteenth and fourteenth centuries new men continued to exert great pressure upon the government for a stronger voice in the disposition of political questions. As we have observed, the year 1343 was the scene for the collapse of concerted patrician resistance to this trend; the perseverance of the new men was finally rewarded when they won a substantial share in public life, thus becoming an integral part of communal politics.[2] They continued to play a critical role in the civic arena through the closing decades of the century. Their participation in the expanded bureaucracy of the government altered irrevocably the political environment of the republic, while their entry into high office encouraged the transformation of the loosely organized commune into a tightly knit territorial state. Their sustained presence in the public world was likewise instrumental in modifying the political behavior and attitudes of certain well-established families. A description of these changes and an attempt to assess the character of novel relationships between new men and patricians can assist us in a search for insight into the intricate workings of the politics of the rising territorial state. Since the process was dialectical, an understanding of politics and the public world can serve as a base for rendering historically intelligible political sentiments coming to the fore after the 1340s.

---

[2] Between 1343 and 1348 approximately half the 270 members of the priorate, the highest communal office, were from families who had never sat in the signory before. Cf. M. Becker, "La esecuzione della legislatura contro le pratiche monopolistiche delle arti fiorentine alla metà del secolo quattordicesimo," *ASI*, 117 (1959), 15-16. For a discussion of the electoral reforms of 1343, see G. Brucker and M. Becker, "The *Arti Minori* in Florentine Politics, 1342-1378," *Mediaeval Studies*, 18 (1956), 96-97. Half the new men were matriculated in the major guilds, and the remainder were enrolled in the *arti minori*. The model for this type of statistical analysis is presented by N. Ottokar in *Il Comune di Firenze alla fine del dugento* (Florence, 1926), pp. 26-27.

THE "NOVI CIVES"

To select the interval from 1343 through the 1380s is to concentrate upon that era when new men exerted greatest influence upon public life. They were not a decisive element in public affairs earlier, when both the rule and the style were patrician and easygoing. The year 1343 witnessed the first great influx and 1348 lent added impetus to this political mobility. The leather bags containing the names of all deemed eligible for the high magistracy of prior were opened to many candidates from "small families" (*famiglie piccole*). These *novi cives* were to be selected for office to replace men of the patriciate declared ineligible as a consequence of strict enforcement of the *divieto*. This restriction was imposed to prevent multiple office holding by men from great clans.[3] Not surprising, therefore, was the persistent challenge to the earlier, relaxed government of an entrenched patriciate.

I

The term "novi cives" is used here to designate a very affluent segment of those immigrants who had only recently established residence in the city, gained Florentine citizenship, and commenced to assume an active part in civic affairs after 1343. Differences between these new men and the older, notable families were of degree rather than of kind. The latter were scions of the most prosperous urban houses, themselves *novi* four or five generations back, whereas the former had only lately come from the thriving families of the Tuscan countryside (*contado*).[4] Both were matriculated in the guilds, masters of their own shops, and employers of labor. Therefore there was fundamental unanimity between these two groups on a variety of economic questions. The same type of accord obtained in agricultural matters, since patrician and new man alike were owners of extensive rural holdings. This compatibility of interests was further reinforced by joint business ventures, partnerships, monetary obligations, and marriage ties.

The character of the *novi cives*, and consequently the tone of Florentine politics, was deeply influenced by changes that had occurred outside the city walls. The environs of Florence had gradually become a microcosm of the city, and during the twelfth and thirteenth centuries the economic and social milieu of the countryside came to resemble more and more that of the metropolis. The *contado* was not the exclusive preserve of the great magnates; much land had come into the hands of the

---

[3] D. Velluti, *La Cronica domestica*, ed. I. del Lungo (Florence, 1914), p. 192.
[4] This statement and the general description that follows is based upon an impressionistic reading of the materials found in the cartularies of the early Florentine notaries. Cf. *Archivio Notarile*, *A* 981–83, *B* 1238, 1473, 1948–50, 2527, *C* 102, *I* 104–5, *M* 293, 490–91, *P* 413, *R* 40, 159. I was unable to locate *L* 76, listed in the inventory as the cartulary of Ser Lapo di Gianni (1298–1327).

free peasants and rural bourgeoisie. Feudal conditions tended to be limited to those less populated districts most remote from the city or to those areas still dominated by the old noble houses of Counts Guidi, the Pazzi of Val d'Arno, and the Ubaldini. Feudal restrictions on person and property were disappearing throughout the countryside. Agricultural labor was hired when available, land was bought and sold in brisk fashion, and estates rented or let for shares to free peasants, rural artisans, notaries, and merchants.

Crafts, trades, and home industries had taken hold in the rural communes and *popoli* of the *contado*; goods were circulated during the course of its manufacture to small shops, each of which, like its urban counterpart, was more or less independent. These developments over a two-and-a-half-century period stimulated diversity of occupation, heterogeneity of production techniques, varieties of skills as well as a wide experience in a mobile, quasi-urban environment that made it possible for men to transfer their sphere of socioeconomic activity from the *contado* to the city with a minimum of trauma. Therefore the *novi cives* cannot be classified as immigrants if the term implies a startling shift in life patterns. Even after they had entrenched themselves in the city, their ties with the *contado* remained firm. So strong were these bonds that the distinction between city and countryside soon blurred.[5]

In Volume One we noted that new men who acquired Florentine citizenship were from the wealthiest and most influential classes of the *contado*. Patterns of migration reveal that this stratum was the first to leave the countryside for the city and that they were soon followed by families only a little less prosperous. This trend, persisting until the middle years of the fourteenth century, had the effect of leaving the poorer elements to cultivate the land. The signory designed communal legislation to dissuade these serfs and agricultural laborers from abandoning their traditional calling and used the power of the courts to prevent them from severing their legal ties with rural Tuscany.[6] The results of a recent study of the countryside support the conclusion that in territories under Florentine jurisdiction, the phrase "Stadtluft macht frei" had little meaning.[7] The new citizens of Florence were not the fugitive slaves and miserable serfs described by historians of a generation ago such as Davidsohn, Pardi, and Caggese, but were rather scions of affluent country families who could well afford to establish residence in the city, purchase real estate and build a dwelling, pay urban imposts over a period of from five

---

[5] E. Fiumi, "Fioritura e decadenza dell'economia fiorentina," *ASI*, 116 (1958), 443–509.
[6] E. Fiumi, "Fioritura e decadenza," pp. 484–87; P. Santini, *Documenti dell'antica costituzione del comune del Firenze* (Florence, 1895), pp. 51, 391.
[7] J. Plesner, *L'émigration de la campagne à la ville libre de Florence au XIIIe siècle* (Copenhagen, 1934), p. 119; N. Ottokar, *Comune di Firenze*, pp. 123 ff.

to ten years, and still have sufficient capital to matriculate in one of the Florentine guilds and open up shop.[8]

In many instances before the new men could be transformed into *veri, antiqui et originari cives*, they had to be sponsored by prominent Florentines who were willing to go surety for them and vouch for their continued good behavior.[9] On other occasions the new men were held responsible for posting a sizable bond.[10] They were also required to demonstrate that they were "true *amatores* of the city" and men with deep commitments to the principles of Florentine Guelfism.[11] Since the atmosphere of the medieval city-state was intimate and personal, the origins, ancestry, backgrounds, allegiances, and opinions of those who petitioned for citizenship were well known to the signory, and when the communal councils voted on these requests this information became a matter of public record. Men who had served the republic well on the battlefield established particularly strong claims on Florence's affection which paved the way to citizenship, and, conversely, those whose loyalties were suspect found themselves confronted with formidable obstacles. Those guardians of political orthodoxy in Florence—the *Parte Guelfa*—kept detailed dossiers on the juridical status, regional ties, and political reliability of the would-be citizens and their families. Since the captains of the *Parte* and other advisory bodies played an important role in the selection of new citizens, the reputation of the aspirant came under careful scrutiny. When a truly prominent applicant petitioned, eminent members of this panel would speak reassuringly about his qualifications.[12]

In late Medieval Florence the entry of the *novi cives* into civic life was a gradual and complex process. There was a protracted interval during which they were given an opportunity to become familiar with the workings of the intricate Florentine political system. Their earliest experiences in this realm came with their participation in guild affairs. These corporations were the very foundation of the Florentine constitutional system, and as such they played a crucial role in communal politics. It was not possible to hold elective office without being inscribed in one of the twenty-

---

[8] See Plesner's telling critique of these older interpretations in *ibid.*, pp. 116-22.

[9] *LF*, 37, fols. 76r-82 (June 21-July 8, 1356). *P*, 43, f. 165 (October 17, 1356) *Ibid.*, 51, f. 8r; *LF*, 37, f. 56 (August 21, 1363). On occasion, as many as eighty-four Florentines acted as *fideiussores* for the *novo homo*.

[10] *P*, 45, f. 105r (December 12, 1357). The amount averaged 200 lire. There is one instance in which the new citizen agreed to make a loan to Florence of 500 florins, and it is interesting to note that he was declared immediately eligible for office. Cf. *P*, 47, f. 98 (December 23, 1359).

[11] *P*, 45, f. 86r (October 23, 1357); *P*, 45, f. 105r (December 12, 1357).

[12] Conversely, the chances of the petitioner would be damaged if an influential Florentine, such as a Rossi, Tornaquinci, or Strozzi, were to speak against him. Cf. *LF*, 34, f. 118r; *ibid.*, 35, f. 10; *ibid.*, 39, f. 211r.

one guilds enumerated in the Ordinances of Justice of 1293. Great political questions were debated in the guild halls as well as in the communal councils so *novi cives* could familiarize themselves with pressing issues of the day. Several times a month the membership was called by the signory to give advice in the *Palazzo Comunale* on a variety of civic matters ranging from an over-all realignment of foreign policy to the most inconsequential details of public administration.

Under the aegis of the guilds some of the most memorable legislation was initiated; it was drawn up by members and presented to the signory by guild captains in petition form and, after being approved by the communal councils, became the law. In drawing up these proposals, the *novi cives* gained first-hand knowledge of civic problems such as the relationship between church and commune, distribution of the republic's grain supply, the feasibility of hiring mercenaries, and procedures to be employed in eradicating tyrannous political factions. The guilds also operated in a judicial capacity, maintaining their own courts and prisons; therefore, *novi cives* were also able to gain valuable experience in the law.

The signory required the *novi cives* to serve a period of political apprenticeship before moving from guild affairs to public office. They were not admitted into the priorate or its colleges, nor, for a period ranging from ten to twenty-five years,[13] were they permitted to serve in the sensitive post of guild captain. These stipulations had the effect of institutionalizing a Florentine *cursus honorum* whereby the novice progressed gradually through lower positions, thus acquiring political experience until finally he was eligible for membership in the supreme magistracies of the republic. He participated in guild affairs, sat in the communal councils, and served in various administrative posts of the city and *contado* before assuming the grave responsibilities of high office. Until the 1340s *novi cives* were rarely entrusted with the charge of carrying out communal foreign policy. Diplomatic missions were staffed almost exclusively by the most renowned patricians, since these men were the best harbingers of the city's prestige. Similarly, offices in the statusworthy Court Merchant and in the most prestigious of all Florentine organizations—the *Parte Guelfa* —were the sole preserve of great tycoons and the aristocratic set.

Entrenched families were willing to see the *novi cives* represented in the commune provided the overwhelming preponderance of power remained in their hands. Since the majority of newcomers were enrolled in the minor guilds, the tendency was to restrict the number of seats open to *minori* in such crucial posts as priorate, colleges, and communal treasury. But in 1343 a serious and sustained challenge was launched against this system of apportionment which had obtained for almost half a century

[13] *P*, Vols. 40–66.

when the new men from the major guilds joined the *minori* and succeeded in gaining greater representation. An epidemic of bankruptcies, an empty communal treasury, and a disastrous experiment with despotism discredited the patriciate and made it difficult for them to resist the demands of the new citizens.[14]

In the past, *novi cives* had pressed hard for a voice in the signory, gaining ephemeral victories in 1293, 1323, and 1328. In part, their dissatisfaction with the status quo and their persistence stemmed from the political backgrounds of these affluent immigrants. Before settling in the city this group had long dominated the social, economic, and political life of their native rural parishes.[15] They had exercised great influence over the local assemblies and established their right to participate in the election of officials empowered to dispense justice and levy taxes. They themselves served as consuls, rectors, and syndics and regularly represented their *popolo* before the various Florentine courts. It was during these sessions that vital issues concerning the recruitment of military forces, the responsibility of the *popolo* for maintaining roads, bridges, and fortifications, and methods for raising communal revenue were debated. These men of the *popoli*, *castelli*, and rural communes zealously guarded their hard-won prerogatives against all who sought to dispute them. They contended against feudal lords and church dignitaries on questions of liability for corvees, ownership of lands, payment of rents, and the right to elect functionaries. They petitioned the signory for prorogation of levies, challenged communal claims that they were responsible for the crimes committed by exiles and criminals in their section of the *contado*, and requested reductions in tax assessments.[16]

Thus, since the new citizens were accustomed to exercising political power in the *contado*, they were not without expectancies in this area upon arrival in the city. They also had much to offer the republic beyond their varied experience on the level of everyday politics, for prominent among their number were many from the learned professions. The

---

[14] For a comprehensive treatment of these bankruptcies, see A. Sapori, *La crisi delle compagnie mercantili dei Bardi e dei Peruzzi* (Florence, 1926). *Tratte*, 1155, contains the names of all bankrupts from the letter 'A' through 'S' and was to be used for the purpose of barring the *falliti* from communal office. The *Atti del Podestà* and the *Camera del Comune* contain additional names and bring the total to 300.

[15] Cf. J. Plesner, *L'émigration*, pp. 63 ff.; *A* 981-83. During the middle years of the fourteenth century many of the new men had sufficient capital to undertake the profitable and vital role of farming communal taxes. See especially *CCE*, 56, f. 190. Cf. also *ibid.*, 58, f. 134; *ibid.*, 59, f. 60; *ibid.*, 172, unnumbered folios; *Scrivano*, 3, unnumbered folios. Less than 5 per cent of those communal officeholders whose descent can be traced had immediate ancestors who were agricultural laborers.

[16] *CCE*, 1 bis. This is the first complete set of treasury records and runs from October, 1342, to July, 1343; it contains a great variety of materials pertaining to relations between the city and countryside. Earlier documents of the *camera* are so fragmentary that they cast little light on this question.

lawyers and notaries who were particularly conspicuous in their ranks contributed a theoretical knowledge of techniques of administration and political procedures. As the functions of communal government became more diverse and complex, the legal training of these *novi cives* became more indispensable to the republic.[17] Throughout the thirteenth and fourteenth centuries the signory's responsibilities mounted as Florence extended her rule over Tuscany, with the consequence that her bureaucracy proliferated. Few members of the patriciate were willing to undertake careers in a civil service that was both underpaid and held in disrepute.[18] Therefore we find the *novi cives* coming to occupy a variety of critical administrative posts, especially in the middle years of the *trecento*, while at the same time being denied entry into the more prestigious offices of the commune, guild courts, and *Parte Guelfa*. Moreover, they were especially vulnerable to attack from the captains of the *Parte,* who demanded they be barred from any public office on grounds that they were unable to establish a bona fide political pedigree. Since the new men, liable for proscription on spurious charges of political heterodoxy, staffed the communal bureaucracy, a political assault upon them undermined the effective force of the emerging public world.

II

In the 1330s the commoner aristocracy and affluent magnates of the greater guilds came to treat public office as if it were their own private preserve. Among the best represented of all the city's families were the Bardi, Cavalcanti, Frescobaldi, Gherardini, Rossi—magnates all. It was to these nobles that the regime turned for advice in matters of foreign policy and communal finance: when special *balìe* (extraordinary commissions) were founded, their names were among the most prominent. Soon the most pressing public problems were dealt with by these *balìe*, and bankers of the houses of Frescobaldi and Bardi joined their *popolani* counterparts, the Acciaiuoli and Peruzzi financiers, in directing affairs of

---

[17] Of all notaries who held communal office between 1343 and 1382, 65 per cent came from families recently migrated to the city. While their numbers increased in the rapidly growing civil service, their representation in the signory declined by half. This statement is based upon a comparison of the number of seats held from 1328 to 1342 with those occupied from 1343 to 1348. The holdings of this group in the funded communal debt averaged 200 florins.

[18] Notable exceptions to this statement are to be found in every prominent Florentine family. However, those who assumed this type of career were frequently the least affluent. For the names of these men, see *CCE*, Vols. 1–30. All employees of the commune were required to pay a tax on their salaries, and, therefore, their names are recorded in the *camera*.

state.[19] During this decade there was a marked tendency to grant concessions to magnates and to be generally mindful of claims of the Florentine aristocracy. This regime represented the interests of a handful of the city's most prestigious guilds, and dominant families matriculated in these corporations were to form a homogeneous patriciate.[20] Until 1340 the signory was secure and self-confident; except for sporadic instances of seditious activity by such magnate families as the Caponsacchi in 1329 or the treasonous negotiations of a Della Tosa with a foreign tyrant, domestic tranquility prevailed.[21]

In this atmosphere of relative internal accord and burgeoning communal prosperity, the trend was toward a fusion of magnate and *popolano grasso* into an elite whose rule would be tolerant of patrician prerogatives and appreciative of aristocratic style. This tendency toward lenient government had long been in evidence and at moments seemed to have achieved genuine stability. Disunity among the Florentine elite, the surge of new men, the intervention of pope or Angevin monarch, humiliating military debacles, and, most telling of all, declining public revenue, each in turn and at critical junctures had served to prevent the consolidation of aristocratic hegemony. The interests of urban magnates were almost identical with those of wealthy *popolani*, and, except for the persistence of violence, little seemed to stand in the way of this amicable fusion.

Soon this government of the guild patriciate abandoned strict interpretation of the Ordinances of Justice and decreed that those who held the dignity of knighthood and had not been classified as magnates since 1293 were to be declared eligible for the highest elective offices in the republic. Shortly thereafter, a special commission was established with authority to create new knights, and in 1335 the statutes of the *Parte Guelfa* empowered the captains to bestow a bounty of fifty florins upon anyone deemed worthy and willing to assume the honors and burdens of knighthood.[22] Throughout its tenure the signory was extremely solicitous of the welfare of all sectors of the Florentine nobility. At no time in communal history were more *grandi* to escape the rigors of communal law through

---

[19] In the early months of 1336, the war against Martino della Scala was directed by the "Sei sulla guerra." Among their number was Ridolfo de' Bardi, Simone della Tosa, Acciaiuoli Acciaiuoli, Giovenco de' Bastari, Celle Bordoni and Simone Peruzzi; Bardi, Peruzzi, and Acciaiuoli were also well represented in the *balìa* authorized to raise revenue. Cf. A. Sapori, *La crisi*, pp. 107–8.

[20] For an assessment of certain features of oligarchical *Signorie*, see M. Becker, "Some Aspects of Oligarchical, Dictatorial and Popular Signorie in Florence, 1282–1382," *Comparative Studies in Society and History*, 2 (1960), 429–34.

[21] *Giudice degli Appelli*, 124, I, f. 25r (February 20, 1329), Feo della Tosa, one of the many condemned on this count, paid 200 lire on September 20, 1337, for judicial dispensation. Cf. *ibid.*, 124, I, f. 22.

[22] F. Bonaini, "Statuto della parte guelfa di Firenze," *ASI*, 5 (1857), p. 41.

grants of judicial dispensation than in those halcyon years immediately preceding the democratization of the Florentine state in 1343.

Clearly, the regime was concerned with the problem of staffing the officer cadre of the citizen army, and the benign policies it advocated were intended to encourage the high-born to serve as knights in the elite cavalry. Despite the lure of subsidy and civic honor this program was fated to fail, yet we must not be misled by our knowledge of the unfortunate outcome into underestimating the enthusiasm with which the signory embarked upon this venture. The regime of the 1330s was willing to recall exiled magnates and restore them to full citizenship if they would put their arms at the disposal of the republic. Grave doubts were voiced concerning the efficacy of mercenary troops, and men remembered that Rome had been great when citizen armies commanded by public-spirited generals had taken the field. Her decline ensued with the enlistment of foreign contingents who fought for gold rather than love of country. A few among the city's magnates were responsive to this type of appeal, and Brunelleschi, Della Tosa, and Ricasoli still led the republic's host; however, these nobles were the exception rather than the rule.[23]

As in earlier days, public policy was predicated upon a curious duality that did little to encourage the maintenance of a military caste. Knighthood and service to the state were accorded their niche in the pantheon of civic virtues, but those who followed these noble callings still found themselves bound by the harsh restraints of collective life. Judicial dispensation and preferential treatment might be meted out to certain nobles, but the Ordinances of Justice remained in effect. Granted the hyperbole of this magnate complaint: "If a horse is running along and hits a *popolano* in the face with its tail; or if in a crowd one man gives another a blow on the chest without intending harm; or if some children of tender age begin quarreling, an accusation will be made. But ought men to have their houses and property destroyed for such trifles as these?" the emotion from which it stems is real enough.[24]

In his justly famous description of "the greatness and state and magnificence of the commune of Florence," Giovanni Villani laments the fact that in 1336–38 there were only "seventy-five full-dress knights." "To be sure, we find that before the second popular government now in power was formed (before 1293) there were more than 250 knights; but from the time that *il popolo* began to rule, the magnates no longer had the

---

[23] G. Villani, *Cronica*, I, 134. At this time over 600 affluent Florentines maintained horses and weapons, and, although they did not usually serve in person, they did send hired replacements. C. C. Bayley, *War and Society in Renaissance Florence* (Toronto, 1961), p. 8.

[24] D. Compagni, *Cronica*, ed. I. del Lungo (Florence, 1889).

status and authority enjoyed earlier, and hence few persons were knighted." The observation "i cavallieri non ebbono stato" was commonplace at this time.[25] To the good burgher Villani, who only despised the lawless among the magnates, this was a tragic portent of military disasters to come.

The need for law and order, the desire to preserve Florentine *libertas* against the machinations of powerful clans, and the persistence of certain features of impartial and impersonal government led to the accumulation of numerous judicial and political restraints upon the magnates. Indeed, these restrictions were lessened during the decade of the thirties, but still no one gained any ostensible civic advantage from magnate status. Therefore nobles continued to petition the government for the privilege of becoming commoners.[26] No attack was made upon the social prestige of the nobility, and yet men were anxious to abandon their magnate status; this type of action demonstrates the incommensurate magnitudes of the *trecento* social and political universes. The guild aristocracy that so admired the code of the nobility was unwilling to abrogate the dread Ordinances of Justice. Nor were they eager to restore all magnates to their full political rights; they were, however, desirous of imitating the way of life of this order and happy to receive the benefits of noble martial prowess.

Giovanni Villani's so-oft-quoted observations pertaining to Florentine magnates and knights are of course relative, based as they are on a comparison of status and authority enjoyed by the nobility in 1336–38 with that of the era before 1293. As informative as this comparison is, it tells us very little about the degree of influence the magnates still exercised during the 1330s. The history of this era suggests that statements by chroniclers that magnates had little status and less authority must be challenged. Granted there was something of a decline, however, we still see affluent commoners of the guilds eagerly seeking to marry into magnate families and priding themselves on kinship with mighty feudatories of the Tuscan *contado*. Nor can we doubt the civic pride taken by these burghers in the most aristocratic of all Florentine organizations—the *Parte Guelfa*. Did not these selfsame commoners consistently elect the scions of magnate houses to represent the commune in the most solemn of public ceremonials? When visiting dignitaries arrived in the city, were they not graciously welcomed and entertained by noble patricians? The very forms and amenities of communal life were replete with the ethos of chivalry,

---

[25] *Delizie degli eruditi toscani*, ed. Fr. I di San Luigi (Florence, 1770–89), 12, 352; G. Villani, *Cronica*, 11, 94.
[26] Cf. Requests of magnates from Certaldo and Colle for popular status; identical petitions were submitted by the house of Galigairi, the Counts Alberti, and the Vecchietti, *P*, 32, fols. 1–2; *LF*, 21, f. 87r (May 14, 1342).

and the artisan and merchant guilds were a part of its pageantry with their costumes, military companies, coats-of arms, and processionals.[27]

Only after 1343 did popular interest in the play of knightly arms diminish. The medieval tournament lost much of its favor, to be greeted with apathy if not scorn.[28] Tenderly and with ample consideration earlier communal society sought to choose from among the spectrum of knightly virtues, retaining variety. Later, the imperatives of the public world became harsher as more men were knighted, not for valor at arms, but rather to inspire awe among peasants of the countryside when they rode out to serve as communal officials. More and more high civil servants bore the honorific title of "knight," so that as the proud term lost meaning in the realm of private style, it acquired greater public significance. Soon the designation failed to evoke admiration from *il popolo,* since it was being widely conferred on many who governed the state and directed the wars of the second half of the *trecento.*

The decline of the Florentine knight can be seen not only from the vantage point of altered communal attitudes toward the magnate; emphasis must also be placed upon changing methods of warfare. The heroic work of the army in the early years of the fourteenth century had been the suppression of insurrection and defense of the Florentine *contado.* For the most part this had been accomplished by a series of relatively brief campaigns waged within easy distance of the city. The militia of the

[27] State ritual prescribed that *milites* should represent the commune. During a later interval, when communal legislation was restrictive and the nobles lost ancient prerogatives, the signory still insisted that important embassies be captained by a *miles:* "Atque fiat responsio per unum militem antiquum qui bene sciat totum et res antiquas." Cf. *CP,* 19, f. 16 (July 21, 1380). This is, of course, not surprising since Florence was not isolated from the chivalric currents of *trecento* Europe. Even the working class desired to emulate the bachelorhood of knights; in 1343 Walter of Brienne permitted them to have their own coats-of-arms, form squads attired in special livery, and fly banners bearing their insignia. Thirty-five years later all of this was to be reviewed by the Ciompi revolutionaries. Upon seizing power, these humble woolcarders were to create *milites* of their own. Cf. C. Falletti-Fossati, *Il tumulto dei Ciompi* (Rome, 1882), p. 172; Marchionne di Coppo Stefani, rub. 566; A. Doren, *Le arti fiorentine* (Florence, 1940), 2, 230–31.

[28] The last great tournaments staged in Florence during the *trecento* appear to have been those of Easter, 1343. No mention is made of major jousts in the writings of Giovanni Villani which treat the subsequent period of Florentine history (to 1348), or in the massive chronicle of his kinsmen Matteo and Filippo, which runs through 1363. Likewise, Marchionne di Coppo Stefani does not note the occurrence of a major tournament, and his chronicle concludes in 1385. Literary men before 1343 referred consistently to the tourney. Among the more prominent literati were Francesco da Barberino (*Documenti d'Amore*), Folgore da San Gimignano (*Le Rime*), and Giovanni Villani (*Cronica,* 10, 128). The tourney of 1343 failed to elicit the enthusiasm of the citizenry. Cf. G. Villani, 12, 8. Much later, in the early *quattrocento,* when literary men such as Leonardo Bruni Aretino were trying to revive certain of the military virtues associated with knighthood, they were contemptuous of the ornamented knight of the mock tournament (the *miles gloriosus*). Cf. C. C. Bayley, "De Militia," *War and Society,* p. 379. The *dignitas* of knighthood came to be intimately connected with civic virtue.

contado, although far from trustworthy, frequently proved to be quite useful, and this force in combination with citizen armies captained by nobles and great feudatories, achieved a succession of notable victories. Long-range campaigns in distant places were beyond the competence of such troops; subsidies and foreign military commanders who led their own contingents seemed an adequate alternative.

During the decade of the thirties the remedy of citizen militia and communal knight became obsolete; no longer could they be relied upon to realize the ambitious schemes envisaged by the new Florentine imperialism. Until then the signory's policy had been largely defensive and only mildly expansionist. Most of the republic's military energies over the previous thirty years had been expanded in fending off dissident exiles, rebellious feudatories, and middling German emperors. For such purposes foot and mounted militia had been indispensable, but during the 1330s Florence promoted a grand design that included alliance with far-off Venice and the dispatch of troops into Lombardy, so that Pisa might be defeated and Lucca conquered and annexed. These plans could only be executed by mercenary armies capable of waging protracted warfare in foreign lands. The issue at stake was no longer the reduction of a single castle in rural Tuscany, but, rather, large-scale warfare throughout north Italy. In major battles of 1341 fewer than a score of Florentine knights saw action, and although the treasury records do indicate that certain *grandi* did continue to serve as captains, the terms of their employment had altered dramatically.[29]

By 1342 they were hired under the same type of contract that prevailed for the city's other mercenaries, and thus native *milites* lost their grandeur and become pensioners of the state. An occasional Buondelmonti, Della Tosa, or Ricasoli might win the acclaim of the crowd for his daring at arms, but it was to the office of the *condotta* that the signory looked for victories over the numerous free-booting companies that streamed into Italy during the middle years of the *trecento.* Soon this office, along with special commissions, was in the business of enlisting the city's would-be enemies under the Florentine banner and paying marauding companies to evacuate Tuscan territory. The warfare of those years seldom brought honor but frequently resulted in victory. The military virtues associated with knighthood found little expression on the battlefield, and in the

---

[29] Among the magnates who filled military posts at this time were Adimari, Agli, Bardi, Bordoni, Cavalcanti, Mozzi, Spini, and Tornaquinci. Cf. *CCE,* 1, fols. 2r–36; *ibid.,* 11, fols. 13r ff.; *ibid.,* 24, f. 48; *ibid.,* 28, fols. 628–42. These magnates received a stipend from the commune for recruiting and leading Florentine troops in battle. *Popolani* from high-born families also served in the same capacity. Albizzi, Bastari, Guicciardini, Mazzingi, Raffacani, Rimbaldesi, Rondinelli, and even Medici were included among their number. *CCE,* 1, f. 28r; *ibid.,* 4, fols. 68 ff.; *ibid.,* 11, fols. 10r–11r; *ibid.,* 21, f. 40; *ibid.,* 24, fols. 40–41.

closing years of the *trecento* they even elicited scorn from such writers as Sacchetti. Fools and knaves, parvenus and the vulgar were awarded golden spurs, but one must not conclude that all Florentines denigrated the virtues of a militant nobility.[30]

Much later the humanist chancellor Leonardo Bruni Aretino implored the Florentines to restore the republic's militia; to him, the year 1351 had been disastrous for his beloved adopted city, for it was then that the signory abolished the last vestiges of a citizen army.[31] Machiavelli's well-known views were much more extreme: he attributed the decline of civic spirit to *il popolo's* repression of the nobility when after 1343 the law was implemented so assiduously. Democratization and a stern regimen stifled martial spirit among the citizenry, and Machiavelli saw the resurrection of the militia as a mechanism for recovering this antique virtue.[32] Certainly this penetrating observer of the Florentine past sensed the leveling effects of the rule of law imposed so stringently beginning with the 1340s. But like others outside the literary tradition of *quattrocento* humanism, he failed to consider fundamental changes in military tactics which encouraged the city to have greater recourse to mercenaries. The Ordinances of Justice and other repressive enactments of *il popolo*, enforced rigorously after 1343, did far less to discourage Florentines from assuming the burdens of knighthood than had the new strategies of war. The remedies of the thirties which sought to restore the *milites* to full political rights proved ineffectual since citizen knighthood had become militarily obsolete. Popular government and the attendant leveling met with less resistance because this once-proud order had deteriorated.

III

The early 1330s, then, had been years of relative harmony for the men of the old patriciate—magnate and high-born commoner alike (*popolano*)—and the signory's policies reflected this cordiality. Only the most affluent sat in the communal councils, and very few new men were able to win entry into this charmed circle. Yet this accord was precarious. By 1338 we can observe a hardening of communal policy toward the magnates and a general transformation of the regime's program which had serious repercussions for the entire privileged class.[33] It meant the dissolution of the

---

[30] F. Sacchetti, *Trecentonovelle*, 168, 213.
[31] C. C. Bayley, *War and Society*, p. 21.
[32] N. Machiavelli, *History of Florence*, ed. F. Gilbert (New York, 1960), pp. 107–11.
[33] The basis for this change was the pressing communal need for revenue in order to mount an offensive against neighboring Pisa. This demand for additional revenue came at a moment when the yield from gabelles (the republic's principal source of income) had declined precipitously. By 1341 the signory was exerting every effort to recover communal property. According to a provision enacted in May of that year much of the

easy, laissez-faire conduct of public life—the gentle paideia. The world of Florentine business underwent its most severe crisis and public revenue declined until it was no longer adequate for the ambitious, imperialistic plans of the republic. Under the impact of these twin pressures, the regime found it necessary to reduce the privileges and immunities of the entrenched classes. Vigorous tax reforms were proposed to revive a declining treasury, but few who sat in the councils were willing to support them.[34] Co-operation among the patriciate was pervasive in periods of prosperity, but with the onset of adversity the bonds became strained. The ruling elite divided sharply on the issue of the feasibility of maintaining the costly alliance with the papacy. Furthermore they were split on the question of the desirability of pursuing the expensive war against Lucca. Many were reluctant to see direct taxes imposed upon their capital and lands.[35] As to the role of the magnates in these troubled years, they ignored many vital communal needs and continued to press for the repeal of the loathed Ordinances of Justice, which increased penalties against them as well as for the establishment of a signory that would be solicitous of their private interests.

In September, 1342, the overwhelming majority of affluent *popolani* and magnates championed the desperate remedy of establishing a dictatorship. Walter of Brienne was installed for life as lord of the city and was granted sweeping powers. In one of his first acts he demonstrated his sympathies toward the magnates by absolving the Bardi, Frescobaldi, Nerli, Pazzi, and Rossi from condemnations incurred as a result of their leadership of the abortive revolution of November, 1340. Eminent members of these families were permitted to return from exile, and they soon numbered among Brienne's most trusted counselors. Adimari, Bardi, Donati, Rossi, and others undertook far-flung diplomatic missions for the new lord of the city. Adimari, Cavalcanti, Rossi, and Tornaquinci held high administrative posts in the Florentine *contado*.[36] Numerous magnates were granted judicial dispensation from convictions on

---

bona et iura communis had been usurped by "magnates et potentes," and since the citizenry was afraid of these haughty and powerful lords, no attempt had been made to wrest the property from them. Now the Officials of the Towers were to have extraordinary authority to recover state property, and any citizen was to have the right to make secret denunciations *(in tamburo)* against predatory "magnates et potentes." Cf. *DP*, 2, fols. 12–12r.

[34] *LF*, 19, fols. 29–187r (June 8, 1340–May 20, 1341).
[35] B. Barbadoro, *Le finanze della repubblica fiorentina* (Florence, 1929) 125 ff.; *LF*, 17, f. 90.
[36] Cf. *CCE*, 1 bis, fols. 130r–249; *Atti del Esecutore*, 17, f. 17r. For the despot's decree absolving the Bardi, Frescobaldi, Nerli, Pazzi, and Rossi from condemnations incurred as a result of their participation in the rebellion of November 1, 1340, see C. Paoli, *Della Signoria di Gualtieri Duca d'Atene* (Florence, 1862), 76. The citation given by Paoli for the document should read: *Balie*, 2 fols. 12–13, instead of: *P*, 32, f. 12.

charges of treason; the Falconieri and Guidolotti had been declared enemies of the Holy Roman Church and rebels against the state in 1304. Now these clans, but recently listed among the despicable Ghibelline nobles of the city, had their citizenship and property restored. The Pulci and Circuli, who had attacked their native city in the company of the perfidious Ghibellines of Pisa, were likewise granted dispensation. A host of rebel magnates had condemnations for capital offenses annulled.[37]

The most vital concern of the Florentine magnates was the abrogation of the Ordinances of Justice, and here, too, their desires were given serious consideration. Although Brienne did not acquiesce completely, he did make substantial alterations in one of its most vexatious clauses: the degree of responsibility for crimes of kinsmen was drastically reduced so that only close blood relations were liable.[38]

Unfortunately for Brienne, the very magnates so frequently recipients of his largess were at best only mildly enthusiastic in their support of his signory, and as soon as popular rebellion erupted in July 1343, they joined the surging mobs in the streets and attacked his palace. Immediately upon regaining its ancient liberties, the government of the republic was taken in hand by a coalition of magnates and *popolani grassi*. The office of prior was now open to Florentine magnates. For the first time since the winter of 1292, Adimari, Bardi, Cavalcanti, Foraboschi, Mannelli, Pazzi, and Spini entered the highest magistracy of the republic. For almost two months these scions of the best families met with their commoner peers to treat the great public questions of the day. *Il popolo* was not ungrateful to these aristocrats for their heroism on that glorious St. Anne's Day, the 26th of July, when they came to the fore and provided leadership so that an undisciplined demonstration could become a successful revolution. It was therefore fitting that these aristocrats should be allocated a generous share of high communal offices. Not since the thirteenth century had such an opportunity been presented to the magnates.

This aristocratic coalition had an unparalleled chance to demonstrate its qualifications for political leadership. The prestige of such magnate families as the Adimari, Bardi, Cavalcanti, Donati, Frescobaldi, Pazzi, Rucellai, and others was at its apogee.[39] Certainly, high-born *popolani*

---

[37] Other ranking families of magnate status granted dispensation for comparable crimes were the Amadori, Corbizzi, Falconetti, and Visconti.

[38] On June 10, 1349, an adviser to the signory proposed that the Ordinances of Justice be re-established as they had been before Brienne had tampered with them. This counselor suggested that all magnates to the sixth degree had been responsible for their kinsmen before the coming of Brienne. *CP*, 1, f. 6.

[39] It appeared reasonable to Giovanni Villani—no warm friend of the magnates—that they should have a share of political offices since they had been the "principali" in the July revolution against Brienne. The chronicler added that the *popolani grassi* "accustomed to governing," supported the "grandi co' quali aveano molti parentadi." Cf.

and *magnati* had previously proven their ability to co-operate politically. There was even some sympathy with demands of magnates for cancellation of the Ordinances of Justice. Based upon the performance of this patriciate, however, one must conclude that few signories in the annals of the republic showed themselves to be so inept and shortsighted. Granted that the circumstances were hardly propitious—the city was faced with a staggering public debt, confidence in the Florentine business world was at its lowest ebb, and unrest among the many workers of the city's *lana* industry was widespread; still, the uncreative and pedestrian quality of this regime's policies remain striking. The legislation enacted during its tenure represented a response to the narrowest of interests and reflected the egoism of the highest echelons of communal society. In actions the ruling patriciate expressed their desire to return to the easy, laissez-faire program of earlier days which at best was suitable only for intervals of great general prosperity. At these times the tendency was to minimize the role of government so that few fiscal burdens and restraints would be placed upon the patriciate. The tax structure was adjusted to increase the income from direct levies which fell on the population as a whole, while imposts on capital and property, which struck the patriciate, were canceled.[40] Such an approach was bound to fail at this time, because communal needs far exceeded the ever-dwindling tribute collected from direct levies. No longer was it possible to finance the business of government in the traditional and time-honored manner; new and daring techniques were imperative if the *camera* was to be rescued from the limbo of bankruptcy. In the face of this challenge, the aristocrats of August, 1343, saw fit to increase the retail sales tax and to reapportion the city so that their own tax assessment would be drastically reduced. This failure to respond to communal needs surely was a factor in demonstrating the unfitness of the magnates to govern.[41] Their political partners, the great *popolani*, so closely bound to the magnates by kinship and business interests, were faced with a stark and painful alternative. Since November, 1342, the treasury had been unable to amortize or even pay interest on the public debt, and therefore the great *popolani*, who were the principal creditors

---

Cronica, 12, 18. Seven magnates were chosen to serve in the highest communal magistracy (the *Quattordici*) along with seven *popolani*. The magnates were Ridolfo de' Bardi, Pino Rossi, Giannozzo Cavalcanti, Giovanni Gianfigliazzi, Testa Tornaquinci, Bindo della Tosa, and the ubiquitous Talano Adimari.

[40] *CCE*, Vol. 2 (this volume of the treasury records covers the tenure of the signory of the *Quattordici*).

[41] For an assessment of the communal fiscal dilemma in August–September, 1343, see M. Becker, "Florentine Popular Government (1343–1348)," *Proceedings of the American Philosophical Society*, 104 (1961), 360–65. This aristocratic regime was unable to pay salaries to communal retainers or honor the republic's commitments to its citizens living in Verona as hostages. *P*, 32, f. 60 (September 16, 1343).

of the republic, were denied the use of their capital as well as return from their investment. Fiscal reforms, even if they involved sacrifice, were, then, mandatory at this time; but judging from the policies pursued by those controlling the *camera*, only the most fatuously sanguine could have believed that they would be initiated by this particular coalition.

The incapacity of magnates to govern effectively was also evidenced by their judicial policies—or lack of them. Much more significant than the annulment of the Ordinances of Justice was the fact that high crimes of magnates went virtually unpunished during the summer and early fall of 1343.[42] The authority of Florentine courts was made almost ineffectual, and as a consequence private rights repeatedly triumphed over public law. Communal properties were widely appropriated by the great clans for personal use, and this was symptomatic of what might be described as the beginnings of a systematic dismemberment of the Florentine state. The bonds of community were in the process of being severed, and the tendency was unmistakably toward dissolution of the commune. The great work of the next regime involved the successful repression of these centrifugal forces and containment of the egoism of powerful clans.

Giovanni Villani contends that at first *il popolo* were satisfied to see the signory in the hands of those magnates who had been so instrumental in ousting Brienne, believing them to be peaceful and law-abiding. Soon, however, this fund of good will was dissipated and the *superbia* of these men became quite evident.[43] The chronicler Stefani observes that the *popolani grassi*, thoroughly disenchanted with their magnate confreres, quickly came to the realization that their interests could be better served if they aligned themselves with masters of the lesser guilds, for these *minori* (*novi cives* for the most part) could be counted upon to be "subservient and reverent" and do the bidding of their social superiors. According to Stefani, the great *popolani* who assumed office after the overthrow of Brienne in 1343 were accustomed to holding the lion's share of public posts, but it was not long before they found themselves relegated to a subordinate role. This seemed unjust since there were 20,000 *popolani* and only 1,000 or so *magnati*.[44] Their loss of representation appeared to be an inevitable consequence of their unfortunate alliance with magnates who would be

---

[42] Giovanni Villani's contention that the high crimes of magnates were not prosecuted by this aristocratic regime (*Cronica*, 12, 19) is borne out by the appropriate volume of the Camera del Comune. Cf. *CCE*, Vol. 2.

[43] Moreover, suspicion among the populace mounted because of the pervasive fear that the magnates were conspiring with neighboring tyrants to the detriment of the city's liberty. Marchionne di Coppo Stefani, rub. 599; Giovanni Villani, *Cronica*, 12, 21. Very shortly certain Bardi, Frescobaldi, and Rossi were exiled because they had been convicted of plotting with Pisa. A Donati was condemned on a similar charge. Stefani, rub. 599, 605; G. Villani, *Cronica*, 12, 32.

[44] Stefani, rub. 588.

satisfied with nothing less than complete hegemony over the *Signoria*. Subsequent communal history was to demonstrate that Stefani's assessment was not far from the truth: the *popolani grassi* did indeed find the nouveaux lesser guildsmen to be much more co-operative as political partners than the magnates.[45]

Certainly, popular feeling against the magnate rulers cannot be an entirely reliable guide in the fixing of responsibility for the misrule of Florence during August and September of 1343. When the rancor of *il popolo* exploded and the mob joined forces with the republic's militia to besiege palaces of the Bardi, Cavalcanti, Donati, Frescobaldi, and Pazzi, certain of the magnates supported the popular cause. Moreover, many *popolani* had sided with the nobles and as officeholders had shown the same incapacity to lead the republic in its desperate hour. The fact remains, however, that the deepest resentments were against the magnate class, and the contempt and disloyalty of leading magnates toward the popular regime of October, 1343-48, did little to repair this opinion. Stefani notes that so intense was the distrust of *il popolo* that "almost all the *grandi*" fled the city and "retired to the *contado* and remained there."[46] Now newcomers to the political arena had an unprecedented opportunity to succeed or to fail.

IV

As we have already observed in the first volume of this study, Tuscan poet and chronicler, from Dante through the young Giovanni Boccaccio and Giovanni Villani, displayed marked ambivalence toward the *novi cives*. On the one hand there was warm espousal of the democratic doctrine of nobility of deeds over lineage, while on the other, the ambition and energies of the parvenu elicited contempt from Dante and his contemporaries. Even the growth and expansion of the polis were regarded as the sinful consequence of avarice and "bestial appetite." The "upstart people" had lowered the tone of civic morality so that Dante and the young Villani pined for a return to the golden times when a homogeneous ruling class was not menaced by discordant elements.

The experience of the late thirties and early forties altered Villani's views, just as that of the fifties and sixties modified the prejudices of Matteo Villani and the mature Giovanni Boccaccio. The older Villani recognized the incalculable damage done the polis by the "grandi e potenti" who sought only to tyrannize the city. It had been the mag-

---

[45] Cf. M. Becker, "Florentine *Libertas*: Political Independents and *Novi Cives*, 1372-1378," *Traditio*, 18 (1962), 393-407. Stefani, rub. 599. The chronicler also notes that at this time many disgruntled magnates entered the service of foreign governments.
[46] Stefani, rub. 599.

nates who were responsible for the betrayal of the republic's *libertà*. If this patriciate was disloyal, not so the *novi cives*. The chronicler appreciated the positive contribution made by this order, but was unable to accept it as a permanent fixture of the Florentine political world; this remained for his brother Matteo. The experience of the early fifties instructed him in the political value of these new citizens. Indeed, they might be lacking in "liberal studies," but they courageously opposed the craven policies of tyrannous aristocrats eager to undermine the sacred *libertà* of the republic. Even Boccaccio, so firm a champion of courtly culture, turned against the once-idealized nobility. By the sixties they were "rapacious wolves of high lineage."[47]

Leading chroniclers and literary men, from Matteo Villani through Franco Sacchetti, depicted the principal threat to the traditional liberty of the polis in different accents than did the men of Dante's time. The political machinations of old and venerable families, not the influx of new people from the countryside, menaced Florentine *libertà*. Alarm over the *bestie fiesolane* was replaced by a pervasive fear that ancient clans such as the Albizzi would establish a tyranny. There was also deep-seated suspicion that these aristocrats were anxious to barter away the polis' cherished freedoms to win private advantage and personal power.[48] The first step in their quest for domination over the signory would involve the ousting of *novi cives* from office. Those in opposition to these intrigues found themselves in the unaccustomed position of defending the new men against their high-born adversaries. No longer were the *novi cives* charged with spreading the virus of factionalism throughout the city and undermining the "Roman inclination towards order and good government"; rather, the Albizzi and that dread bastion of the Florentine aristocracy—the *Parte Guelfa*—were held responsible for the many ills besetting the republic.[49]

Economic policies favored by the *novi cives* were in part the cause for this transvaluation of values whereby they gained stature in the

---

[47] See the incisive study of Giorgio Padoan, "Sulla datazione del 'Corbaccio,'" *Lettere Italiane*, 15 (1963), 1–27, and "Ancora sulla datazione e sul titolo del 'Corbaccio,'" *ibid.*, 199–201.

[48] M. Villani, 8, 103; Stefani, rub. 720, 726. The fears expressed by the chroniclers were echoed by the advisers to the signory who urged that the government be wary of the action taken by its patrician ambassadors lest the city lose its *libertà* at the hands of secular rulers and ecclesiastical princes. Cf. *CP*, 1, unnumbered folio (March 14, 1355). Spokesmen for the colleges admonished the government to restrain the Albizzi in order that they remain subject to the communal regime. Cf. *CP*, 12, f. 100 (April 8, 1373). Similarly, they beseeched the priors to make certain that the captains of the *Parte* submit "to the will of the commune." *CP*, 8, f. 55r (March 18, 1367).

[49] The captains of the *Parte* were accused, in the council halls, of fomenting suspicion among the citizenry, creating disunity and acting in such a manner as to discredit the Guelf cause in Florence. Cf. *CP*, 2, f. 159r (January 20, 1360); *ibid.*, 4, fols. 101r–103 (September 24, 1363).

eyes of their contemporaries. Entry of the new men into communal government on a large scale in 1343 altered the tone of Florentine politics but did nothing to disrupt the socioeconomic base of republican society. Approximately half of their number were matriculated in the greater guilds, and these, coupled with the older officeholders, also from the *arti maggiori*, meant that the seven greater guilds could count upon holding three-fourths of the seats in the signory. The remainder were occupied by new men from the fourteen minor guilds who were selected from the most affluent segment of the artisan, shopkeeper world.[50]

This distribution of offices was maintained until 1378 and served to guarantee the political hegemony of the *maggiori*. The silk guild (*Por San Maria*) more than doubled its representation in the signory over the preceding fifteen-year period, and holdings of the new men from this rapidly burgeoning major guild in the funded communal debt averaged the considerable sum of 142 florins. The wool guild (*Lana*) likewise increased its allotment of high communal offices, and the new men from this guild also owned extensive *Monte* holdings. The shares held by *novi cives* matriculated in the twenty-one guilds (major and minor) averaged the impressive sum of fifty-seven florins. The tax assessments of this new group of officeholders stood in a ratio of five to six and a half in comparison to those imposed upon members of the urban patriciate.[51] Therefore we should not be surprised to find that these wealthy newcomers, possessors of extensive capital and themselves employers of labor, were in substantial agreement with the patriciate on many aspects of communal economic policy. All the guild masters joined forces to stamp out rebellious movements among Florentine workers in the years between 1343 and 1345. The new government stripped *il popolo minuto* of the privileges and unaccustomed status recently conferred upon it by the ousted despot, Walter of Brienne.[52]

In formulating agrarian policy this signory rigidly adhered to the traditional program and remained unsympathetic to any innovation threatening the interests of great landed proprietors. After 1348 the regime enacted various ordinances designed to depress the wages of agricultural laborers and buttress the authority of their masters.[53] The

---

[50] The holdings of these men in the funded communal debt of 1345 averaged fifty-seven florins. G. Brucker and M. Becker, "*Arti Minori*," p. 101.
[51] M. Becker, *Florence in Transition*, 1, 190–221.
[52] *Atti del Capitano*, 17, f. 72. For a further consideration of this question, see M. Becker, "Oligarchical, Dictatorial and Popular Signorie," 425–29.
[53] N. Rodolico, *Il Popolo minuto (1343–1378)*, (Bologna, 1899), pp. 173–74. For fines against agricultural laborers who violated these ordinances, see *Ufficiali del Biado*, 102, 12, fols. 1–8 (August 13–September 1, 1353). For records of payments made by these

incidence of taxation on those who owned land in the city and countryside remained virtually unchanged throughout this period. On the vital question of monetary policy the new government followed the lead of merchants of the wool guild and reformed the Florentine coinage system: the value of the gold florin in which merchants received payment for cloth was augmented, while the silver coinage paid to workers was depreciated.[54] Vintners, ironmongers, hosiers, and doublet-makers willingly gave their support to petitions presented by greater guildsmen.[55] A seller of oil and a coopersmith favored a request by the wool guild asking that their rectors be granted immunity from communal law.[56] The new representatives in the government also championed the cause of hard-pressed Florentine banking houses and as a result the government was able to win precious time for these harassed companies so that they might postpone making restitution to their numerous creditors.[57]

This consensus on fundamental economic problems did not preclude the existence of certain areas of disagreement. But these tended to be peripheral, and while they did serve to alienate some elements of the patriciate from the *novi cives*, there was a substantial segment of older families who were not dissuaded from seeking the adherence of the new men. According to the testimony of the usually well-informed chronicler, Donato Velluti, who was much involved in communal politics at this time, these political notables actively sought to win support of the new men recently enrolled in the minor guilds when they favored repeal of certain legislation adversely affecting the *minori*: laws to reduce their representation in government.[58] Therefore, despite the presence of such vexing questions as establishment of price ceilings on goods and services, enforcement, or lack of enforcement, of antimonopoly legislation, and the sensitive problem of the authority of guild consuls over those who followed a trade without troubling to enroll in any of the city's minor guilds, there were patricians who realized that

---

men, see especially *CCE*, 70, fols. 11–30r (April 6–30, 1358). In 1383 the character of Florentine legislation pertaining to agricultural laborers was altered radically and the signory offered many inducements to these men to farm in the *contado*. Cf. *P*, 72, f. 161r; *LF*, 41, f. 1164.

[54] G. Villani, 12, 97; *Statuti della Repubblica fiorentina*, ed. R. Caggese (Florence, 1910–21), 2, 279.

[55] *LF*, 23, f. 4r; 26, f. 7; *Duplicati Provvisioni*, 4, fols. 27, 103.

[56] *P*, 48, f. 133; *LF*, 36, f. 39r.

[57] M. Becker, "Florentine Politics and the Diffusion of Heresy in the Trecento," *Speculum*, 34 (1959), 62–63.

[58] *La Cronica domestica*, ed. I. del Lungo (Florence, 1914), p. 242.

a liaison with the *novi cives* could be founded upon a mutuality of interests.[59]

The leaders of the *novi cives* after 1343 constituted an elite drawn from the upper echelons of manufacturers and traffickers in domestic goods and services. This wealthy group soon gained the confidence of many of their social superiors with whom they had much more in common than with the humble artisans and shopkeepers of the city. Michele di Jacopo Arrighi, armorer, was one of Florence's affluent creditors, who championed the cause of popular government. When the aristocratic captains of the *Parte Guelfa* challenged the authority of the signory, Michele spoke before the advisory councils exhorting the priors "to recover their honor and obtain their will." In the company of the popular Ricci leaders and a prominent new citizen, the grocer Niccolò Delli, Michele spoke for implementation of the law of 1366 whereby lesser guildsmen (principally *nouveaux*) were accorded representation in the captaincy of the Guelf party. During the war against the papacy, the armorer stood firm in support of alliance with the church's dread enemy Bernabo Visconti, urging strict adherence and militancy against papal lieutenants. While the republic was negotiating with the church for peace, Michele spoke against the restoration of the inquisition in the polis.[60]

Another armorer who also followed a hard line toward the papacy was Simone di Biagio. Even as peace negotiations with the Holy See were being consummated, he spoke in favor of conserving "unity" with the Visconti. Going beyond this, he recommended Florence give aid to the redoubtable Bernabo. His most germane contribution to legislative discourse, however, was staunch advocacy of reduction in interest rates. Like many another new man, he approved of equalization of the tax burden: "Et quod fiat equatio inter cives pro solutione pecunie" was his principle. To this end he persistently urged the signory to enact an *estimo*. Needless to say, few aristocrats believed this course viable. Biagio was sympathetic to the plight of communal creditors, always contending the "fides communis" be conserved. When the treasury was unable to meet *Monte* obligations, he suggested a meeting between creditors and government to search out alternatives. Later he pro-

[59] On the problem of antimonopoly legislation, see M. Becker, "La esecuzione della legislatura," pp. 8-29. On disputes concerning the jurisdiction of guild consuls, see *Atti del Esecutore*, 29, fols. 196r-197; *ibid.*, 40, f. 112.

[60] On Matteo di Jacopo Arrighi, see *CP*, 8, fols. 58, 59r; 14, f. 89; 15, fols. 86r, 92-93r; *CCE*, 38, f. 49; *LF*, 24, f. 83. For numerous other *novi cives*, affluent creditors, and supporters of popular government, see M. Becker, *Florence in Transition*, 1, 221-23. Among these were Niccolò Delli the vintner; Valeriano Dolcibene, ironmonger; Tellino Dini, used clothing dealer; Giovanni Goggio, grain importer, and so on. Cf. also G. Brucker, *Politics and Society*, pp. 41-56 for these and other *nouveaux* figures and L. Martines, "La famiglia Martelli e un documento," *ASI*, 117 (1959), 29-43.

posed that monies derived from judicial condemnations be employed to reduce the *Monte* debt. He appealed to patriotic impulses in calling upon fellow citizens to loan capital to the treasury without demanding interest. Exhibiting solicitude for "iura communis," he advocated, like numerous *novi cives*, strict controls over public properties. Perhaps his most vehement declamations were reserved for the theme of "iustitia" ("vigorose fiat iustitia"). To Biagio, justice meant punishment of the guilty "especially the overpowerful" ("maxime maiores"), not merely the "parvos sed magnos."[61]

The doublet-maker Francesco Bonaiuti shared these sentiments, supporting a provision granting the signory additional authority to seize and send to trial malefactors. More crucial was his advocacy of a law whereby criminous great burghers (*popolani grassi*) could be deprived of certain key political rights by being compelled to assume magnate status. Essentially, this barred the *popolano* from sitting in the priorate or either of its colleges (in a word, the highest elected magistracies of the republic—the signory). His distrust of the Florentine nobility was revealed when he opposed a law permitting nobles to have one of their number in the sensitive post of the *regulatores*. This newly created office performed important bureaucratic tasks in the *contado* where aristocratic influence might be most intense. The general problem of office holding in rural regions also engaged the doublet-maker. Here again he opted for legislation designed to limit the influence of great families, favoring strict enforcement of the *divieto* over *contado* offices. Such a law would prevent individuals from the same family from holding office simultaneously or in rapid succession.[62]

Bianco di Bonsi was extremely active in the signory and, although *nouveau*, served in the high post of prior in 1353, 1356, 1365, and 1378. In 1359 he was chosen for the most prestigious elective position, *gonfaloniere* of justice. Like so many other newcomers, he was experienced in treasury work. If there is a single proving ground for the *novi cives*, it is the *camera*. As a group their work in the treasury makes them understanding of and sensitive to economic needs of an emerging territorial state. In Bonsi's case he espoused fiscal interests of the polis against traditional immunities and liberties of the church. Following a hard line calculated to promote public imperatives, he spoke out in favor of state appropriation of numerous bequests to pious foundations and religious companies. Later he supported more extreme measures,

---

[61] *CP*, 15, f. 129; 16, fols. 35r, 104, 124; 18, fols. 51, 63r, 117r; 19, f. 84r; N. Rodolico, *I Ciompi* (Florence, 1945), p. 193.
[62] *P*, 43, f. 151; *LF*, 34, fols. 115, 118; *P*, 44, f. 55; *LF*, 34, f. 121.

counseling on behalf of the election of public officials to impose forced loans upon the Tuscan clergy.[63]

The merchant Frozzo Casini likewise took a stern stand on matters ecclesiastical, having little sympathy for time-honored privileges. He would not recognize the clergy's claims for immunity from communal jurisdiction; nor was he tolerant of others violating laws of the republic. He supported strengthened magistracies possessing greater powers, particularly over crimes of violence. In conjunction with this, he, too, advocated increased authority of public officials over communal property. In the company of other new citizens and their patrician adherents, he espoused imposition of the *estimo*. Also he saw the main prop of public order in a firm alliance between *populus et artes*. Here again sentiments of the public-spirited found an echo in this small merchant championing an accord between the "people and the guilds": in concert they might save the state from the machinations of the overmighty.[64]

The political career of Giovanni di Ciari, a well-to-do dealer in used clothing (a respected *trecento* occupation) illustrates the perils of supporting communal authority. The family was counted among the chief rate payers of the S. Spirito quarter of the city, and Giovanni served as prior in 1351, 1356, and 1361 while intermittently sitting with the college of the Twelve. In the early fifties he spoke for strict justice against the warring Ubaldini feudatories of Tuscany. A few years later, as representative of the colleges, he entered the celebrated debate racking the city concerning benefit of clergy, siding with the priors against the pope. In this instance he counseled the government to write to the pontiff "defending the justice done [by communal magistrates] in the case of the priest Bricciolo." Giovanni also contributed to the discourse on public finance, urging the signory to elect "cives artifices" (citizen artisans and masters) to investigate modes for raising needed revenues. The war with Pisa, bitterly opposed by the church, engaged Giovanni's talents; he served on a *balìa* directing the conflict and staunchly supported it. In 1367 he received a commonplace reward: the aristocratic Guelf party struck him down. In that year he was declared *ammonito* which to all intent and purpose branded him a political heretic. Suffering proscription, his civic career terminated in dishonor, he was visited with the dread political ostracism.[65]

This was no isolated happening. Those *novi cives* who spoke for the claims of the emerging public world or served in its burgeoning admin-

---

[63] *LF*, 40, f. 284; *CP*, 4, f. 88; *CCE*, 54.
[64] *CP*, 16, fols. 59r, 68r, 69r, 128; 18, fols. 28, 136.
[65] *CP*, 1, part 2, f. 8; *DP*, 6, f. 25; *Prestanze*, 2, f. 3 (1355); *CP*, 1, part 2, f. 3; 2, fols. 4, 20; *P*, 51, f. 1; *ibid.*, 56, f. 112r; *CCE*, 68, f. 135r.

istrative machinery threatened aristocratic privilege and ecclesiastical liberties. Men without clan connections or membership in powerful *consorterie* ran great risks in seeking to implement impersonal government that could only menace entrenched interests. Francesco Alderotti spoke vigorously for taxation of the clergy and was declared *ammonito*. His brother Matteo was an official in charge of the sale of church property and a firm supporter of the *artifices*. Proscription and exile were his lot. Two members of the *nouveau riche* Asini family likewise were declared *ammoniti*; their fate was quite typical of that befalling *novi cives* who advanced large sums of capital to the treasury, served as tax farmers, and acted in a variety of bureaucratic roles. An identical destiny confronted the affluent notary Ser Albizo di Messer Filippo da Barberino, civil servant and creditor of the treasury. The two sons of Bindo Benini were also declared *ammoniti* for hostility toward the *Parte Guelfa*. Later, in the revolution of 1378, one was made a knight of *il popolo*. Simone Bertini was an early victim (1358) who had repeatedly purchased communal gabelles on vendors of foodstuffs, fulling mills, and so on. Another was the druggist Ugolino di Bonsi, key treasury official and substantial government creditor. Niccolò di Bartolo del Buono regularly acted as a tax farmer for minor gabelles as well as serving in a plethora of public offices, from that of magistrate over a rural commune to ambassador to the Romagna. Shortly after he spoke before the signory, urging concord and union among citizens, he was visited with political ostracism. Certain of the Davizzi, among the most important holders of *Monte* shares, likewise suffered in this manner as did the extremely affluent Petriboni bankers. Still other victims were the Ferratini, Gucci, Guidetti, Perini, Rinuccini, and others.[66]

Such a figure as Giovanni Dini, druggist and importer of spices, was justly celebrated in his own lifetime for civic service. Included among those especially commended by the signory for acting to conserve the liberty of Florence against the machinations of the church, he was granted immunity from a ban of excommunication. (How efficacious such a grant was must remain unanswered.) He was a member of the *balìa* of Eight, later called the "Eight Saints," who guided the republic in its desperate war against the Holy See, and in 1378 was rewarded by

---

[66] On the Alderotti, see *P*, 64, f. 137; *CP*, 16, f. 24. On the Asini, see *Estimo*, 8, f. 3 (1352); *Monte*, 442, f. 47 (1361); *CCE*, 192; *Cambio*, 12, f. 26r. For Ser Albizo, see Stefani, rub. 765; *CCE*, 77, f. 21. On the sons of Benini, see P. Conti, *Il libro segreto della ragione di Piero Benini e compagni* (Florence, 1937); *CCE*, 73, f. 68. For Simone Bertini, see M. Villani, 8, 31; *CCE*, 81, f. 3r; *Monte*, 437, f. 67; *CCE*, 173, f. 21. For Del Buono, see M. Villani, 8, 31; *CCE*, 25, f. 61r; 29, f. 274; 33, f. 200; *CP*, 1, part 1, f. 22r; *Scrivano, piccolo*, 2, f. 2. These and other political casualties will be dealt with in volume 3 of this study.

il popolo for service to the state with the patent of knighthood. It was he and his confreres who were later to be commended by Machiavelli for caring more about their country than about the welfare of their own souls. Like so many other *novi cives* and patrician reformers, he championed impersonal government and the strict rule of law, favoring legislation against carrying deadly weapons as well as challenging the sanctuary churches offered the criminous. Irregularities in legislative procedures also attracted his attention; he saw to it that private petitions were not voted upon unless submitted to scrupulous examination by the signory. In foreign policy he demonstrated abiding concern for Florentine interests. Older ideologies played little part in his thinking, so that, for him, the correct course was always to surmount immediate difficulties: this might involve shifting alliances or even assuming unpopular risks and responsibilities. Dini was credited by the chronicler Stefani with having revealed the existence of a conspiracy against the state. He also suffered ostracism as did so many other public-spirited men.[67]

For the most part we have concentrated only on names of politically active *novi cives* from the initial letters of the alphabet. The list could be multiplied many times, but the inferences to be drawn would be little altered. The new men were gaining a reputation for being responsible citizens and trustworthy political allies of those seeking to make public order prevail over special privilege and private rights. These harbingers of impersonal government had assumed challenging and dangerous roles in new, uncharted times.[68]

Problems confronting the republic in 1343 were novel and complex. The tone and style of Florentine politics were transformed; never again would it be possible to reconstruct the Guelf political system which had served the city so well over many generations. Fissures had been discernible as early as 1340, but now not even the most sanguine of Florentines could hope to avoid a breach between the twin bulwarks of the Guelf confederation—the papacy and the kingdom of Naples. The city was unable to sustain its time-honored role as financial fulcrum of this alliance because bankruptcy was imminent. A similar fate lay in store for many of the great Florentine banking houses; Neapolitan barons and high clergy were no longer the commune's Guelf friends but rather her nagging creditors whose demands could not be satisfied. There were other forces that were working to erode old Guelf ties: persistent papal support for the claims of the deposed, much despised

---

[67] Stefani, rub. 752, 781, pp. 354, 400; *P*, 60, f. 148 (January 21, 1373); *ibid.*, 64, f. 19 (April 22, 1376); *LF*, 40, f. 52; *CP*, 12, f. 129r; 15, f. 81r.
[68] Especially pertinent in this context are the careers of numerous judges and notaries to be treated in the next volume.

despot, Walter of Brienne; policies followed by the Holy See in making appointments to the Tuscan church; meddling of the Inquisitor in secular affairs; sweeping juridical claims of ecclesiastical courts; and the untimely death of the military captain of the Guelf forces, King Robert of Naples, in 1343.[69]

At this juncture, captains of the twenty-one guilds, two-thirds of whom were *novi cives*, responded to the crisis by presenting two petitions to the signory which were adopted by the councils and became part of the statutory law of the realm. These measures were designed to prevent the impatient prelates and Neapolitan barons from using the ecclesiastical courts to press their claims for restitution.[70] During the interval from 1343–47, a combination of old and new men from the guilds acted in concert to strengthen the prerogatives of secular tribunals. They also made radical innovations in the communal credit structure aimed at averting the city's impending bankruptcy. In the face of bitter ecclesiastical censure, the communal debt was funded and declared to be both negotiable and interest bearing.[71] Throughout the decade of the 1350s speakers for the college of the *gonfaloniere*, where new men had their greatest representation, persisted in advocating policies that brought the republic into sharp conflict with her old allies. They voiced their disapproval on the matter of sending subsidies to the papal legate and called upon the signory to withdraw contingents of Florentine cavalry stationed in the kingdom of Naples.[72] Spokesmen for this college bitterly opposed an alliance with the Holy See because they believed it would constitute a breach of Florence's treaty obligations with Milan. Consistently they admonished the signory not to take any action that might antagonize the powerful Visconti despot and

---

[69] On the question of the relationship between the city's banks and the papacy, see Y. Renouard, *Les relations des Papes d'Avignon et des compagnies commerciales et bancaires de 1316 à 1378* (Paris, 1941). For a detailed analysis of the economic motives behind the split between Florence and the papacy, see A. Sapori, *La crisi*, pp. 117 ff. On papal policy toward Brienne, see L. Leoni, "Breve di Clemente VI en favore di Gualtieri di Brienne, duca d'Atene," *ASI*, 22 (1875), pp. 181 ff. The clergy made extensive loans to Brienne in 1342. Cf. *CCE*, 1 bis, f. 297r; *ibid.*, 2, f. 4r. On the role of church tribunals and the inquisition in Florence, see M. Becker, "Some Economic Implications of the Conflict between Church and State in 'Trecento' Florence." *Mediaeval Studies*, 21 (1959), 1–16.

[70] A. Panella, "Politica ecclesiastica del comune fiorentine," *ASI*, 2, part IV (1913), 327–65; A. Sapori, *La crisi*, pp. 197 ff.

[71] B. Barbadoro, *Le finanze della repubblica fiorentina* (Florence, 1929).

[72] *CP*, 1, 2, f. 25; *ibid.*, unnumbered folio (March 12, 1355). Tellino Dini's statement to the signory expresses the view held by the new men: "Non placet nullo modo legam factam cum legato." Dominus Tommaso Altoviti rejected this proposal in favor of a "lega cum ecclesia." His suggestion was seconded by the prominent patricians Carlo Strozzi and Andrea Bardi. Cf. *CP*, 4, f. 103r. Marco Strozzi urged the Florentines to send troops to Naples as recompense for the many services rendered to them in the past by the king.

urged the government to maintain a strict neutrality in the hostilities between Milan and the papacy.[73] These views clashed with traditional propapal sentiments and caused sharp cleavages among the citizenry. During the 1360s and 1370s successful papal efforts to re-establish dominion over the Patrimony altered dramatically the tone of foreign policy discussions held by the signory. Leading *novi cives* such as Giovanni Goggio, Ricco Taldi, and Tellino Dini openly advocated an alliance with Milan to serve as a counter to the ever-growing power of the papacy in territories bordering the republic.[74] Suspicion of ecclesiastical designs against the city's *libertà* mounted throughout this interval, and by 1375 the church was looked upon as the principal threat to Florentine liberty. Despite assurances by Avignon that the papacy had no territorial ambitions in Tuscany, the new men remained unconvinced and continued to press for the adoption of alternatives far removed from those of traditional Guelfism.[75]

Advocacy of a foreign policy independent of ancient ties with the papacy and Naples placed the new men in opposition to the more conservative elements of the patriciate captained by Piero degli Albizzi, Carlo Strozzi, and, later, Lapo da Castiglionchio. These *ottimati* believed passionately that the republic's interests could best be served by integrating communal policy with that of the Holy See. In 1359 Piero degli Albizzi, backed by the *Parte Guelfa*, induced the signory to ally with Cardinal Albornoz, the papal legate. According to the testimony of Matteo Villani, the citizenry were outraged by this maneuver; such prominent *novi cives* as Tellino Dini advised the signory to dispatch an ambassador to the curia in order to reverse policies initiated by the *ottimati* and the legate.[76] The chroniclers Villani, Stefani, and Velluti concurred in the judgment that the Albizzi faction and Guelf captains were motivated by a desire to aggrandize themselves: rich ecclesiastical benefices and lucrative administrative posts in the papal states were tempting rewards; therefore the *bene comune* was neglected

---

[73] Giovanni Dini advised the signory not to send a subsidy to the papal legate because it might offend Milan. Cf. *CP*, 12, f. 119r. The same sentiments were voiced by the guild captains. Cf. *CP*, 7, f. 6. Ricco Taldi stated that if for any reason it became necessary to send troops to aid the papacy, the government should first take counsel with the citizenry. *CP*, 12, f. 72r. Schiatta di Rocco proposed that the government not contract an alliance with any lord or commune "maiori" than Florence. Cf. *CP*, 10, f. 114.

[74] *Ibid.*, 9, fols. 21–65.

[75] Communal counselors expressed fear that the Holy See might absorb lands belonging to neighboring Lucca and Arezzo and that papal lieutenants might intervene in the domestic affairs of Siena and other Tuscan communes, thus destroying the *libertà* of their citizenry. Cf. *CP*, 12, fols. 66–67. Speakers also accused the church of aiding the rebellious Florentine feudatories, the Ubaldini clan, in their war against the city. *Ibid.*, 12, f. 77r.

[76] *Ibid.*, 2, f. 44. See also footnote 72.

and the *libertà* of the republic placed in jeopardy.⁷⁷ It was the propapal *ottimati* who posed the chief threat to republican liberty, while the *novi cives* and their allies were counted among its staunchest defenders. Three years later the self-same controversy arose again over the feasibility of war with Pisa. The church and *ottimati* vigorously opposed this risky venture, while the blacksmith Andrea Donati, the oil vendor Andrea Terii, the vintner Francesco Fabrini, the goldsmith Nerio, and others of their station enthusiastically championed this undertaking.⁷⁸

The same *novi cives* who tended to be suspicious of the propapal machinations of the Albizzi faction and wary of foreign entanglements were also hostile to the ancient liberties, prerogatives, and immunities enjoyed by the Tuscan church. They were anxious to reduce the authority of ecclesiastical courts so that clergy might be brought under communal jurisdiction. They also disputed the time-honored right of sanctuary and favored imposing harsh penalties upon criminous clerics.⁷⁹ However, the greatest pressure these men exerted was in the area of tax reform. Here *novi cives* attacked the invidious standards of the medieval commune when they demanded that taxes and imposts fall equally upon clergy and laity.⁸⁰ Another suggestion entailed the appointment of communal officials who were to supervise the execution of wills and administer the endowments of pious foundations and religious confraternities. This zeal for reform was not confined to things ecclesiastical but radiated into many other sectors of civic life. The affluent butcher Schiatta di Ricco called upon the signory to redistribute the tax burden so that greater equality would prevail among the citizenry; this involved new assessments commensurate with the wealth of each particular quarter of the city. Ricco also suggested that the signory elect special officials to review the system of tax rates.⁸¹ The grocer Niccolò Delli entreated the signory to force those who owed money to the commune to make immediate restitution. As spokesman for the college of the *Dodici*, he pressed for the equalization of forced loans (*prestanze*); this was an ever-present problem, and Delli's sentiments were shared by numerous *novi cives* who advised the signory on economic matters.⁸² More sweeping fiscal innovations were advanced

---

⁷⁷ D. Velluti, *La Cronica domestica*, p. 253.
⁷⁸ *CP*, 4, f. 96; *LF*, 36, fols. 130r–135. The statements made by the chroniclers Velluti (p. 240) and Filippo Villani (11, 102) are borne out by the records of the advisory councils to the signory. We note that Piero degli Albizzi, Carlo Strozzi, and the Guelf captains consistently advocated peace. Cf. *CP*, 3, f. 14; *ibid.*, 4, f. 33r; *ibid.*, 5, fols. 4–4r.
⁷⁹ *Ibid.*, 1, 2, fols. 132–133; *ibid.*, 3, f. 8; *P*, 63, fols. 70r–73; *LF*, 40, f. 150.
⁸⁰ *CP*, 4, f. 97; *ibid.*, 14, fols. 48–57r.
⁸¹ See footnote 69 and *CP*, 10, f. 114.
⁸² *P*, 60, f. 1; *ibid.*, 64, f. 129; *CP*, 5, f. 108r; *ibid.*, 11, f. 106.

by the *gonfaloniere* Recco di Guido Guazza, by far the most radical of those *novi cives* whose opinions are recorded in the minutes of the communal legislative debates. This maverick later became infamous in the eyes of his compatriots for vigorously and successfully championing a drastic reduction in the interest rate on the funded communal debt. Stefani contends that this was the most extreme step taken by the government in over a century, and Guazza's name was recorded in the diary of the Curiani family, owners of extensive *Monte* stock, as being "Gonfaloniere di *Ingiustizia*." This inveterate foe of entrenched privilege was first noticed when he spoke up boldly in favor of taxing clergy and raising the amount of the bond that nobles of certain Florentine territories had to post.[83] Shortly thereafter he proposed legislation authorizing the commune to sell property of the Tuscan church; he was counted among the signory's most ardent supporters during Florence's war with the papacy. For his novel opinions and enthusiasms, he was promptly excommunicated by the Church; two years after this ban was proclaimed, he rose in the councils to argue against the re-establishment of the inquisition in Florentine territory. Guazza was the first speaker to congratulate Filippo di Cionetto Bastari for his daring oration imploring the signory to oust the propapal Albizzi family from their commanding position over Florentine politics.[84]

The *novi cives* warmly espoused state authority as a restraint against the entrenched strength of great families who tended to be a law unto themselves, and legislation enacted under their aegis reflects this deep concern. They were most anxious to curb the lawlessness prevalent among these *potentes* so that inhabitants of the city and *contado* might live in peace and tranquility. In 1346 two artisans spoke in favor of legislation designed to curtail the power of very great clans: these *potentes* were to be prohibited from contracting marriages with the families of any foreign prince, lord, or baron since such an alliance would inordinately increase their status. Any offspring from such a union was to be automatically barred from exercising any jurisdiction and was to be required to pay the heavy fine of 1,000 florins.[85] The government also acted to fix severe penalties against any patrician who lawlessly usurped ecclesiastical property.[86] The following year the doublet-maker Domenico Dante counseled the enactment of a provision

---

[83] Technically, Guazza does not qualify as *nouveau* since his family sat in the signory earlier. His is included because he, like others, belonged to families out of public office for over half a century. I wish to thank Professor Brucker for this fact. Cf. *ibid.*, 12, fols. 3, 10r–11; *P*, 64, f. 17; *LF*, 40, f. 230; Stefani, rub. 881–83; D. Marzi, *La cancelleria della repubblica fiorentina* (Rocca S. Casciano, 1910), p. 100.
[84] *CP*, 12, f. 10r.
[85] Cf. M. Becker, *Florence in Transition*, 1, p. 223.
[86] *P*, 33, f. 18r.

canceling permission to bear arms formerly granted by the commune to certain great families; this was to be done because of the "lamentations" of the citizenry concerning the terrible violence being committed against them daily by the *potentes*.[87] In 1352 a petition was presented by several "peace-loving *populares*" which was seconded by two notaries new to the Florentine political scene. It stated that any commoner who behaved in a lawless manner could be declared a magnate by a vote of the signory and captains of the twenty-one guilds (two-thirds of whom were *novi cives*). The effect of making a citizen a magnate was to deprive him of many of his political rights. For example, he was not to be permitted to sit in the signory or to hold other critical posts. This petition was amended and then enacted with this preamble: ". . . in order to conserve and defend the liberty and innocence of the commoners, the poor, the weak and the clergy," those who were convicted under this law were not only deprived of high office, but were not permitted to live in the same section of the city as their kinsmen.[88] The threat of vendetta or reprisal by relatives of lawless Florentines encouraged the government to take steps to weaken the *consorteria* (family ties) of powerful clans. In 1361 there were further inroads into the authority of great families when a law was enacted compelling all those who had formerly been classed as *magnati* (nobles) but whose legal status had been transformed by action of the signory to that of *popolani* (commoners) to appear before the priorate and renounce their *consorteria*. Florentines whose status had been altered in this way were not to be permitted to hold office in the signory for two decades.[89] Other severe measures were taken to reduce the influence of the patriciate over communal courts: anyone seeking dispensation from a verdict of these tribunals was obliged to present a petition to the signory which required a three-fourths vote for approval, then ratification by a two-thirds vote of the communal councils.[90] Legislation of this type was implemented by various directives issued by the signory to the judiciary stating that sentences were not to be suspended; special officials were elected to enforce this mandate. The coopersmith Guido Pizzini, the doublet-makers Augustino Cocchi and Francesco Bonaiuto, the furrier Piero Neri del Zancha, the grocer Giovanni Dini, and the hosier Andrea Niccolini were but a few of the many *novi cives* who enthusiastically battled for the supremacy of communal law over time-honored prerogatives of the established patriciate.

[87] *DP*, 7, f. 66r.
[88] *P*, 39, f. 192.
[89] *Ibid.*, 68, f. 164.
[90] *Ibid.*, 43, f. 1.

The *novi cives* warmly supported the Ordinances of Justice, which increased the penalties on lawless nobles and required this class to post bond as a guarantee for their good behavior. One of the first measures taken by the popular signory of 1343 was to restore these "most fortunate ordinances," which had been abrogated by the preceding regime. The government was also much concerned with their vigorous enforcement.[91]

In 1349 the wine merchant Federigo Soldi, the notary Ser Jacobo Gherardi, and three other new men, Jacobo Mezze, Francesco Benini, and Puccio Carletti, favored extending the liability for any crime committed by a member of a noble house to his kinsmen even as distant as the sixth degree.[92] The hosier Augustino Cocchi spoke in behalf of legislation requiring all nobles who desired to serve abroad to first obtain permission of the government.[93] The notary Ser Piero Guccio supported the proposal that would reinstitute the practice of permitting commoners to deposit secret denunciations against lawless *magnati* in a special box affixed to the door of the court of the Executor of Justice.[94] Spokesmen for the colleges favored the exaction of special taxes to be levied against the nobility of the *contado* and, in the company of Recco di Guido Guazza, suggested that this class be compelled to increase bond.[95] Particular suspicion was harbored against certain noble families who had a long history of disloyalty to the republic and who were excessively given to acts of violence and brigandage. By a provision of the signory and the councils, the Adimari, Bostichi, Della Tosa, Donati, Gherardini, Giandonati, Rossi, and Visdomini families were singled out for special retribution.[96] At the same time, certain members of less powerful and more law-abiding noble houses were permitted to renounce their status and enroll in the ranks of the commoners in order to avoid restraints imposed upon the *magnati*. By a special decree of the popular regime in October, 1343, 530 Florentine nobles were permitted to change their class affiliation.[97] This practice was continued, and in the summer of 1349 an extraordinary commission was appointed by the signory to select those *magnati* considered most worthy of commoner status. Many of these new *popolani* changed their names, separated themselves from their consorts, and relinquished their coats-of-arms; yet popular distrust of these former

---

[91] *P*, 32, f. 73.
[92] *CP*, 1, 1, f.5. Cf. M. Becker, *Florence in Transition*, 1, p. 225.
[93] *LF*, 24, f. 20.
[94] This measure was designed to prevent crimes by nobles against "libertatem et statum popularium." The magnate Piero Foraboschi spoke against its adoption. Cf. *P*, 48, f. 30.
[95] *CP*, 1, 2, f. 130r; *ibid.*, 6, f. 118.
[96] *P*, 37, f. 99; *LF*, 30, f. 46.
[97] Stefani, rub. 595; G. Villani, 12, 23.

grandi and *potenti* persisted.⁹⁸ In 1371, two *novi cives*, Bernardino Cini Bartolini and Ser Nigio Ser Giovanni seconded a proposal to extend the political disabilities imposed upon former *magnati*.⁹⁹ By these measures the signory was able to reduce the number of nobility, set strict limits upon the political participation of former members of this class, and weaken the force of dynastic ties, while at the same time buttressing communal prerogatives. This movement was intensified during the 1370s, when the *novi cives* played an even larger role in communal politics. By the summer of 1378 this trend had broadened into a frontal assault which divested the *magnati* (referred to anachronistically in the pertinent documents as "milities") of other ancient rights and destroyed the effective force of their clan ties.¹⁰⁰

The tendency to exalt the authority of the state at the expense of the privileges of the great families was a dominant theme during those intervals when the *novi cives* were well-represented in the government. This motif was implicit both in the many condemnations handed down by the republic's courts against those lawless *magnati* and *popolani* who appropriated communal rights and property for their own use and in the numerous attempts of the various popular signories to compel the culprits to make restitution of their usurpations. In 1344 the courts fined 16 members of the Bardi family a total of 3,000 florins on this count. The Buondelmonti and Pazzi were condemned to pay 5,161 lire and 3,249 lire, respectively, on similar charges, while the eminent Rossi and Della Tosa were obliged to restore extensive communal properties to the treasury.¹⁰¹ The following year a provision was enacted stating that the republic was desperately in need of revenue, and the signory was enjoined to recover "the property and rights of the city so that Florence might continue to live in *libertate et iustitia.*"¹⁰² In 1349 three new men counseled the enactment of even more stringent legislation framed to achieve this end, and such speakers from the college of the *gonfaloniere* as Antonio Niccoli and Andrea Fei continued to urge further reforms in this area.¹⁰³ Special commissions were created whose chief function was the preservation of perquisites of the republic and strengthening the jurisdiction of civil tribunals. The founding of these *balie* and the extension of their prerogatives were enthusiastically advocated by Recco di Guido Guazza and other new men. Soon these *novi cives* gained the support of certain public-spirited opponents of the factions such as the political in-

---

⁹⁸ Stefani, rub. 748; *P*, 40, f. 39.
⁹⁹ *Ibid.*, 58, f. 164.
¹⁰⁰ *Balie*, 16, fols. 2r–6; *P*, 66, f. 31; *LF*, 40, f. 298.
¹⁰¹ *CCE*, 6, fols. 72r–89; *ibid.*, 7, fols. 115–17; *ibid.*, 17, f. 6r; *P*, 33, f. 43.
¹⁰² *DP*, 5, f. 64.
¹⁰³ *CP*, 12, f. 175; *LF*, 29, fols. 23–24.

dependents Giovanni Magalotti, Filippo di Cionetto Bastari, Caroccio Alberti, Andrea Francesco Salviati, Francesco Vigorosi, and, last but not least, Salvestro de' Medici.[104]

The chronicler Stefani was particularly well-informed about the events of these years, since, in addition to serving on the *balìa* of the *Dieci della Libertà* and later acting as a fiscal officer for this commission, he also was a key Florentine diplomat and was frequently in attendance at communal council meetings. He tells us that the *Dieci* forced great families to restore possessions of the republic, and this information is substantiated by documentary evidence. But what is much more significant, the chronicler calls attention to the steps taken by this *balìa* to undermine the authority of the great lords in the *contado*.[105] This movement to extend republican jurisdiction into the outer reaches of the countryside and to bring these remote territories "under the arm of communal justice" was accelerated in the late 1370s and early 1380s and culminated in 1384 with the destruction of the liberties, immunities, and exemptions of the great Florentine feudatories, the Counts Guidi and Ubaldini.[106] Stefani provides us with an insight into the motives of the new men whose energies contributed so much to the rise of state power. This group, according to the chronicler, harbored a deep resentment toward those *grandi* and *potenti* who used their privileged position to commit numerous extortions against their inferiors.[107] Stefani and an anonymous *priorista* made particular mention of those nobles and mighty commoners who used the church courts and the power of ecclesiastical office to oppress the less powerful.[108] These patricians held a monopoly of high church positions in Tuscany, and it was this group, in the opinion of the signory of July, 1375, who exploited the Florentines—"especially the *populares* and artisans *sub calore iusticiae*." Through their actions these lawless and factious men threatened the liberty of the city and prevented the people from conducting their affairs in peace and tranquility.

V

Like the sentiments of the chroniclers Matteo Villani, Velluti, Stefani, and Morelli, those of the Florentine chancellor Coluccio Salutati, foremost humanist of his generation, reflect a fundamental reinterpretation of

---

[104] These men were all instrumental in displacing the Albizzi and Ricci from communal politics. Stefani, rub. 731; *P*, 60, f. 2r; *ibid.*, 64, f. 17. For their political opinions, see especially *CP*, Vol. 12.
[105] E. Fiumi, "Fioritura e decadenza," p. 492.
[106] Stefani, rub. 588; *CP*, 12, f. 175.
[107] M. Becker, "Un avvenimento riguardante il cronista Marchionne di Coppo Stefani," *ASI*, 117 (1959), 137–46.
[108] N. Rodolico, *I Ciompi* (Florence, 1945), p. 42; Stefani, rub. 616.

the character of the republic's politics.[109] No longer were the *novi cives* depicted as the principal threat to the proper conduct of civic life. Instead the intransigent, factious, propapal segment of the urban patriciate were considered to pose the most serious challenge to the orderly workings of communal politics. These immoderate men, in the opinion of Salutati, were responsible for the enormities committed in the name of traditional Guelfism. Using the prestige and power of the *Parte Guelfa*, nobles and great *popolani* sought to control Florence and formulate policy that would assure the triumph of the propapal cause. This would necessarily involve catapulting the philopapal Albizzi faction into power through devious techniques of political proscription. Any who withstood this tide were denounced as "Ghibellines" and driven from office. It was this stratagem that provoked an undeclared civil war in the city of Florence.

In this campaign of vilification, *novi cives* and their adherents were logical targets since their objectives frequently clashed with those of the captains of the *Parte* and the Albizzi faction. The popular government of 1343, which reduced the influence of the great families, extolled the impersonal force of communal law, and promoted a foreign policy independent of Avignon, was anathema to the propapal patricians who had so long ruled the city as if it were their own private preserve. Beginning with the fall of 1346 and ending disastrously with the summer of 1378, these patricians repeatedly worked through the organization of the *Parte Guelfa* to subvert the various popular regimes that held power intermittently. Giovanni Villani contended that the legislation passed in 1346 was expressly designed by the Guelf captains to oust *novi cives* from the government and to break the hold of the twenty-one guilds over civic affairs. This was to be accomplished by barring from public life *novi cives* who failed to fulfill their communal fiscal obligations or whose ancestors were not native-born Florentines.[110] In this way the rule of the "antichi e originali" citizens would be restored, and those men of "unknown and insufficient origins" were to be removed from the lists of candidates eligible for communal office when, in the opinion of "true citizens," they were judged to be unworthy of such high honor. Giovanni Villani saw this as the first move in a calculated plot to stifle the political aspirations of the new men. The dénouement soon followed when in January, 1347, the captains of the *Parte Guelfa* initiated even more sweeping legislation to weaken further the power of the newcomers and their political allies and thus put an end, once and for all, to the popular regime. Anyone whose forebears had sympathized with the Ghibellines or who came from territories under Ghibelline domination or who was not reputed to be "a true

---

[109] E. Garin, "I cancellieri umanisti della repubblica fiorentina da Coluccio Salutati a Bartolomeo Scala," *Rivista Storica Italiana*, 71 (1959), 185–95.
[110] G. Villani, 12, 72; *P*, 34, f. 93r; *LF*, 26, fols. 93r–94r.

Guelf and lover of the *Parte* of the Holy Church" was to be declared ineligible for office in the republic.[111] Those who did assume communal posts in violation of this edict were to be fined the exorbitant sum of 500 lire. At first there was extensive public support for this type of legislation, even among the *novi cives* and their friends; apparently, few of these men believed they would be affected by these measures, for were they not *amatores* of the *Parte Guelfa*?[112] Did they not stem from the most prosperous rural Florentine families? Had they not despised the pro-imperial Ghibellines and did they not share the prejudices of the aristocracy against foreigners who resided within the city walls?[113] Soon, however, it became evident that the anti-Ghibelline, anti-alien legislation would be used not only against the *novi cives* but also against dissident members of the patriciate, enemies of the captains of the *Parte Guelfa*, supporters of popular government, opponents of propapal foreign policy advocated by the Albizzi, and political independents who refused to ally with any faction.

Major chroniclers agreed that the intent of these laws was admirable and even favored amendments to buttress them, but they were deeply disturbed by the partisan and factious spirit in which they were enforced. Accusations of political heterodoxy on grounds of Ghibellinism were soon made against men from all social strata, and by 1378 few felt secure. The tense atmosphere of these times encouraged the formulation of a fundamental question that was to have broad implications for subsequent political orthodoxy and right to membership in the Guelf party. The medieval commune was composed of a cluster of quasi-autonomous bodies and institutions. The *Parte*, the most prominent of these, asserted its authority to select its own members. As with many medieval legal questions, conflicting precedents could be cited because of the in-

---

[111] G. Villani, 12, 79; *LF*, 26, fols. 127–28. This measure barely gained the necessary two-thirds majority required for passage.

[112] The initial measure of January, 1347, had several safeguards that were designed to protect the new 'artefici.' Cf. G. Villani, 12, 79. The word 'artefici' (in Italian) or 'artifices' (in Latin) is used to describe men whose occupations range from small-scale producers of goods to the great industrial entrepreneurs. According to Villani, as soon as it became evident that the *Parte* wanted to use this type of legislation to overthrow popular government in Florence, two-thirds of the members of the priorate wished to annul the anti-Ghibelline laws, but the power of the captains was so great that this was impossible. Cf. G. Villani, 12, 92. The new men disfranchised by these laws were Bartolo di Gruerio; Lorenzo Buonaccorsi; Gallo di Rossi, recently of Poggibonsi; Iacobo Faloci, also of Poggibonsi; Neruzzio, a hosier; and Francesco Guerrio, a carpenter. The only patrician affected was Uberto Infangati, a banker, and he was restored to communal office two years later. In 1360 he was sentenced to death for treason in absentia. Cf. *CCE*, 20 fols. 20–20r; *ibid.*, 22, f. 61r; *ibid.*, 23, f. 18; *ibid.*, 25, fols. 78r–86.

[113] The *novi cives* were never anxious to extend the rights of citizenship. Cf. *P*, 66, f. 57; *LF*, 26, fols. 93–94r.

formal and *ad hoc* character of the communal constitution.[114] In 1349 the *Parte*'s claim was placed in jeopardy when the signory arrogated to itself the right to confer Guelf status upon worthy individuals and groups.[115] During the next few years the signory used this power when it accepted petitions of families who contended they had been excluded from the *Parte* and unjustly accused of being Ghibellines; the signory ordered the *Parte* to admit them.[116] The communal councils acquiesced to requests from syndics of rural communes, newly integrated into the Florentine state, that the inhabitants be recognized as "veri et originali guelfi," despite the fact that Ghibellines had previously lived in these areas.[117] In 1354 Florence sent ambassadors to San Gimignano to reorganize the territory; upon their return, the signory acted upon the advice of its emissaries and conferred the benefits of citizenship upon the populace. Henceforth, the men of this region were to be known as "guelfi populares, veri, originari et antiqui."[118] Captains of the *Parte* responded to these challenges by raising the matriculation fee so that anyone applying for admission, whose ancestors had not been enrolled, was required to pay 100 florins. Since this sum was equivalent to twenty-five years rent on the average artisan's shop, this measure was designed to be an effective deterrent to all but the most affluent.[119] The signory continued to assert its right to receive men into the *Parte Guelfa* and maintained that it alone had authority in these matters. Further, it declared that the captains could not accept members unless prior approval was obtained from the signory.[120] There were other issues dividing the *Parte* and the signory: the most delicate of these was the question of economic autonomy. In 1351 the communal councils enacted a provision authorizing the signory to elect state auditors to review accounts of the *Parte* reaching back over two decades. This problem had disturbed the rapport between the *Parte* and earlier popular regimes; its persistence emphasized the ambiguous character of communal governments in which the boundary between the authority of quasi-independent bodies and the force of public law tended to become a twilight zone. Nowhere was this dilemma better illustrated than in the bitter dispute over the fiscal autonomy of the *Parte*.[121]

Giano della Bella, patrician leader of the popular regime of 1293–95,

---

[114] *Diplomatico*, Strozzi (November 21, 1311); *Diplomatico*, Spedale degli Innocenti (July 30, 1325).
[115] *P*, 45, fols. 113–14r.
[116] *Ibid.*, 37, f. 23.
[117] *Ibid.*, 39, f. 202.
[118] *CP*, 1, 2, f. 5; *P*, 40, f. 137.
[119] *Parte Guelfa*, numeri rossi, 1, f. 31.
[120] *Statuti del Capitano* (1355), 11, bk. I, rub. 201; *P*, 37, f. 22r.
[121] *Ibid.*, 38, f. 226; *ibid.*, 39, f. 15r.

had been among the first to challenge the warrant of the *Parte* to deprive Florentines of their right to hold office on charges of Ghibellinism. During the middle years of the fourteenth century, the controversy still raged around this crucial question. Did the signory or the *Parte Guelfa* have ultimate jurisdiction in this matter? The legislative debates of 1354 disclose that Florentines were far from united on this question, with the *novi cives* and their allies favoring the signory. In the years immediately following the Black Death, the Ricci clan assumed leadership of the popular party and continued in this role until the end of the 1360s. During these two decades they tended to support measures advocated by the *novi cives* to reduce the influence of the *Parte Guelfa* over communal politics and favored the supremacy of the signory. Uguccione dei Ricci, spokesman for this group, consistently urged the signory to assume responsibility for protecting the liberty of the city against the intrigues of those who threatened the independence and sovereignty of the republic.[122] He included among the foes of *libertà* intransigent feudatories, lawless nobles, avaricious emperors, and designing popes. He was a militant partisan of a pragmatic foreign policy free from commitments to the old Guelf allies—the Holy See and Naples—and a resolute defender of communal sovereignty against the claims of quasi-independent institutions. The assumption of this posture placed him in the vanguard of those who opposed the *Parte Guelfa*. Antagonism mounted when he supported an alliance with the Ghibelline Visconti; this enraged the Albizzi leadership of the *Parte*. He then actively encouraged the Florentines to take up arms against neighboring Pisa and continued to exhort the signory to press on for total victory over its archrival. While his exertions were loudly applauded by the *novi cives* and won Uguccione much popularity among the masses, they were scorned by the prominent oligarchs Piero degli Albizzi and Carlo Strozzi, whose desperate attempts to make peace were vigorously backed by the *Parte* and the papacy.[123]

The *novi cives* were anxious to gain representation in all communal bodies and institutions and looked to Uguccione for leadership. In 1358 they won a singular victory when Uguccione successfully led an assault against the preponderance of aristocratic influence in the *Parte Guelfa;* the proportion of representation accorded the nobility in the captaincy was substantially reduced and the number open to the *novi cives* from the major guilds was increased.[124] Eight years later he again took up the cause of the new men, and, for the first time in communal history, those from the minor guilds were given two seats in the sacred precincts of the *Parte*. A series of provisions were enacted in the winter of 1366 justifying

[122] *CP*, 1, 1, f. 4; *ibid.*, f. 51r; *ibid.*, f. 110.
[123] Cf. footnote 84 and *CP*, 2, f. 119r; *ibid.*, 8, f. 57.
[124] *P*, 45, f. 189.

this radical step; fear was rampant among the citizenry since "even true Guelfs" were being accused of Ghibellinism and driven from public life. By adding new men to the captaincy, the signory hoped to preserve "the good and peaceful state of the city" and defend the "libertà" of its denizens. Before such accusations could be made in the future, they had to be investigated and verified by five of the seven captains from the guilds. Uguccione and his partisans contended that the *Parte Guelfa* desired to enslave Florence, make the inhabitants her vassals, and, thereby, destroy the "buono stato" of her artisan and merchant classes. But the presence of *novi cives* in the supreme magistracy of the *Parte* would prevent this and preserve the *libertà* of the citizenry—"especially the artisans and merchants."[125] A new rapport was emerging between the *novi cives* and those elements of the patriciate hostile to the philopapal, Albizzi-led Guelfs, which had the effect of drawing these men together into a *parte popolare*. When the chief Guelfs of the city objected to receiving new men from the minor guilds into their ranks, Uguccione threatened to assemble the merchants, artisans, and *il popolo* together in a parliament; this, he insinuated, would be the beginning of revolution in Florence.[126] When the captains of the *Parte Guelfa* were charged with having "defamed and injured the priors," Uguccione was quick to suggest that these evil men be punished for their *superbia* and that representatives from the seven major and fourteen minor guilds be called upon to fix the penalties. At this time the Ricci and other popular leaders were coming to rely more upon support of the artisans and "middling citizens" (*modici cives*), new to the political scene, who were consistently in attendance at legislative debates.[127] They urged the communal councils to grant these new men a share of the important posts in the *contado* and advised the signory to consult with the newcomers on formulation of foreign policy. The Ricci and their followers counted upon these new men to be a force "for the public good and the conservation and increase of liberty"; it was hoped

---

[125] *Ibid.*, 54, f. 133r; D. Velluti, *La Cronica domestica*, p. 249. Tommaso di Mone, seller of grain, speaking for the *gonfaloniere*, contended that adoption of these measures would unite the city, strengthen the "populus," and increase the security "of the middling and minor citizenry" (*mediorum et minorum con civium*). Cf. *CP*, 8, f. 1.

[126] The terms used by Uguccione, as reported in the chronicle of Velluti (p. 250), are "i popolari, artefici" and "I popolo di Firenze." These men were to defend "il bene comune" against "le famiglie popolari grandi." Cf. also Stefani, rub. 695. Uguccione's brother Rosso exhorted the signory to elect citizens who were "amatores statum et communis" to conserve the *libertà* of Florence. Cf. *CP*, 8, f. 23r.

[127] *Ibid.*, 8, f. 57. Rosso also criticized the injustices committed by the captains against the lower orders, and he and his brother Uguccione spoke on behalf of legislation favoring the lesser guildsmen. *Ibid.*, 7, fols. 25r, 80, 87. The term "modici cives" first appears in the *Consulte e Pratiche* when the government was urged to convoke an assembly of these men who are described as "sapientes, delectores communis." *Ibid.*, 5, fols. 116r–119r. For a similar request by Uguccione, see *ibid.*, 7, f. 18 (September 27, 1365).

that in the process they would bring honor to the merchant class and stymie the tyrannical aspirations of the *Parte Guelfa*.[128]

Out of the struggle against the *Parte* emerged the most renowned of all *trecento* Florentine popular leaders. Salvestro de' Medici had consistently been an audacious speaker for political causes that were bound to win him the enthusiastic adherence of the *novi cives* from the greater and lesser guilds. In 1363 he boldly proposed that revenues from certain properties belonging to the church be assigned to the republic and that the clergy be compelled to make extensive loans to the communal treasury. In the following year, during another session of the councils, he attacked the philopapal *Parte Guelfa* for its attempt to drive a new citizen from public life for his alleged Ghibelline sympathies; enraged, he went on to suggest that the government should conduct an inquiry into this type of nefarious practice and punish the provocateurs. At the moment when Uguccione was bitterly castigating the *Parte*, Salvestro called upon the prior to resist the machinations of the evil *capitani* who were seeking "to gain control of the city of Florence." Like the Ricci leader, he then entered a plea for unity between merchants and artisans in order that they might "avoid being divided by those who desired to seize power."[129] Along with other popular leaders such as Tommaso Strozzi, Giorgio Scali, Benedetto Alberti, and Filippo di Cionetto Bastari, he advocated that the new middling citizens play a more decisive role in communal affairs; particularly, he desired that they be consulted on the conduct of diplomatic relations with the papacy and be included in the captaincy of the *Parte*. There was little doubt that the advice these *novi cives* offered the signory and Guelf councils would parallel the opinions held by Salvestro and other popular figures: under no circumstances should Florence ally herself with the Holy See; nor should the *Parte* be permitted to continue its reckless proscriptions. These views were anathema to the Albizzi leadership of the Guelfs, and the offense was compounded when Salvestro and the new citizens reopened an old wound in the body politic by again championing an alliance with Ghibelline Milan.[130] Suspicion of papal ambitions in Tuscany persisted and further intensified the hostility of popular leadership; now, more than ever, these men were coming to favor an aggressive, antipapal foreign policy. Salvestro's speeches in the council halls indicate he was the most impassioned spokesman in this cause.[131] Throughout Florentine history there had been others who had assumed a similar stance but they had uttered their sentiments under very different

---

[128] *Ibid.*, 8, fols. 70, 89r; *P*, 54, f. 86r (December 12, 1366).
[129] G. Brucker, "The Medici in the Fourteenth Century," *Speculum*, 32 (1957), 17–18.
[130] *CP*, 12, f. 172r (November 12, 1374); f. 160r (October 31, 1374).
[131] In 1376 he proposed that the government confiscate all ecclesiastical property if the pope did not meet Florentine demands. He went on to suggest that these lands be sold and that the revenue be employed to wage war against the papacy. Cf. *ibid.*, 14, f. 85.

historical conditions. In the late thirteenth and early fourteenth centuries the new men were only perfunctory participants in civic life; however, by the 1360s and 1370s this order provided a substantial political base on which a program could be grounded. Since their entry into Florentine politics in sizable numbers in 1343, the influence of the *novi cives* had been expanding, and their political behavior indicated they would make trustworthy confederates in the chronic struggle to preserve *libertà*.

VI

In the minds of many Florentines, the Albizzi faction and the *Parte Guelfa* stood condemned as the subversive arm of the Holy See plotting to undermine the republic. At the start of the 1370s, the Ricci chiefs were also accused of harboring the same treasonous designs. According to Stefani, Uguccione was bribed with tempting offers of rich ecclesiastical benefices if his kinsmen forsook the cause of the *parte popolare* and joined the Albizzi to bring Florence into the papal camp.[132] As long as these two great clans opposed one another, the republic and its *libertà* were secure, since each was strong enough to prevent the other from completely dominating the machinery of state. However, once a coalition was formed there was the problem of checking its power in order to block the rise of a propapal despotism. If the republic was to be saved, the *parte popolare* would have to be reconstituted as the one force capable of fighting for "the welfare of the commune" (*il bene di comune*).[133] It would then be necessary for them to restrain the political influence of the great clans and, thereby, preserve the rule of public law, communal jurisdiction, state property and rights, and the impersonal machinery of government. The events of January, 1372, justified the worst fears of Stefani and his public-spirited contemporaries: the Ricci did indeed ally with Carlo Strozzi, Bonaiuto de' Serragli, and other prominent members of the revivified Albizzi faction. Strozzi saved the prior Bartolo di Giovanni Siminetti from bankruptcy, and the latter in turn coerced his colleagues into passing a law raising the *Parte Guelfa* authority to unprecedented heights. Michele di Vanni di Ser Lotto, who had labored long and hard with Piero degli Albizzi to ally Florence with the Holy See, was also instrumental in forcing through this legislation.[134] The *Parte* was granted autonomous status and freed from all governmental checks; no measure could be enacted against this organization without obtaining its consent.

[132] Rub. 726.
[133] *Ibid.* For a discussion of the tendency to use the phrases "pro bono communis" and "pro communi bono" interchangeably, see N. Rubinstein, "Political Ideas in Sienese Art," *Journal of the Warburg and Courtauld Institutes*, 5 (1942), 184–85; L. Minio-Paluello, "Remigio de' Girolami's *De bonocommuni*," *Italian Studies*, 11 (1956), 56–59.
[134] D. Velluti, *La Cronica domestica*, p. 253; Stefani, rub. 730.

The laconic Stefani bitterly observed that the merchants and artisans of the city were now indeed the slaves of the tyrannical Albizzi-Ricci faction. His pessimistic sentiments were echoed by the counselors to the signory, and when in April of the same year a new priorate entered office it sought to undo the work of the factious leadership of the *Parte Guelfa*.[135] Sitting in the signory were four *novi cives* and four nonfaction men; only the *gonfaloniere* of justice was a follower of the Albizzi. It was this combination of new men and political independents, backed by Salvestro de' Medici, Giovanni Magalotti, Giovanni di Luigi Mozzi, Luigi di Lippo Aldobrandini, and other popular leaders, who now advanced a far-reaching program for conservation of the republic's *libertà* against their adversaries.

The fundamental legislation enacted by this most democratic of all Florentine regimes was initiated by the *artifices* and *populares* of the republic. The composition of the government from April, 1372, to July, 1375, indicates that the *artifices* were the *novi cives* and the *populares* were the nonfactious independents who now resolutely battled *per il bene di comune*. In documents of the period, this coalition referred to itself as "*artifices* and *populares*" who were "*zelatores* of the popular status of the city."[136] The phrase "popular status of the city" implied the existence of a political atmosphere free from the inordinate influence of the *Parte Guelfa* and the factions. It also connoted a respect for statutory law and the verdicts of communal courts. It postulated impartial assessment and collection of taxes, curtailment of ecclesiastical immunity and privilege, and equality before communal magistracies. Peculation of public funds, revenue delinquencies, and crimes by the powerful against the poor and the weak were not be be tolerated. To this end magistrates were enjoined to obey the letter of the law and not to be swayed by personal considerations. Extensive syndication of all state functionaries became the order of the day. Special officials and new rectors were to be chosen by the signory to buttress public authority in Florentine territories. Other officers with extraordinary powers to enforce governmental edicts were to be elected.[137] The collection of direct taxes was to be regularized and important reforms were to be made in the Florentine treasury. Communal accountants

---

[135] The description of the events offered by Stefani in rub. 731 of his chronicle is substantiated by the records found in Volume 12 of the *Consulte e Pratiche*. See especially folio 10, which contains a report of the famous speech made by Filippo di Cionetto Bastari before the signory, calling upon the citizens to defend the "statum popularis" against the Ricci and Albizzi. The same judgment is expressed by Giovanni di Pagolo Morelli in his *Ricordi*, ed. V. Branca (Florence, 1956), p. 25, when he condemns the Ricci and Albizzi for not allowing the "artefici" and the men "di piccolo affare" to live in peace.
[136] *CP*, 12, f. 13.
[137] *Ibid.*, 12, f. 55r. These men were to preserve the city "in sua libertate." Cf. *ibid.*, 12, fols. 14, 36r.

were selected to protect the estates of minors and to recover usurped properties. Finally, the intractable, lawless elements among the patriciate were to be driven out of political life so that artisans and *populares* might live and work in peace.[138]

The regime of 1372 also proclaimed itself the defender of Florence's most treasured possession—its *libertà*, "whose price no one could estimate."[139] In order to preserve this precious inheritance, it would be necessary to eradicate all factions and divisions within the city. To this end, the signory acted favorably on a petition presented by the "artisans and *populares*" barring leading members of the Ricci and Albizzi houses from public life for a protracted interval. Shortly thereafter, the scope of this law was extended and harsher terms were laid down—again at the behest of artisans and *populares*.[140] At the same time as the signory limited the authority of great families, it acted to enhance the political prestige of new men from the lesser guilds in a most dramatic way. In April, 1372, *minori* were admitted into the *Mercanzia*, the august council of the High Court of the Merchants, for the first time in communal history. Even the relatively democratic Stefani was shocked when the signory accepted the petition requesting elevation of parvenus into the hallowed precincts of this magistracy, and he commented bitterly that the artisans had gained much in past years as a result of conflicts between the Ricci and Albizzi. With the founding of the new signory, he protested, they were entering those halls where only "the most solemn, most experienced, and most wise merchants of Florence" ought by right to sit.[141] Lapo da Castiglionchio, principal publicist for the aristocratic ethos of the *Parte Guelfa* and the archenemy of popular government in Florence at this time, bemoaned the many rewards and honors bestowed upon these unworthy upstarts and later blamed them for the many ills that befell the commune. The laments of Lapo were uttered in the palace of the Guelf party and in letters to his son, but as a member of the *balia* and counselor to the signory he did not oppose the admission of the *novi cives* into the *Mercanzia*; rather, he piously orated that the government should do what was useful for the commune and the guilds.[142] The records of the debates

---

[138] F. Perrens, *Histoire de Florence*, 4, 523; *Diario di anonimo fiorentino*, ed. A. Gherardi (Florence, 1867), p. 494; *Capitoli*, 11, fols. 72, 76, 80.
[139] *P*, 60, f. 2r.
[140] *Ibid.*, 60, f. 157. Under no circumstances was this provision to be suspended.
[141] Rub. 734. See D. Velluti (p. 241) for a description of the effect that factionalism had upon the new men from the lesser guilds. On the seating of these men in the *Mercanzia*, see G. Bonolis, *La giurisdizione della Mercanzia in Firenze nel secolo XIV* (Florence, 1901), p. 82. The petition that initiated this legislation was presented by the "artifices" of Florence. Cf. *CP*, 12, f. 20 (April 21, 1372).
[142] *Ibid.*, 12, f. 20. For the private opinions of Lapo on this question see L. Mehus, *Epistola o sia ragionamento di Messer Lapo da Castiglionchio* (Bologna, 1753), p. 162. For a description of his political outlook, see P. J. Jones, "Florentine Families and

of the councils from 1372 to 1375 indicate that there were other speakers with the same commitments as Lapo who were reluctant to talk against the new men. There was also a misleading unanimity among speakers on the feasibility of establishing an extraordinary commission to repress the overweening power (*maioritas*) of the great families.[143] Even though the Ricci and Albizzi formally agreed to abide by this proposal, they did not abandon their old political grudges and consuming ambitions. Deprived of the authority of public office, they turned away from the signory and embraced the *Parte Guelfa* as the most effective means for realizing their aspirations.

Novi cives and their confederates were firmly entrenched in public life and continued to dominate the signory until 1382. Not satisfied with having reduced the influence of the Albizzi and Ricci over communal affairs, these men now sought for a broader distribution of public offices. The officials elected to investigate usurpation of the commune's rights and properties by the great families soon learned that these selfsame Florentines were also guilty of violating the *divieto*. This ancient legislation prohibited members of the same family from holding high office simultaneously and fixed an interval during which an individual was declared ineligible for re-election; it also prevented the nobility from occupying certain key posts. These enactments gave an impersonal tone to the conduct of civic affairs since they restricted the power of large old families and encouraged the political mobility of *novi cives*. In the judgment of Matteo Villani, it was the *divieto* more than any other single type of legislation, which was responsible for the rise of the new men.[144] The lists of candidates for office inscribed in the *Tratte* reveal that during the seventies large numbers of patricians were barred from office because of the effectiveness of the *divieto*. If one member of the Strozzi family sat in the priorate, fifty of his kinsmen might be denied entry. But like so many other statutes the *divieto* was frequently observed in the breach.[145] Records of the legislative debates before 1372 suggest that enforcement

---

Florentine Diaries in the Fourteenth Century," *Papers of the British School at Rome*, 24 (1956), 191–92.

[143] *CP*, 14, f. 14. Only Uguccione dei Ricci spoke out against this proposal, complaining that it was an illegal measure taken at the behest of private citizens who acted without communal authorization.

[144] M. Villani, 8, 31.

[145] E. Sestan, "Il comune nel trecento," in *Libera Cattedra di Storia della Civiltà Fiorentina: Il Trecento* (Florence, 1953), p. 27. For charges against two members of the Albizzi family accused of violating the *divieto*, see Stefani, rub. 739. The chronicler was one of four communal officials who investigated this matter, and he was convinced of their guilt. Documents in the *Sindacato del Podestà*, 20, fols. 43–45 substantiate this. A summary of these materials can be found in G. Masi's *Il sindacato delle magistrature comunali nel secolo XIV* (Rome, 1930), p. 112.

of the *divieto* was closely tied to other political considerations. The *Parte Guelfa* repeatedly used the tactic of pressing for anti-Ghibelline legislation in order to force the signory to accept a relaxation of the *divieto* against the patriciate and opening certain offices to them.

This curious connection between legislation on the *divieto* and measures against Ghibellines served further to tangle the already complex web of communal politics. When the *Parte* threatened to enforce rigorously the provisions against Ghibellines, the signory proposed that the communal councils agree to a redistribution of offices so that the patriciate might be better represented. Upon occasion the *novi cives* would dissent, and since a two-thirds majority was necessary for passage of legislation, the ameliorative efforts of the signory would be frustrated. It was the presence of new men in government that reduced the number of posts open to older families. In the 1350s, Donato Velluti justified his support of anti-Ghibelline legislation on the grounds that only one of his relations had been declared eligible for office over a four-year period. In his estimation, the term "Ghibelline" was synonymous with the phrase *novi cives* and it was these pushy upstarts who were responsible for his family's dilemma.[146] During subsequent decades the more factious leaders who dominated the *Parte Guelfa* saw the new men as wholly contaminated with the virus of Ghibellinism. Opposition of the *novi cives* to the Albizzi-sponsored papal alliance intensified this animosity, and in the 1370s the *Parte* struck venomously at this group when it ostracized the most prominent of their number on the spurious charge of Ghibellinism.[147] The popular party, led by the Ricci during the fifties and sixties, tended to be just as obdurate in their support of the *divieto* and in their hostility to propapal alliances and anti-Ghibelline legislation. But in 1372 when the Ricci deserted their old political allies and joined the camp of the Albizzi they reversed roles and became ardent proponents of political proscription and extreme partisans of the philopapal policies of the *Parte Guelfa*. The new men, better represented in the signory than at any time since 1347, turned their energies toward conserving popular government. The *Parte Guelfa* had conducted in past times campaigns of vilification and abuse which contributed greatly to the decline of earlier popular regimes. The

---

[146] D. Velluti, *La Cronica domestica*, p. 241. Even those Florentines most hostile to the new men agreed that there were no bona fide Ghibellines in Florence at this time. Cf. "Discorso d'autore incerto (1377)," in G. Capponi, *Storia della repubblica di Firenze* (Florence, 1930), 1, 593. ". . . e veramente ognuno era diventato guelfo d'animo, di volere e di ogni suo pensiero. Potessi dire che a Firenze non fusse alcuno ghibellino che non fussi antichi nobili rubelli: ma della gente comune mezzana e minore di che nazione si fusse tutti di volontà erano guelfi."

[147] Among those accused were Ugolino di Bonsi, seller of spices; Manente d'Amedeo and Valeriano Dolicibene, vintners; Giraldo di Paolo Giraldi, tanner; and numerous others referred to in the judicial records. Cf. especially, *Atti del Esecutore*, Vols. 785, 790.

new men of 1372, much more experienced in the tactics of political warfare, adroitly sought to contain the *Parte* and to eradicate factionalism. Formerly they had attempted to achieve these ends by allying with the Ricci; now they hoped to accomplish them through increasing the impersonal force of government by undermining the political influence of great families of the *Parte Guelfa*. The *divieto* was indeed a powerful weapon in their hands, and by coupling it with the ingenious technique of conferring noble status upon their political adversaries, the *novi cives* could look forward to disfranchising the more hostile elements of the city.

Partisans of the Albizzi-Ricci coalition numbered approximately one-sixth of all Florentines eligible for communal office. The personal and intimate character of urban life made it difficult for men to camouflage their loyalties and political affiliations; therefore it was easy for *novi cives* to seek out their enemies. Ouster of the Albizzi and Ricci from the signory was the first step and was followed by repeated attack against their adherents. These faction men were seen as opponents of the government—revolutionaries, if you will—whose leaders had been barred from public office and whose only remaining political bastion was the *Parte Guelfa*, and even this encampment was becoming insecure. The Florentine state was drifting toward war with the papacy, and by 1375 the philopapal sympathies of the *Parte* bordered on treason. The *Parte* stood against the powerful tide toward war that was coming to be popularly regarded as a crusade in defense of Florence's sacred liberty. When the Albizzi and their followers, from the vantage point of the *Parte*, hurled charges of Ghibellinism against the *novi cives* directing this war for the preservation of the republic, they were placed in the position of seeking to crucify men regarded by the masses as secular saints. *Novi cives* such as Giovanni Dini and Guccio di Dino Gucci were in fact numbered among the "Eight Saints" who demonstrated that they preferred the safety of their country to the salvation of their own souls when they undertook leadership of the government in war. For their heroic efforts, both suffered excommunication at the hands of the church and abuse from the *Parte*. In July, 1378, however, knightly status was bestowed upon these two patriots by a grateful *popolo*. Other new men were also to be dishonored by the papacy and *Parte* only to receive accolades at the hands of the people. Events from 1372 to 1378 tended to make heroes of new men like Tommaso di Mone, also one of the Eight Saints; Niccolò Lapozzi, an official chosen to defend the *libertà* of the city; and Recco di Guido Guazza, proponent of the confiscation of ecclesiastical properties. All these men were excommunicated by the church and attacked by the *Parte*. Andrea di Feo, a paving contractor; Maso di Nero, a ropemaker; Francesco di Geri, an ironmonger; and many others held important offices at this time and suffered assaults from the *Parte*.[148] It was the new men who were the patriots and unequivocal champions of the Florentine republic, while the Guelf patriciate were seen as enemies of the government and perpetrators of sedition.

The overwhelming majority of Florentines eligible for high office during the middle years of the *trecento* were neither extreme Guelf partisans nor committed members of factions; rather, they were political moderates who counseled caution and compromise in most things. Despite their capacity to temporize on a variety of issues, they remained firm in their patriotic commitments to the defense of *libertà* and republican government. They understood well the pragmatic character of Florentine politics and recognized that on the day-to-day level there must be compromise in order to insure survival of the republic. This conciliatory attitude extended even to the burning question of the *divieto* and enforcement of anti-Ghibelline legislation. During the fifties and sixties these moderates favored relaxation of the *divieto* and opposed the extensive use of political proscription. They hoped to reconcile the great families to existing constitutional order by easing stipulations of the *divieto* and, thereby, to convince them it was unnecessary to denounce the *novi cives* as political subversives in order to gain a larger share of communal offices. At the same time they sought to placate the *novi cives* by reducing the threat of political proscription while upholding the principle of the *divieto*. The moderates suggested that the law be suspended for short periods of time, and then only as a temporary measure.[149] The chronicle of Donato Velluti serves to clarify the political dilemma of men of moderate stripe: they were most anxious to remain in the good graces of the *Parte* and yet avoid antagonizing the *novi cives*. Velluti, who wrote about the adverse effect of the *divieto* upon the political ambitions of his own large family, rose in the council halls to exhort the signory to mitigate its most drastic features. In the same speech he urged that priors meet with captains of the *Parte* and reform the anti-Ghibelline legislation. This he did in the company of other Florentine moderates such as Stefano del Forese, Giovanni Lanfredini, and the ubiquitous Giovanni Geri del Bello. These middle-of-the-roaders won their point in 1354, and the captains ceased proscribing Florentine citizens until 1358. In January of that year, new and more terrible procedures were introduced by these captains who, in the opinion of Matteo Villani, desired to intimidate the signory and establish themselves as "little tyrants" over the city.[150] The extreme Guelfs who successfully advocated this reign of terror were overtly propapal and employed the new techniques of political persecution to force through an alliance with the

[148] *Ibid.*, 800, f. 4r.
[149] *CP*, 1, 2, f. 72.
[150] *Ibid.*, fols. 72–73. M. Villani, 8, 31.

papal legate in 1359. Despite efforts of the moderates, the attacks were intensified, and in April 1363, Matteo Villani himself fell victim to the intrigues of the captains on the tired charge of Ghibellinism.[151] His proscription and subsequent dismissal from office revealed the vulnerability of nonfaction men who counseled moderation and stood as political independents. The partisans and allies of the great clans were either represented in the *Parte* or had a voice in the powerful political cliques of the city; in this way they were able to achieve a modicum of security. Now the threat of disfranchisement encompassed the independents as well as the *novi cives*. As much as any other factor, this common insecurity welded these two groups together and induced them to unite against their mutual adversaries.

Few Florentines were optimistic about the outcome of what was now frankly spoken of as "la guerra cittadinesca" raging between the faction men and their opponents. The political confidence of the moderates was giving way to a pervasive sense of despair. Even the most sanguine of Florentine chroniclers, Velluti, could only hope that Divine Providence would end this "citizen war" before it brought his beloved city to ruin, but he seriously doubted that his prayers would be answered.[152] Matteo Villani's history concludes as a diatribe against those men of "pessima e iniqua condizione" who imposed capricious tests of political orthodoxy upon virtuous citizens. Even more vitriolic was his polemic against those captains of the *Parte* who were willing to betray Florence's sacred liberty in exchange for high ecclesiastical office.[153] But the independents sitting in the communal councils at this time were intent upon finding positive remedies for this intolerable situation. No longer did they offer the soothing balm of compromise to the great oligarchs, for it was evident that the Albizzi and *Parte* would not be easily reconciled to the existing constitutional order. Stefani maintained that the citizens felt they were now at the mercy of the evil Guelf captains.[154] In January, 1364, Giovanni Geri del Bello, advisor to the signory, charged the captains were unjustly defaming "good citizens" who were known to be ardent supporters of Guelfic principles. He then called upon the priorate to act as "savior" (salutificator) of the beleaguered citizenry. Others speaking on this question, who became prominent in the government after 1372 as political independents, were Barna di Valorino Curiani, Niccolò Alberti, Bernardo Bigliotti, and the candid Salvestro de' Medici; they, too, recognized that the signory had

---

[151] G. Brucker, "Trial of Matteo Villani," pp. 49–50.
[152] D. Velluti, *La Cronica domestica*, p. 241; G. Capponi, *Storia della repubblica*, Vol. 1, p. 593.
[153] G. Brucker, "Trial of Matteo Villani," pp. 53–55.
[154] Stefani, rub. 674. Stefani's contention is supported by the fact that large numbers of prominent citizens were being persecuted by the *Parte*. Cf. rub. 743; *Atti del Esecutore*, Vols. 752, 790.

to stand as a buffer against the tyrannous aspirations of those who sought to overthrow the popular and free status of the city.[155]

Many of the men the *Parte* denounced as Ghibellines were notaries who held a variety of administrative positions in the city and countryside. As early as February, 1347, less than a month after enactment of the initial laws against Ghibellines, when the first proscriptions took place, a number of these officeholders were charged with political heterodoxy.[156] These notaries constituted the hard core of the Florentine bureaucracy, and without their continued participation in civil life it would have been difficult to carry on the daily business of government. The notary performed those routine political tasks which most directly impinged upon the daily life of the citizenry, ranging from the enforcement of verdicts of the courts to the maintenance of walls, bridges, and roads. It was these men who conducted investigations of such sensitive questions as the peculation of communal funds and the usurpation of state property. They also handled the payment of mercenaries, the collection of many different but equally unpopular communal levies, and acted as conservers of the republic's rights. In the course of these manifold activities they were subject to a plethora of pressures from those desiring a reduction in their tax assessment, a lowering of their *gabelle*, certification of payments alleged to have been made on behalf of the commune, title to disputed property, the squelching of investigations, and favorable action in the matter of the exercise of extralegal authority by the great patricians of the city and *contado*. If these lesser officeholders could resist the threats and blandishments of the overmighty, then impersonal government would indeed have some opportunity to survive in Florence. In enforcing the verdicts of the courts and carrying out the letter of the law, these notaries risked incurring the enmity of powerfully entrenched interests and even the disfavor of their own fellow citizens. Their problems were compounded since they were, for the most part, *novi cives* of modest origins and, therefore, contemptible to those whose *dignitas* and pride of blood set them above the rule of communal law. It can be suggested that the antipathy of the *potentes* toward state functionaries was directly proportional to the officeholder's lack of status and to the frequency with which the exercise of his duties interfered with the interests of the aforesaid patricians.

That lesser men of state came under the concerted attack of the dynasts implies that the political importance of minor posts frequently was not commensurate with the humble title used to designate the routine character of their function. These men were pickets on the boundary line that separated public law from private rights. The signory could not afford

---

[155] *CP*, 5, f. 7. Benedetto di Geri del Bello, Giovanni's brother, was proscribed by the *Parte* in 1377. Cf. Stefani, 770.
[156] *Atti del Esecutore*, 79, fols. 7–7r.

to regard these political careerists, bureaucrats, and civil servants as pawns to be sacrificed in artfully waged civic games without suffering a considerable attrition of its own authority. Matteo Villani held the controversial post of official over the funded communal debt when he fell victim to the machinations of the *Parte*. Other officers of the Florentine treasury who suffered an identical fate were Giovanni Parenti and Michele di Puccio.[157] Communal officials over the grain supply, the shops of the *Platea*, those in charge of the assets of bankrupts, syndics over judicial officers, reviewers of the accounts of the republic, rectors over communal property, those empowered to enforce the city's sumptuary laws, tax collectors, and a host of other civil servants who served in numerous key positions throughout the Tuscan countryside were all casualties of the bitter political vendetta being waged by the *Parte Guelfa* against Florentine officialdom.

In 1366 the *Parte* struck at the most prominent of the republic's bureaucratic luminaries when it ostracized Niccolò di Ser Ventura Monachi, chancellor of the commune, on the shopworn charge of Ghibellinism. This time the signory rose up and defended Monachi with a will. The sentence of the *Parte* was canceled by action of the priorate and communal councils. Because of his laudable character, his sincere faith, his great prudence, and his faithful labors on behalf of the republic, the chancellor was restored to the full honors of his office and his rightful place among the Guelf hosts of Italy.[158] Unfortunately for Monachi, however, the case was far from closed, and during the following decade the political persecution of this leading civil servant was resumed. His tribulations bring to light the complex interplay of personal motives behind the attacks on Florentine bureaucrats. Monachi had incurred the hatred of Bonaiuto de Ser Belcaro, of the patrician house of Serragli, for being the instigator of an accusation brought against the latter in the Court of the Executor. It was alleged that when Bonaiuto had been prior in 1372, he exerted pressure upon the government to grant a certain rural commune, in which he had an interest, a substantial reduction in its tax assessment. The unnamed men who presented this indictment, presumably inspired by Monachi, are referred to in the copy of the charges as peaceful merchants, artisans, and guildsmen—good citizens all. It was their contention that Bonaiuto had accepted a bribe and acted to defraud the republic of

---

[157] *Estimo*, 307, f. 1; *P*, 36, f. 69. Another leading Florentine bureaucrat, Donato del Ricco, a lawyer, was also struck down by the *Parte*. In 1366 he spoke in favor of adding two minor guildsmen to the Guelf captaincy. Three years later he opposed sending a subsidy to the Holy See, and in the following decade he counseled that Florence make war "viriliter" against the church and under no circumstances should the commune settle for anything less than complete victory. Cf. *P*, 54, fols. 81–83; *CP*, 10, fols. 107, 129r; *ibid.*, 14, fols. 78r, 86; Stefani, rub. 775.

[158] D. Marzi, *La cancelleria*, pp. 99–101.

its rightful revenues.¹⁵⁹ There were great outcries of popular discontent when the magistrate failed to convict Bonaiuto on this count, so convinced of his guilt were the Florentines. Three years later Bonaiuto was chosen chief of the priorate by the Florentine system of lots and thus not in a position to be revenged. Monachi was deposed from the office of chancellor, and in 1378 this "truthful, loyal man," outspoken foe of that sect of "criminal men" who loved to proscribe "against every dictate of reason," was finally branded Ghibelline.¹⁶⁰

The figure behind Monachi's disfranchisement in 1378 was Lapo da Castiglionchio, the most vigorous and most despised of all proponents of Guelf orthodoxy. Married into the highest echelons of the Florentine aristocracy—Bardi, Cerchi, Amieri, Cavalcanti—claiming direct descent from the most ancient of the Tuscan feudatories, loathing trade and tradesmen, this *grande* prized "the lordly life" (*la vita signorile*) which prevailed in those happy days when his patrician forebears had ruled Florence. For him commerce was degrading and true grandeur possible only for those who never stooped to the vile *arti* or *mercanzia*, but conducted themselves like the nobility of old, preferring country life, estate management, and the chase, to the meaner pursuits of the city. For the most part, urban life was without honor and never bestowed "great fame" on those families who deserted their ancestral heritage. Lapo's model Florentine family was the Ricasoli, who, like the Castiglionchi, were "noble, venerable and great men," contemptuous of the new vulgar pursuits and who held tenaciously to the old ways, maintaining themselves in "grandeur" in the countryside. Indeed, it was true that in recent times some of the Ricasoli had become merchants, but they had only trafficked in the noble wool trade with foreign lands and not in "base merchandise." Unlike the *nouveaux riches*, the Ricasoli, Bardi, and Peruzzi were merchant pilgrims engaged in the virtuous business of the *arte della lana* and not in petty affairs or usurious transactions.¹⁶¹

Lapo's zeal for the traditional was matched only by his contempt for the new order and its principal harbingers, the *novi cives*. Had not some of these upstarts been vassals of the Castiglionchio family who had gone to the city, made their fortunes in base trades, and then acquired the precious right of citizenship? Now these new men of *piccolo affari* sat in the communal councils and were too presumptuous to heed the wise advice of their betters. Lapo bemoaned the fact that these parvenus had become so powerful a force in Florentine politics by 1373 that it had become necessary to

---

¹⁵⁹ *Atti del Esecutore*, 675, f. 32; Stefani, rub. 749; *Parte Guelfa*, numeri rossi, 5, f. 49.
¹⁶⁰ Stefani, rub. 735. Monachi's own guild, the judges and notaries, conducted an investigation into his proscription and stated that it was clearly illegal. Cf. D. Marzi, *La cancelleria*, pp. 101-2.
¹⁶¹ L. Mehus, *Epistola*, pp. 43-45, 147-48; P. J. Jones, "Florentine Families," pp. 191-92.

grant them very important concessions. He wondered whether it was ever truly possible to dissolve the bonds of fealty. Were not these new men indeed still vassals in the sight of God, since their ancestors took an oath that bound them to their lord in perpetuity? But nowadays the new men have forgotten their ancient ties and no longer have "the old love" for patrician families such as the Ricasoli, Serragli, and Castiglionchi. The same men who lacked respect for the prerogatives of the patriciate were also without reverence for Holy Church and were, therefore, to be numbered among her Ghibelline foes who richly deserved the political fate which the *Parte* had in store for them.

Lapo, eminent canon lawyer and lecturer on the Decretals; his brother, Alberto, captain of the *Parte Guelfa* in 1366 when the first attempt was made to proscribe Monachi; and his nephew, Simone di Francesco da Castiglionchio, who denounced Matteo Villani as a Ghibelline, were among the most rabid partisans of Guelf political orthodoxy.[162] The traditional meaning of Ghibellinism, with its emphasis upon strict loyalty to the imperial cause, was alien to Lapo and his generation, for was not the papacy itself looking for an alliance with the emperor which would help to restore the Holy See to Rome? By their definition, Ghibellines did not revere the patriciate, were in sympathy with the *novi cives*, and were without devotion to Holy Mother Church. To Lapo and his cohorts, the government that waged war against the papacy from 1375 to 1378 had departed so far from these Guelf principles that it deserved to be stigmatized as Ghibelline.[163]

[162] D. Marzi, *La cancelleria*, p. 100; G. Brucker, "Trial of Matteo Villani," 50–51. Tribaldo da Castiglionchio was also high in the councils of the *Parte*, and in 1354 he spoke for the enactment of anti-Ghibelline legislation before representatives of the commune. Cf. *P*, 41, f. 63. The case of Alberto suggests that holding high office in the *Parte* was not without its advantages. He was convicted by the communal courts for peculation of state funds when serving as a *castellano* in the Florentine *contado*. He petitioned the signory for judicial dispensation and it was granted. Cf. *ibid.*, 42, 133r (October 9, 1355). Lapo himself was accused of using a public trust—in this instance, his position as Florentine ambassador to the papal court—to advance the interests of his own family. Specifically, the charge involved his willingness to compromise his city in return for benefices to be conferred upon his nephew, Simone di Francesco. Cf. *Atti del Esecutore*, 510, fols. 29–30r (June 29, 1367). Despite the concreteness of the allegations, Lapo was exonerated on all counts. In 1377 he was made a *savio* of the *Parte* for life. Cf. Stefani, rub. 775.

[163] Lapo writes in a bizarre manner of the origin of the names "Ghibelline" and "Guelf." The former stems from "gerentes bellum" against the Holy See, while the latter is derived from "gerentes fidem" to the church. Cf. R. Davidsohn, "Tre orazioni di Lapo da Castiglionchio," *ASI*, 20 (1897), 225–46; L. Mehus, *Epistola*, p. 78. Lapo consistently favored very close ties with the church. In 1367, when an alliance with Milan—the foremost papal antagonist at this time—was being hotly debated in the government, Lapo argued that the priors "in no way ought to remove Florence's obedience and devotion from the Roman church." If the papacy desires an alliance against Milan, Florence should not decline, for disobedience to the will of the pope is dangerous to the well-being of Guelf cities. Cf. *CP*, 9, f. 22r. The following year he counseled that it

Prior to 1375, the attacks of the *Parte* were sporadic rather than sustained, but after the outbreak of the war against the papacy they were intensified until they became an all-out assault directed against the state itself. At a time when the signory was telling the populace that Florence was engaged in a struggle to preserve her liberty against the onslaughts of her mortal enemies, the rapacious papal lieutenants, Lapo was contending that the republic had embarked on an evil venture against an invincible enemy which was certain to end disastrously unless the Florentines sued for peace.[164] In the language of Virgil, whom he so much admired, Lapo "had hardened his heart to the internecine strife" and was willing to use the power of the *Parte* to drive those political independents and *novi cives* who were enemies of Mother Church from the government so that this unholiest of wars might be terminated. But the signory was not content to sit idly by and turn the other cheek while its membership was suffering political proscription. The government countered with the most refined and artful techniques of political character assassination calculated to discredit Lapo and his ilk. The Ricasoli and Serragli were charged with being "ferocious and lawless nobles," and the ultimate weapon was used when they, along with the Castiglionchi, were accused of being Ghibellines.[165] So successful was this campaign of vilification that in June, 1378, when the populace rioted, it was against these obstreperous aristocrats that it moved with torch and ban of exile.

The hero of this coup was Salvestro de' Medici, who acted *pro parte popularium mercatorum et artificum* to protect "the merchants and artisans, the poor and the weak" and all those who desired to live in peace, free from the menace of the fierce nobility. The *Parte* was accused of promoting dangerous innovations and fomenting violence which had swept

---

would not "be useful to make an alliance with Bernabo [Visconti] *qui natura repugnat guelfum ghibellino inimicho (sic)."* He went on to advise the signory not to ally with the Holy Roman Emperor or to vote him a subsidy until His Majesty promised to do the will of the church. Needless to say, Salvestro de' Medici and such leading new men as Tellino Dini, ironmonger; Ricco Taldi, coopersmith; and Schiatta di Ricco, pork butcher, were not in agreement with the opinions of the doctrinaire Guelf. Cf. *ibid.*, 10, f. 38r; *ibid.*, 9, f. 22r.

[164] He went on to state that even though the forces of the church might be driven out of Italy, the Holy See would remain there "in facto et jure. Et ideo pax sine intermissione procuretur." Cf. *ibid.*, f. 65 (December 26, 1377), The speaker for the *gonfaloniere* expressed an antithetical view when he called the papal vicars "vulpini." Another spokesman from the same college castigated the iniquitous Tuscan prelates and called them "rebelles" and "hostes" of the commune. Cf. *ibid.*, 15, f. 29 (August 14, 1377); f. 47 (October 17, 1377). The entry for May 11, 1376, in the *Diario di anonimo fiorentino,* p. 308, calls the Florentines "veri cristiani eletti da Dio" to contest the authority of the papacy. It is well to remember that the antipapal teachings of the Fraticelli were intense at this time. Cf. M. Becker, "Politics and Heresy," pp. 71–73.

[165] *Atti del Esecutore*, Vols. 752–806. In Salutati's opinion, Lapo would have done well to remain a man of letters. Cited by P. J. Jones, "Florentine Families," p. 192.

the city to the brink of revolution. Through its flagrant and unscrupulous use of proscription, the *Parte* had caused "scandala" and instigated a reign of terror among the citizenry. Therefore, in order to restore the city to that free and peaceful condition so necessary for the well-being of the artisans and merchants, the *Parte* was to be stripped of its authority and the contentious nobility to be vigorously persecuted. To this end, legislation sponsored by Salvestro was promptly enacted and a special commission established to rule over the city. Two-thirds of the membership of this *balìa* were *novi cives*, and they were enjoined to remove the yoke of the *Parte* from the shoulders of the citizenry. One of their first measures was to declare Lapo a rebel and to deprive his clique of their political rights.[166]

The new men and the political independents had achieved a *concordia ordinum* which enabled them to strengthen the machinery of state. Brought together by the fiery hostility of factions and the animus of the *Parte Guelfa*, personal antagonisms, suspicions, and social prejudices tended to erode. These two groups co-operated in advancing a program that exalted the authority of the signory to unprecedented heights. More intensively than ever, they employed state power to reduce the influence of great families over the Florentine church, contending that these patricians were using ecclesiastical courts to exploit "artisans and *populares*." Then they proceeded to attack clerical tribunals, which in their opinion had been responsible for much injustice and oppression; a provision was enacted permitting any citizen to appeal from a verdict of these courts to the signory. The government also sought to render ineffectual the authority of the inquisition in territories under Florentine jurisdiction. State officials replaced clergy in certain instances as executors of last wills and testaments. Ecclesiastical tax immunities were revoked, clergy were compelled to pay heavy imposts, and numerous church properties were confiscated by the state to be sold or rented to the Florentines. The signory treated the problems of usury, the licensing of pawnbrokers, and the taking of interest as matters to be dealt with by public law without any concern for traditional ecclesiastical prerogatives. Never before had the *divieto* been used with such telling effect to preserve authority of the state against the might of old families. A protracted campaign was conducted by the signory to rectify certain economic abuses prevalent in civic life so that communal rights would prevail over private interests.[167]

By 1378 this *consensus omnium bonorum* had not only resulted in strengthening the government as a buffer against the aggressive aristocracy, but it had also altered markedly the status of new men. The latter

---

[166] C. Falletti-Fossati, *Il tumulto dei Ciompi* (Florence, 1882), p. 328. Lapo's home was one of the first to be burned and three years later he died in exile.
[167] Cf. especially, *CP*, Vols. 14–15; *P*, 63, fols. 70r ff.; *P*, 66, fols. 1–53.

were in a position where they could justly claim citizenship, not merely because they had satisfied legal technicalities or economic requirements, but rather on the grounds that they had fulfilled the moral expectancies of their society. Petrarch in defining the term "cives" wrote, "By citizens, of course, I mean those who love the existing order; for those who daily desire change are rebels and traitors, and against such, a stern justice may take its course."[168] It was the *novi cives* and their allies who best met Petrach's definition.

This transvaluation of values whereby the *novi cives* who had been regarded as the sowers of civic discord in the age of Dante, only to become the defenders of the commonwealth three generations later, found expression in the lives and writings of the eminent humanists of the late fourteenth and early fifteenth centuries. To Coluccio Salutati, Florence was a city of "merchants and artisans," not of soldiers, knights, and nobles, for without trade and industry the city could not hope to survive. It was the moderate guildsmen, great and small, who had acted to help preserve the liberty of the people against the excesses of the *Parte Guelfa* and the *superbia* of the nobles.[169] This view was imbedded in Florentine historiography until challenged by Machiavelli at the beginning of the sixteenth century. In the early *quattrocento* the prominent humanist Leonardo Bruni Aretino praised those popular regimes which the Greeks called "democratic" because it was only under this type of government that liberty and equality before the law could be safeguarded: "All our laws aim only for this, that the [Florentine] citizens may be equal because true liberty has roots only in equality."[170] This just condition could only be maintained, according to Bruni, if the most powerful families were prevented from monopolizing public office. Poggio Bracciolini, leading exponent of the classics and a successor of Bruni in the Florentine chancellery, extolled trade and commerce because it was only through these activities that cities gained the wealth that made possible their splendor, beauty, and art. He canonized bourgeois virtue by arguing that the desire for riches was good since it was natural to all men, and he condemned those who preached disrespect for material possessions as hypocrites.[171] Finally, it should be noted that Coluccio, Bruni, and Poggio,

---

[168] *Epistolae Seniles*, 14, 1, to Francesco di Carrera (November 28, 1373). The relevant passage is cited by Jacob Burckhardt in *The Civilization of the Renaissance in Italy* (New York, 1958), 1, 28.

[169] E. Garin, "Cancellieri umanisti," pp. 194–95. The same point of view is expressed in the *Diario di anonimo fiorentino*, pp. 291 ff.

[170] E. Garin, "Cancellieri umanisti," p. 200; H. Baron, *Humanistic and Political Literature in Florence and Venice at the Beginning of the Quattrocento* (Cambridge, Mass., 1955).

[171] E. Garin, *L'umanesimo italiano* (Bari, 1952), pp. 59–60; H. Baron, "Franciscan Poverty and Civic Wealth as Factors in the Rise of Humanistic Thought," *Speculum*, 13 (1938), 16 ff.

along with their fellow humanists Carlo Marzuppini and Benedetto Accolti, were all *novi cives,* and each in turn was elevated to the exalted office of Chancellor of the Republic. Unlike their famous predecessors Brunetto Latini and Monachi and their *trecento* literary prototypes Dante, Compagni, and the Villanis, each of whom suffered political persecution at the hands of their compatriots, the latter-day humanists lived out their lives secure in the service of the state. That they were born in Arezzo, Terra Nuova, or Stignano in Val di Nievole was the occasion neither for scorn nor ridicule nor political proscription.

THE *MONTE* FROM ITS FOUNDING (1343–45) UNTIL THE LATE FOURTEENTH CENTURY

At the risk of being overly solicitous for the well-being of the reader soon to be led through a maze of economic data, I would like to repeat something of the earlier description of public finance and the founding of the funded communal debt or *Monte*.

Even at the height of Florentine prosperity (1336–38), the total income of the commune was barely sufficient to cover half of the republic's ever-mounting expenditures. This circumstance stemmed from the costly wars Florence was compelled to wage throughout the fourteenth century.[1] Previously, the armies of Florence had been drawn from the populace, and the budget had reflected this fact. In 1303 the communal debt had been trifling; within a generation, however, it had increased to a grand total of 450,000 florins, which was in excess of the amount the city could hope to raise from all revenue sources over a sixteen-month period. Giovanni Villani tells us the outlay for troops averaged 140,000 florins between 1336 and 1338. As a bitter afterthought he adds that this exorbitant sum did not include pay for mercenaries hired by the republic to fight the disastrous campaigns in Lombardy. By 1342 the public debt had reached 800,000 florins. In the same year the number of mercenaries enrolled in the Florentine armies was twenty times greater than citizen levies. These military expenses, more than any other

---

[1] For bibliography on this and other questions concerning communal finance, see M. Becker, "Problemi della finanza pubblica fiorentina della seconda metà del Trecento e dei primi del Quattrocento," *ASI*, 133 (1965), 434–66; G. Brucker, *Florentine Politics and Society*, pp. 403–8. On the origins of the *Monte*, see B. Barbadoro, *Le finanze della repubblica fiorentina* (Florence, 1929), pp. 629–87. For a treatment of the *Monte* in the *quattrocento*, see L. Marks, "The Financial Oligarchy in Florence under Lorenzo," in *Italian Renaissance Studies* (New York, 1960), pp. 123–45. Cf. also G. Brucker, "Un documento fiorentino sulla guerra, sulla finanza e sulla amministrazione pubblica (1375)," *ASI*, 115 (1957), 169; E. Fiumi, "Fioritura e decadenza dell'economia fiorentina," *ASI*, 117 (1959), 427–502; A. Sapori, *L'età della rinascita* (Milan, 1958), pp. 149–54. For the military background, see C. C. Bayley, *War and Society in Renaissance Florence* (Toronto, 1961), pp. 3–58; M. Becker, "Economic Change and the Emerging Florentine Territorial State," *Studies in the Renaissance*, 13 (1965), 7–39.

single factor, brought on the formation of the consolidated public debt, and their continued incidence caused this debt or *Monte* to surge ever upward. By the end of the fourteenth century it totaled over 3,000,000 florins, and by the middle years of the fifteenth century, when Florence incurred new liabilities through the formation of the *Monte delle Doti*, it climbed to the astronomical figure of 8,000,000 florins. The way in which it accumulated, and its sharp ascent, remain neglected facets of Florentine history; yet to understand the emergence of new loyalties and the rise of a new political mentality, we must treat the *Monte* with the respect it merits.

An increase of public indebtedness from 47,275 florins in 1303 to 3,000,000 florins in 1400, and finally 8,000,000 florins just two generations later, of course would contribute to the irreversible decline of medieval political and economic structures. New allegiances and bonds would be created; private interests would diminish in the face of a mounting concern with state affairs. In communal society, the church, nobility, confraternities, *Parte Guelfa*, and great guilds with their affluent burghers had provided capital and credit; until then money and credit had been almost exclusively in the hands of these orders and medieval corporations, for the commune had little wealth. By the fifteenth century, however, the state had become the largest consumer of capital with a rentier class investing heavily in the interest-bearing public debt. There was a movement from a private system of multiple economies—lay and ecclesiastical—toward the formation of a more unitary public fiscal structure. The management of this debt affected not only the fortunes of the citizenry but even the well-being of the Florentine business community that was employing *Monte* shares as negotiable instruments.

The story of this funded communal debt occupies a central position in the writings of the major chronicler, Matteo Villani, and it is not surprising to discover that he was also a *Monte* official.[2] The chronicler Stefani, our best source for the events of the 1370s, believed that the reduction of interest rates on the debt was the single most important measure to be taken by the government in over a century.[3] In the *quat-*

---

[2] G. Brucker, "The Ghibelline Trial of Matteo Villani (1362)," *Medievalia et Humanistica*, 13 (1960), 52–54. For materials pertaining to Matteo's political career and patrimony, see *LF*, 34, f. 26r (September 11, 1355). Cf. also *Estimo*, 8, f. 77; *Prestanze*, 83, f. 18; *Monte*, 442, f. 59. His experience with the *Monte* adds dimension to the observations he makes in his chronicle (M. Villani, *Cronica*, ed. F. Dragomanni [Florence, 1844–45], 8, 71). Another chronicler much involved in state fiscal matters was Donato Velluti, keeper of the best domestic chronicle for the middle years of the *trecento*. Cf. *La Cronica domestica*, ed. I del Lungo and G. Volpe (Florence, 1914); *LF*, 23, f. 15r (May 26, 1344).

[3] Stefani, rub. 883–84. For his career as a communal financial official, see *Prestanze*, 368, f. 1r; *CP*, 14, f. 87; *CCE*, 158, unnumbered folio (February 27, 1374). For additional biographical detail, see A. Panella, "Per la biografia del cronista Marchionne di

trocento, when communal councils spoke of the *Monte* as "the heart of this body that we call city. . . [which] every limb, large and small, must contribute to preserving . . . ," and described the same *Monte* "as the guardian fortress, immovable rock and enduring certainty of the salvation of the whole body and government of your state," they were indulging in much more than ponderous metaphor.[4] It was indeed an exact, if flowery, description of the economic heart of a new organism—the Renaissance territorial state. We might begin by asking this question: How much was the sum of 8,000,000 florins? The answer, if we employ the tax returns of 1427, would be that it was an amount of money approximately equal to the total wealth of the Florentine populace. In other words, the state debt had grown until it was equal to the entire capital of the Florentine citizenry; thus the entire state budget would not suffice to pay the carrying charges.[5] Next we might inquire into how and why this curiously modern system of deficit finance gained such momentum in the years just before the Black Death.

The medieval system of gabelles, or indirect taxes, was inadequate to underwrite the military expenses of the commune, and what is more, between 1339 and 1342, the years immediately preceding the founding of the *Monte*, returns from the gabelles decreased alarmingly.[6] It was evident that the days of an ever-expanding economy were at an end. This is not to suggest, as several modern economic historians have done, that Florence was caught in the irreversible grip of a terrible depression. Nothing could be farther from the truth: rather, it is to propose that the halcyon days of the medieval upswing were waning. It is important to realize that the economy remained viable, and was in fact to demonstrate an astounding resiliency. However, beginning in 1339 we witness a general deterioration in the returns from gabelles. The republic's revenue from her single most important impost, the customs toll, had reached 90,200 florins by the year 1337. Very soon, however, it tapered off and then plunged precipitously. In the following year it returned 83,500 florins, and by 1343 the income had fallen to 68,000 florins. The city's

---

Coppo Stefani," *ASI*, 88 (1930), 241–53; M. Becker, "Un avvenimento riguardante il cronista Marchionne di Coppo Stefani," *ASI*, 117 (1959), 137–46.

[4] L. Marks, "The Financial Oligarchy in Florence under Lorenzo," in *Italian Renaissance Studies* (New York, 1960), pp. 127–28.

[5] P. J. Jones, "Florentine Families and Florentine Diaries in the Fourteenth Century," *Papers of the British School at Rome*, 24 (1956), 197, n. 113.

[6] Evidence for this statement is derived from the figures presented by Giovanni Villani in his *Cronica*, 11, 92, for the biennium 1336–38. For returns from the customs toll for 1343, see *CCE*, 5, f. 18. It is important to note that when this gabelle was sold on January 13, 1339, it brought in 14,200 florins less than it had yielded in 1336–38. Figures for the gabelle on wine, contracts, salt, and other communal levies are taken from *CCE*, 2 bis, *passim*.

most lucrative tax was the levy on the sale of wine: it averaged 58,000 florins between 1336 and 1338, but by 1342 it had dropped to 36,000 florins. The returns from the gabelle on contracts show a similar fluctuation during these critical years: for the biennium 1336–38 it had totaled 20,000 florins annually, but within four years it had lost two-thirds of its value. The impost on salt averaged 14,450 florins for the interval 1336–38, but by 1342 it had plunged to 4,679 florins. Comparable patterns of steep decline are evinced by the many other communal levies, and judging from these crucial indicators of communal well-being, we can conclude that the bottom of the curve of state finances was reached late in 1342.[7]

The decline in public revenues is but one of the many indexes that can assist us in determining the locus of the darkest part of the communal depression. As early as 1339 the signory had found it extremely difficult to farm out Florentine taxes. The annual auctions had been able to turn up very few publicans willing to advance money to the treasury for the right to collect certain of the imposts. Moreover, many of those who had purchased this right were unable to make payment because the yield had fallen far below its anticipated level. Therefore the signory was compelled to establish special commissions for the purpose of collecting those taxes that could no longer be farmed out. The yield from rural imposts was also dwindling, and groups of tradesmen and shopkeepers such as the vintners and butchers tearfully petitioned the signory for tax relief. Villages and hamlets were likewise unable to fulfill their obligations to the commune, and their syndics railed against the evil times, lamenting the failure of crops and calling for a redress of grievances. The number of small landowners in the *contado* had declined, and as a result the commune acted to reduce the rural property tax by some 75,000 lire.[8]

By 1341 it had become apparent that unless the fiscal structure of the Florentine commune were altered drastically, the state faced bankruptcy. In January of that year the government announced that revenues from indirect taxes were no longer adequate to finance the republic's military ventures. At that moment it was suggested that lands and capital be taxed. The overwhelming resistance to this proposal is a fact of

---

[7] The records of the *Camera del Comune* indicate that this occurred in November of that fateful year, and it was at that time that Walter of Brienne, short-lived despot of the city, enacted a decree declaring a moratorium on communal debts. The treasury balance was just above 15,000 florins, barely enough to meet the daily exigencies of government. Cf. A. Sapori, *Le crisi della compagnie mercantili dei Bardi e dei Peruzzi* (Florence, 1926), pp. 148–51; *CCE*, 2 bis, f. 7.

[8] B. Barbadoro, *Le finanze*, p. 616; A. Sapori, *Le crisi*, p. 138. Among purchasers of communal imposts who were unable to meet their obligations to the treasury were the buyers of the *gabella portarum*, the gabelle on wine, cattle, mills, hawkers of foods, and the levy on communal property. Cf. *CCE*, 2 bis, fols. 157r–158r, 187r, 219, 313.

particular significance for an understanding of the economic mentality of Florentine politicians.⁹ Tradition and economic interest dictated a policy that formed the basis of the Florentine Renaissance state. The elite—both new and old—held strongly to conservative communal fiscal thinking: the government must be financed through indirect taxes and *prestanze*.¹⁰ The latter were loans by private citizens at rates of interest well above those realized from landed investment. Fifteen per cent was not at all uncommon. Instead of paying taxes, then, an affluent Florentine lent money to the republic—and gained a sizable income. Ironically, the government could not hope to repay the principal on these loans unless new sources of taxation were unearthed. Much has been made of the feeble efforts to discover these new sources, but the fact remains that even after they were found they were not tapped appreciably.¹¹ This essentially is the way the *Monte* came into being and grew until it became the very "heart" of public life.

I

Revolution broke out in late September, 1343; *il popolo* were enraged against certain high-born commoners and their magnate colleagues who had collaborated in that most aristocratic of all Florentine regimes, which

---

⁹ After 1315 the dreaded *estimo* was suppressed, and only under the despotism of Charles of Calabria (1325–28) and Walter of Brienne (1342–43) was it revived. Cf. M. Becker, "Some Aspects of Oligarchical, Dictatorial, and Popular *Signorie* in Florence, 1282–1382," *Comparative Studies in Society and History*, 2 (1960), 434–38. The greater guildsmen who completely dominated the signory at this time repeatedly rejected the imposition of the *estimo*, as well as any levy on the guilds themselves. Cf. *LF*, 14, ff. 41r–43, 45; *ibid.*, 19, f. 118; *ibid.*, 20, f. 59.

¹⁰ Time and time again, advisers to the signory urged the government to impose new gabelles or to ask for voluntary loans; only when these remedies were exhausted would the speakers consent to discuss more drastic alternatives. In the matter of gabelles the tendency was to oppose the *gabella mercantie* and other imposts that fell most heavily upon the *arti maggiori* and to favor levies on such commodities as wine, bread, or meat. In 1351 Uguccione Ricciardi made a novel suggestion to the signory: Instead of imposing a tax on *mercantie*, compel the citizens to serve in the Florentine garrisons without pay. Jacopo Banco Puccio, another speaker, much preferred exacting money through voluntary loans and then hiring mercenaries. When the most democratic of all Florentine regimes (1378–82) was finally able to enact direct taxation, the advisers to the signory demanded that taxpayers be given interest; in effect, this converted an *estimo* into a *prestanza*. Cf. *CP*, 1, part 1, and *CP*, 17, *passim*.

¹¹ The *catasti* of Florentine citizens in 1427 yielded 25,341 florins, of which less than one-quarter was contributed by commercial wealth. The *contadini* paid in over three times this amount. See P. J. Jones, "Florentine Families," p. 187; G. Cavalcanti, *Istorie fiorentine*, ed. G. di Pino (Milan, 1945), 4, 8; P. Berti, "Nuovi documenti intorno al catasto fiorentino," *Giornale Storico degli Archivi Toscani*, 4 (1860), 32–62. The text of the enabling act founding the *Catasto* was published by O. Karmin, *La legge del catasto fiorentino del 1427* (Florence, 1906), pp. 11 ff. It should be noted that the interests of the major guildsmen were insured by the proviso that eight of the ten officials in charge of assessing this tax were to be elected by the major guilds.

governed from late July of that year until late September.[12] A vengeful citizenry demanding a swift and terrible justice teemed into the streets and soon overran the broad piazzas. The Adimari, Acciaiuoli, Bardi, and many other patrician clans implicated in the recent fiscal and military disasters lost what contemporary chroniclers spoke of respectfully as "lo stato." The term connotes much more than power and patrimony, signifying, in addition, political grandeur capable of intimidating men. Undisputed hegemony of the Florentine aristocracy was discontinued; a democratized communal regime turned to the demanding unfinished business of the times.[13]

The two crucial areas of civic life were defense and maintenance of fiscal integrity. Before considering the latter—the main concern of this chapter—it might be well to suggest possible connections between these matters. If Florence persisted in her grandiose imperial schemes of the 1330s, whereby the city sought hegemony over Tuscany, solvency of the fisc would not be achieved. The democratic signory ruling after 1343 pursued a defensive, unambitious foreign policy. The implications of this novel program were clear: a sizable reduction in military outlays would permit treasury funds to be used for restitution to the creditors of the republic. Of course it would be essential that revenue from the many communal imposts prosper. Soon the republic benefited from a substantial reduction in costs for mercenaries and a startling recovery in revenue from indirect levies. Solvency was tantalizingly close.

Only two months after the installation of this democratic signory, steps were taken to fund the communal debt. On the 29th of December, 1343, the two councils of the republic approved a law authorizing the consolidation of all outstanding governmental obligations.[14] The name of a communal creditor, plus the amount of his credit, was to be entered in one of four ledgers appropriate to his quarter of the city. This Herculean work of the Commission of Eight and its notaries produced four mammoth registers containing over 8,000 names of citizens designated as communal creditors. The Commission was instructed to survey communal records dating back as far as 1326 to ascertain the extent of indebtedness. All this was to be done with a view toward immediate payment of interest and, hopefully, the amortization of principal.

Early in 1344 the councils ratified a proposal that income from levies on salt and wine be utilized to satisfy the claims of communal creditors.

---

[12] Stefani, rub. 588; G. Villani, 12, 18–19.

[13] Also represented in the highest offices were the patrician houses of Albizzi, Antella, Bordoni, Brunelleschi, Cavalcanti, Della Tosa, Frescobaldi, Gianfigliazzi, Peruzzi, and so forth. Cf. *I Capitoli del Comune*, ed. C. Guasti (Florence, 1893), 2, 57 ff.; G. Villani, 12, 22; *DP*, 4, f. 1 (August 2, 1343).

[14] *P*, 32, f. 88r. A commission of eight and a notary were appointed to initiate the Herculean work.

Too quickly it was evident the republic lacked sufficient funds for this laudable purpose. Already the gabelles on salt and wine were pledged for payment of other governmental obligations, since the treasury assumed liability for the outstanding commitments of preceding regimes when the democratized signory was installed. These stemmed from monies owed Mastino della Scala, the republic of Venice, the government of Pisa, and the many loans of the recently deposed dictator of the city, Walter of Brienne. Consequently the ordinances of early 1344 decreeing that income from gabelles on salt and wine be utilized for restitution to the citizenry were temporarily suspended.[15] Not until October of the following year did the funding of the public debt begin. The establishment of the *Monte Comune* or "mountain of indebtedness" and disbursement of interest started at that time. The mainstay for the *paghe* or interest payments was income from the two aforementioned gabelles (after prior commitments were met), coupled with a portion of the customs toll.

Given subsequent developments, it could be inferred that the regime did not intend to amortize the *Monte Comune* but only to make interest payments. However, since income from gabelles on salt and wine and custom tolls rose, it would appear the government had reason to believe both principal and interest might be paid. Payment was contingent upon receipts holding up and military expenditures remaining modest. Such was the case in the short run, with the total yield of the two gabelles reaching 55,000 florins.[16] The burden was lessened since interest rates were set at only 5 per cent in February, 1345, while the amount of the public debt had been scaled from 800,000 florins to 500,000 florins. Therefore only 25,000 florins would be required each year to meet interest payments. This would still leave a balance sufficient to amortize the debt at a rate of 5 per cent per annum. That amortization did not occur is no indication of the intent of the founders of the *Monte*.

By 1345, then, the public debt had been funded and the *Monte* firmly established. Citizen holdings in the *Monte* were declared negotiable and can be likened to shares of stock. The effect of actions by the signory between December, 1343, and February, 1345, was to reduce the total of the state debt by a very sizable margin—somewhere between 30 and 40 per cent. Communal indebtedness finally seemed manageable. Further, these steps were taken when communal revenues burgeoned, so that the situation looked quite promising. Military expenditures also

---

[15] B. Barbadoro, *Le finanze*, p. 639; *P*, 32, f. 94r (January 19, 1344); *Capitoli*, 18, f. 50 (July 24, 1344).
[16] In point of fact, just before the advent of the Black Death they brought in 58,000 florins. *CCE*, 9, f. 39r; *ibid.*, 9, f. 59r; *ibid.*, 10, f. 89; *ibid.*, 11, f. 33r; *ibid.*, 14, f. 18; *ibid.*, 25, f. 104r.

continued to be very modest; thus in October of the same year the treasury paid its first interest.[17] The chief shareholders were of course the many great guildsmen who had made forced and voluntary loans (*prestanze*) to the *camera* since the 1320s. Although the debt was funded, men of the *arti maggiori* would not realize their earlier expectations, since the original loans had been contracted at two and three times the new interest rates. The reduction was significant, yet the creditors would receive interest only three years after the treasury, confronted with bankruptcy, declared a moratorium. That this happy recovery took place over so short an interval could not have been predicted by the most sanguine of government counselors. Likewise, the most pessimistic would hardly have prophesied the plague and wars soon to overtake the city. These catastrophes were to unhinge the *Monte* from its moorings and propel it into uncharted seas with unforeseen consequences.

II

After 1345, when the consolidation of the public debt was achieved, this mountain of indebtedness came to dominate the formation of public policy as did no other issue. As a consequence of its establishment a new relationship emerged between the affluent citizen and the political community. No longer was it possible to follow the easy, laissez-faire program dictated by the casual rule of the patriciate. The government was compelled to strain every resource and talent to meet the mounting interest payments. No longer were individual loyalties explicable in terms of clan allegiances, church ties, participation in the Guelf party, guild affiliation, membership in a tower society, or religious confraternity. Instead, those enjoying full political rights (guild masters or at least guild matriculees declared eligible for high communal posts) became involved as never before in the life of the republic. By the 1350s virtually every Florentine active in civic affairs was a large shareholder in the *Monte*. This continued over the balance of the century and well into the middle years of the *quattrocento*. Large blocks of *Monte* stock were listed among the prime assets of the great Florentine companies and their directors.[18]

As citizen capital invested in the burgeoning *Monte* soared and its impact on the public world increased, so, too, did citizen concern with politics. There was a brisk traffic in *Monte* shares, with price fluctuating like the ebb and flow of political tides. When the *Monte* for dowries was founded later, the very progeny of the average citizen depended

[17] *LF*, 83, f. 125 (October 11, 1345).
[18] For a sizable sample of mid-*trecento Monte* holdings, see *Monte*, Vols. 485, 681, 682, 683, 684, and 685.

upon the ability of the state to weather Milanese invasions and survive chronic Italian war. During an age when a suitable dowry was a necessity, the winning of a husband depended upon the ability of the state to honor its commitments. The *Monte* had much to do with the creation of an audience for the civic humanists and artists of the early Renaissance, since Florentines, personally involved in the destiny of the polis, were vitally anxious about their politics and longed to believe in the durability and magnificence of a new entity—the Renaissance State. By 1380 there were some 5,000 Florentines holding *Monte* stock. This was perhaps one-twelfth of the population—a total approximating the propertied class of the polis.[19] The novel type of political discourse initiated by the humanist chancellors Coluccio Salutati and Leonardo Bruni Aretino, and coming to fruition in the person of the most renowned of all Florentine public servants, Niccolò Machiavelli, reflected the interests of men in the growing cult of the state. The citizen's well-being and his very economic survival were tightly bound to this new organism. To glimpse the enthusiasm with which increases in the value of *Monte* shares were greeted and the grief when decreases were announced is to appreciate that to the Florentines of the late *trecento* and early *quattrocento* the state was indeed no mere abstraction.[20]

Earlier, in medieval Florence, one's destiny was less influenced by government fiscal policy; the bonds of society tended to be intimate and personal rather than political. At the apex of that society was a configuration of bedazzling, shifting, and frequently conflicting loyalties. Generally, political leadership was furnished by a select business patriciate who underwrote public policy with their private fortunes by means of short-term loans to the government. It was the Acciaiuoli, Bardi, Frescobaldi, Peruzzi, and a score or two of other houses who financed the more spectacular Florentine political adventures of the recent past. These fifty or so families were the backbone of the *camera* as well as directors of the republic's destiny.[21]

Until the early 1340s the polis was administered by them as if it were a giant holding company: when prosperity prevailed and communal income was swollen by returns from gabelles (indirect imposts),

---

[19] Stefani, rub. 883–84. Figures given by the chronicler are borne out by a count of the creditors. All statistics of this type can only be approximations since duplication of names and other difficulties intrude. A 10 per cent margin of error would not be excessive. Matteo Villani explains something of the mechanism of this change: When interest rates go up men sell land and business and buy *Monte* stock (8, 71). Cf. also G. Cavalcanti, *Istorie fiorentine* (Florence, 1839), 2, 203. For speculation in *Monte* shares by the *Tavola* of the Medici bank, see R. de Roover, *The Rise and Decline of the Medici Bank 1397–1494* (Cambridge, Mass., 1963), p. 263.
[20] N. Rodolico, *I Ciompi* (Florence, 1945), p. 188; G. Brucker, *Florentine Politics and Society*, pp. 19–21.
[21] M. Becker, *Florence in Transition*, 1, 92–121; A. Sapori, *Le crisi, passim*.

then constraints of government and public law slackened and the tone of the regimen became laissez-faire and casual. If prosperity receded or defense proved inadequate, the alternatives were dictatorship or popuular government. The hope was that despot or democratized regime could tighten the rule and initiate stern measures to extricate the city from fiscal bind and military crisis. When peace and recovery were in prospect, these experiments in impersonal government were terminated and Florence reverted to the casual rule of an easygoing patriciate willing to loan money to the treasury at high interest rather than raise tax rates.[22] Certainly there was broad support for such a relaxed regime, and the brevity of the rule of popular government (1293–95, 1323–25, 1328–29) was related to the ground swell of discontent provoked by increases in public imposts. Great guildsmen and clerics closed ranks when popular governments threatened their privileged position.[23] The Guelf party, religious confraternities, Tuscan church, and other quasi-public bodies of the medieval polis were hardly anxious to see their traditional status undermined by strict enforcement of communal law.

After 1343, however, the return to casual government became increasingly difficult, for as public indebtedness grew, mounting obligations to communal creditors had to be met. Therefore few sources of revenue could comfortably be overlooked; modest treasury surpluses and short-term loans were insufficient. Communal law acquired a new force, with an ever-more-impersonal political regime the end product. Until the middle years of the *trecento*, when pressure intensified, the commune could ease the fiscal bind by exhorting the Tuscan clergy to vote a benevolence, or requesting the guilds to pay a special assessment, or proposing that the *Parte Guelfa* grant a subsidy. But after the mid-*trecento*, only trifling amounts could be collected from these antique and familiar sources, for the budgetary demands of the republic were doubling and tripling.

The first of the major conflicts, the Pisan war (1362–64), cost more than 1,000,000 florins, and the War of the Eight Saints against the papacy (1375–78) left a legacy of indebtedness approaching 3,500,000 florins. Very soon the outlays for these two wars were dwarfed by the cost of late *trecento* conflicts with the Visconti of Milan. By the 1380s the hire of mercenaries averaged 100,000 florins a month, a modest portent of things to come. In the early *quattrocento* disbursements ran double and sometimes triple that awesome figure.[24] In the interim there was the persistent and nagging drain of bribes for marauding companies to leave Florentine territory unravaged, or of costly subsidies

---

[22] M. Becker, *Florence in Transition*, 1, 89–122.
[23] M. Becker, "*Signorie* in Florence, 1282–1382," pp. 421–38.
[24] M. Becker, "Finanza pubblica fiorentina," pp. 434–35.

voted those luminaries from the north—the German emperors. Problems were compounded by the pursuit of costly imperialistic policies championed by leading Florentines during the 1380s and again after 1402. In the *quattrocento* staggering *prestanze* were exacted to enable Florence finally to overwhelm her small but fierce neighbor, Pisa, and go on to win a port and even an empire. There were also the various expenditures necessary to shore up the shifting and uncertain alliance systems so ingeniously constructed by the Florentines.

In the face of mounting communal budgets (over the century military outlays increased by 1,000 per cent), medieval corporate guilds and politico-religious bodies, of the caliber of the Guelf party, lost much of their ancient authority. That they lingered must be a tribute to Florentine conservatism and nostalgia; that their power dwindled as their fiscal contribution lessened expressed the hard, socioeconomic realities of the public world. If there is a truism concerning Florentine political experience, it would be: If organizations or groups do not contribute manifoldly to the *camera*, then their power will be attenuated and influence decimated. Nowhere was this more evident than in the world of the Florentine guilds. (The converse is of course true.) Possibly one illustration will suffice: Before the 1340s guilds were among the principal purchasers of communal gabelles. The structure of the system of tax farming until that date was predicated upon the willingness and ability of the *arti* to advance limited sums of money to the *camera* on the security of anticipated revenue. After this date the commune itself was obliged to collect all important indirect levies. Communal bureaucracy usurped the prerogatives of the medieval guilds and these *arti* lost prestige.[25]

Anticipating the narrative, it was the *Monte* and its management that became the single most important economic determinant of public policy. Private citizens (fifty or so patrician clans), medieval corporate guilds, honorific organizations (religious confraternities) and their ilk, or even quasi-political bodies such as the Guelf party could no longer be relied upon to alleviate the chronic budgetary deficits. As we shall see, during the 1350s interest rates on the *Monte* were made much more attractive; at 15 per cent annually it was possible to attract an abundance of new capital into the *camera* from other sources. Each year, then, hundreds of *novi cives* were enlisted in the growing legions

---

[25] *CCE*, Vols. 1–28 (1348) contain records of regular purchases of the major gabelles. Beginning with the 1350s only the most modest levies continued to be farmed (rural markets, imposts on food vendors, and so on). Communal "domini gabellarum" and other state officials now regularly assumed responsibilities for collection of indirect taxes.

of the commune's creditors.²⁶ With the advent of the sixties and intensification of Tuscan militarism, deficit spending insinuated itself more deeply into the scheme of the republic's expanding budgetary operations. The Florentine treasury began regularly to borrow large sums of money directly from the capital of the *Monte*. These funds were not disbursed to the creditors of the polis but were employed for the hire of mercenaries. This fiscal stratagem continued to be practiced with alarming frequency over succeeding decades. Confronted with staggering military commitments, the signory proposed legislation authorizing the officials over the *Monte* to make loans to the *camera* until they became the mainstay of the republic's budgetary program.²⁷

At the end of the century, Florence's obligation for interest payments to *Monte* creditors alone stood at 190,000 florins per annum, almost two-thirds the normal revenue the polis could hope to enjoy from standard sources. Public policy, then, had to be shaped so the signory could support this ever-more-onerous obligation. In a single year forced loans totaled just above 1,300,000 florins, and much of this sum was incorporated into the *Monte* as a long-term addition to the public indebtedness.²⁸ Tax policies pertaining to the *contado* and subject territories were altered in order to bring in new revenue that might in turn be diverted to *Monte* creditors.²⁹ Even after these radical fiscal alterations were completed the commune still was unable to make regular interest payments. The necessity to divert funds to *balìe* in charge of waging the protracted wars had not abated.³⁰

Public life began to cluster around the funded communal debt, until the officials of the *Monte* came to be numbered among the most influential and revered of the state's elected officers. Florence was well on the way to becoming a giant corporation in which the middling and affluent citizenry had invested a very substantial portion of their patrimony. Anything adversely affecting the welfare of the republic perforce dealt a cruel blow to the private fortunes of the citizenry, for in fact the two had become inseparable.

If there was a perceptible shift in the pattern of Florentine invest-

---

²⁶ The first entries are for late May, 1353. Cf. *CCE*, 47, fols. 154 ff. Also *ibid.*, 54 fols. 174r ff; *ibid.*, 77, fols. 140 ff.

²⁷ Not surprisingly the bulk of monies borrowed was assigned as "introytus conducte stipendiariorum" for hire of troops. Cf. *CCE*, 125 (May–June, 1368) through 133 (September–October, 1369) for protracted reliance on this technique.

²⁸ *PC*, 9 (1393). See also *ibid.*, 18, for the year 1403, when *prestanze* amounted to more than 1,200,000 florins. The total of all forced and voluntary loans over the decade of the 1390's approximates 5,000,000 florins.

²⁹ M. Becker, "Finanza pubblica fiorentina," pp. 460–62.

³⁰ For the share of the *estimo* on the *contado* diverted to the *balìa* of Ten, ten soldi per lira, see *CCE*, 231, f. 21 (July 23, 1386). This *balìa* had its own treasurer. Cf. *ibid.*, f. 248 (April 30, 1389).

ment after the middle years of the *trecento,* it was in the direction of greater concentration of wealth in the public sector of the economy. Generalizations concerning the dramatic and relentless onslaught of economic decline after 1343 are less frequently advanced by present-day economic historians.[31] Few scholars would disagree that Florentine capitalism, even though variously defined, was still vigorous in the thriving polis of the late *trecento* and early *quattrocento.* Those marked changes apparent in communal economic life by the mid-fourteenth century were not the result of a protracted medieval slump or the consequence of irreparable damage done the manufacturing and commercial community by the recent recession. In the short term, the recession of the early forties did have a serious impact, but this crisis though deep was brief, not long impairing the entrepreneurial and civic spirit of Florence's business community. Their élan persisted notwithstanding ravages of the Black Death, Pisan war, new plagues, War of the Eight Saints, proletarian revolution, and, finally, the terrible contests with the Visconti lords of Milan.[32]

The life of the polis was undeniably altered as a result of military and economic debacles of the early 1340s, with business failures and foreign policy disasters undermining the older, gentler style of governing. The confident psychology that buttressed the protohumanism of the earlier prosperous era was discredited in the public world only to be recaptured by sentimentalists. This dramatic subversion of the paideia of the older polis did not sap the energies of the ruling mercantile community. Their economic vitality did not flag, nor political will crumble. On the contrary, in a world where older ideals and values were threatened and sometimes undermined, civic consciousness assumed a more intense and exaggerated form, with patriotism and imperialism its hallmarks. In the welter of crumbling traditional expectations, allegiances and loyalties to the commune grew even more pervasive and ferocious.

---

[31] Armando Sapori is cautious in his recent appraisals of economic conditions in this decade. Evidence he has published on the stability of urban rents in the 1350s and income from the customs toll in the 1360s would support the position offered in this volume. Cf. his *L'età della rinascità, secoli XIII–XVI* (Milan, 1958), pp. 355–56. Still he insists on a timorous and regressive capitalism for late *trecento* Florence, with Francesco Datini as its *Angst*-ridden representative. This stands in contrast with the heroic age of the merchant pilgrims, the Acciaiuoli, Bardi, and Peruzzi. For recent bibliography on this question, see W. K. Ferguson "Recent Trends in the Economic Historiography of the Renaissance," *Studies in the Renaissance,* 7 (1960), 7–26.

[32] To carry such costly wars to a successful conclusion is hardly evidence of Florentine loss of vitality or civic health. E. Fiumi, no sympathizer with theories of urban recovery, presents statistics concerning city population indicating rapid urban recovery from the Black Death to 1380. In 1350 the figure stood about 53,000, while in 1380 it rose to 70–75,000. Cf. his "Fioritura e decadenza dell'economia fiorentina, *ASI,* 115 (1958), 468–70.

This aggressive ruling order, strongly committed to a public world, were the creators of a new Florentine empire.

In the eighty years between the nadir of Florentine fortunes (1340) and its apogee (1420), we witness an activism perhaps unparalleled in the annals of a city-state bourgeoisie since the halcyon days of the Roman Republic. Heroic undertakings never could have been achieved by a bourgeoisie paralyzed with *Angst* and guilt. This was a confident class, possessed of sufficient patrimony and willing to invest millions of florins in the awesome tasks of defense and conquest.[33] This, too, was the stage for the most spectacular profusion of civic art since ancient Athens. Accomplishments in patriotic letters and proud historiography matched the outpourings of a splendid public world created by such artists as Donatello, Ghiberti, Brunelleschi, and Masaccio.

If depression was not prolonged and there was no substantial exodus to the land by frightened and discouraged businessmen, if the ruling order did not embrace *rentier* status as economic historians have maintained, what crucial transformations, if any, can be discerned in the economic life of the polis? The Florentine business community's investment in the *Monte* induced the flow of capital into the communal treasury so that a novel economic system, characterized here as "state capitalism," emerged. The significant transformation was from the multiple private economy of the late Middle Ages, where investment in the public fisc was limited, and wealth remained in the hands of quasi-public institutions such as the Guelf party, guilds, or religious confraternities, to a Renaissance economy in which a large proportion of Florentine capital was invested directly in the state and public fiscal policy became the critical economic determinant.

III

To return to the economic narrative of the years around the establishment of the *Monte,* the popular government of 1343 revealed itself to be an imaginative although conservative signory. The imaginative quality of its rule is attested to by the bold and unprecedented step of installing the funded debt—intense ecclesiastical opposition notwith-

---

[33] A. Sapori, in his "Medioevo e Rinascimento, spunti per una diversa periodizzazione," *ASI,* 115 (1957), calls attention to the creative character of late medieval capitalism, the work of the private sector of the economy, without acknowledging the possibility of a comparable transformation in the public economy as a hallmark of the early Florentine Renaissance. On the crucial question of rents on urban shops, Sapori presents evidence that does little to confirm a bleak hypothesis of flagging energies. Cf. *Studi di storia economica* (Florence, 1955), 3d. ed., pp. 320–22. He takes a very cautious view of the alleged decline of the wool industry. Cf. *Studi di storia economica (Secoli XIII–XIV–XV),* (Florence, 1956), Vol. 1, 544 ff.

standing. Many in Florence, clergy and laity alike, contended heatedly that payment of interest on government loans was usurious and therefore sinful.[34] The conservative character is evidenced by the regime's reluctance to initiate new types of revenue measures as well as to renounce fiscal obligations of its predecessors. Even the burden of debts contracted by the late and unlamented tyrant Walter of Brienne was assumed. Among its first acts was a provision announcing the intention to assume responsibility for Brienne's loans. Simultaneously with the funding of the public debt, the signory elected a commission to fix Brienne's obligation to the citizenry.[35] A decree of 1344 created bureaucracy to this end.

To meet these liabilities the popular government was compelled to be more efficient in its management of communal patrimony, forcing *magnates* and *potentes* to disgorge public revenue and property. At no time in communal history was the law enforced with greater impersonality against an overbearing and overmighty nobility whose status had once been ample guarantee for preferential treatment.[36] The need to guard scrupulously the public interest if fiscal obligations of the commune were to be met had become a constant in civic life.

From 1345 until late July, 1349, the treasury was able to make restitution to communal creditors. The gabelle on wine, a fraction of the customs toll, and a portion of the salt impost were assigned to the *capsa conducte* (war chest). This division of the *camera*, installed in 1343, was devoted solely to the hire of mercenaries. Over these years the *capsa conducte* could be financed with only a fraction of the total state revenues, since military expenditures averaged a modest 5,500 florins monthly. For the first time in almost a generation the defense budget was pared down to 70,000 florins a year. It was a nominal outlay—between one-quarter and one-fifth of the republic's income; only a few years before it had reached four-fifths of the commune's total revenues.[37] The achievement of stringent economies was possible only after Florence renounced imperial ambitions (1343) and retreated into isolation within her reduced Tuscan domain. Florence ceased to cut a figure on the Italian scene, contenting herself with loss of territories laboriously accumulated over so many decades. Despite savings accruing from disavowal of extravagant imperial ambitions, income from indirect levies had to recover appreciably from the low of 1342–43 before creditors could receive interest on *Monte* shares.

[34] For the debate on the licitness of *Monte*, see R. de Roover, "Il trattato di fra Santi Rucellai sul cambio, il monte comune e il monte delle doti," *ASI*, 111 (1953), 3–34.
[35] *P*, 32, fols., 98–992.
[36] M. Becker, *Florence in Transition*, 1, 203–10.
[37] M. Becker, "Finanza pubblica fiorentina," pp. 434–36.

The period after 1343 was just such an interval of zestful gain in communal finances. Indeed, a striking characteristic of the republic's economy was its ability to survive catastrophe, endure shock, and finally to reassert unbounded energies. For the balance of the *trecento* and the first quarter of the *quattrocento*, Florence suffered adversities as varied as they were punishing. Repeated famine, plague, bankruptcy, depression, invasion by free-booting companies, proletarian revolution, the sustained menace of the Visconti colossus, and, lastly, the anguish of fratricidal Italian wars with the church were not only endured but surmounted. Each time, Florence recovered her confidence, recouped her forces, and asserted her fiscal vigor. The year 1343 was the start of a communal recovery, one in a series of energetic upsurges, duplicated again immediately after the Black Death, just after the Pisan war, at the close of the Ciompi revolution, and, ultimately, in the blackest hours of the interminable wars at the turn of the century.[38]

When Walter of Brienne decreed his infamous moratorium on payment of interest to the republic's creditors on November 20, 1342, the *camera*, with a balance of only a few thousand florins, was virtually bankrupt. Income from all indirect levies had fallen alarmingly in the years just before this nadir in communal finances.[39] But soon this gloomy trend was in the process of dramatic reversal: the best index of communal well-being, the customs toll, rose to 68,000 florins in 1343, and when it was auctioned to tax farmers two years later it brought in 75,000 florins. Just before plague struck Florence in 1348, it reached 79,000 florins. The gabelle on contracts returned only 7,322 florins in 1342–43; by January 1, 1344, it yielded the commune 17,166-2/3 florins; a year later it was up to 18,500 florins. The impost on wine was sold for 36,000 florins on December 10, 1342; that same day in 1344 it was purchased for 44,000 florins. By January, 1348, it had climbed to 47,465 florins. The salt tax had tumbled from 14,450 florins in 1336–38 to 4,073 florins in 1342–43. With steady increments between 1343 and 1347, it reached 14,000 florins, just 450 florins less than the peak it had recorded in 1336–38.[40]

---

[38] In my next volume I shall treat the movement of the Florentine economy of the second part of the *trecento* in considerable detail. According to the frequently authenticated statistics of Giovanni Villani, urban population stood at 90,000 in 1338, fell to 75,000 in 1340, only to rise again to 80,000 in early 1347. This reversed a trend of population decline in force since 1300 when the number stood at 105,000. Urban growth is suggested for the first time in half a century for the five years before the Black Death. E. Fiumi, who stresses severe economic decline, presents evidence that cannot be subsumed under his hypothesis. Cf. his "La demografia fiorentina nelle pagine di Giovanni Villani," *ASI*, 108 (1950), 78–92.

[39] For finances under Brienne, see M. Becker, *Florence in Transition*, 1, 161–64.

[40] For returns on the salt tax, see *CCE*, 6, f. 45r; *ibid.*, 9, f. 59r; *ibid.*, 14, f. 77r. For the customs toll, see *ibid.*, 5, f. 18; *ibid.*, 6, f. 47; *ibid.*, 7, f. 115; *ibid.*, 14, f. 18; *ibid.*,

THE *MONTE*

Comparable gains were also registered by the entire battery of communal imposts, and it is clear that one of the two conditions essential for making restitution to communal creditors had been met. Returns from the gabelles on communal mills and fisheries were up, along with the imposts on hawkers on foodstuffs. The tax on cattle and on the sale of meat also spiraled. Even the levy on pawnbrokers—a sign of weal or woe, who can tell?—likewise ascended. But perhaps most significant of all was the recovery demonstrated by the *estimo* on the *contado*. By early 1348 it had more than recovered the value of just a decade before.[41]

In such a thriving milieu the signory could support payments to *Monte* creditors with relative ease; nor was it necessary to impose new taxes or substantial forced loans. Throughout its five-year tenure the popular government exacted fewer *prestanze* than any other communal regime within recent memory.[42] Suddenly, however, this veritable arcadian interlude was terminated; by March, 1348, the terrible pestilence had descended upon Florence, and within a half-year perhaps one-third of the populace were stricken with bubonic plague and pneumonia. Judging from the records of the *camera* and the courts, social disorganization was widespread. It is difficult to determine the extent to which this dislocation affected the collection of communal levies. Possibly the very low figures recorded in May–June, 1348, were the result of prevailing disorder rather than an index of economic decline. The fact does remain, however, that the customs toll of March–April, 1348, was less than one-quarter the amount registered during the preceding two months. Normally, receipts for January and February represented a low for this particular gabelle. Starting in March–April, there was an ascent so that income by May–June should have been substantial. The gabelle on salt yielded 4,064 florins in January–February, only to fall to 2,700

18, f. 102; *ibid.*, 25, f. 104r. For the gabelle on wine, see *ibid.*, 9, f. 394; *ibid.*, 10, f. 84; *ibid.*, 11, f. 33r; *ibid.*, 25, f. 104r. For the gabelle on contracts, see *ibid.*, 10, f. 108r; *ibid.*, 11, f. 34; *ibid.*, 14, f. 18; *ibid.*, 17, f. 6. For the yield of the lesser gabelles, see *ibid.*, 12, f. 41r; *ibid.*, 11, f. 34; *ibid.*, 23, f. 26; *ibid.*, 10, f. 107; *ibid.*, 16, f. 102r; *ibid.*, 10 f, 9, Since these taxes were auctioned off during this interval, the increased income that accrued to the commune resulted from the judgment of buyers who believed that economic conditions were going to improve. I have been unable to find significant increases in rates of the gabelles that would account for their greater yield between 1343 and 1348.

[41] *Ibid.*, 10, fols. 9, 107; *ibid.*, 11, f. 34; *ibid.*, 12, f. 3; *ibid.*, 16, f. 102r; *ibid.*, 23, f. 26; *ibid.*, 24, f. 47. In 1348 the *estimo* on the *contado* was fixed at slightly above the 29,000 florin figure for which it had been sold. *CapP*, 12, f. 211r; *P*, 35, f. 114 (March 27, 1348).

[42] The treasury records (*CCE*, 2, Vols. 2–30) indicate only six modest *prestanze* for those years. Part was used to satisfy old treaty obligations to the Della Scala. *LF*, 26, f. 90 (September 13, 1346).

florins in the two months immediately following the onset of pestilence. By May–June of that same year intake had plummeted below 1,000 florins. The gabelle on wine recorded a figure of 13,824 florins in January–February, 1348; with the coming of plague it dropped almost 50 per cent. The behavior of this gabelle, however, over the next year or so was almost as tipsy and unpredictable as that of bibulous Arno inhabitants attempting to forget the ravages of the plague.[43]

Communal income was at a new low. The totals of the *entrata* (intake) of the *camera* for the last eight months of the plague year reveal that receipts did not rise much above 14,000 florins for any month.[44] Meanwhile, military outlays were climbing steadily and with the abatement of plague were doubling and tripling. In May–June, 1348, the outlay was only 8,161 florins; during this same interim in the following year it reached 17,391 florins, and by 1350 it was above 30,000 florins.[45]

IV

The pressure of declining communal income and escalating military expenditures induced by the bitter war with the Tuscan feudatories of the Ubaldini clan caused the commune to default on interest payments to *Monte* creditors. The signory had proclaimed a moratorium in 1349 when the *camera* was depleted and the *capsa conducte* almost empty. A number of stopgap and ineffectual remedies had been suggested so that the treasury might have ample revenue: allow convicted criminals to assign their *Monte* credits to the treasury in lieu of paying condemnations, or let all who apply for citizenship be required to make payments into the treasury of the *Monte*. Such proposals, even if implemented, could be expected to garner only a few hundred florins for a beleaguered treasury when in fact many thousands were required. Even seizure of certain of the properties of pious foundations and religious confraternities could contribute only modestly to the budgetary deficit.[46]

The regime limped along not honoring its *Monte* commitments until early 1351 when dramatic action was initiated to triple and even quadruple treasury income. First, the rates of communal gabelles were

---

[43] By January–February, 1350, it stood at approximately 17,000 florins; in March–April, at over 35,000 florins. Although this gabelle was raised by one-half, the increase exceeds that figure. Also, a decline of one-third in population leads to the conclusion of a substantial gain in *per capita* consumption. Cf. *CCE*, Vols. 37–38.
[44] It remained steady at about that figure, with September–October a few thousand florins lower. *Ibid.*, Vols. 27–30.
[45] *Ibid.*, 27 (May–June, 1348); *ibid.*, 33 (May–June, 1349); *ibid.*, 39 (May–June, 1350).
[46] *Ibid.*, 45 (January–February, 1353).

doubled so that the *camera* was assured an annual income of 360,000 florins—a substantial sum. A return of this magnitude was 60,000 florins above that enjoyed by the republic in the most prosperous of all recent bienniums, 1336–38, and this at a time when Florence's population was depleted by approximately one-third.[47] The first substantial yield from the augmented gabelles was paid into the *camera* in March–April, 1351. At just this moment, two additional sources were being tapped: urban real estate and the Tuscan clergy. The latter were compelled to make payment to a special "Camarlingho del Cherichato di Firenze," and direct taxes on city property (the *estimo*) were levied for the first time since the unhappy days of Brienne, with the commune realizing 20,000 florins from these two sources in a single month.[48] The *estimo* remained in force over the next two years, and although the treasury records are not complete for this biennium, the *entrata* for the period for which documentation survives averaged just under 70,000 florins for each two-month interval—a sizable return for the *camera*.

Matteo Villani, continuator of his brother Giovanni's chronicle—the latter being among the first victims of the Black Death—was quite knowledgeable about communal finances in general and the *Monte* in particular, since he regularly served as *scrivano del Monte*. He held this post over the entire decade of the fifties and entered all interest payments made to communal creditors in the appropriate state ledgers. The chronicler informs us the *Monte* reached better than 600,000 florins, an increment of 100,000 florins over a period of five years.[49] Interest payments would have been a maximum of 30,000 florins annually if rates had remained at the original 5 per cent, but this figure was soon altered. A signory whose membership was first among the principal shareholders in the *Monte* would not be unsympathetic to raising the rate. Further, it was argued by governmental advisers that in order to attract new capital to the *Monte*, interest should be doubled or tripled; returns on business and even in land investment frequently exceeded the 5 per cent figure.[50]

In March–April, 1351, Donato Velluti, esteemed jurist and keeper of a domestic chronicle, the leading personage in the nine-man priorate, was elected to the highest communal magistracy—*Gonfaloniere di Giustizia*. It was his boast that during his two-month tenure, interest payments to creditors of the republic were resumed. The main source of

---

[47] M. Villani, 1, 53. For a translation of the relevant chapter from Giovanni Villani's chronicle, see R. Lopez and I. Raymond, *Medieval Trade in the Mediterranean World* (New York, 1955), pp. 71–74.
[48] *Scrivano*, 11, f. 29r (March–April, 1351).
[49] M. Villani, 3, 106 and n. 3.
[50] *CP*, 2, 62r (April 1, 1355); *CCE*, Vols. 47–54 (1353–54).

communal revenue, the customs toll, was diverted to these ends. But very soon the *camera* was again on the threshold of lean times; intake from the *estimo,* enacted earlier that year, decreased.[51]

The *Consulte e Pratiche* are the Latin shorthand accounts of the numerous discussions and debates held before the signory. This valuable source commences again in the mid-*trecento* after a lapse of almost half a century. The history of the first half of the *trecento* must be less explicit as to particulars, for the loss of this most precious of all runs of Florentine public documents is irreparable. With the advent of the 1350s and the reappearance of this source, more dimension can be lent to the economic experience of the polis.

In late July and early August, 1351, a great debate on communal finance was held before the signory. By then the commune was feeling the strain of preparations for a new war with the Visconti. Additional money was needed to fortify and garrison the territories of Pistoia, Prato, and Scarperia. The first of many speakers was Domenico da Certaldo, and he voiced a sentiment shared by many: Let the treasury raise the necessary funds in the time-honored fashion, through imposition of gabelles. He reasoned, as numerous advisers in the late thirteenth century had done before and were to do again and again, that levies on foodstuffs and other essentials provoked less dissension among the citizenry; therefore they were to be preferred over direct taxes on capital and property. Surely, the advice was politic if one believed that only the affluent among the citizenry need be placated, and this was his audience in the council hall, since the prosperous alone were afforded representation at this time.[52] Not surprisingly, the gabelles were most unpopular with the disfranchised lower orders (*il popolo minuto*), since they were a regressive tax falling on the consumer. It was not the unanimity or support of this class that Domenico sought, but the "cives meliores," whom all knew must remain "ad unionem et sint uniti."

Giovanni Giani and Messer Berto Frescobaldi also exhorted the signory to look to the union of these citizens, and thereafter a variety of time-honored remedies were put forth by the politically experienced counselors. Simone Peruzzi, speaking for the majority, advocated imposing interest-bearing loans (*prestanze*) as well as increasing gabelles. Other speakers, no matter what remedy they proffered for communal ills, avoided mention of the vexatious direct levies. Let there be, said Messer Tommaso Altoviti, voluntary loans made gratis to the government. Uguccione Ricci offered the novel though not universally popular suggestion that the citizenry themselves agree to ride forth from the

[51] *La Cronica domestica,* p. 38.
[52] *CP,* 1, part 1, fols. 22–23 (July 30–August 1, 1351).

city and garrison the beleaguered fortresses at Pistoia, Prato, and Scarperia; persumably this would reduce the costs for mercenaries. A few of the speakers favored collecting taxes on merchandise entering the city, and one proposed doubling the customs toll.

A less than startling observation on the sociology of the budget might be: The lower the status ranking of an adviser to the signory, or the closer the ties between a particular patrician speaker and the populace, the greater the likelihood for favoring the principle of direct taxation on capital and property. The college of the *Gonfalonieri,* most democratic of all branches of the signory, was the first to champion an *estimo,* a *sega,* or a hearth tax as a corrective for fiscal ills. The signory continued debate on the merits of these various imposts for the next thirty years, with no single measure more likely to provoke disaffection and acrimonious debate than the introduction of the *estimo.*[53] As we shall see, failure to re-enact a direct tax in later years had surprising consequences.

Despite the aversion of affluent counselors, the signory continued to hold debates on the merits of the *estimo*. Influential statesmen such as Uguccione Ricci, Niccolò Alberti, Berto Frescobaldi, along with a hundred or so of the prosperous guildsmen, were selected regularly to serve in one or more of the financial positions created to strengthen communal machinery during the middle years of the *trecento*. Because of wide experience in various areas of public finance, they learned to appreciate the impossibility of operating with traditional economic measures while at the same time discharging the republic's obligations to the holders of *Monte* shares. The more extensive an individual's experience in the field of public finance, the greater the probability of his realizing the need for greater revenue. Knowledgeable officials no longer embraced antique formulas with such certainty. Less frequently did they offer the signory sage advice as to the need for living within her means by reducing expenses, or agree generously that a minuscule levy on weights and measures might be enacted. Many who were to make cause with the *parte popolare* (the most malleable element in the political community) had wide-ranging experience in republican finances, having served in key fiscal posts.[54]

There was, then, always some support for the *estimo,* although it remained unpopular with a large segment of the monied patriciate. In 1351, as we have noted, and again in 1352, under the pressure of war with the Visconti, the direct tax was imposed so that over the next few

---

[53] For examples of opposition to direct taxation during the 1350's, see *LF,* 30, 52r; *ibid.,* 31, fols. 35, 37.
[54] *Cursus honorum* of leading bureaucrats and treasury officials will be treated in detail in Volume 3.

years the treasury was the beneficiary of increased revenue. When the strain was eased, the exaction of this levy was discontinued. But again in 1355, when Tuscany was menaced by the awesome prospect of a German emperor and his hosts, an *estimo* was enacted and officials appointed to oversee its collection. The debate preceding proclamation of the enabling act was heated and prolonged, however. Already in December, 1354, the signory had assembled an expert panel of advisers.[55]

Uguccione Ricci, experienced in public finance and soon to be one in the vanguard of the *parte popolare,* spoke at the outset: The *populus* of Florence must preserve its *libertas;* therefore the priorate and a commission of Eight, authorized to raise revenue, were to do what would be suitable for the preservation of *libertas.* First, let them install new gabelles; if that did not work, then taxes on property should be imposed. Luca Fei, also knowledgeable in matters of public finance, followed the same line. Niccolò Alberti, of comparable background, took a more cautious tone, but the substance of his comments was identical: Augment the gabelles; if this proves unsuccessful, re-impose an *estimo.* Only Filippo Machiavelli, among the other speakers, opted for increasing gabelles as the sole remedy. The same session saw Uguccione speak once again, this time in his capacity as communal administrator of the gabelle on salt. Addressing the signory, he counseled "that it did not seem useful to raise the gabelles." One can only conjecture the reasons behind his statement: perhaps the point of diminishing returns was reached, since the rates of these imposts had already been increased at least 100 per cent over the last four years.[56]

Hostility against imposition of the *estimo* remained intense. In January, 1355, a tanner named Salvestro Lapi, one of several to view economic problems from the vantage point of humble social position, exhorted the signory to reimpose the *estimo.* This plea was without equivocation and the first of many democratic fiscal proposals advanced by minor guildsmen. But neither Salvestro's nor Uguccione's suggestion was followed. Although the enabling act, establishing machinery for the *estimo,* was approved by the communal councils, the levy itself was never collected. Instead it was assessed and immediately afterwards converted into a forced loan. By April, 1355, the first returns of this new *prestanza* were entering the treasury.[57] The original estimate, which had been made in order to fix an assessment for a property tax, was employed as a base for determining the size of an individual's loan. In this way the impost was converted into a profitable interest-bearing *prestanza,* with the government, to the delight of principal

---

[55] *CP,* 1, part 2, fols. 101r (December 19, 1354).
[56] *Ibid.,* fols. 101r–102.
[57] *Ibid.,* 118r (January 24, 1355).

rate payers, assuming liability both for payment of interest and restitution of principal.[58]

As early as 1353 the many names of communal creditors with the amount of their outstanding loans were entered in the records of the *Camera del Comune*. The sums were ample, and the creditors corresponded to the mid-*trecento* ruling class of the polis; in fact it would be difficult to distinguish between high officeholders and those advancing capital to the communal treasury. This affluent governing order made the sizable loans to officials charged with hiring communal troops and paid subventions to emperors, prelates, and marauding companies. Indeed, it would not be exaggerated to suggest that between 1353 and 1362 these monied Florentines underwrote the expanded communal budget. This was an enlarged, altered group, different from the previous generation, when a score of old families controlling select companies placed their resources at the disposal of the *camera*. As has been observed, communal budgets in the earlier period were not inordinately high, so little reason existed for expanding the creditor class. Consequently, the great Florentine business houses, the Acciaiuoli, Bardi, Frescobaldi, Peruzzi, dominated the political life of the polis while supporting the *camera* with short-term loans.

With the middle years of the *trecento* the military and foreign budgets were escalated some tenfold; therefore contributions from the patriciate were inadequate. Now new citizens with new fortunes made handsome loans to the *camera*.[59] Their presence was felt more immediately in the conduct of foreign policy. Diplomatic relations were not controlled by a few entrepreneurial families, but rather by the broad and sometimes shifting spectrum of the old and new upper classes of the Florentine guild world. Ensuing policy became a curious amalgam of defense and aggression dictated by practical considerations rather than ideological commitments. Within a generation Florence was to win dominion of much of Tuscany, making her the principal power in north Italy next to Milan. Finally she humbled even Milan, aided by what Machiavelli termed the republic's best ally—death—when the Visconti were struck down. The cost was enormous, but it increased citizen involvement with the state.

In March, 1355, the chronicler Matteo Villani proudly announced that those making the *prestanza*, based on assessments of property taxes, were to have receipts from gabelles assigned them for payment of interest. The rate, moreover, was to be 10 per cent, with the well-to-do

---

[58] *CCE*, 68, f. 127r (November–December, 1357). In this volume of the treasury records notation is made that on April 29, 1355, lists of *estimo* rate payers were drawn up who were in fact creditors.
[59] See chapter II.

being permitted to pay the assessment of the less fortunate ("impotenti"). In return for this payment they were to collect interest, and eventually the principal was to be restored. The chronicler, still a *Monte* official at this time, viewed this as an exemplary device, for would not the commune be in the enviable position of being able to raise revenue without strain ("senze fatica")? Let all know, he unctuously announced, that this heroic maneuver is recounted for the sake of future generations, to demonstrate that the commune was determined to keep faith with these creditors. For did not direct and indirect levies occasion only enmity ("molte mortali nimicizie tra cittadini"), "grave confusion," and even provoke many to flee into exile rather than pay the cruel tribute?[60]

Again, in 1358, despite the success of this new tactic, additional funds were required. The signory readily acknowledged what had been standard practice during the last years when gabelles were not raised and the *estimo* not imposed: Those who lent money to the commune were to receive *Monte* shares. This time (June 16–18, 1358) the treasury was authorized to offer 300 florins of *Monte* stock to any new subscriber willing to loan 100 florins in cash to the commune.[61] In effect, through this transparent device, interest rates were boosted from 10 to 15 per cent. The result was to attract new capital to the *Monte,* soon to be affectionately labeled "The Three for One *Monte.*" The government continued to pay 5 per cent of the *Monte Comune,* funded in 1345; 10 per cent on *prestanze,* levied from 1353 to June, 1358; and 15 per cent to new *Monte* subscribers—a most attractive investment.

Matteo Villani began to entertain second thoughts as to whether the tactic of June, 1358, would prove a satisfactory solution for the chronic budgetary deficits. Not long before he had lauded the regime for ingeniously converting the *estimo* into a *prestanza,* and in principle this differed little from the action taken by the signory in June, 1358; although only one of degree, the change was disturbing enough to induce misgivings in Matteo. The rate of interest was increased 50 per cent, and he feared this would have grave consequences for the future of the funded debt. As an official over the *Monte,* Matteo was aware the commune could have an enduring source of revenue only if direct levies

---

[60] See footnote 2 and Matteo Villani, 4, 83. A lively traffic ensued whereby speculators paid assessments for the less affluent, collecting interest and finally recovering capital. Minor *prestanza* levies of two florins or less were canceled if the citizen agreed to pay only a part (usually one-half) into the treasury, relinquishing claims for interest or capital. Cf. G. Brucker, "Documento fiorentino," p. 168.
[61] M. Villani, 8, 71. The last large-scale loans from this series were collected by the treasury. CCE, 88 (March–April, 1362). Loans were inscribed immediately in a fifteen per cent *Monte, CCE,* 71, fols. 166–166r (May–June, 1358); G. Brucker, *Florentine Politics and Society,* p. 95.

were imposed or the rates of direct imposts increased. It was not from a sense of charity or affection for the republic that citizens volunteered to loan capital; rather, they were moved by the desire for quick gain. Avariciousness, moralized Matteo, was far from the "ancient and good customs of our ancestors," yet it was a fact of his times, if not of human nature.[62]

This moral glance backward to the arcadian world of an idyllic Florence occasioned the chronicler's prophetic observation: High interest rates would encourage capital to forego business opportunity in favor of investment in state bonds. His was an early intimation concerning the origins of what soon becomes one of the most brisk trades in Florence—speculation in *Monte* shares. The value of this public stock rose and fell with the success or failure of Florentine arms, the making and unmaking of alliances, the crowning of emperors, elections of popes, and the information passed on to the signory about the collection of gabelles or condition of the *camera*. Few were sufficiently troubled as to the licitness of this trade in the eyes of God to refuse *Monte* interest payments or to make restitution to the treasury. This is not surprising; even the principal religious orders of the city were in violent disagreement on this score, with Dominicans taking a severe view and Franciscans displaying lenience.[63]

In the following year, 1359, a portion of the tax on salt and the customs toll was assigned to these *Monte* creditors. The value of the old *Monte* shares, paying only 5 per cent, was of course falling, and advisers to the signory exhorted the government to buttress public credit by setting attractive interest rates.[64] Five per cent compared unfavorably with returns from more conservative investments, whereas 15 per cent was difficult to resist. Therefore from 1358 through 1364, as interest rates were raised, sizable amounts of private capital were placed in the *Monte*. This interval can be viewed as the second stage in the shift from an economy of a pervasively private character to one dominated by the exigencies of state finance. The first period closed with the formation and funding of the original *Monte* (1343–45), composed of government obligations contracted to finance foreign policy objectives over the past quarter of a century. The loans contributing toward the formation of this first *Monte* were funded at a modest rate. The second interval was markedly different, with capital readily available because the regime provided so attractive an incentive. The

---

[62] M. Villani, 8, 71.
[63] M. Villani, 3, 106. So commonplace was the practice of making contracts which were in fact bets on whether the *Monte* would rise or fall, that the signory placed a 2 per cent tax on such transactions. Cf. Stefani, 732. This does not suggest excessive fragility of economic conscience on the part of substantial numbers of Florentines.
[64] *CP*, 2, fols. 41–64 (February–April, 1359).

acceleration of the flow resulted not only from the structure of the communal tax program, but also from the creation of the state as an object for profitable investment. The rub of course was that such investment could involve serious risk; the state debt was climbing alarmingly and the structure of public credit was erected on a most fragile base.

V

The commune went to war with neighboring Pisa in 1362, and almost at once there was talk among governmental advisers of imposing an *estimo*.[65] Prominent popular leaders such as Jacopo Alberti favored this step, with new citizens such as Jacopo Banco Puccio in hearty accord.[66] Clearly there was anxiety about continuing the practice of expanding the "Three for One *Monte*"; perhaps a revision in the tax system was in order. Should this practice persist, it would inflate the carrying charges of the public debt until no regime would be capable of meeting them regularly. As it was, almost all revenue from the gabelles was already designated for the hire of troops. In point of fact the government was already engaged in the tortuous practice of raising money by forced loans in order to make interest payments to *Monte* subscribers. Soon this sleight of hand developed to such an extent that a *prestanza* was imposed to pay back interest on another *prestanza* or to furnish *Monte* creditors interest. As long as all communal income from indirect levies was committed for the hire of mercenaries, only additional unpledged revenue from direct taxes would serve to ease the dilemma.

At the height of the costly war with Pisa, after protracted discussion before the signory and much political maneuvering in the communal councils, the government did reactivate the *estimo*. Further, the regime installed intricate machinery for its collection, taking the serious and rather expensive step of hiring a foreign judicial official "ad faciendum extimum civitatus Florentie."[67] Again, however, at the critical moment the imposition of the direct tax was abandoned. Government counselors proposed instead that panoply of weary and inefficacious pre-

---

[65] Almost immediately, interest payments to *Monte* creditors were suspended. A special *camerarius peditum comitatus* was appointed to collect payments from county villages and hamlets in lieu of military service. CCE, 91, f. 90r (September–October, 1362); *ibid.*, 98, f. 233r (November–December, 1363).

[66] CP, 4, f. 94 (September, 1363); *ibid.*, 5, f. 2r (January 3, 1364). Not all Alberti agreed; Niccolò advised: "Quod extimus non fiat ad presens." *Ibid.*, 5, f. 3r (January 8, 1364).

[67] The magistrate elected was Messer Pino Charde. CCE, 90, f. 189 (December 30, 1364).

scriptions: Let communal property be recovered; grant no new tax immunities; require even the exalted Guelf party to pay its proper share of imposts; punish all tax delinquencies severely; elect only "boni et experti cives" as governors of the gabelles; auction off certain public holdings; and, finally, compel the signory to reduce expenses and live within its means. Of course there was ardent advocacy for extraction of revenue from the church with Salvestro de' Medici, soon to be a hero of *il popolo minuto*, espousing this position with a vengeance. He exhorted the signory to commandeer bequests to churches, religious companies, and pious foundations to satisfy pressing communal needs. There were even some who recommended that the signory enforce with added rigor communal sumptuary laws against luxury-loving women so that more revenue might be acquired.[68]

None of these recipes, even if expertly expedited, would garner sufficient revenue. The answer was of course the time-honored one of the *prestanza*, and from June, 1362, to August, 1364 (the war years), sixteen of these forced loans were levied. The grand total of this new borrowing was 1,013,000, much of it incorporated into the *Monte* at the rate of three for one.[69] This represented a continuation of the practice legalized in 1358 whereby the *camera* was authorized to pay 15 per cent to its newer creditors. Again, of course, the effect of such a strategy was to add a sizable increment to the already swollen public debt.

Based upon a complete set of the treasury records for 1367, the carrying charges on all communal *Monti*, both old and new, was 135,414 florins, and although it is impossible to determine the exact total of the communal indebtedness, it can be suggested that since better than half a million was borrowed at 5 per cent, which would mean that 25,000 florins was earmarked for payment of interest to old *Monte* creditors. This would leave a balance of approximately 750,000 florins outstanding if the commune paid 15 per cent on all other indebtedness.[70] This

---

[68] For Salvestro's customary forthright opinions, see *CP*, 4, f. 73 (July 6, 1363). For a call to enforce sumptuary legislation more rigorously, see *ibid.*, 4, f. 55r (May 19, 1363). In August, 1363, a provision was enacted whereby the treasurer of the republic could appropriate certain bequests made to religious companies from 1345 to 1363. Cf. *P*, 51, f. 7 (August 21, 1363). Monies were to be used to pay communal creditors; the treasury even borrowed from the notary in charge of funds of the Cathedral. *CCE*, 95, f. 100. (May 18, 1363).

[69] The wars of the early *trecento* left only a small residue of indebtedness. Even a conflict with so formidable an adversary as Castruccio increased the debt by only 50,000 florins. Cf. B. Barbadoro, *Le finanze*, p. 630, n. 1. *Prestanze* were levied at a frantic pace throughout the Pisan war. Cf. *Prestanze*, Vol. 13 (June, 1362) through Vol. 109 (July, 1364). In June of the following year advisers to the signory expressed concern as to whether there were sufficient funds in the treasury to pay interest on the public debt.

[70] *CCE*, Vols. 117-22. If the figures of Gene Brucker for 1378 can be projected back, my estimate is very modest. Capital invested in the 15 per cent *Monte* (Three for One) was three and one-half times greater than that invested in the original *Monte* (*Monte*

latter figure is something of an underestimation, since many debts were contracted at only 10 per cent. It does permit us, however, to establish the lower limits for the total communal debt: 1,250,000 florins. Since my purpose is not to fix with precision the sum of burgeoning interest obligations on the government, but rather to indicate that the figure was indeed substantial, representing as it did an increase of 125 per cent within the span of less than twenty years, this approximation may be satisfactory.

In August, 1364, during the course of Florentine discussions about acceptable terms for concluding the war with Pisa, Carlo Strozzi, a leading banker and political leader, voiced the sentiments of many patricians when he urged that hostilities be terminated so that Florence might be freed from "intolerable expenses." Salvestro de' Medici, one of the blunter government counselors of this or any other time, posed this cruel alternative to the signory: Either raise the necessary revenue or make peace with Pisa.[71] Shortly thereafter the Pisans did capitulate and the Florentines were able to conclude a most advantageous treaty. At once the cry was raised by Florentines as diverse as the lofty patrician banker Piero Guicciardini on the one hand and the *nouveau* Francesco del Benino on the other to discharge the city's large mercenary force. Talk in the communal councils focused on the theme of honoring the commune's commitments to its citizenry.[72]

They felt that under all circumstances the signory must strive to maintain "faith" with the republic's patient creditors. Should Florence fail in this, the honor of the commune would be irreparably damaged and the city held up to scorn. Many of the old economic clichés were paraded forth: levy a new *prestanza* so that interest payments can be met; elect a special officer "ad alienandum bona et possessiones communis Florentie"; make more stringent laws to prevent nepotism and fraud in the treasury; have the officers of the *Monte* subtract all unpaid taxes from the holdings of the delinquent *Monte* creditors; and finally, open up the funded debt to foreign investors. This last suggestion was received with much enthusiasm, and shortly thereafter the first very substantial deposits were accepted by the treasurer of the *Monte*. In this instance it was Giovanna, daughter of Charles, Duke of Durazzo, who invested 40,000 florins in the funded debt. Needless to

---

Vecchio) at 5 per cent. Investment in the Two for One *Monte* at 10 per cent was almost five times greater than in the *Monte Vecchio*. G. Brucker, "Un documento fiorentino sulla guerra sulla finanza e sulla amministrazione pubblica (1375)," *ASI*, 115 (1957), 169.
[71] *CP*, 4, 94r.
[72] *Ibid.*, fols. 60r ff. (November 13, 1365).

say, this money was turned over at once to the eager communal creditors.[73]

The years following the Pisan war saw a strong upsurge in the collection of communal imposts, both in the city and *contado*. The customs toll registered approximately 60,000 florins in 1365, increased to 63,000 florins in the next year, and by 1367 registered 69,000 florins. Also, over this three-year period Florence was the unaccustomed beneficiary of a respite from war, so that expenses for troops were not staggering. The total for a year was less than the figure recorded during any two-month period of the war against Pisa. There was agitation for the reduction of *Monte* principal as well as for regular payment of interest. A special section of the treasury was installed in January, 1367, entitled "Capse Quattor Clavium pro Diminutione Montis."[74] Deposits from foreign creditors, a percentage of the customs toll, levies on the nobility of the *contado*, returns from rural *estimi*, delinquent *prestanze* from patricians of the houses Acciaiuoli, Bardi, and Gherardini, and even condemnations for violations of the sumptuary laws were assigned to the "Introytus" for this *Capse* of the "Four Keys." Unhappily, by summer, 1368, favorable conditions no longer obtained, for receipts available to the funded debt dwindled. The signory instructed the *camera* to resort to a practice destined to have lasting impact upon the structure of communal finance.

The *camera* commenced to borrow enormous sums from the *Monte* to support the republic's expanding military commitments. This became commonplace in the 1370s—little more than fiscal sleight of hand. The façade of the *Monte* was left intact, or at least remained recognizable, but the furnishings and interior were radically renovated. Perhaps a topical analogy will serve better than a metaphor: what occurred can be compared to the operation of the American social security system. Interest was to be paid on a principal that was persistently deployed for current budget operations. In other words, for the balance of the life of the republic and well beyond, the treasury borrowed capital from the *Monte*, trying, though frequently unsuccessfully, to make interest payments. In this way the *Monte* was systematically stripped of its capital. Through the first year, from September,

---

[73] The rate was fixed at 5 per cent; that many princes and prelates did invest in the *Monte* indicates foreign confidence in the viability of the public economy. *CP*, 8, 62 (March 31, 1367). A few years earlier Mastino della Scala deposited 50,000 florins in the funded debt. *CCE*, 94, f. 101r (June 13, 1363).

[74] *Ibid.*, 117 (January 1, 1367). As early as November, 1367, discussion on reduction of the state debt began. Money was to be deposited in this special section of the treasury to be used for purchase of *Monte* shares; for appropriate references to discussions as well as the passage of an enabling act, see G. Brucker, "Un documento fiorentino," p. 169. For the initiation of borrowing from *Monte* capital, see *CCE*, 125.

1368, to August, 1369, money borrowed averaged 5,000 florins a month,[75] and this was only a harbinger of things to come; in less than a decade the *camera* was borrowing five times this amount annually. The drain on capital of the *Monte* was so great that the façade itself was in danger of crumbling.

Prompting this ingenious tactic of deficit financing were the crushing burdens placed upon the treasury resources by the decade of war 1369–78. Previous and lighter campaigns in 1369 for the annexation of the territory of San Miniato al Tedesco were financed by a new 10 per cent *Monte* (*Monte dell'uno due*) and subsequently by thirteen forced loans, some totaling as much as 40,000 florins.[76]

Again, a leading counselor, Simone di Rinieri Peruzzi, proposed the imposition of that dread remedy, the *estimo*. There was so little support for this measure that it was not even brought to a vote.[77] Better to borrow principal from the already established *Monte*, create a new 10 per cent *Monte*, or impose interest-bearing forced loans than suffer the loathed direct levy. Shortly thereafter a spokesman suggested a new remedy: Let the citizenry lend money to the commune without interest.[78] Such a proposal indicates something of the anxiety provoked by the now commonplace solution of inscribing an entire series of *prestanze* in the books of the escalating communal debt.

By March, 1372, conditions had so deteriorated that governmental advisers were compelled to entertain the bleak prospect of suspending interest payments to communal creditors. Needless to say, a consensus was hardly possible. One counselor to the signory stated his judicious preference: Make no further forced loans; suspend interest payments on the *Monte* instead. Ostensibly the money saved could be employed for the new Florentine war with the Ubaldini feudatories to the north. However, such fiscal sleight of hand, whereby money was borrowed from *Monte* capital to pay creditors interest, would inflate the debt beyond recall. Recco di Guido Guazza, no conservative in matters of communal fiscal policy, did not equivocate: Suspend payment of interest and principal to holders of *Monte* stock. Many speakers were more moderate but demonstrated the same concern. Let restitution of interest be suspended for six months, suggested Messer Bindo de' Bardi. Alessandro Albizzi opted for only a two-month suspension, but ad-

---

[75] *Ibid.*, Vols. 127–32. A similar situation obtained from July, 1372, to August, 1373, when 74,457 florins were transferred from the coffers of the *Monte* to the officials in charge of hiring troops for the republic. During the war with the Ubaldini, which broke out shortly thereafter, the amount involved reached almost 100,000 florins. Cf. *CC*, 149–63.

[76] *Prestanze*, Vols. 138–97. First returns are recorded *CCE*, 130 (March 18, 1369).

[77] *CP*, 9, 110r (May 15, 1369); *ibid.*, 2, f. 64 (April 2, 1359).

[78] *Ibid.*, 11, f. 134 (January 11, 1370).

vocated the imposition of additional *prestanze*. Other speakers advanced what had become a most popular remedy for the many communal crises: Let the countryside and its inhabitants be taxed.[79]

V

Thus throughout the sixties and seventies communal councilors were concerned about the ability of the government to honor its fiscal obligations. The persistent question plaguing the signory since 1349, when first the suspension of interest was decreed, remained the hardy perennial: how to unearth new sources of revenue to assist in defraying the spiraling costs of the *Monte* without imposing undo hardship (a relative term) upon the republic's principal rate payers, who were, incidentally, the ruling order.

Between that time and the early 1380s the debt climbed to the grand total of 2,500,000 florins. Confronted with this imposing obligation, only the imperceptive continued to advocate such traditional remedies as strict enforcement of communal sumptuary laws, an increment on license fees of pawnbrokers, or tighter policing of communal food markets, for returns from such imposts were picayune.[80] Only revenue from direct levies on urban property and capital could relieve the republic's monetary bind without further inflating the debt. But communal councilors remained adamant toward measures likely to prove unpopular with their guild constituency. Untapped, however, was the most abundant fiscal resource of the republic—the extensive territories under its sovereignty, the countryside, and Tuscan towns.

Recently, economic historians have sought to discredit the thesis advanced by an older generation of scholars. In the late nineteenth century, Gaetano Salvemini, R. Caggese, and others stoutly asserted that Florence practiced ruthless exploitation of her domains. Present-day revisionists have championed a contrary thesis: The relationship between city and countryside was not exploitive in the least; in fact, it was nothing short of idyllic.[81] No doubt there is much to be said for this latter-day interpretation, provided we limit its application exclusively to thirteenth- and early fourteenth-century experience. For then

[79] *Ibid.*, 12, f. 10r (March 18, 1372).
[80] It might be possible to realize 1,000 florins through raising the gabelle on nobles or an additional few hundred from stricter enforcement of sumptuary laws or a tax on citizens *extra muros civitatis*. All this was inconsequential given the rapidly escalating debt. For upping of gabelle on nobles, see *P*, 50, f. 104 (February 15, 1363). For suggestions on raising money for violations of sumptuary laws, see *CP*, 4, f. 55r (May 19, 1363). For special impost by *regulatores* on citizens residing outside the city walls, see *CCE*, Vol. 162, unnumbered folio (October 20, 1374).
[81] For the most recent summary of the revisionist view of the Tuscan *contado*, see E. Cristiani, *Nobiltà e Popolo nel Comune di Pisa* (Naples, 1962), pp. 151–61.

communal budgets were minimal and a substantial part of the citizenry took up arms in their own defense; the commune was, therefore, free from the chronic need for revenue. The dominant tone of this type of society, as we have seen, was laissez-faire, and since military campaigns were fought by small forces over limited terrain, they were relatively inexpensive. With lower costs of government, the late medieval republic could well afford a loosely administered and lightly taxed *contado* over the early years of the *trecento*. But unfortunately the public debt and extravagant warfare were to do much to undermine this gentle regimen after the decade of the 1340s.

VI

Under the aegis of Brienne in 1342–43, administration over the *contado* and subject territories was tightened. No longer was it easy for a rural commune or rustic parish to continue to be delinquent in its obligations to the republic for ten or even fifteen years. With unaccustomed zeal the Florentine despot compelled the countryside to pay direct taxes long outstanding, post security for future fiscal reliability, imprison exiles residing illegally in the district, repair roads and bridges, and provide castle guard and cart service.[82]

Impersonal government in the polis achieved added momentum in subsequent years when a legion of new officials exercised stricter fiscal authority over the *contado*. The office of Defender of the *Contado*, created to prevent spoliation of the countryside by the overrich and overbearing, was converted into a magistracy charged with the protection of public property and punishment of tax delinquencies. The *bargellini* likewise became a magistracy devoted to the defense of public assets and the exaction of revenue from the countryside. Broader powers were bestowed upon the *Capitano del Custodia* so that rustics now regularly felt the full force of this official's authority.[83] The post was designed to supervise the activities, or inactivities, of locally elected officers, generally referred to as "rectors." Elected by the inhabitants of villages and hamlets, they were to be liable if outlaws or citizens, under the ban of exile, established residence within the confines of the country community. They were subject to fines whenever they failed to

---

[82] *CCE*, 2 *bis*, is the appropriate volume of treasury records for this interval and contains numerous citations against *popoli* and rural communes for failure to honor their commitments to the republic. Unpaid *estimi* and condemnations for negligence dated back to the 1320s and were collected in 1342–43.

[83] *CP*, 8, f. 287 (January 11, 1367); *ibid.*, 12, f. 57 (September 30, 1372). For later activities of communal officials in *contado*, see *Sommario delle riforme leggi e ordini dell'ufitio conservatori del contado* (Florence, 1553). For harsh justice dealt out by the *Defensor*, see *CCE*, Vol. 202.

report the incidence of a crime to the judiciary and police of the city. It was their duty to inscribe the names of all people in the *contado* liable for the *estimo* or for the tax on nobility. They were also enjoined to protect communal property and required to turn over proceeds from rebel property in their district to the *camera*. Finally, if they failed to post ample bond guaranteeing their good conduct in office, they were to be prosecuted by the dread Executor of the Ordinances of Justice of the Republic.[84]

There were numerous other Florentine bureaucrats supervising the manifold activities of country life. The magistrates of the Court of the Grascia held session even in remote places, overseeing the pricing of foodstuffs, while officials over the *Plateas* supervised the operation of country markets, and officials over the communal grain supply attempted to discourage the smuggling of this precious commodity from Florentine territories. There was also continued strict enforcement of legislation requiring peasants to do castle guard and furnish carts for the rural militia.[85] There were, of course, the roads to be mended, bridges to be kept in repair, and walls to be built. And although the nature and extent of labor services extracted by the state from the *contado* cannot be easily assessed, the treasury records indicate that beginning with the early 1340s rural communities were under increasing pressure to perform them.[86]

The magistracy of the "regulatores" was installed in 1352, and soon it became the principal arm of the republic in the *contado*.[87] First, these officers were to deal with the manifold problems associated with the exaction of indirect taxes on the *contado*. Only a few years later, responsibility for fixing the totals of the *estimo* to be paid by country hamlets were conferred upon the *regulatores*. Soon they assumed the role of collecting obligations owed the republic by the rural nobility. More crucial was their function of assessing the number of knights and foot soldiers each country town would be expected to furnish the commune. This magistracy came to work in close collaboration with the officials over the *Monte*, since a large portion of the revenue they collected was immediately earmarked for interest to communal creditors. Periodically, they were expected to confer with officials over the

---

[84] *Ibid.*, Vols. 77–94. Very significant is the assignment of condemnations against rural citizens to a special section of the treasury for the diminution of the *Monte*. Cf. *ibid.*, 189, unnumbered folio (June 25, 1379). Moreover, fines against castellans and other rural officials were assigned for restitution of interest on the funded debt. *Ibid.*, 192 (November–December, 1379).

[85] *Ibid.*, Vols. 34–35, 42, 79–80.

[86] *Ibid.*, Vols. 4–24. For failure to do militia duty or send foodstuffs, see *CCE*, Vols. 79–80, 85.

[87] See *Archivio dei Sindaci*, B., IV, 5, f. 1r where the connection is made in a latter-day hand between the decline of oligarchical hegemony and the rise of new bureaucracy.

Monte to determine the *contado's* share of the republic's fiscal burden.[88]

A marked tendency, after the middle years of the *trecento*, was conversion of taxes, once deemed personal, into territorial obligations. Formerly the gabelle on nobility residing in the *contado* was assessed on the holdings of the individual noble. Now it was imposed on his lands, and the rural parish in which the estates were located was responsible for unpaid levies. Although ownership of such lands frequently changed hands, with title devolving upon men of nonnoble status, the tiny communities were nevertheless forced to assume responsibility for exaction of this gabelle. By the 1370s country communities were paying fixed sums into the *camera* so that an impost, once a personal tax, came to be fixed as a territorial levy.[89] Over the same period the gabelle on wine falling on the *contado* was likewise converted into a territorial obligation. Villages and hamlets paid fixed sums into the *camera* instead of exacting daily imposts on wine consumption.[90]

When the issue of borrowing money from the *Monte* was heatedly debated in May, 1367, an adviser to the signory suggested that the *camera* determine whether the customs toll was being collected from all artisans plying their craft outside the city walls. Within a decade speakers were proposing that vintners practicing their trade in the environs of Florence and its domains pay a tax to the *camera* on the wholesale purchase of wine. Butchers were also to pay a substantial gabelle on all meats sold in rustic shops and markets. In addition, the signory was urged to obtain assurance that the innkeepers of the *contado* would pay the gabelle on wine and be responsible for collection of a special assessment on inns and taverns. These instances disclosed that the growing call for government regulation over country life was prompted by the state's chronic need for revenue—a demand occasioning a self-conscious paternalism, if not a calculated mercantilism.[91]

Beginning in the fifties and gaining momentum over subsequent decades was the implementation of a rugged program designed to increase the city's share of *contado* wealth. First, the rate of the rural *estimo* was revised upward. In the halcyon biennium 1336–38 it had been only ten soldi per lira. By 1355, however, it was collected at a rate of fifteen soldi per lira; five years later the figure rose to twenty

---

[88] For close ties between the *regulatores* and the *Monte* officials, see *CP*, 9, fols. 3, 10.
[89] *CCE*, 117 (January–February, 1366).
[90] *Ibid.*, 116 (November–December, 1365).
[91] On the suggestion that "Gabellae portarum ad tassandam artifices extra civitate Florentie" be investigated, see *CP*, 8, f. 77. For other proposals treating innkeepers, butchers, and vintners outside of the city, see *ibid.*, 14, f. 89r (October 3, 1377); *ibid.*, 15, f. 100 (April 10, 1378).

soldi, and in the sixties it fluctuated between thirty and forty soldi.[92] The return from this rural *estimo* averaged 30,100 florins during the years 1336–38, and complaints from the countryside reveal there were some who believed the burden of this tax to be oppressive.[93] Just after the Black Death, with country population diminished from one-third to perhaps a half, and a proportionate decline in productivity, the rural *estimo* yielded the Florentine treasury 35,355 florins.[94] Therefore the incidence of taxation on rural survivors of the plague had risen by almost one-half. Shortly thereafter, communal revenue officers were placing two direct levies on the *contado* each year, one designated as an "estimo ordinario" and the other "estimo straordinario." At the close of the century, when treasury records were more ample, the exact intake of the *camera* from these *estimi* can be calculated: in a lean year the total exceeded 41,000 florins and during a more prosperous period, 50,000 florins. The total income of the treasury from all direct and indirect levies averaged 300,000 florins a year over the second half of the *trecento*, so it is apparent the *contado* is being called upon to pay an ever-greater share. In 1336–38 the *estimo* on the *contado* accounted for only one-tenth of the republic's income from all direct and indirect taxes; by the end of the century, however, the proportion had risen to one-sixth. Later, a variety of other imposts were placed on the *contado*, with the burdens of the countryside becoming ever-more onerous.[95]

Comparable patterns can be detected if returns from other rural levies are calculated. The old rate of the gabelle on wine produced in the *contado* was revised upward. The figure in 1336 was only ten soldi, but during the decade of the fifties it doubled and finally, in the subsequent decade, reached thirty soldi *pro congio*.[96] By late *trecento* this impost yielded the treasury an income approximately equal to that of the ordinary *estimo* on the *contado*, with the return twice that of a half century ago. The yield from the gabelle on meat in the *contado* had averaged 4,400 florins for those prosperous years of the early *trecento*; then rates were increased, and if we take into account the decline in population, the return of 5,716 florins for the year 1357 represented a jump of over 100 per cent. Identical gains were registered by

[92] *CCE*, 45, f. 14r (January–February, 1353); *ibid.*, 70, unnumbered folio (March–April, 1358); *ibid.*, 139, unnumbered folio (December 16, 1370).
[93] G. Villani, *Cronica*, 11, 92; B. Barbadoro, *Le finanze*, p. 201; E. Fiumi, "Sui rapporti tra città e contado," *ASI*, 108 (1950), 36–37.
[94] Communal income from this direct levy increased each year during the decade 1348–58.
[95] M. Becker, "Finanza pubblica fiorentina," pp. 461–62.
[96] *CCE*, 30, f. 255r (November–December, 1348). The rate was unchanged throughout the decade of the forties; it was only with the advent of the fifties that this gabelle on the *contado*, like so many others, was raised dramatically. Cf. *CCE*, 45, f. 75r (January–February, 1353); *ibid.*, 77, unnumbered folio (May–June, 1359).

a variety of other rural imposts, ranging from the levy on country markets to the gabelle on rural nobility.[97] In 1364, with the debt mounting as a consequence of the Pisan war, the signory resorted to the unusual expedient of imposing a forced loan on the *contado*. Indeed, this was an exceptional measure, with this form of taxation generally reserved for the city; the countryside, unlike the city, did pay an *estimo*. The forced loan was assessed at approximately three times the urban rate and enriched the *camera* by 19,175 florins in a single month.[98]

Communal policy toward the republic's territories was, then, increasingly dictated by budgetary deficits and the pressing need to underwrite the inflated communal credit structure. If sufficient funds from the *contado* were collected to pay mercenaries, the customs toll and other gabelles formerly deployed for this purpose could be at the disposal of the treasurer of the *Monte*, with communal creditors receiving full interest payments. One method for achieving this end was the exaction of money from the *contado* in lieu of rural militia duty. This seldom collected obligation became a regular feature of state fiscal policy, and after 1351 the rural quota was raised.[99] Despite stiff payments, the inhabitants of the *contado* were not released from militia duty. Over the following generation rural communes and parishes were regularly fined for failure to dispatch troops or supplies to some distant Florentine outpost.[100] Still other onerous obligations were pressed upon the *contadini* with increased efficiency by a vastly expanded communal bureaucracy. A special *estimo* of two soldi was imposed for the

---

[97] The gabelle on nobles had been 2,000 florins in the biennium 1336–38. On December 22, 1351, it was doubled by action of the communal councils. The tax on rural markets was 3,400 lire in 1351; three years later it was up some 600 lire, and by 1360 it totaled 5,277 lire. Cf. *ibid.*, 45, f. 84 (January 30, 1353); *ibid.*, 53, f. 107 (April–May, 1354); *ibid.*, 83, unnumbered folio (May–June, 1361).

[98] *Ibid.*, 103, unnumbered folio (August 2, 1364). A certain Niccolò Cassini was elected treasurer of this *prestanza*, and it was assessed at thirty soldi per lira. The rate of the *estimo* on the *contado* was soon upped to forty soldi per lira. The old rate (1336–38) had been only ten soldi per lira. Cf. G. Villani, *Cronica*, 11, 92; *CCE*, 139, unnumbered folio (Dec. 16, 1370). At the close of the decade of the seventies, an *estimo* levied on the *contado* at the rate of forty soldi per lira was expected to produce 20,000 florins in revenue. The same amount could have been garnered by the state in the biennium 1336–38, with an *estimo* imposed at only ten soldi per lira. In order to obtain the same yield, the signory had quadrupled the rates, and this burden was borne by a much depleted population. For a study of rural population at this time, see E. Fiumi, "La demografia fiorentina," pp. 89–94.

[99] *CCE*, 39, f. 75r (Dec. 29, 1351): "Tassatio quinque peditum pro centenario"; *ibid.*, 57, f. 2 (February 23, 1353). Giovanni Catallini Infangati was *camerarius tassationis peditum*, which was imposed at a rate of fifteen soldi per lira. The return from this tax was 20,915 lire during the first two months of his tenure.

[100] As we have noted, condemnations were visited on country communities by a variety of communal officials, from the captains of war to the regular city magistrates; *ibid.*, 53, f. 89 (May 16, 1353); *ibid.*, 85, f. 133 (September 19, 1361).

maintenance of rural roads, bridges, and gates, with another decree for the construction of walls and fortifications. On the eve of the Pisan war, in a two-month interval, some 560 tiny communities were required to pay a battery of ancient obligations thought to have lapsed long ago. If a country parish failed to furnish the proper-size contingent for castle guard or neglected to repair a wall or maintain fortifications, the *regulatores* promptly imposed fines. Income from these condemnations was directly assigned for payment of interest on the *Monte*.[101]

The signory continued exhorting *regulatores* to seek additional revenue in the *contado*, and these officials began prosecuting rural communes for ancient delinquencies. By the late sixties, hundreds of hamlets were compelled to pay a certain percentage of their *estimo* for past breaches of the law, with offenses ranging from failure to send candles to the Baptistry in honor of Florence's patron saint, to spoliation of public property. Such fines were then placed in the special section of the treasury accounts entitled "The Four Keys," to be disbursed to communal creditors.[102]

More lucrative were the myriad assessments placed on subject cities. At first they were required only to maintain garrisons of mercenaries and to furnish military subsidies. Soon these obligations were converted into cash payments; between 1353 and 1368 Pistoia's contribution to the Florentine *camera* increased 50 per cent. San Gimignano was even less fortunate; her tax was doubled over the same interval. Bibbiena's tribute soared by one-half within two years. The commune was collecting over 100 knights annually from a single region—the Valdinievole.[103] By the early 1370s these subject cities were virtually

---

[101] *Ibid.*, 137 (July–August, 1367), section entitled, "Introytus quatuor clavium." For condemnations just before the Pisan war, see *ibid.*, 89 (May–June, 1362).

[102] *Ibid.*, 122.

[103] In the early fifties Pistoia was supporting a garrison of forty *equites ultramontanni*. The stipend for each knight was twenty-six lire a month, and the total disbursement, including that to foot soldiers, was approximately 2,800 lire for a two-month interval. Soon Pistoia was making additional payments into the *camera* in the form of subsidies for defense. In 1354 these totaled 7,000 lire. CCE, 52, f. 70r (April 1, 1354); *ibid.*, f. 215 (December 22, 1354); *ibid.*, 69 (January–February, 1358). Proposals that Florence should exact special imposts and levy *prestanze* on such communities as Pistoia and Volterra were justified in the light of the "multa beneficia" conferred by the republic's benign rule. The subject people ought to be grateful and Florence "cum iusticia pecuniam procuretur ab eis." Cf. CP, 15, f. 116 (May 19, 1378). On Bibbiena, see CCE, 119, unnumbered folio (June 27, 1369). San Gimignano is the subject of a recent monograph by Enrico Fiumi, *Storia economica e sociale di San Gimignano* (Florence, 1961). Fiumi demonstrates the profound crisis Florentine fiscal policy produced in that small community. The incidence of taxation increased almost threefold from the late dugento to the early *quattrocento*, and San Gimignano incurred severe budget deficits. The author wryly observes that by 1435 imposts were being placed even on locks and keys. Cf. pp. 160–64, 189–91. For San Gimignano's earlier tax assessments, see CCE, 106, entire volume; *ibid.*, 118, entire volume.

incorporated into the Florentine fisc. The treasurers of San Miniato were now Florentine citizens paying receipts directly into the *camera* of the republic. Revenue from customs tolls, gabelles on wine, salt, and other commodities, and even levies on contracts were transferred directly to Florence. Over the next few years the rate of taxation doubled and sometimes even tripled. Meanwhile the military subsidy extracted from subject cities increased some 70 per cent when the signory decreed that a special tax should be collected over and above the so-called *tassa ordinaria*. Subject cities could not hope to meet their crushing responsibilities to Florence; soon their treasuries ran sizable deficits.[104] New taxes, new debts, and a stern program of Florentine mercantilism did little to encourage the economic growth of these towns. Out of the ever-widening claims of the Florentine treasury were forged the links of empire, with the pattern of exploitation of *contado* intensifying in the late *trecento* and early *quattrocento* further accelerating this transition.[105]

VII

The search for revenue was to lead to the integration of Florentine territory and the rise of empire; this consolidation and imperial triumph notwithstanding, the fiscal drain on the *camera* persisted. Disquieting was the precipitous drop in customs receipts, as well as in yields from other major gabelles. Difficulties were compounded since Florence became embroiled in a series of wars, each conflict proving more costly than the last. The war of the Eight Saints (1375–78) required outlays of 2,500,000 florins—some eight times the total annual revenue collected by the commune from all principal imposts. From the

---

[104] Soon after the thwarting of the rebellion of San Miniato, Florentine officials were empowered to collect all the important gabelles and to supervise the fiscal administration of this subject town. By 1371 revenues from the courts of San Miniato were being paid directly into the Florentine treasury. Cf. *ibid.*, 135–40 (1370–71). The communities under Florentine dominion were consistently incurring debts by their steady borrowing from the *camera* of the republic. On the subject of mercantilism, see R. Davidsohn, "Blüte und Niedergang der florentinischen Tuchindustrie," *Zeitschrift für die gesamte Staatswissenschaft*, 85 (1928), 225–55. For additional bibliography, see M. Becker, "The Republican City State," p. 50. By the end of the *trecento* a tax was placed on each piece of imported cloth. Even inexpensive varieties were being excluded from the Florentine market. E. Fiumi has graphically described the impact of Florentine legislation that imposed gabelles on goods exported by citizens of San Gimignano to any other town than the Arno republic. Cf. E. Fiumi, *Storia economica*, p. 185.

[105] Neither Fiumi nor any other investigator of Tuscan rural history has drawn inferences as to the possible effects of Florentine economic policy upon the *contado* and its many towns. In the case of San Gimignano, the one community whose *trecento* history has been carefully analyzed, the heavy tax burden laid on this subject town by her masters certainly discouraged economic development. Florentine tax policy also resulted in ever stricter regulation of those who plied minor trades in the *contado*.

start, many in the signory realized that new revenues must be unearthed if victory was to be gained. One speaker's proposal was not without irony: Let monies be extracted "sweetly and modestly" from the inhabitants of the Florentine countryside. In this instance "dulciter et modeste" referred to the levying of an *estimo* on the *contado* at the high rate of thirty soldi per lira, as well as to the imposition of a gabelle on wine "in comitatu" at a figure establishing a new mark for that impost—forty soldi *per congio*. Additional revenues were to be realized when a tax was placed on wine sold in wholesale lots. Also, keepers of rural inns were subject to sizable taxes based upon the amount of their retail trade.[106]

Again the familiar reluctance to impose an *estimo* on the city prevailed. Advisers to the signory were aware that returns from a few new gabelles on the *contado* would be too meager for treasury needs. Once more the government was instructed to rely upon that aged remedy for fiscal ills—the forced loan. During the three years Florence warred against the Holy See, twenty-five *prestanze* were levied, thereby augmenting the funded debt by at least half a million florins.[107] As early as the winter of 1375–76, counselors to the signory stolidly proclaimed the treasury should pay interest to those making *prestanze*. The all too familiar cycle commenced: new money must be borrowed to repay old creditors.

By June, 1376, governmental advisers were lamenting that expenses of war were nothing short of *intolerable*. Again pressure mounted for exaction of new imposts on the *contado*. Those whose xenophobia encouraged them to seek for a conspiratorial explanation of fiscal problems were convinced the crisis had been provoked by foreign investors. According to them, these aliens bought into the *Monte*, then exported gold from the city under the pretext that it was only payment received for interest. These hypothetical villains were collecting small sums from the *Monte* and exporting precious bullion by falsifying treasury receipts to serve as export licenses. Of course foreigners purchased *Monte* stock, but the few who had substantial holdings were great prelates and lords, too well known to employ successfully such subterfuges. Strong support likewise existed for increasing the tax rate upon rural nobility, but this too was not a genuinely helpful remedy. Even at best, income from this source seldom rose above 4,000 florins, averaging the scant sum of 2,000 per annum.[108]

Borrowing money from capital invested in the *Monte* entailed less dissension and became chronic with the onset of the War of the Eight Saints. Accelerating in 1377 and 1378, the *camera* was regularly trans-

---

[106] *CP*, 14, f. 89r (October 3, 1377); *ibid.*, 15, f. 100 (April 10, 1378).
[107] *Prestanze*, Vols. 240–343; *CCE*, Vols. 172–80; G. Brucker, "Un documento," p. 168.
[108] Cf. footnote 97.

ferring 50,000 florins a month from *Monte* deposits and placing it in the accounts of officials charged with the hire of mercenaries. The largest reserve of untapped revenue still exempt from many communal imposts was the patrimony of the Tuscan church. Never before had the moment been more propitious for the spoliation of these ecclesiastical estates. Anticlerical sentiment was at its zenith, with the Florentine signory leading twenty-one states in battle against papal troops and lieutenants. Earlier, communal taxation of clergy was sporadic; during intervals of popular government, however, the signory made inroads into traditional ecclesiastical immunities and liberties. Popular ardor cooled shortly thereafter, and the more oligarchical regimes were again considerate of time-honored rights, but at that hour the wealth of the Tuscan church was in jeopardy, since the signory was democratized, the costs of war were escalating, and aintipapal feeling was intense. At first, speakers before the signory suggested that clerics contribute "just as other citizens" (*sicut alii cives*); next, a special impost of 30,000 florins was proposed. Soon, however, these moderate voices receded and the call came for mass appropriation of church lands.[109]

On the eve of war the outlay for troops stood at 25,000 florins a month. With the onset of hostilities it almost tripled, so that advisers to the government were anxious about payment of interest to communal creditors. Confronted with the certainty of a rising budget, their anxiety was not misplaced. November, 1376, witnessed the decision to elect officials charged with selling or leasing ecclesiastical property. They acted promptly, for in January, 1377, records of the first payments were entered in the treasury registers. Some of the lands may have been acquired as a consequence of straw transactions, with the church employing agents to make payment so patrimony might remain intact. Among the first to gain title (at least at law) was Lapo da Castiglionchio, a most vociferous advocate of ecclesiastical causes. Several thousand others took this unrivaled opportunity to acquire valuable real estate at bargain rates. Indeed, this lure served to democratize society, with all classes participating—patrician, newcomer, and even prosperous peasant.[110]

The next years saw the acceleration of leasing, confiscation, and alienation of ecclesiastical holdings. Only with the end of war in the summer of 1378 did the signory agree to the principle that restitution be made. Through a complex series of maneuvers, the Florentine government assumed liability for substantial tracts of land now lost to the church. The exact value of appropriated holdings cannot be

---

[109] *CP*, 14, fols. 57r–105r (June 14–November 18, 1376).
[110] For records of first payments by purchasers, see *CCE*, 175 (November–December, 1376); *ibid.*, 176, unnumbered folio (January 20, 1377).

determined; judging from the total of the debt assumed by the commune from that source, the figure was close to 220,000 florins. After intricate negotiation in the early 1380s, the government agreed to pay the church 5 per cent interest on the value of its unrecovered patrimony. Although the obligation was scaled down, interest payments stood at 12,000 florins annually, and 220,000 florins was the increment to the state debt.[111] Further escalation followed when new *prestanze* were levied and the practice of borrowing from capital invested in the *Monte* continued.

Just before the outbreak of the revolution of the wool workers (the Ciompi), the signory was again regaled with sage fiscal counsel. As usual, contradictions abounded; Confiscate more ecclesiastical property, then new *prestanze* will not be required; impose *prestanze* and desist from appropriating church property; levy new taxes on Pistoia and Volterra, but treat subject territories moderately. Perhaps the most tantalizing suggestion was advanced during a session of the signory in May, 1378: Procure money but don't touch the purses of the citizenry. Soon after, need for revenue was so pressing that communal councilors advised the regime to impose *prestanze* promptly to avert immediate peril.[112]

In the next few weeks the revolution of the Ciompi exploded, and in its wake pronouncements of a new fiscal program. The florin was not to be worth more than sixty-eight soldi. Formerly cloth manufacturers had profited from an increase in the value of this gold coin and an attendant depreciation of silver currency, for they received income for merchandise in gold while paying workers in silver.[113] *Prestanze*, hitherto so profitable to the guild elite, were not levied for six months. Meanwhile preparations were to be undertaken for the imposition of an *estimo*. The most radical proposal of all entailed a plan for amortizing the *Monte*. Over a twelve-year interval the original investment of each creditor was restored; a fund was established from monies saved as a consequence of amortization and reduced interest. Ideally, funds were to be sufficient for repayment of principal over that twelve-year interval.

Past management of the *Monte* especially incensed the Ciompi revolutionaries. Their animus was focused upon the notary Ser Piero Ser Grifi, originator of various schemes for increasing interest rates, the "Three for One *Monte*" being his pet creation. In reprisal the rebels declared him ineligible for any public office; later a sizable portion of

---

[111] *PC*, Vols. 1 (1384)–6 (1390).
[112] The call for imposition of *prestanze* also included the suggestion that the citizenry of Pistoia and Volterra be liable. Cf. *CP*, 15, f. 108r (May 6, 1378).
[113] G. Brucker, *Florentine Politics and Society*, p. 383.

his patrimony was confiscated. Other decisions of the revolutionary junta involved prohibition of export of grain from the *contado* and lowering of the tax on processors of this necessity. Between announcing a program and implementing it, the distance was as between two galaxies.[114]

Despite the regime's proclaimed opposition, *prestanze* continued as the primary source of revenue.[115] Revolutionary government found it simpler to change treasury personnel than to initiate novel financial practices. Magnates could easily be ousted from positions of fiscal responsibility, but to create machinery for an *estimo* was intricate and time-consuming. To compensate for lack of income the commune continued collecting rents from confiscated ecclesiastical property as well as conducting outright sales. Although some 20,000 florins was realized during July–August, 1378, the treasury was confronted with its deepest crisis since 1342–43. The War of the Eight Saints added 2,500,000 florins to the state debt, and *Monte* shares fell to a new low when they were traded on the market at 13 per cent of their face value.

In early September, 1378, an end was made to the experiment of the Ciompi when representatives of the wool workers were expelled from government and a moderate, albeit democratic, regime was installed. This time the masters of the fourteen lesser guilds were accorded extensive power. Confidence in the stability of a social order returned and a general business recovery ensued. Receipts from the gabelle on contracts reached their nadir during June and July, 1378, but by November–December of that year were up some 400 per cent. The first half of the following year saw them continue to prosper, until in January–February they reached 2,220 florins—a figure approximating the total reached just before the outbreak of the Ciompi. Receipts in June–August, 1379, topped 4,200 florins, a very respectable sum.[116]

At first this democratized regime was satisfied to continue exacting *prestanze*; soon, however, it was clear other remedies were mandatory. A legislative debate held in late September, 1378, revealed general agreement among speakers that the commune maintain "faith with its creditors." The precipitous drop in the value of *Monte* shares was disquieting; it became necessary to find new sources of income. The first speaker suggested creating an extraordinary commission of fifteen men charged with distributing the tax on salt so that the treasury would enjoy an income of 30,000 florins. Coupled with this was the dire expedient of an *estimo* on the city. The usual vigorous opposi-

---

[114] For a statement of objectives by the Ciompi leadership, see *P*, 67, fols. 1–13; *LF*, 40, fols. 301–7 (July 21, 1378).
[115] *CCE*, 185 (July–August, 1378); *ibid.*, 186 (October–November, 1378).
[116] *Ibid.*, Vols. 186–190.

tion ensued, so that shortly thereafter the suggestion was made that "pauperes et impotentes" be exempt. In mid-October troubled councilors returned to this controversial theme; Ser Niccolò Ser Ventura exhorted the signory to take steps so that the *"fides communis* should be observed *in facto montis."*[117] Patriotism lent resonance to his discourse: Citizens must stand firm, supporting the commune in her dark hour; they must make the most telling of sacrifices—accepting a reduction of interest rates. His proposal was indeed moderate: Let the rate of interest paid the holders of *Monte* shares be reduced one-third. Even then, new sources of revenue would have to be unearthed if interest was to be paid regularly.

Benedetto Alberti, patrician by birth and popular leader by conviction, concurred: The republic must keep faith with communal creditors. This outspoken Florentine political leader soon to dominate economic discussions before the signory was reluctant to opt for an *estimo* on the city. Because it provoked disaffection, he and other prominent advisers remained wary, favoring a direct tax "only if it were absolutely necessary."[118] The usual tired proposals followed: Let there be a new tax on salt, or better yet, an extraordinary impost on the *contado*. Both expedients were adopted, with the tax on the countryside fixed at the high rate of forty soldi per lira; still the revenue crisis persisted. There was talk in the advisory councils of raising the figure above that imposing level. Even this fell short of resolving the crisis.

Revenues continued sparse; late in 1378 the signory dramatically convoked in solemn session a panel of eminent jurists who ventured opinions on the feasibility of amending sacred regulations concerning administration of the funded debt. These experts were unanimous that no change should be countenanced: the consequences for the treasury were continued high interest rates at a time when new revenues were still unavailable.[119] Again the option of imposing an *estimo* was entertained, this time more seriously, since communal bankruptcy was a real possibility.

Cumbersome machinery for the extraction of the *estimo* was installed in the first months of 1379, so that by late October the first receipts entered the treasury. Special officers for each quarter of the city were regularly making payments into the *camera*.[120] At first, receipts were channeled into the general fund, but late in November they were credited to the account for hire of mercenaries entitled "Introytus depu-

---

[117] *CP*, 16, f. 35 (October 19, 1378).
[118] *Ibid.*
[119] *Ibid.*, 16, fols. 43–43r (November 8, 1378).
[120] *CCE*, Vols. 189–92.

tatus ad capsam conducte." Soon they constituted the largest portion of income available for the purpose. Clearly, plans had misfired. Thus in October–November, 1380, 95 per cent of all income from the *estimo* was diverted for troops, with petty sums remaining for holders of *Monte* shares.[121]

Treasury shortages were severe in 1380 and pressure for restitution to *Monte* creditors still intense. Proposals to utilize funds from criminal condemnations for the benefit of *Monte* creditors involved only trifling sums. Even as the first *estimo* was being collected, a suggestion for converting this direct tax into an interest-bearing forced loan was introduced. Such a stratagem was unoriginal, but coming at this time its approval was a brake on the democratic thrust toward reorganization of the fiscal base of the republic. Some governmental advisers advocated the *estimo* be converted into a non-interest-bearing loan; the majority, however, favored some interest for use of citizen capital. The end of the year saw the treasury collecting from eight different levies, euphemistically described as *estimi*. In fact these were interest-bearing loans, and the following January the treasury discontinued the subterfuge, establishing a treasurer of *prestanze* charged with collection.[122] Income was still used for mercenaries, and when costs rose unexpectedly the treasury again resorted to the venerable practice of borrowing from *Monte* capital. In January–February, 1380, the sum reached 100,000 florins; for the balance of the year receipts from the customs toll and other gabelles pledged for payment of interest to *Monte* shareholders also went for the same cause.[123]

Large-scale borrowing was soon discontinued, however, as was the practice of assigning certain monies intended for *Monte* interest to the *Introytus honorum presbiteriorum*. (This was a special account set up by the treasury to pay clergy for properties confiscated during the War of the Eight Saints.)[124] The "fides communis" stood in jeopardy with speakers calling for new taxes to allow the treasury to dispense a meager one denarius per lira interest a month—only 5 per cent per annum. Still, an *estimo* might provoke "scandala" (grave discord), and the responsible popular leader Uguccione Ricciardi Ricci advocated that certain citizens be deputized to raise sufficient revenue, but "not through an *estimo*." His popular confederate Benedetto degli Alberti concurred adding that money should be collected from Florentines, but always with "the hope of repayment." New citizens and *minori* still favored direct taxes, but not the patrician leadership of the democ-

[121] *Ibid.*, Vols. 191–92.
[122] *Ibid.*, Vol. 199.
[123] *Ibid.*, Vols. 193–98.
[124] *Ibid.*, Vol. 197.

ratized regime. The armorer Simone di Biagio, among the first to favor an *estimo* because it would make the tax burden more equal, still believed loans should be made "without interest," with only the principal to be restored. Speakers candidly acknowledged the "impotentia communis," expressing dismay that the *camera* was unable to meet its obligations to the clergy or its own citizens—yet practical advice was not forthcoming.[125]

In April, Cipriano Duccio Alberti spoke before the signory proffering the familiar solution: Let money be procured "by the usual means," but this time effort to obtain maximum income from public properties and rural wealth should be intensified.[126] High returns from the "officials over communal properties" attest to the success of the program with systematic collection of imposts on rural Tuscany commencing in 1379. Delinquent taxes on salt and wine were recovered. The treasury collected levies outstanding since 1354; harsh justice was dealt the *contado* nobles from the houses of the Ubaldini of Barberina, Uberti of Figline, Gherardini, Ricasoli, and Scolari. By 1380 communal accountants (*rationerii*) with extraordinary powers were in full operation. Rural communes remiss in their tributary obligations made restitution. The rural nobility were also liable for exceptional imposts, and a special *balìa*, the *Otto della Guardia*, placed new taxes on towns in the *contado*. With the rate of the rural *estimo* at the high of forty soldi per lira, additional direct taxes (*extimi extraordinarii*) were ordered and became a regular feature of the regimen of city over countryside.[127]

In the polis the same strict rule was practiced, with the returns collected by the magistrates over public property (*Officiales bonorum rebellium* reaching the unprecedented total of 1,200 florins for July–August, 1381.[128] Again the armorer Simone di Biagio spoke, this time admonishing the signory to see that the officials holding "full power" ("plena balia") for recovery of public property exercised their mandate "sine aliqua exceptione sicut fuit intentio populi" ("without any exception just as the people intended"). The chronicler Marchionne di Coppo Stefani, active in politics at this time, advised that all be forced to pay their "debentes communi" ("communal obligations") and that full power be given the "officiales bonorum, rebellium"; if these proved in-

---

[125] *CP*, 18, fols. 90 ff.; *N. Rodolico, I Ciompi* (Florence, 1945), p. 193.
[126] *CP*, 18, f. 104r.
[127] Cf. *CCE*, 187, unnumbered folio (January 2, 1379). For the beginning of systematic collection of other outstanding imposts such as the gabelle on country nobles or the rural *estimo* back to 1355, see *ibid.*, 190, unnumbered folio (July 21, 1379); *ibid.*, unnumbered folio (November 14, 1379) and (December 5, 1379). For the "introitus" of the *Otto*, see *ibid.*, Vol. 188. For the *rationerii*, see *ibid.*, 187, unnumbered folio (January 20, 1379), and continuing through 193 (January–February, 1380).
[128] *Ibid.*, Vol. 202.

sufficient the *estimo* should be the remedy. Salvestro de' Medici, outspoken popular hero, reiterated this counsel, adding that expenses for mercenaries should be reduced. Benedetto degli Alberti was of the same mind, except that he recommended reducing the number of mercenaries rather than their term of service. Later that year other councilors proposed that added power be given *rationerii extraordinarii* to obtain revenue; only if this failed should imposition of an *estimo* follow.[129] A commission of Eight was appointed with instructions to tap new sources. The two bold measures that followed were bound to antagonize: a levy was placed on oil used in processing wool, embittering influential manufacturers, and a tax of one-half florin was imposed on each yoke of oxen, distressing farmers. Returns were still inadequate.[130]

Although the fiscal bind of the treasury persisted, these measures accelerated the trend toward more impersonal and stricter government. The experience of the years after 1378 indicates that juridical and political attitudes could be modified more readily than economic habits. The machinery of government and force of public law were strengthened, communal bureaucracy became more effective, but the principle of direct taxation had to be abandoned. The stage was set for an easy solution: consolidation of the *Monte* and a reduction of interest rates.

Although carrying charges would be reduced, deficits must continue, for tax income would be insufficient. The treasury would continue to rely upon interest-bearing forced loans, with more citizen capital flowing into the public fisc and the state debt reaching monumental proportions. If direct taxation of urban capital and property had been effected and the original plan of 1378 to amortize the *Monte* implemented, the new state economy essential for the formation of attitudes associated with the Renaissance might well have been forestalled.

IX

The autumn of 1380 was the scene for the last confrontation of the men of the polis with the problem of the debt. The chronicler Marchionne di Coppo Stefani, little given to hyperbole, opined that in a hundred years of history there had never been a more crucial political decision than the one now to be made.[131] Once more the armorer Si-

---

[129] *CP*, 19, fols. 84r–87r.
[130] N. Rodolico, *I Ciompi*, pp. 188–89.
[131] Stefani, 883, ". . . e non credo, che già cento anni, niuna così gran cosa si facesse colle fave, come questa; perocchè la somma era grande de danari e la quantità degli uomini, e femmine grande."

mone di Biagio spoke first, this time for the college of the *gonfalonieri*. He and his colleagues favored imposing a forced loan at 5 per cent as well as reducing interest rates on the *Monte* to the same figure. This could only stir up opposition, damaging the reputation of any regime brave enough to implement it. Although the creditors were not receiving that modest return, any official acknowledgment by the government that rates were cut by two-thirds or even one-half would have the effect of further depressing the market in shares and obliterating whole paper fortunes. Not surprising, then, Benedetto Alberti's familiar plea that the government reduce expenses for the hire of mercenaries and that if any fortress is useless it be evacuated. If these savings are insufficient and if the consent of creditors can be obtained, then discussion of the reduction of interest rates can commence. Uguccione de' Ricci was just as cautious, again advising the government to reduce expenses.

The apothecary Giovanni Dini voiced the apprehension of the commission of the *Otto della Custodia* when he stated: "Concerning the matter of the *Monte* let nothing be said, lest it appear that the commune wishes to break faith." The speaker for the college of the Twelve Good Men urged the signory first to limit "omnes expenses" and next to hold a formal meeting on the *Monte* problem with all who participate sworn to secrecy. Rosso Ricci, so experienced in communal politics, could only urge the republic to keep faith with the creditors. The blunt Salvestro de' Medici was one of the few to speak in early October without equivocation for reduction of interest. There were others who would resort to taxes on oxen, oil, or the wine of the *contado*.

Timorousness among the advisers and commissions delayed policy formulation. However, revenue was required for subsidies to marauding companies, to secure the new alliance with Milan, and to rebuff the threat of foreign conquest of Arezzo. In political discussion expressions of deep concern "pro securitate libertatis et status presentis civitatis Florentie" were commonplace. In December, 1380, resistance proved less formidable; the old debts were canceled, then consolidated into a new *Monte*. The new "mountain of indebtedness" assumed full liability for all governmental obligations, this time at the modest rate of 5 per cent a year.[132]

As we have seen, Stefani opined this was the gravest single measure taken by any signory over the course of the fourteenth century. In a *ricordanza* (memorial) kept by the Curiani family, owners of substantial *Monte* holdings, the name of the high magistrate (*Gonfaloniere di Giustizia*), Recco di Guido Guazza, was entered as "gonfaloniere di

[132] *CP*, 19, fols. 41r–84r.

ingiustizia," for he was seen as perpetrator of this horrendous act.[133] The new *Monte* of December, 1380, was responsible for all outstanding loans, but, to the dismay of the good burghers, at reduced interest rates. In order that carrying charges might be further reduced, provision for amortization was made: a certain proportion of the customs toll (1,000 florins a month), the retail tax on wine (32,000 a month), the return from a new assessment of one-half florin on each yoke of oxen used to cultivate land in the *contado*, plus the yield from the other new impost on the production of olive oil, were each to be devoted to the lofty purpose of debt retirement.[134]

Despite well-intentioned efforts the debt continued to mount and the hope of amortizing the new *Monte* proved illusory. The vision of the ruling *minori* and their patrician adherents was heroic, but the treasury records show that nothing beyond the reduction of interest rates was translated into action. By March–April, 1381, the commune was imposing new *prestanze*, thus further inflating the public debt. Even the more popular leaders of this democratic regime no longer championed any revision of the revenue structure. Any shift toward reducing the inflated indebtedness by initiating direct levies on urban wealth and property had been forestalled. This postponement obtained for better than forty years.

The consensus favoring 5 per cent interest for government loans prevailed only through the early eighties. With an end to the democratic experiment of 1378–82, demand from communal creditors grew, and by June–July, 1383, income from major gabelles was employed for interest. Again the commune relied on new *prestanze* and loans from capital of the *Monte* treasurer. Meanwhile, heavier gabelles were imposed on wine produced in the *contado*, and a special section of the treasury, the *Introytus capse condepnationum*, was established, with the bulk of receipts derived from fines against rural inhabitants. A series of *extimi extraordinarii* were also levied so that in June, 1383, the treasury was collecting four *estimi* at rates of ten soldi, eleven soldi, twelve soldi, and 22 soldi per lire.[135] The government also assumed liability for property confiscated by the democratic regime of 1378–82. The signory was authorized to realize higher mint profits on coinage, and this together with added income from the countryside was intended to reimburse those whose patrimonies had been appro-

---

[133] N. Rodolico, *I Ciompi*, p. 188.

[134] B. Barbadoro, *Le finanze*, p. 672; N. Rodolico, *I Ciompi*, pp. 188–89. The oil taxed was of a quality employed in manufacture of wool.

[135] *CCE*, Vol. 213. Cf. also *ibid.*, Vols. 225 (June–July, 1385) and 230 (April–May, 1386) for comparable tax pattern in the *contado*. At the same time certain revenues pledged for interest payments to creditors were being employed for hire of mercenaries. *Ibid.*, 228 (December–January, 1385–86).

priated earlier. This was no durable solution, since shortly thereafter this income was diverted for war.[136]

In February–March, 1384, leading families in the city subscribed to special short-term loans. These included the Alberti, Castellani, Medici, Panciatichi, Rinuccini, and other financiers of the polis.[137] This expedient also increased the indebtedness of the city. With the start of the Visconti war, the customs toll, salt tax, wine impost, and a dozen other staples of the public fisc pledged for restitution were again spent for mercenaries. Treasury balances improved slightly between 1382–84, but they were never substantial. In October, 1387, they were dangerously low, totaling a few hundred florins. Meanwhile the spiral of indebtedness climbed; in the winter of 1385 the treasury was collecting seventeen *prestanze* simultaneously.[138]

X

Interminable talk in the advisory councils over the decade resulted in a myriad of trivial modifications in the tributary system. The two subjects dominating political discourse at this time were those hardy historical twins, war and taxes; this lack of creativity was prompted by the reluctance of the larger communal councils to co-operate with even modest proposals of the signory. Only in the next decade was the need to obtain the approval of these bodies suspended. In 1393 the government founded a special council of Eighty-one who alone had authority over the imposition of new taxes.[139] Further, they were empowered to assign 60,000 florins annually for interest to *Monte* creditors. The persistence of war again disrupted plans, and over the next years payment was regularly suspended. Good advice was still forthcoming, until, at the end of the century, Filippo Salvi voiced deep frustration observing that many in the government either carped at or rejected proposed reforms but never made positive proposals.[140]

If the weight of the debt only increased, not to be lessened by political action, yet there was no despair among the citizenry. The practice of allowing the affluent to pay the forced loans of the middling citizens, thereby gaining title, continued. So, too, did the strategy of

---

[136] Stefani, 927. We observe the onset of this diversion to the special *capsa* for hire of troops beginning in early 1385. Cf. *CCE*, Vol. 223, and footnote 135.
[137] *Ibid.*, Vol. 217.
[138] *Ibid.*, 223, unnumbered folio (February 27, 1385); cf. also *ibid.*, 239 (October 1, 1387). Communal income pledged for reimbursement for confiscation of church property was also diverted for war. *Ibid.*, 225 (January, 1388).
[139] *Balìe*, 19, fols. 18r–20r.
[140] I wish to thank Professor Anthony Molho for permitting me to read his manuscript "The Florentine Oligarchy and Balìe of the Late Trecento."

permitting a citizen to pay only a portion of his *prestanza* assessment. If a Florentine chose this option, then the treasury paid him neither interest nor principal. In effect, he was paying a direct tax.[141]

Most encouraging to the creditors was the firm character of the public economy as measured by treasury receipts. The steady flow of the customs toll, gabelles on wine, salt, contracts, and other indicators of communal well-being engendered confidence among the creditors of the republic. At intervals of surcease from war the treasury was able to resume interest payments.[142]

Over the last decades of the century realization grew that the precious *libertas* of the polis was hinged on the capacity of government to sustain public indebtedness. As early as the 1370s Antonio Pucci, the accomplished poet, linked the liberty of the republic with the well-being of the *Monte* and citizen wealth.[143] This awareness of a novel relationship between private and public worlds was ministered to by regimes unable to alter the fiscal base of the republic. Only by borrowing citizen capital could the government have sufficient funds. Ironically, fiscal conservatism led to new social and economic ideas soon expressed in the arts and historiography of the early Florentine Renaissance. Humanist scholars and artists would discover the bond between a healthy public fisc and private affluence. To the extent that individual identity depended upon patrimony, the citizen must have faith in the vitality of the state in order to believe in the durability of his own family and its progeny.

---

[141] R. de Roover, *Medici Bank*, p. 23.
[142] Throughout the decade of the 1380s tax receipts remained well above the ample figures in 1336–38 and the late 1350s. Even if rates were raised and inflation persisted, the increase was significant in the next decade except for 1390 and 1391. Income from this critical gabelle held up well. A comparable pattern can be discerned in returns for the salt tax. Only in the year 1386 was there a sharp dip, but recovery immediately sets in. *PC*, 1–15 (1384–1400).
[143] "Centiloquio," canto XCI (1373) in *Delizie degli eruditi toscani*, ed. Fr. Ildefonso di San Luigi (Florence, 1785), 6, 185–86, especially verses 83–94.

THE RENAISSANCE TERRITORIAL STATE AND CIVIC PERSPECTIVE

IV

In the late 1360s and 1370s there was a profusion of patriotic poetry, sermons, and prophetic writings. The tone of this vernacular literature was strikingly at variance with that of an earlier generation. Dante and his contemporaries tried to order the chaotic political landscape of the early fourteenth century by employing the ideals and ideal types of the medieval world. They hoped to achieve unity of historical materials by utilizing traditional ideologies in evidence in Italian historiography from the mid-tenth-century days of Otto I until the late *dugento*. The last great north Italian works to structure successfully events of their own times in terms of papal or imperial themes were the writings of Dante's contemporaries, the Paduan Albertino Mussato and Ferreto de' Ferreti of Vicenza. Neither scholastic modes for order and numeration nor symmetrical grouping of seeemingly disparate events around some charismatic figure such as pope or emperor proved effective. Likewise, medieval science, astronomy, and even astrology no longer seemed capable of furnishing ordering principles.[1] The same can be said for doctrines of courtly love and the promptings of chivalry. Surely, Dante's own poetry stands as a stunning tribute to the ultimate failure of the application of medieval chivalric strategies to the world of contemporary history. The difficulty was not limited to poetry. As we have observed, major Florentine chroniclers confronted the problems of subsuming historical experience of their time under any political, religious, or ethical schema from the medieval world. Favorite sources for earlier writers were eclipsed as the classics jostled with Eusebius and the Scriptures.

With the mid-*trecento* we see novel efforts by Florentines to lend meaning to their political experience by connecting citizen identity with a polis whose durability was being projected for the first time. Florence is not to be viewed as an inconsequential link in the great chain of medieval, political entities; rather, she will be depicted as standing secure

---

[1] N. Rubinstein, "Some Ideas on Municipal Progress and Decline in the Italy of the Commune," in *Fritz Saxl 1890–1948* (London, 1957), pp. 165–81; E. Mehl, *Die Weltanschauung des Giovanni Villani* (Leipzig, 1927), pp. 161–71.

and separate from any hierarchical order. Recent history confirms this feeling of apartness, for the Arno republic believed herself deserted by her old medieval allies, the Angevin monarchy of Naples and the papacy of Avignon. The latter's insistent support for the claims of Walter of Brienne, even after his ouster, served to initiate distrust, while the former's lack of sympathy toward a beleaguered business community in the 1340s turned good will into suspicion. A decade later old Guelf friendships were invoked in vain by Naples and Avignon; the recall of these pleasant memories seemed to Florentines only a prelude to requests for subsidies and troops. Axiomatic among chronicler and poet was the conclusion that the once-sacred agents of the Guelf alliance were not reliable. The pope was accused of supporting the "cause of the tyrant Visconti"; further, he had not deterred Emperor Charles IV from entering north Italy and disturbing Tuscan equilibrium. The kingdom of Naples could not even police itself, so extensive was the anarchy. Communal councils remained unmoved despite attempts by speakers to stir smoldering Guelf ashes by recalling the once-ample assistance of the Guelf king.[2]

The foremost poet of his day, Franco Sacchetti, portrayed Florence as a sainted personage, divinely chosen to lead the peoples of Italy into a new age. A less fierce but still glowing patriotic light illuminated the poetry of Antonio Pucci in his celebration of the polis' splendid victory over Pisa in 1364. Parenthetically, he was the first literary man to note how significant the growth of the *Monte* was for the expansion of the state. Standing without peer as an appreciator—almost a lover—of the material abundance of a thriving polis, who accepted the wealth of Florence with sensual delight, he celebrated the glories of its wool manufacture in the same tone as he extolled the beauty of its female inhabitants.[3]

Whole groups of prophecies composed in the seventies and eighties made the polis an object of religious veneration. Even the most agitated mystic appeared to find rest and some solace in the contemplation of this blessed *civitas*. Hope for political reform as well as for spiritual *renovatio* focused on the state: under Florentine leadership Italy will be renewed and peace and *libertas* assured; later, Florence, the "new great city" and "daughter of Rome," would work to heal the dread

---

[2] For Marco Strozzi's statement, "in recompensatione servitorum . . . ," see *CP*, 2, f. 141 (December 18, 1359). For a vote rejecting a provision requesting payment for troops to be dispatched to Naples, see *LF*, 36, f. 42 (February 26, 1361). Valuable for recent bibliography is P. Partner, "Florence and the Papacy 1300–1375," *Europe in the Late Middle Ages*, ed. J. Hale (London, 1965), pp. 81 ff. Cf. E. Léonard, *Histoire de Jeanne I*re*, reine de Naples*, 3 vols. (Paris, 1932–37).

[3] On this colorful figure, see Feruccio Ferri's valuable study *La poesia popolare in Antonio Pucci* (Bologna, 1909).

schism; soon the "bella città" will extend her rule over her neighbors, bringing happiness and *libertas* to those opposing the Lombard Visconti of Milan. Predictions casting Florence in the role of savior and agent of *renovatio* multiplied, coming to cluster around political leaders like Cosimo de' Medici.[4] Anonymous enthusiasts joined with clerical mystics in exhorting the citizenry, "true Christians elected by God," to undo the "heinous work of the carnal church." Sober politicians advised the signory to elect only those "zealous for the liberty of Tuscany." Speakers in the council halls saw the polis as defender of the sacred liberty of Arezzo, Perugia, Bologna, and other towns. The government was cautioned not to make peace with its adversary unless the liberty of these cities was assured. *Libertas* was the most precious of all possessions and the sole reason why the commune might break its solemn word. Such an ideology had become the exclusive property of the Arno city, and in its name *superbia* must be repressed and righteousness exalted.[5]

At mid-*trecento* there was mounting anxiety concerning the durability of this *libertas*. Government advisers cautioned the signory not to submit to any lordship, lay or ecclesiastical. Instructions to ambassadors emphasized that treaty arrangements never jeopardize *libertas*. Certain leading public figures were perturbed by this narrow conception of *libertas*, for it seemed to be little more than a parochial assertion of sovereign rights. Traditional Guelf ideology saw the *libertas* of individual communities as subordinate to universal Christian liberty. Lapo da Castiglionchio intoned the most stanch defense of this venerable position. His speeches of the 1360s and 1370s, however, were bizarre formulations of ideals he himself barely understood.[6] Certainly, many were shocked by the glaring violations of ecclesiastical liberties in the name of their secular counterpart. Disappointment was widespread when Florence repudiated old medieval ties, but the fact was that new loyalties and a more intense assertion of sovereignty always carried the day in the communal councils. Individual sympathies for the financial plight

---

[4] Cf D. Weinstein's soon-to-be-published study "The Myth of Florence and Prophecy," in *Italian Renaissance Studies*, Vol. 2.

[5] Caution was always given ambassadors or the signory that "in nicchilo diminuit libertatem communis." Advice was proffered regularly to act so that Perugia, Lucca, Pisa, Bologna, or Siena remain "in libertate." Treaties were made and oaths of loyalty taken "salva semper" the liberty of the polis. Extensive evidence is found for this in the earliest surviving records of the *trecento Consulte e Pratiche*. Cf. especially *CP*, 1, unnumbered folio (March 14, 1355); *CP*, 5, fols. 66r, 103 (May 4–July 5, 1364); *CP*, 10, fols. 43, 94r, 99r (November 24, 1368–April 28, 1369).

[6] R. Davidsohn, "Tre orazioni di Lapo da Castiglionchio," *ASI*, 20 (1897), 225–45, presents a sample of his quixotic oratory. Compare with the insights into the failure of papal policy by one of its key designers in the second half of the *trecento* as described by G. Romano, "Niccolò Spinelli diplomatico del secolo XIV," *Archivio Storico per le Provincie Napoletane*, 26 (1901), 400–529. Cf. also G. Brucker, *Florentine Politics and Society*, pp. 226–27.

of the papacy or the Guelf kingdom of Naples persisted, but seldom were benevolences or subsidies voted.

With the early 1350s, foreign policy discussions predominated. Although weeks and months might be spent analyzing the ethics of particular alternatives, the decision was almost a foregone conclusion. After 1353, when the Florentines signed a neutrality pact with the Ghibelline Visconti of Milan, the signory could not easily be persuaded to take any action that might jeopardize the pact. Therefore Florence remained responsive to the needs of the polis even when this meant reversing older programs hedged with Christian sanction. Her concern came to be the establishment of a belt of neutral or friendly cities surrounding her lands. *Libertas* came to imply freedom of her neighbors from domination by a foreign lord. To distinguish between this new ideology and imperialism was a delicate matter. In the name of just such principles, Florence embarked upon a cruel program of expansion, finally terminating in early *quattrocento* with the acquisition of Pisa and Livorno. Renaissance chroniclers applauded this rousing defense of *libertas*; earlier, medieval chroniclers were willing to condone expansionism only if undertaken for Christian ends.

At mid-*trecento*, however, few were at ease with a change in policy that upset traditional political values and styles. There was no large bloc of confident aristocracy, secure in their beliefs and graceful in gesture. Rather we see a mixed elite of *novi cives* and sympathetic patricians never standing together in lyric pose, for the exigencies of an increasingly public world made the loss of older, gentler ways more poignant. The political tone could only be awkward and tense. The need for revenue necessitated strict enforcement of public law; it also encouraged the extension of bureaucratic controls. Despite contempt for the less affluent newcomers, their presence was essential for staffing minor administrative offices. Many a Florentine preferred to pay a fine rather than serve in some remote post. Resentment against broadening the franchise and liberalizing communal policy on citizenship persisted. Yet although individual magnates vituperated democratization, actions of government tended in the aggregate to respond to practical imperatives. Although debate might be heated and extensive, substantial majorities regularly supported egalitarianism.

The day-to-day political psychology was characterized by an irritability; divisions deepened and factiousness intensified. No matter what the tactic or strategy employed to disfranchise, the fact remains that the number of citizens eligible for public office was on the increase in every decade from 1350 to 1400. The numerous petitions presented to the signory by aspirants for Florentine citizenship disclose the effective way in which practical needs triumphed. The candidate for this high honor agreed to purchase extensive property within the city walls, construct a suitable dwelling, enter his name on the communal tax rolls, and submit proof he had paid communal imposts for at least a decade. He would, moreover, be liable to all forthcoming *prestanze*. Finally, he would buy into the *Monte*. In this way the value of shares in the funded debt would be bolstered. Although there was opposition to these requests, hundreds of petitions were approved by the signory.[7] Too compelling were the advantages for a polis with an impoverished treasury, an expanded debt, and a burgeoning bureaucracy. That so many successful aspirants were notaries and professional men whose talents could benefit the republic was no coincidence.

Sympathies for a casual regimen proved durable, but when the issue was joined they were seldom strong enough to win the battle. There was still nostalgia for a loosely administered *contado*, and although over the fifties and sixties there was opposition in the councils to direct levies on the countryside, it seldom carried the day. Reluctantly, councilors supported a stricter rule over distant areas, for, confronted with mounting budgets, it was no longer possible to countenance widespread tax evasion.

I

Democratization paralleled the increasing attraction of the public world. As early as the mid-1350s the architect Francesco Talenti multiplied the distance between single pillars to achieve greater space in the Cathedral. Meanwhile, the commune's favorite church, Sta. Croce, assumed the appearance of a single hall, so wide were the apertures of the arcades. The Loggia dei Lanzi (1376–92), where political ceremonial was performed, stood as the most monumental, open Gothic hall yet built in Italy. No more democratic, secular piece of architecture ever dominated a Renaissance polis while at the same time permitting the citizenry, great and small, to participate in the political ritual.[8]

Florence was compared to beauteous ladies by poet-politicians and politician-poets. In a sermon Franco Sacchetti spoke of our beloved "Donna" as awaiting her Scipio, whom he compared with "Our Saviour." Was not, asks Sacchetti, His passion and death undertaken "per la libertà de l'anime nostre"? The wording of this appraisal of Christ's mission was not lost on a patriotic audience.[9] Leading clerics from Giovanni dalle Celle and Luigi Marsili in the seventies to Giovanni Domi-

---

[7] Cf. Chapter II of the present volume and the many petitions by those desiring a status identical to that of "antiqui cives" in *P*, Vols. 40–49, and *LF*, Vols. 34–36.

[8] F. Antal, *Florentine Painting and its Social Background* (London, 1948), p. 127.

[9] F. Sacchetti, *Opere*, ed. A. Chiari (Bari, 1938), 2, 277–82.

nici in the nineties lauded "la più onesta usanza della patria." Patriotic poetry by great clerics heaped fulsome praise upon a citizenry whose polis was the nearest possible approximation to the *civitas Dei*.[10]

Novel phrases such as "contra utilitatem publicem" or "contra voluntatem populi" appear regularly in the minutes of the advisory councils to the signory. There are "rebelles et hostes publicae" and "inimici status." The true "fideles" were the guildsmen of the *arti* who had to stand against the treacherous foes of *buon governo*. A special commission was elected to imprison and execute all who act "contra statum." These officials had "custodia" of the "statum." It is "necessitates status" that prevented Florence from sending aid to an ally. This awareness of the boundaries of this republican, political world was heightened after the forties with the bitter, anti-despot reaction to Walter of Brienne. Tragic experience fortified allegiances to the *status popularis*; only once was there report of statements in favor of installing a despot recorded in the minutes of the advisory councils.[11]

The demands of the public order grew more intense over the second half of the *trecento*. By the early 1380s the Tuscan clergy had lost many of their medieval immunities and liberties. The ancient rights of benefit of clergy and sanctuary had been systematically denied; the Tuscan church was making regular contributions to the public fisc. The republic confiscated large tracts of ecclesiastical land, and although some liability was finally assumed for this clerical patrimony, restitution was made only sporadically. The signory sought to dominate the court of the inquisition as well as to extend the authority of public courts into areas once the sole preserve of ecclesiastical tribunals. So successful was this extension of public power that by the early fifteenth century it was hazardous to prosecute on a charge of usury in a church court, since the plaintiff was required to post a sum exactly equal to that for which he was bringing suit. This money was to be deposited with a public magistrate, and if the plaintiff emerged victorious in the state court, this money was forfeited to the defendant.[12]

Two organizations closely associated with the Italian church were likewise much reduced in stature. Starting in the middle years of the

---

[10] Giovanni Dominici, *Regola del governo di cura familiare*, ed. D. Salvi (Florence, 1860), p. 136, and his poem in Vol. 13 of Giovanni Lami's *Deliciae eurditorum* (Florence, 1743), pp. 82–100.

[11] In the debate concerning whether extensive power should be conceded to Pandolfo Malatesta, Simone Rinieri Peruzzi rose to voice his opposition. Recollecting the horrors of the despotism of Walter of Brienne, he spoke to his fellow councilors of "la dolcezza della libertà, e come da lui erano stati trattati e che conoscessono la dolcezza della libertà, e che volessono vivere e morire in essa." F. Villani, 11, 69. Coluccio Salutati was bitter against the tyranny of the Visconti, and, like Boccaccio, even castigated Petrarch for accepting their hospitality. *Espistolario*, 1, 90, 97, 99, 141.

[12] *Statuta populi et communis Florentiae* (Freiburg, 1778), 1, 124–25.

fourteenth century the signory began to hedge the authority of those quasi-political bodies, the religious confraternities, until they were almost under state domination. Not only did the signory appoint captains to govern the most prominent of these groups, but the communal councils enacted laws putting the public treasurer in charge of the assets of the confraternities. By the 1370s direct fiscal supervision was the order of the day.[13] With the advent of the fifteenth century these lay religious companies were expressly prohibited from engaging in any political activity, no matter how trivial. If this proviso was violated the chancellor of the republic was to confiscate all the fraternities' assets and distribute them among the poor.[14] Much more significant than the extension of state hegemony over the many confraternities was the reduction of power of that most intractable of medieval organisms—the *Parte Guelfa*. The religious confraternities could upon occasion be used by those who sought to undo a communal statute against the Tuscan church, but the *Parte Guelfa* could and did serve as the arm for the city's nobility and the papacy of Avignon. As we have observed, by the late seventies many of the great patricians of Florence had come to champion a philopapal policy. The *Parte Guelfa* was utilized to check communal policies considered inimical to the interests of the Holy See. In 1375, when war erupted between Florence and the papacy, the *Parte* stood in direct opposition to official governmental policy. So adamant was the *Parte* and so obdurate its foes that a divided Florence was the consequence. Cleavage within the ranks of influential political men weakened the signory and made it difficult to resist the revolutionary demands of the wool workers set forth in the summer of 1378. Events of the late seventies and early eighties encouraged public-minded Florentines to scale down the *Parte*'s role until by late *trecento* its functions were principally ceremonial. No longer were the aristocratic captains of

---

[13] Severe regulation of the confraternities commenced at the height of the Pisan war, when the *camera* was sorely pressed for funds. Cf. *P*, 51, fols. 7–7r (August 21, 1363). The connection between the growth of government regulation and the rise of the public debt becomes increasingly clear when we learn from this provision that all bequests from last wills and testaments made to these bodies were to be paid into the Florentine treasury and certain of their assets were to be sold by the state. Monies realized were to be used to satisfy the claims of communal creditors. Two years later the government reserved the right to examine the accounts of these bodies, even though they were under the direct jurisdiction of the Bishop of Florence. *P*, 52, f. 151 (May 30, 1365). For examples of statutes of these confraternities, see *Testi fiorentini del dugento e dei primi del trecento*, ed. A. Schiaffini (Florence, 1926), pp. 34–54. On the general theme of these organizations in north Italian history, see G. Monti, *Le confraternite medievali dell'Alta e Media Italia* (Venice, 1927), 1, 147–93; 2, 23–25.

[14] R. Caggese, *Firenze della decadenza di Roma al Risorgimento di Italia* (Florence, 1913), 2, 360. For an instance earlier than that cited by Caggese, see *LF*, 41, f. 90 (February 18, 1383). After 1415 it was necessary to have the permission of the signory before a religious company could be organized. Cf. *Statuta Populi*, 3, 42.

this venerable, medieval, quasi-public organization to carry substantial weight in the political dialogues of early Renaissance Florence.[15]

The second half of the *trecento* was also the stage for vigorous assertion of public rights over the antique prerogatives of great feudatories of remote Tuscany. Within three decades the patrimonies of the mighty Counts Guidi and Ubaldini were finally declared subject to direct public levies. Other usurpations of seigneurial rights followed despite longstanding treaties between polis and feudatory in which the state had solemnly agreed to respect the prerogatives of the lords.[16] In the 1340s a program was initiated to regain "iura communis" entailing scrupulous implementation of public law against feudatories usurping state property for private use.[17]

Though the signory never denied the right of vendetta, it came to be strictly limited to the principals in any blood feud. After the 1330s this honorable recourse tapered off, and since responsibility for revenge devolved upon the most status-worthy magnates and haute bourgeoisie, the force of law served to modify violent behavior at the highest stratum

---

[15] Judging from representation accorded the *Parte*, it reached the apogee of its *auctoritas* in the late 1360s and early 1370s. Cf. *CP*, Vols. 9–12. Shortly before, legislation had been enacted requiring that the Guelf captains be present at all important sessions of the communal councils. Cf. U. Dorini, *Notizie Storiche sull'Università di Parte Guelfa in Firenze* (Florence, 1902), pp. 28–39.

[16] In a single month, the Counts Battifolle were fined the grand total of 52,473 lire, 10 soldi, for usurping public property. Formerly these extensive holdings spread over three rural parishes and had been acknowledged by the commune as the private patrimony of these feudatories. *CCE*, 161, unnumbered folio (July 7, 1374). In the territories of the Counts Guidi (the Commune of Romena) and those of the Ubaldini (the Podere Fiorentina), the *signori* enjoyed jurisdiction and exemption from the communal *estimo*. In the early 1380s these lands were subject to all obligations. Cf. E. Fiumi, "L'imposta diretta nei comuni medioevali della Toscana," *Studi in onore di Armando Sapori* (Milan, 1957), 1, 338; *PC*, 1, (1384).

[17] M. Becker, "Florentine Popular Government (1343-1348)," *Proceedings of the American Philosophical Society*, 106 (1962), 373–77. Many of the feudatories of the great Tuscan house of Ubaldini became subjects of the commune shortly after the republic waged her last great war against these nobles in the early 1370s. *CCE*, 169, unnumbered folio (November 21, 1375). For arrangements between Florence and other *signori* during these years, so critical for the formation of the territorial state, see *CCE*, 171, unnumbered folio (April 12, 1376); *LF*, 41, f. 101r (April 28, 1383). On this general but neglected theme, see G. Soranzo, "Collegati, raccomandati aderenti negli stati italiani dei secoli XIV et XV," *ASI*, 119 (1941), 3–35. What the commune could not gain through coercion, she was to achieve with subsidies. In a discussion held by the advisory councils before the signory on September 5, 1380, speakers suggested that the Tarlati clan and other great feudal lords in the vicinity be visited by discreet diplomats "ad exhortandum eos. Et cum pecunia subveniantur." *CP*, 19, f. 63. Cf. also *Delizie degli eruditi*, ed. Fr. I. di San Luigi (Florence, 1770–1789), 7, p. 191.

On the problems of magnate lawlessness, see *Giudice degli Appelli*, Vols. 121–25. During the decade of the 1330s there were seventy-two Florentine families inscribed among the city's *magnati*. Of this number, forty-six stood convicted of grievous breaches of communal law. Each of these houses averaged four convictions for high crimes ranging from assault to homicide and treason.

of society. Aristocratic prejudice against seeking justice in the courts of the republic rather than in the streets and piazzas of the city was also receding. Over the second half of the *trecento* certain of the most lawless magnates became pensioners of the commune, placing their skill at arms at the disposal of the polis rather than at the call of their violent *consorteria*.

Many rural nobles succeeded in enrolling among the ranks of the commoners, while others sold their lands to the commune and relinquished their proud titles. In Tuscany the status of vassal had become rare in the late Middle Ages. Only a few generations before, the designation "homo alterius" was considered advantageous since such an individual could avoid liability for certain communal imposts.[18] Indeed, the feudal structure of society was influenced by tax policies of the polis. When levies tended to be territorial rather than personal, nothing could be gained by assuming the status "homo alterius," for now the tax was placed on a district instead of on noble proprietors. By mid-fourteenth century a transformation was in process: rural communes and parishes were held responsible for a variety of imposts. The nexus between country person and urban government was tightening. In the past the great nobles and landlords collected gabelles on wine and taxes on rural magnates. Now the communities performed in this capacity.

Scores of Tuscan nobles renounced their *consorterie*; standing up in the courts of the republic they rejected family ties, since it was no fiscal advantage to be a country magnate. The Pazzi of Valdarno, the Counts of Certaldo, the Becchi of Castro Fiorentino, and hundreds of others petitioned to be numbered among the city population of Florence. As rule over the *contado* tightened, so, too, did the bonds between rural people and polis.[19] Needless to say, removal of these names from rural tax rolls eventually increased the burden of small parishes and villages.

In the city, too, there was progressive transformation of the character of the magnate order. The noble house of Ricasoli renounced its magnate status, changed its name to Bindacci, and was declared "populares." The Della Tosa were henceforth to be known as the Bilisardi; the Donati, as the Bellincioni; the Buondelmonti, as the Montebucini. These are but a few of the threescore or more of noble houses voluntar-

[18] The advantage accruing to those declared "homines alterius" and thus exempt from certain Florentine imposts disappeared almost entirely over the first years of the *trecento*. Cf. E. Fiumi, "Fioritura e decadenza dell'economia fiorentina," *ASI*, 116 (1958), 482-83. Significant was the fact that tributary obligations were becoming territorial rather than personal and that increased communal income was being employed to pay interest to communal creditors. *CCE*, 130 (March-April, 1369).

[19] When the rate of the *estimo* on *contado* was raised it became extremely advantageous to be enrolled as a citizen of the polis. Cf. Ser Lapo Mazzei, *Lettere di un notaro a un mercante del secolo XIV*, ed. C. Guasti (Florence, 1880), 1, 74-75. For the imposition of an extraordinary *estimo* of 25,000 florins on the *contado*, see p. 181.

ily to shift their status from partially disfranchised magnate to fully participating citizen.[20] Further, many magnate individuals petitioned the signory insisting they and their ancestors had always been "peaceful and law-abiding denizens of the city of Florence." Some beseeched the rulers of the city to take special cognizance of the fact that "as far as the mind runneth back, their forebears had lived as law-abiding merchants," being duly matriculated in one of the republic's greater guilds. Now, because a distant consort, for whom they had been compelled to go surety, committed a heinous crime, they were being persecuted. From whom could they seek redress of grievances and a modicum of protection at this trying moment unless it be the signory?[21] Their assessment of the legal possibilities open to them was sound; as the power of the polis increased, so, too, was protection of public law extended. Over the fourteenth century the number of petitions by individuals requesting the right to bear arms declined. The signory was also exceedingly reluctant to confer this prerogative upon medieval corporate bodies, retainers of ecclesiastical courts, and high-born nobles. Fines for carrying concealed weapons were increased 100 per cent, rising from twenty-five to fifty lire for carrying a long sword. The once estimable activities of jousting and sword play became less prestigious. Later, when the tournament was revived, it was the ceremonial and decorative that entranced *quattrocento* Florentines.

Like the order of magnates, the republic's guilds also underwent significant alteration in the second half of the *trecento*. Egalitarianism was evident among the *arti:* for the first time, in the 1340s, affluent dyers were declared eligible for the office of consul in the august wool guild. Added recognition was afforded the silk weavers and dyers by the *Por San Maria* guild, while the artists who had entered the guild of physicians and apothecaries as dependants of the *membrum* in 1314 achieved greater independence. Upon occasion, although the victories of members of the *arti minori* might be merely juridical, this did not render them inconsequential. All guilds and guildsmen were subject to prosecution for violating communal ordinances against monopolies after 1343. No longer did the city's seven major guilds stand virtually exempt from these stern pronouncements. The imbalance between major and minor guild representation in the Court Merchant was also adjusted in the early seventies. At that time lesser guildsmen were permitted to have

---

[20] *Statuta Populi*, 1, 446–47; *Balie*, 5 (1349). For a discussion of taxation as a force in encouraging magnates to seek *popolani* status, see E. Fiumi, *Storia economica e sociale di San Gimignano* (Florence, 1961), pp. 189 ff.

[21] Cf. G. Brucker, *Florentine Politics and Society 1343–1378*, pp. 155–56. Very important were the payments made into the treasury by many who were granted the coveted *popolani* status. Again the monies acruing from these former magnates were diverted to communal creditors. Cf. *CCE*, 89–95 (May–June, 1362—May–June, 1363).

free recourse to both the Court Merchant and the state tribunals. No slight advantage, this, since litigation was frequently tortuous in lower guild courts as well as in those of the major guilds to which appeal was permitted.[22]

The irony is that at a time when greater legal parity between major and minor *arti* was achieved, the guild political system was entering a decline. The familiar pattern of state intrusion into the workings of another set of medieval corporate bodies was evident. Officers of the republic were charged with responsibility for substantial parts of the communal food supply, undertaking import of certain commodities, even fixing prices and arranging for sale. The consuls of such energetic minor guilds as the butchers' were stripped of much of their authority; in the eighties—only a decade after the installation of such officials—a special commission (*balìa*) was formed to oversee general guild operation. With the advent of the *quattrocento* the cornerstones of the pluralistic medieval commune suffered a loss of prestige and, even more significantly, an attrition of income. A century before, artisan, mercantile, and industrial corporations had been among the principal props of the communal treasury. Like other quasi-political organizations such as the *Parte Guelfa* or the religious confraternities, they could furnish needed revenue for communal ventures. As we have noted, the republic's budget escalated dramatically over these years, until by the first third of the *quattrocento* the treasuries of the guilds were so meager the state could place little reliance on their resources.[23] The coming of the Medici in 1434 heralded a decline in the scope of jurisdiction of both Court Merchant and guild tribunals; in their stead, state courts assumed a larger measure of control. With the close of the *quattrocento*, the elaborate system of guild matriculation and surveillance was seriously undermined. Again state authority intruded rudely into the once-sacrosanct, semiautonomous world of medieval corporate bodies.[24]

Such an intrusion can in part be related to a more assertive mercantilism. Economic interests were looking to rulers of the republic for state support; increasing competition from north Europe encouraged this greater dependency. Expanded trade with eastern Europe was a promising counter to diminished opportunities to the north and west.

---

[22] M. Becker, "La esecuzione della legislazione contro le pratiche monopolistiche della arti fiorentine alla metà del secolo quattordicesimo," *ASI*, 117 (1959), 8–28; A. Doren, *Le arti fiorentine*, translated by G. Klein (Florence, 1940), 2, 70.

[23] For the depleted condition of the treasuries of the *arti*, see G. Canestrini, *La scienza e l'arte di stato* (Florence, 1862), p. 156. On the new authority of public officials over the *arti*, see *CP*, 21, fols. 53, 56–56r; *CCE*, 230, f. 4r (April 21, 1386); A. Doren, *Le arti fiorentine*, 2, 105.

[24] R. Pöhlmann, *Die Wirtschaftspolitik der florentiner Renaissance und das Prinzip der Verkehrsfreiheit* (Leipzig, 1878), pp. 48–49; A. Doren, *Die florentiner Wollentuchindustrie vom vierzehnten bis zum sechzehnten Jahrhundert* (Stuttgart, 1901), pp. 418 ff.

The Low Countries and Continental neighbors in the world of finance had only too well absorbed their economic lessons from the north Italians. The gap in fiscal techniques and economic strategies was narrowing so that the century-old advantage of the Florentine businessman was less pronounced.

For the second half of the fourteenth century the correspondence (*missive*) of the Florentine chancellery houses copies of letters dispatched by the signory in support of the myriad of enterprises of Florentine merchants trading and banking from the Balearic Islands to the exotic capitals of eastern Europe. Distant and precarious ventures of these businessmen required state support if profits were to be realized. This becomes apparent in the correspondence commencing with the late seventies when Florence's favored position was threatened; foreign competition and the hostility of the papacy were handicaps too severe for the republic's traders to overcome without government help.[25]

Increasingly the city's manufacturers called upon the signory to afford them protection from ruinous foreign competition. In October, 1393, the first general legislation was enacted establishing a sizable duty on the importation of fine foreign cloth. Over the next years the consuls of the once-so-proud wool guild acknowledged that further state action would be necessary if the guild and its membership were to prosper. Similar requests were made by other cloth guilds during the first part of the *quattrocento*.[26] Certain of the leadership of the major guilds had concluded that the *arti* could not sustain their competitive position on the European market unless they were protected at home by increased tariffs. That the earliest reforms were introduced during the tenure of Maso degli Albizzi, when first he came to dominate the formulation of political policy in October, 1393, indicates that powerful elements in communal politics opted enthusiastically for the imperatives of proto-

---

[25] The concern of the signory for winning advantages for Florentine bankers, merchants, and industrialists is indicated by the ever-greater number of discussions on this topic as well as the growth of communal diplomatic correspondence devoted to promoting the republic's mercantile interests abroad. Cf. especially *Missive della Prima Cancelleria*, Vols. 17–35. On the decline of Florentine foreign trade during the 1370s, see *Cronica fiorentina di Marchionne di Coppo Stefani*, ed. N. Rodolico, *Rerum Italicarum Scriptores*, new ed., 30, Part I (Città di Castello, 1903–1955), rub. 675. The best available index for assessing the vigor of this foreign trade are the receipts from the customs toll. In 1368 they stood at 196,395 lire, whereas in 1377 they totaled only 93,806 lire. For the figures on the earlier year, see *CCE*, Vols. 122–27, and for the latter year, see *CCE*, Vols. 176–81.

[26] C. C. Bayley, *War and Society in Renaissance Florence* (Toronto, 1961), pp. 71–72. R. Davidsohn's, "Blüte und Niedergang der florentinischen Tuchindustrie," *Zeitschrift für die gesamte Staatswissenschaft*, 85 (1928), 225–55, so frequently cited as an authoritative study on the Florentine cloth industry, is much in need of revision. For evidence pertaining to demands by the consuls of the *Lana* guild for protection, see LF, 51, f. 203 (May 30, 1418); *ibid.*, f. 206r (June 9, 1418).

mercantilism. Moreover, two of Florence's major wars, one against Pisa in the 1360s and the other against the same adversary in the early fifteenth century, were fought in response to the exigencies of manufacture and trade. These conflicts were burdensome, but Florence finally wrested control of the littoral from her sturdy neighbor and was soon constructing and building galleys to further the Mediterranean ambitions of her great *mercatores*.[27]

Florentine protomercantilism emerged as a sustained response to the needs of a business community that had once been ministered to by the powerful guilds. Yet another impulse propelling this mercantilism was the increased requirements of an expanded polis. In the same year that the signory proffered protection to her merchants (1393), legislation was also enacted prohibiting citizens from insuring merchandise carried on foreign ships; the public interest could best be served if capital was prevented from leaving the *patria*. At the same time a law was passed making anyone who exported more than fifty gold florins from the lands of the republic liable for prosecution.[28] A comparable motive lay behind Florentine legislation aimed at preventing a citizen from selling *Monte* shares to foreigners. The polis was extremely reluctant to make interest payments to noncitizens who it feared would drain precious bullion from the republic's reserves. By 1397 Tuscany was enclosed by a veritable tariff wall to protect home manufacture and conserve precious income of the *camera*.

Increased state participation in the economic life of the polis promoted enlargement of communal bureaucracy. Over the half century between the popular revolution of 1343 and installation of the regimen in 1393 the number of officials employed by a single public agency—the treasury—had quintupled. In one year 100 highly trained functionaries were required to carry out intricate *camera* operations. Prominent among their number were experienced lawyers, trained notaries, and accountants; fifty-eight commissioners were necessary to draw up contracts for the hire and provision of troops. Collection of a single gabelle —the customs toll—demanded the efforts of eighteen civil servants, whereas the gabelle on contracts required twelve men. Many officials in charge of indirect levies rendered daily reports to the *camera*. Twenty agents and clerks were employed by the communal bureau for importation and sale of grain. Additional recruits served as commissioners over the meat and fish supply, making contracts for import and fixing prices.

---

[27] For appropriations dedicated to these ends, see *PC*, Vols. 27–40.
[28] R. Piattoli, "Le leggi fiorentine sull'assicurazione nel medioevo," *ASI*, 90 (1932). 208–11. For a discussion of this problem, held by the advisors to the signory in August of 1395, *CP*, 31, f. 107r. Cf. also G. Canestrini, *La scienza*, p. 131, on legislation against alienating shares of *Monte* stock.

Even the new commitment of the republic to education involved the appointment of six learned men as directors over the *Studio*. This Florentine institution of highest learning was financed in part by monies collected under an extended and more regularized tax system affecting communal pawnbrokers. The need for more bureaucrats rose.

Multiplication of fiscal posts induced qualitative as well as quantitative change. At mid-*trecento* outstanding public men were managing the complex workings of the funded communal debt. This entailed formulation of public tax policy, administration of remote districts, and even making peace and war. Among their lesser functions was licensing of pawnbrokers and service as guardians for orphan children.[29] The *regulatores* were another set of officials conspicuous in public service with the 1350s. At first they treated accounting problems attendant upon administration of the *contado*. Soon these key appointees were meeting with the signory to adjudicate critical questions pertaining to tax assessment and rates of indirect levies. They and their battery of notaries and scribes inquired into problems of imposing rural quotas for militia service and castle guard, while at the same time determining and collecting obligations from great Tuscan feudatories. By the early seventies they were meeting with the signory to explain the merits of a particular tax bill or discuss the advantage of repossessing certain public properties.[30] In this area activity was intense, with the courts regularly restoring appropriated properties to the public fisc. Special judges and notaries were selected to adjudicate cases arising from collection of the principal communal gabelles. Additional notaries were enlisted to oversee collection of the *estimo straordinario*, soon to become a regular feature of state fiscal policy over the *contado*. Identical developments

---

[29] By the 1360s their number had quadrupled, and by the 1370s they were handling such diverse matters as the licensing of pawnbrokers and the operation of a credit bank for the republic's mercenaries. By 1377 these officers in charge of the communal debt were also serving as guardians of orphaned minors. At a meeting of the advisory councils to the signory it was suggested "pro utilitate pupillorum" that the patrimony of these children remain "in the hands of the commune." It would then be invested in the funded communal debt "cum interesse." It should be observed that earlier the role now performed by the state had been filled by one of the city's many confraternities. Cf. *CP*, 15, f. 54r (November 13, 1377).

[30] On the early history of the *regulatores*, see *Archivio dei Sindaci*, B., 4, 5, f. 1r. The date given for the beginnings of effective administration by the *regulatores* in this source is 1352. On their participation in sessions of the government, see especially *CP*, Vols. 6, 12, 14.

The office of defensor was originally created by the signory to check the spoliation of the *contado* by *magnates* and *potentes*. By 1367, however, the function of this vastly expanded office had been altered: now its members were regularly dispatched to the environs of the city in order to punish tax delinquents and protect communal property. *CP*, 12, f. 57. The office of *bargellini* underwent a similar evolution. *CP*, 8, f. 28r (January 11, 1367). On the fiscal role of the *Capitano del Custodia* and his staff, see *CCE*, 33, f. 71 (May 14, 1349).

attended the imposition of what was euphemistically called an "extraordinary tax" on designated subject cities. For the gathering of this impost new notaries were required; so, too, were special accountants for registering the yield of imposts upon the territorials (*districtuali*). Increased staffing of the *Grascia* reflected the varied duties it was called upon to perform. These ran the gamut from collection of petty debts to enforcement of more detailed codes concerning the sale of victuals. These responsibilities were coupled with their traditional, more colorful, duties of fining prostitutes who solicited outside prescribed districts and enforcement of the more complex communal sumptuary laws.[31]

A host of administrators supervised the legion of castellans heading garrisons in the more numerous castles and fortresses of the republic. These *officiales castrorum* were busily occupied managing public monies employed to underwrite this expanding operation. Simultaneously throughout the burgeoning Florentine empire the number of vicars and captains, podestàs, and other rectors was markedly increased. This thrust was accelerated with the election of new magistrates for such recently acquired cities as Arezzo, Pistoia, Prato, San Gimignano, and Volterra. Commensurate with this increased administrative responsibility was the development of elaborate procedures for reviewing the activities of the republic's bureaucrats. Over the generation after 1340 a review of the financial activities of a vicar or a captain had become a veritable legal *tour de force*.[32] So many facets of communal life were under tight supervision and regulation that the search for qualified civil servants was arduous. Such trifling activities as control over the vending of fish or determining the value of gifts betrothed couples might exchange required experienced personnel. If the position of the minor bureaucrat remained insecure, it only intensified the difficulties of recruitment. As long as so many of their number were vulnerable to charges of political deviancy leveled by such quasi-autonomous bodies as the Guelf party, government operations were disrupted and the role of civil servant thankless and dangerous. Only after the revolutionary years from 1378 to 1382 did statal machinery become sufficiently robust to protect public servants from the snares of factionalism and the accusations of political heterodoxy. Without ample legal and constitutional defenses, the impartial rule so essential for safeguarding administrative

---

[31] *Statuta Populi*, 2, 241–49; 261–62.
[32] The treasury records indicate that the number of officials compelled to make restitution of communal monies increased tenfold since the early 1340s. If one looks into the many volumes of the *Atti del Esecutore*, one is immediately struck by the long and involved procedure that came into vogue in the mid-*trecento*. On the theme of syndication, see G. Masi, *Il sindacato delle magistrature comunali nel secolo XIV* (Rome, 1930). There are special runs of documents housed in the Florentine archives yet to be examined on this neglected theme. Cf. *Sindacato del Capitano e Podestà*, Vols. 1 ff.

personnel remained ephemeral. Judicial persecution, vendetta, proscription, and excommunication done by influential magnates, ecclesiastical hierarchs, and the *Parte Guelfa,* if continued, must sever the political fabric of a newly risen territorial state.[33]

A secure office-holding class coming to resemble over the years a civil service was the response to a political climate dominated by managerial problems. The politics of ideology was receding, and as a result fewer dramatic choices obtruded themselves. Passion for an emperor, love for the pope, loyalty to a foreign prince, affection for Guelf and Ghibelline principles, no longer influenced public debate with such force; nor did these traditional enthusiasms continue to divide citizen from citizen with the old intensity. Class differences once evidenced by the violent life style of a haughty magnate tended to blur as the lawlessness of this order was suppressed. In the blander political climate of a managed polis, the age of sharp civic personality faded. Fewer Corso Donatis, Giano della Bellas, and Guido Cavalcantis are visible; the political poetry is not animated by medieval ideologies but, as we have seen, firmly fixed to the state and even subservient to its interests. The prickly, many-faceted personality of the Dantesque world is no longer typical. Men a century earlier suffered severe cases of multiple loyalties with ties to pope, guild, *consorteria,* and so forth. Now the ideal type has the possibility of greater unity with his overarching loyalty to polis.[34]

Even the communal magistracy was losing dramatic character; formerly rectors of the republic had either been celebrated as senatorial apostles or damned as progeny of Lucifer. Now they came and served in monotonous succession, forgotten, seldom to be named in memorable histories of the times. The once-grand offices of *podestà, esecutore,* and *capitano del popolo* lost their splendor and were incorporated into the ranks of the lusterless but efficient bureaucracy. High matters of state were no longer under their purview so that their tenure was spent reviewing uninspired testimony on citizen crime, activities of petty bureaucrats, and the thousand and one other painful details of enforcement.[35]

By the 1380s influential citizens were deeply conscious of the evils of demagogism and dangers of factionalism. Only a few years before, a schism among the city's elite had encouraged the aspirations of lower-

---

[33] U. Dorini, *Notizie storiche sull'università di Parte Guelfa in Firenze* (Florence, 1902), pp. 32–33.

[34] Cf. M. Becker, "Dante and His Contemporaries as Political Men," *Speculum,* 41 (1966), 665–80.

[35] The once-glorious magistracies became objects for ridicule. Boccaccio, Pucci, and Sacchetti, among others, composed satires on the theme. Cf. F. Novati, *La giovinezza di Coluccio Salutati* (Turin, 1898), pp. 90 ff.

class revolutionaries. The generation that lived through the Ciompi revolt understood well the need for a politics based on consensus. Such a desideratum was the more apparent in that political problems gravitated around techniques of fiscal maneuver. Oligarchical unity at the top was much prized, whereas individual acts of virtuoso statesmanship were suspect. Such a conformity did pose disquieting questions to humanist historians. Leonardo Bruni Aretino, chancellor and narrator of the history of his adopted polis, saw the dilemma. A cohesive and harmonious ruling cadre was essential for a healthy republic. But such a polis would suffer the defects of its own virtues: in time of crisis—the entire late *trecento* and early *quattrocento*—the need for consensus slowed decisions and weakened requests for citizen sacrifice. Humanistic education with its stress upon proportion might even make the untoward act ugly, and yet throughout Bruni's writings is the high sensitivity to the anomaly. Bruni judged that the cost of unanimity was high, for it discouraged that rarest of qualities among political men—leadership. In a society largely immunized against the individualistic political act, a plain-speaking man exposing unpleasant economic and diplomatic realities must be regarded as a disease if not a menace.[36]

Fiscal policy was the prime topic of communal discourse in the 1380s. Foreign policy decisions could be realized only after cautious appraisal of the relative expenditures necessary for alternate goals. The technicalities of tributary and administrative decisions were demanding, so that old methods of choosing public officials by lot were gradually abandoned; democratic results notwithstanding, this method did not furnish the polis with expert personnel. The *divieto*, once fiercely championed to prevent overrepresentation in the government by men from the same clan or a too rapid succession in office by a single individual, was likewise relaxed. This prohibition limited too severely opportunities to select experienced public officials. Elaborate election procedures for certain critical posts were canceled, and service in the treasury and *Monte* became appointive. Comparable changes were initiated for administrative positions in the *contado*; here experience and technical know-how counted for much when confronting complex problems of rural finance. All this counteracted the hardening of social prejudice against the "new citizens," for they, in the company of recruits from subject territories, were too essential to be discriminated against.[37]

[36] See the remarkable speech by Rinaldo Gianfigliazzi in which he requests the indulgence of his listeners in the councils for talking so frankly and contends that present dangers (1399) seem to justify even telling the truth. Cf. *Istoria fiorentina*, trans. Donato Acciaiuoli (Florence, 1861), pp. 582–87.
[37] As one would expect, the least attractive communal posts were most in need of staffing. The records of the *Camera del Comune* show that long before the office of castellan was opened to lower guildsmen (the mid-1360s), remote *castelle* were staffed

The character of political discourse in the advisory councils to the signory was ever more intricate. Suggestions and countersuggestions concentrated on details of administration and procedure. Attention and expertise were lavished upon alternate strategies for imposing special varieties of forced loans. The merits of the case might be decided on issues such as whether the *prestanza* should be levied geographically—that is, upon a city district—then subdivided according to the wealth of its inhabitants, or directly imposed on a state-wide basis. The question of interest rates remained abrasive; the technicalities were baffling, since the various government obligations were consolidated at different rates. Still more complex were considerations of deferral of interest payments upon one series of loans in order to employ the monies for restitution to other creditors. The problem of whether a particular tax should be converted into a forced loan and then incorporated into one of the existing *Monti* was frequently at issue and rendered still more intricate by the fine distinctions among types of *Monti*. Explanations of these alternatives and statements of their merits and demerits could be undertaken only by knowledgeable public men. Implementation of complex policy required skilled civil servants.[38]

Later, the single office Cosimo de' Medici allowed himself to be elected to was membership on the *Monte* board. The only position in the Florentine administration ever occupied by his grandson Lorenzo (the Magnificent) was a seat on the same board. Although few could match the almost legendary fiscal accomplishment of Cosimo, we do observe a greater appreciation for the abilities and character of more ordinary civil servants. One of the neglected transvaluations to occur between the world of Giovanni Villani in the early fourteenth century and that of the Florentine biographer Vespasiano da Bisticci of the late *quattrocento* was the radical reassessment of the role of bureaucrat. To early *trecento* chronicler and poet, the bureaucrat was unendurable and his cunning in filching money from the citizenry rivaled only Aristotle's skill in philosophy. The idealized portraits of civil servants whose talents were managerial suggest the new paideia of the *quattrocento*.[39] The antique virtues of the magnanimous hero were displaced by the

---

by *novi cives*. Volume Three will treat the personnel of the Florentine bureaucracy and administration in great detail.

[38] Spinello di Luca Alberti, treasurer of the *Monte*, was one such figure. Affectionately known as "Spinello della Camera," he was the most influential administrator in Florence during the second half of the *trecento*. N. Rodolico, *I Ciompi* (Florence, 1945), p. 95. Cf. F. Villani, *Cronica*, ed. F. Dragomanni (Florence, 1845), 11, 82.

[39] See Vespasiano da Bisticci, *Vite di uomini illustri del secolo XV*, ed. P. D'Ancona and E. Aeschlimann (Milan, 1951), pp. 380, 444, 530. For biographies of Ser Filippo di Ser Ugolino Pieruzzi, Lorenzo Ridolfi, and others, cf. also L. Martines, *The Social World of the Florentine Humanists*, p. 7.

prudent qualities of adroit financier and merchant. Earlier medieval republics had also confronted difficult fiscal problems, but such confrontations were not circumscribed by an aura of reverence. In early *quattrocento* Florence the performance of technical civic roles was elevated to the status of an ideal, becoming an integral part of humanistic education. The portrait of the "good politician" by Vespasiano was composed with veneration for this new unheroic style. Modes of recording and celebrating a political act grew responsive to a new paradigm of *buon governo*. Yet Machiavelli demonstrates a self-conscious ambiguity: on the one hand he understood and indeed performed the role of good bureaucrat, but on the other, he yearned for the heroes of old with their individualistic and violent political styles.

II

Again we see that the rise of public power augmented the need for civic men and officeholders. It is ironic to note that this need intensified after 1382 at a time when the area of political decision was constricting and the government more elitist at the upper echelons. The term "elitist" as applied to the political world of the late *trecento* should not be confused with similar terms used to describe earlier styles of rule. At the onset of the fourteenth century political power devolved upon a few select families; unless confronted with prolonged crisis they could govern with a minimum of bureaucracy and coercive power. Budgets were small and the public debt trifling. Spectacular acts of political reprisal did occur, ending in exile and banishment. But consistent enforcement of law was a tense alternative in the commune where immunity, ecclesiastical liberty, and privilege prevailed. The oligarchical signory of this earlier day was personal and not founded upon bureaucratic and rationalized political structure.[40]

Popular government after 1343 weakened traditional prerogatives by extending the rule of law. Again in the eighties when power was concentrated in fewer hands an "elite" asserted itself in the signory, but the structural base of the polis was so firm and ample that alterations at the top involved no withering away of public power. Unlike earlier coups seeking to undo the authority of the polis, the coming to power of Maso degli Albizzi in 1393 entailed changes only at the highest echelons of government. Unity of political direction continued and centralization with its attendant growth of bureaucracy was accelerated. Those at the top were unlike their predecessors who had sought actively to under-

---

[40] For a definition of the term "oligarchical," see M. Becker, "Some Aspects of Oligarchical, Dictatorial, and Popular *Signorie* in Florence, 1282-1382," *Comparative Studies in Society and History*, 2 (1960), 421-39.

mine the constraints of law and render bothersome public courts ineffectual. These earlier elites formed types of antigovernments aiming to gratify the laissez-faire aspirations of a patriciate by dismantling the administrative system and communal bureaucracy.[41]

How different were the problems and political responses of those called to govern in late *trecento* Florence; the need to underwrite and manage the debt and to sustain the administrative machinery imposed burdens upon any coterie seeking to shape the politics of the republic. In the 1380s communal councils were edgy, displaying reluctance to approve revenue measures. Florentine respect for the letter of the law did not permit any signory to by-pass constitutional practice or offend public opinion. The appointment of extraordinary commissions (*balìe*) was the favored remedy. Just a generation ago the chronicler Giovanni Villani warned his fellow citizens of the dangers of such *balìe*: ". . . for experience has shown that they caused the death and the humiliation of our commune."[42] This message was at least half-remembered. *Balìe* were selected, with communal councils exercising substantial control. After 1393, however, a special commission was authorized to staff the most important of these *balìe*, the *Dieci*. The Albizzi rulers could control the selection of the special commission of the *Ottantuno*. Here we observe two tendencies at work: release of the *balìe* from tight supervision of the communal councils and maximizing of the managerial role of the Albizzi and their adherents. Crucial to any consideration of this intricate problem is the sustained respect for legal forms and constitutional imperatives demonstrated by early Renaissance Florentines. *Balìe* continued to serve for stated periods under conditions made explicit in provisions enacted by the communal councils. Moreover, the same councils continued to function in many of the traditional ways. Authority at the top was more centralized, and the possibilities of influence multiplied; the *balìe* grew more important, and their terms of office were lengthened. All this served to give greater continuity and more intense managerial direction to political life without engendering feelings of political impotence among the citizenry.[43]

The *Ottantuno* also exercised controls over finances, being authorized to impose *prestanze* "with interest or without" (*cum interesse et sine*). These *prestanze* could be garnered "by any means whatsoever" (*per viam cuiuscumque*). Despite this authorization Florentine scruples per-

---

[41] M. Becker, *Florence in Transition*, 1, 174–75.
[42] For materials on the *balìa*, I wish to thank Professor Anthony Molho for permitting me to read his manuscript, "The Florentine Oligarchy and the Balìe of the Late Trecento," soon to be published in *Speculum*.
[43] For an incisive disquisition of the Florentine penchant for legality in the election of *balìe* and other matters of constitutional practice, see N. Rubinstein's *The Government of Florence under the Medici 1434 to 1494* (Oxford, 1966), pp. 1–31.

sisted, with communal councils being called upon to approve tax policies. Again it is true that such confirmation was less readily sought after 1395, indicating that the thrust toward centralization and greater fiscal control by the signory was increasing. That confirmation was sought even intermittently and that over the next seven years the communal councils were called upon to ratify proposed changes in the disposition of the *Monte* speak for an abiding respect for law and institutional republican practice. In early *quattrocento*, when war with the Visconti ended, the mandate of the *Ottantuno* was revoked; affection for traditional political forms still flourished. But less than a decade later a more awesome body was established—the Council of a Hundred and Ten. Two forces were at work: the demands of war and finance, and the lively affection for republican forms. Centralization proceeded in no simple linear fashion, for the matrix of republican sensibility offered resistance.[44]

Past history served to favor the formation of particular, extraordinary magistracies. The *Otto di Guardia* resembled the exceptional magistracies of the early *quattrocento* in that it was created to confront special problems; the difference lay in its protracted tenure. The *Otto* was founded in the autumn of 1378 just after the failure of the Ciompi revolution. It was hoped this magistracy would assist the new government in repressing any insurrection or political sedition. Vast juridical authority might be employed against the enemies of the regime both foreign and domestic. With unlimited tenure the charge of these officials was soon extended to encompass supervision over state bureaucracy as well as judicial power over rural parishes and *popoli*. Later, that elegant observer of republican institutions, Francesco Guicciardini, concluded: ". . . if the fear of this magistracy had not restrained the evil doers in Florence one would simply not have been able to live."[45]

Emergence of greater coercive power, exercised by an extended bureaucracy, capped at the top by *balìe* and special magistracies, was in part a consequence of negative factors. Much that might have operated to retard this trend toward centralization was in decline. As we have seen, affluent greater guildsmen were unified by the memory of that terrible moment in the summer of 1378 when the wool workers rebelled and set up a new government. An insurrection of this magnitude was readily interpreted as a visitation of God's wrath provoked by the factious and treasonous behavior of the patriciate. There was ample justifica-

---

[44] See G. Pampaloni's valuable study, "Gli organi della repubblica fiorentina per le relazioni con l'estero," *Rivista di Studi Politici Internazionali*, 20 (1953), 261–96.
[45] Quoted by G. Antonelli in his useful study "La magistratura degli Otto di Guardia a Firenze," *ASI*, 112 (1954), 3–23. From Guicciardini's *Storia fiorentina*, ed. G. Canestrini (Florence, 1859), p. 47.

tion for seeing in this a mundane counterpart of the theological view of history: division among the ruling order in the polis throughout the 1370s surely weakened the patriciate and encouraged the political ambitions of a more class-conscious community of workers.[46]

If this cataclysm etched upon patrician political conscience the need for relinquishing certain prerogatives, the failure of the revolt acted to demoralize *il popolo minuto*. It was the most recent worker rebellion in Florentine history, so that any regime was more secure with an enervated proletariat at heel. Yet another experience of those years made its mark upon Florentines who were later called to govern. The democratized signory installed in September, 1378, and lasting until 1382 was led by men of exceptional talents whose political styles were strongly individualistic. Almost to a man they suffered either exile or death; the tragic political fortunes of reformers or demagogues made the political milieu much blander. Men of strong conviction such as Tommaso di Marco Strozzi and Benedetto di Nerozzo Alberti, along with outspoken leaders like Simone di Biagio, were less evident on the political scene; problems of government focused less on ideology, as rule came to be conceived of in managerial terms. Minutes of the advisory councils to the signory show a dramatic transformation: the role of ideology subsided after 1382. Acceptance of this transformation was encouraged because spokesmen from the two extreme wings of the political spectrum stood discredited. Radical popular leadership had injected the issues of cutting interest rates on *Monte* shares or according recognition to new artisan organizations; such questions could only bring ideology to the fore. On the right, the captains of the Guelf party had introduced theoretical questions highly disturbing to public conscience. Before 1382 doctrinaire concerns of allegiance to pope or emperor and the always divisive issue of loyalty to the principles of Florentine Guelfism were perennials on the agenda. Nothing had agitated the sensibilities of political men more than the topic of whether to brand a citizen as politically heterodox. On the other side there was the disturbing practice of depriving a suspect individual of his political rights by designating him a "supermagnate."

After 1382 the republic was usually able to remain aloof from the contest between Pope Urban VI and his rival, the antipope, Clement VII. The signory and advisory councils debated in a calmer atmosphere; a consensus favorable toward maintaining spiritual ties with Urban prevailed, but this did not preclude displaying the respect due a "great

---

[46] G. Brucker, *Florentine Politics and Society*, pp. 336-96. The chapter is entitled "The Demise of the Regime, 1378."

lord" (*magnus dominus*) when Clement's ambassadors visited the city.[47] The souls of Florentines were no longer in jeopardy, because the damning choices between allegiance to the Holy See or maintenance of alliance with political schismatics (Ghibellines) were removed. In a polis where traditional religious conflict was receding, self-dramatization based on divided loyalties was also less frequent and more difficult. Political heresies like those disseminated by the Spiritual Franciscans, which had served to agitate sensibilities, were on the wane after 1382.[48] The outlook of advisers to the signory was marked by caution and a recognition of the need for regional security. Means and ends were articulately discussed in terms of "salute respubblica"; councilors set moderate and attainable objectives before the signory: Florentine influence must operate to maintain friendly and stable governments in Tuscan lands. Division and discord can only invite predatory outside powers to intervene and upset an equilibrium so favorable to Florence.[49] Strong consensus prevailed when the need for security and even trade advantage dictated more energetic programs of imperialism. The onset of protracted war, first against Giangaleazzo Visconti (1388–1402), then Pisa (1402–6), then Ladislaus (1409–14), then Filippo Maria Visconti (1406–28), and, lastly, Lucca (1429–33), served to unite the citizenry in a sustained enterprise of self-defense and imperialism. The unity of political ego was simpler to sustain, for choices were not so complex.

When Giovanni Dominici, the Dominican, counseled his disciples on just and appropriate modes of political behavior, he struck the familiar note of shunning factionalism. His reasons were novel and commanding: Not only must one follow this course "for the common good," but also for profound spiritual cause. Remember well, "no partisan goes into paradise" (*niuno partigiano va in paradiso*)! His admonition concludes with this apostrophe: "Neither a Guelf nor Ghibelline be." Far removed from traditional Florentine Dominican thinking is this voice. One has but to recall the philopapal accents of less than a generation earlier given pictorial form in the frescoes of the Spanish Chapel. In late

---

[47] *Diario di anonimo*, ed. A. Gherardi in *Documenti di storia Italiana pubblicati a cura della R. deputazione toscana di storia patria* (Florence, 1876), p. 474: "Oratores Clementis moneantur quod abstineant a visitatione ecclesiarum, quando officia celebrantur divina; et hoc suggeratur eis curialiter per hospitem a seipso. Et audiantur et honorentur tamquam oratores magni domini."

[48] The signory followed a policy of stern repression after that date. Cf. M. Becker, "Florentine Politics and the Diffusion of Heresy in the Trecento," *Speculum*, 34 (1959), 260–75.

[49] See the poetry of Giovanni da Trebbio, herald of the signory, in F. Flamini, *La lirica toscana del rinascimento* (Pisa, 1891), p. 55: "La division che 'n te, Fiorenza, è nata/ fra' cittadini odiosi e malcontenti,/ di tutto il senno spenti,/ all'animo m'induce pena dura."

trecento the new civic theology intruded into the message of this most influential Dominican of the polis.[50]

This steady, political view, free of the flame of older expectancies, was further encouraged by disappointment with the church hierarchy. To place hopes in pope and curia at a time of schism would be foolhardy.[51] Ser Lapo Mazzei, mild-mannered notary and confidant of the merchant Francesco Datini, was to muse thus: Throughout the land they say that the pope will be received in Florence and it shall be a great event. Many times has it been said that His Holiness is the fortress and defense of our commune; this I can hardly believe.[52]

The possibility of glorious intervention by a *deus ex machina* was minimal, and although Giovanni Dominici tried to give assurance that *paradiso* was accessible to the "just" political man, experienced office-holders knew otherwise. To his fellow civil servants the perennial office-holder Franco Sacchetti counseled patience so that the trials of public responsibility could be endured. Unlike political men of Dante's generation, he placed a premium upon experience. At the end of his life Sacchetti allowed himself the luxury of raising a troubling question. In an imposing letter written while holding office in Faenza, dispatched to a fellow *podestà*, Agnolo Panciatichi, he ruminated as to why he ever pursued a public career. Had it been a desire for humiliation that induced him to don the "pilgrim's cap" and leave family and hearth to serve among ignorant rustics? Why had he not abandoned himself to a life of merchant ease and wealth? The answer came when he realized that whatever form our lives take we must confront "contrary things." Does not Petrarch tell us in *De vita solitaria* that the least of the monks of Camaldoli have less hardship than a public man, even if he be "magior Signore." The world of the polis is, then, a proving ground "nostro purgatorio," and while it is surely no *paradiso*, it is endowed with great dignity and worth.[53]

There was distrust of religious enthusiasms of penitential groups; the solidity of the "everyday" world proved more resistant than the lure of the ecstatic. In 1399, when tens of thousands of zealous *Bianchi* surged into Tuscany, Florentines emphasized the social content of their message while remaining skeptical about the miracles performed. This religious assemblage were no fanatics; nor did they, like the Flagellants of old, wield scourges. Their plea was for *misericordia* and *pace*; no summons was issued for the massacre of Jews or for taking up arms against

---

[50] Giovanni Dominici, *Regola del governo di cura familiare*, ed. D. Salvi (Florence, 1860), p. 78.
[51] F. Sacchetti, *Opere*, ed. A. Chiari (Bari, 1938), 2, 103–4.
[52] Ser Lapo Mazzei, *Lettere di un notaro a un notaro mercante del secolo XIV*, ed. C. Guasti (Florence, 1880), 1, 104.
[53] F. Sacchetti, *Opere*, pp. 104–6 (December, 1396).

the Mohammedans of the East. When their history was written by Tuscan admirers, little attention was given to the claim that the Bianchi had resurrected a dead man; what was stressed were their good works.[54] The Florentine *anonimo* who chronicled their sojourn in the lands of the republic tells of the lies and artifices done by certain Bianchi so "molta gente idiota" would believe them.[55]

III

A strengthened political organism, call it *lo stato*, commune, polis, or *civitas Florentiae*, was also capable of furnishing greater security for its civil service at home. The elite at the top of the broadly based pyramid could rely upon legal forms such as *balìe* or the use of special electors *(accoppiatori)* to ensure greater continuity. Meanwhile, clearer political boundaries were being delineated in public administration. But yet another factor far removed from elite control and unrelated to the interior history of bureaucracy intruded in the 1380s. From that time through the *quattrocento* Florence experienced a decline in social mobility. The boundaries of *lo stato* were not challenged by *novi cives* seeking to stretch the constitutional fabric so they might win a greater share of political power and prestige. Their fathers had contributed heroically to the formation of *lo stato*, but their creation was not subject to dramatic alteration because no influx of *novi cives* was imminent. The impersonal and legalistic qualities of the emerging public world owed much to that earlier generation. That it maintained a regular and stable form is connected with the decline of pressure for admission into the upper echelons. The need for support of the war effort and the attendant underwriting of the public debt also acted to prevent the machinery of state from atrophying. Thus at a time when the force of impersonal government was no longer generated by assertive *novi cives*, it was strengthened by the exigencies of war and the budget.

As an indication of the diminution of mobility we observe that whereas the number of households increased from 10,000 to approximately 13,000 between 1350 and 1380, from 1380 until 1404 there was little increment.[56] That the interval from the fifties to the eighties was

---

[54] Giovanni Sercambi, *Le cronache*, ed. S. Bongi in *Fonti per la storia d'Italia*, 20 (Lucca, 1892), p. 307; Coluccio Salutati (*Epistolario*, 3, 351–53) makes no mention of miracles but, rather, of the work done by the penitents in reconciling enemies and achieving general pacification.
[55] *Cronica volgare di anonimo fiorentino*, ed. E. Bellondi in RIS, 28, 2 (Città di Castello, 1915–1918), p. 240.
[56] Indeed urban population was in the neighborhood of 70–75,000 in 1380 and 70,000 in 1526. E. Fiumi, "Fioritura e decadenza," *ASI*, 115 (1958), 468–70. For population of the city in the sixteenth and early seventeenth centuries, see K. J. Beloch, *Bevölkerungsgeschichte Italiens* (Berlin and Leipzig, 1937), 1, 16–18.

the locus of startling economic recovery and expansion for the Florentine guild world, whereas the next era was characterized by a loss of momentum, is suggested by a variety of indicators. After the 1380s there was a strong tendency for the customs toll to level off. The curve of this tax was duplicated by that of other major gabelles. For example, the salt impost struck its high in the same year as did the customs toll (1385). A final statistic that might prove telling concerns the ratio of those matriculating in the guilds by hereditary right as compared to those who were *nouveaux*. In the earlier period the ratio of new to old was 73 per cent to 27. For late *trecento* and early *quattrocento* the figures were almost exactly reversed, with 72 per cent old and 28 per cent *nouveaux*. No conclusion should be drawn asserting the onset of economic decline; rather, the evidence points to a stasis.[57]

When Coluccio Salutati exalted the "chain of laws" (*legum catena*) serving to bind the citizenry together, he voiced a view commonplace among those of north Italy interested in politics and law. A notable transition in the meaning of *carità* wherein it was stripped of its Christian connotations is at the very linguistic center of the decline of late medieval admonitory culture. The strengthening of associative bonds is a leitmotif clearly visible in the literature and politics of the stern paideia. To contend that this chain of laws transcends "ties of kinship, parentage and even friendship" is to explicate the motif. To draw the conclusion that we owe everything to country and that parents, brothers, even children, stand for less than the relationship holding between citizen and polis is to announce the claims of a revivified public world in revolutionary accents. The question is not whether Coluccio Salutati was *sincere* or whether we should take his assertions at face value and employ them to describe the realities of everyday political life. Perhaps the suggestion that *sincerity* is an invention of Rousseau and the Enlightenment will not be considered too facetious. The core of late *trecento* education involved writing *pro* and *contra* on a myriad of topics. Instead, what is worthy of recognition is that statal imperatives were given literary form. Salutati defined *libertas* as "equality before the law," and then asserted the pre-eminence of that law over individual interest. When he spoke of "the sweet rein of law," it was no bizarre figure of speech but simply that law served to prevent the *libertas* of the republic from degenerating into tyranny. This insight would still be jejune if it were not coupled with Salutati's keen appreciation of the role bureaucracy must play in protecting citizen liberty. The very hall-

---

[57] A. Doren, *Le arti fiorentine*, 1, 262. Using the same indicator for the period from 1471 to 1530, social mobility underwent further diminution, with the ratio of old to new standing at 89 to 11. Cf. R. Mousnier, *La Renaissance en Italie au XVIe siècle* (Paris, n.d.), p. 23.

mark of Florentine republicanism was an administration staffed by thousands (*"Milia sunt hominum, qui nostram rem publicam administrant, qui communitatis intra limitata tempora magistratibus nobis consulunt nosque regunt, nec solet populus Florentinus subesse paucis aut umquam passus est servire domi, qui foris semper pro libertate quondam non sua, sed aliorum, nunc autem etiam pro libertate propria bellum gerit. . . ."*) who were responsive "to the well-being of those they serve."[58] Without such esprit the regime would have declined into tyranny.

Recent tragic history had instructed the aged Boccaccio and the young Filippo Villani that only fools favor the tyranny of a foreigner over "the sweet yoke of a law" to which they were happily accustomed. Sad experience showed Donato Velluti and Giovanni di Pagolo Morelli that the days of vendetta and bloody tourney were anything but romantic. Better to settle feuds by appealing to the courts of the polis rather than resorting to cold steel. Civic humanists like Salutati and Bruni were already surmising that citizen behavior in the public world was more virtuous than its private counterpart. Not only did the contemporary world possess dignity, but it was also the arena in which the citizen would be educated. He would gain in virtue to the extent that he pursued the "public good." In the first quarter of the *quattrocento* Bruni contended that the uniqueness of the Florentine constitution rested in the opportunity it furnished citizens for public debate rather than private violence. *Quattrocento* historians from Bruni and Poggio through Machiavelli wrote a new type of history wherein the polis pre-empted the stage. Actions of individuals were relevant only insofar as they contributed to an understanding of the collective political behavior of a *civitas*.

Unlike its medieval forebear, the polis of the early Renaissance cannot be defined in terms of its particulars—corporate bodies, quasi-autonomous organizations, political cliques, or even personalities. The observation has recently been made that in medieval times words like *lo stato*, *il comune*, or simply *Firenze* could be adequately understood.[59] To begin at the very circumference of medieval public life and to try to reach its center would be difficult even for those with a trained historical eye. Indeed, it is relevant to ask whether there was a fixed center. Were the essentials of this world discernible in the tower societies, religious confraternities, knightly companies, ecclesiastical-political organi-

---

[58] The quotation is from Peter Herde's "Politik und Rhetorik am Vorabend der Renaissance," *Archiv für Kulturgeschichte*, 47 (1965), 182–83.
[59] Cf. footnote 42. On legal aspects of this transformation, see F. Ercole, *Da Bartolo all'Althusio* (Florence, 1938), pp. 49–118. F. Calasso treats medieval and humanist contributions to the concept of man as the subject of a juridical order in his *Introduzione al diritto comune* (Milan, 1951), pp. 181–205.

zations, or corporate guilds? The fully developed medieval chronicle of Giovanni Villani treats communal society and politics in a manner reminiscent of a Flemish painting wherein each minute detail possesses its own reality. The total architecture of the chronicle must always be recalled since the reader will be lost if he attempts to establish firm relationships between the historical phenomena described therein. Within a frame the magic realism of the late Middle Ages, with its nominalist faith in the reality of particulars, can function. Perhaps the best image to bear in mind when considering this theme is that of the cluttered, overarticulated city of late medieval Tuscan painting, alive in its particulars and without a fixed center.

Since the polis did not have a life of its own where explicit and noncontradictory demands were made, chroniclers and diarists could easily assume an ambivalence toward it. Alternately, praise or blame was heaped on this political entity, so like an organism was it, with certain parts functioning smoothly while others boggled. Communal imperatives were always challenged by the dictates of private morality. The individual could not readily identify with the commune: first, because his loyalties were multiple; and second, because his private standards were in conflict. The inability to subscribe unqualifiedly to the present was magnified by the persistence of visions of a golden past. This encouraged chronicler and poet to judge their contemporary public world as a fall from mythic prosperity or Christian grace. The bounds of the commune were marked by avarice and pride in time of crisis; their polar opposites, charity and love, prevailed only when the commune succeeded. The geography of the historically represented polis was irregular, matched only by the uncertain and shifting perspective of communal artist or chronicler. Thus what was relevant to the commentator was the interior spiritual quality of the citizenry, for they alone were bearers of the city's fate. Medieval historiography perforce directed its angle of vision toward the individual.

Contemporaries saw very different qualities in the Renaissance polis. It was considered an identity in itself, significant by virtue of transcending the very particulars composing it. Possessed of a vital energy, there is little need for it to seek self-justification. Earlier it had been the virtuous citizens who made possible the "good commune"; now it was the "good polis" that made possible civic virtue. The state conferred nobility upon citizen, and he in turn could be relied upon to be one of the many "cittadini del reggimento e amatori della libertà."[60] Florentine public men of the first part of the *quattrocento*, from Bruni through Matteo Palmieri (*Della vita civile*, 1438–39), stressed the role of polis

---

[60] N. Rubinstein, *Government of Florence*, p. 70.

as educator of men; the first tracts since antiquity on the political education of children were composed by those in the circle of the civic humanists. The substance of the discourse was frequently novel: To be of human flesh is to understand instability and inconstancy. Perfection and "the immaculate life" are not possible to mortals. Rent by despair of the human condition, I recall ancient history and the excellence of noble and glorious deeds. Then I realize that in the world of the best republic lies the highest possibility open to men; therein one is able to live with dignity ("*con degnità possono vivere*").[61] We have come full circle when the public world proffers the explicit option of stability to the individual. It is in this sphere that heroism is possible, and the contemporary sculpture of Donatello stands at the political heart of the city to remind all of this dramatic fact.

On a more mundane level, statal forces have operated on Gregorio Dati so that he accepts uncritically the authority of polis with its officialdom. When composing Book IX of his *L'Istoria di Firenze*, he would say: "L'uficio e balìa e autorità è potenzia di detti Signori è grande sanza misura; ciò che volessono potrebbona necessari mentre che dura il loro uficio." Here he has appraised the effects of bureaucratization and centralization. Throughout his history runs the assumption that this government is supreme and independent, independent of universal church or higher ethic. The idea of civil disobedience was alien to his world, for *lo stato* was a transcendent good.[62]

"The power of the *Signore*," which is "great beyond measure," was, in Dati's judgment, employed fully only "extremely infrequently in certain necessary cases. . . ." Generally the government followed "the written ordinances of the commune." Here we observe a sensitivity to parallels rather than conflicting trends in the life of the polis. The increasing ascendancy of a centralized regime, staffed by an elite and utilizing an accomplished bureaucracy, was not interpreted as defiance of the legalistic intricacies and constitutional niceties constructed and refined over almost two generations. All regimes, from that of Maso degli Albizzi, his son Rinaldo, and later Cosimo de' Medici (1434), showed pious regard for this political legacy. A strong state, then, did not lull old scruples or undermine traditional forms.[63]

---

[61] M. Palmieri, *Della vita civile* in *Prosatori volgari del Quattrocento*, ed. C. Varese (Milan–Naples, n.d.), p. 355. For relationships between various writers and classical sources, see L. Rainaldi, "Di una fonte comune della 'Vita Civile' di Matteo Palmieri e del 'De educatione liberorum' di Maffeo Vegio," in *Giornale Storico della Letteratura Italiana*, 130 (1953), 495–507. Here the author argues that the uniqueness of the work is in its focus upon the formation of the citizen.
[62] *L'Istoria di Firenze di Gregorio Dati dal 1380 al 1405*, ed. L. Pratesi (Norcia, 1904), pp. 73 ff.
[63] In Volume Three this theme will be treated at great length.

Appreciation of a supreme and independent polis with a life and momentum of its own did not deter Florentines from pursuing constitutionalism. Statal claims must operate in a milieu where legal precedent merits respect. Civic humanists and historians responsive to the imperatives of power and the norms of law were to make only modest contributions to theoretical problems. Employing either classical or medieval standards of accomplishment, even the most generous of our present-day scholars would be pressed if called upon to cite significant contributions of civic humanists in the realm of theory. The halcyon days had passed with the deaths of Dante, Marsiglio of Padua, and the politically oriented scholastics. Humanists of the early Florentine Renaissance found something different in the ancient classics. Familiar texts of Aristotle and new ones of Quintillian were mined not for speculative insights but for clues as to appropriate modes for educating and persuading the citizenry. History, rhetoric, and the civic education of children (even women) were to serve as a bridge between private interests and demands of the public world. Bruni tells us that "no kind of learning can be more fitting to man than to understand what is a city and what is a commonwealth." He argued that politics (a concern for public life) is the most suitable subject for eloquence. His preference is for Aristotle over Plato, for the former "appears to support those things which participate in ordinary life and practice, not to invent things which are strange and abhorrent and of no use to it."[64]

The new humanism nourished the citizen ego by conferring fame upon the wise counselor and patriot. History would satisfy the yearning for immortality by recording great deeds. The public world was projected in so beguiling a form that it seemed to possess such amplitude that it offered options for happiness and virtue unknown to those who dwelled only in the cramped recesses of self. The possibilities of structuring self so that a harmony obtained between public and private worlds was at the core of this classical revival. The two Florentine chancellors, Bruni and Poggio, legitimized the citizen quest for wealth and even certified the acquisitive instincts as natural to man and redounding to the advantage of the polis. Religious concern was relegated to the private world where it could operate with force and conviction. When speaking politically and historically—the realm of public discourse—affairs of conscience were not suitable subject matter.[65]

---

[64] Leonardo Bruni Aretino, *Humanistisch-Philosophische Schriften*, ed. H. Baron (Leipzig and Berlin, 1928), pp. 45–73.

[65] As the imperatives of the public world became more commanding, Florentine historians from Bruni through Machiavelli and Guicciardini emptied out problems of conscience. There was a deliberate separation of public and private morality, with a clear and sometimes anguished awareness that the requirements of the former may do grave violence to the latter. See the celebrated advice of Gino di Neri Capponi, conqueror of

Central to the thinking of the civic humanists of the first part of the *quattrocento* was the conviction that man was "a weak being, incapable of achieving anything. Perfection can only be reached in a civic community." In Bruni's elegant introduction to his translation of the *Politics* of Aristotle, the thesis is upheld that human activity bears fruit only in proportion to the number of people deriving benefit from it. Labor and wealth must therefore be highly valued if their ends are social.[66] Since the time of Petrarch there had been a tendency to value emotions harshly condemned by medieval ascetics and stoics. Petrarch himself had waged a modest campaign to rehabilitate at least a part of Epicurus' damaged reputation, while Salutati, after long meditation, decided there were praiseworthy passions. In his last work, *De laboribus Herculis*, unfinished at the time of his death, he dealt with mythic lovers in a sympathetic manner. Instead of discoursing on the traditional plane of sensuality, he elevated the discussion to a more esthetic and heroic level.[67] It was, however, the persistent demands of community that finally prompted a fundamental re-evaluation of the philosophy of emotionality. Observations by a Petrarch or Salutati could only be idiosyncratic since there was no enduring set of social and political conditions to provide a frame around which a coherent tradition could be structured.

Frank acknowledgment of claims of the polis provided a base for this transvaluation of values. Reasoning from the exigencies of the state, the spectrum of human emotion—from ambition, to the desire for wealth, and, finally, to the quest for glory—was legitimized. Civic humanists from Bruni and Poggio to Machiavelli and Guicciardini attempted to rescue primal drives from Stoic censure and Christian ambivalence in order to reinstate them untarnished in the new pantheon of civic virtues. Poggio, writing in 1428 and 1429, has a speaker in his dialogue *De avaritia* heap invective on the hypocrisy of monks, arguing that the desire for money is natural and even socially beneficial. "One cannot tolerate the objections raised by hypocrites, parasites and coarse men who are running after food under the cover of religion. These people do not work and take no pains and preach

---

Pisa (1406), to his son: Appoint men of wisdom to *balìa* of Ten who are more interested in the welfare of their own souls. R. Sereno, "The Ricordi of Gino di Neri Capponi," *American Political Science Review*, 52 (1958), 1121.

[66] E. Garin, *Filosofi italiani del Quattrocento* (Florence, 1942), p. 113; *Humanistisch-Philosophische Schriften*, p. 164.

[67] C. Salutati, *De laboribus Herculis*, ed. B. Ullman (Zurich, 1951), 2, 493–508. For Petrarch, see *Rerum memorandarum*, ed. G. Billanovich (Florence, 1945), pp. 166–69; *Invective contra medicum*, ed. P. Ricci (Rome, 1950), p. 64; *Le Familiari*, ed. V. Rossi (Florence, 1934), 2, 162. For Boccaccio's comments, see *Commento alla Divina Commedia*, ed. D. Guerri (Bari, 1918), 3, 45–46.

that others ought to seek poverty and despise earthly treasures! We cannot build our cities with these pseudo-men who can afford to be lazy only because our labours keep them alive."[68] The appreciation for wealth leads Poggio to understand that society in any meaningful sense would be impossible if men isolated themselves in a cocoon of economic self-sufficiency. Like the good doctor in the Chekhov play, the civic humanist understands that one's energies would be utterly consumed by the struggle for survival. Worse yet, "All splendour, all beauty, all charm would disappear from our cities. There would be no more temples, no more monuments and no more art. Our whole existence as well as that of the state would be disrupted if everyone endeavoured solely to provide for his own necessities. . . . For the commonwealth, money is the nerve of life and those who lust for money are its foundation."[69]

Similar re-evaluations of emotions and drives tended to justify the once-base "ira" until it became a type of heroic fury. Soon *superbia* was seen as an ingredient of the martial spirit and satisfaction of the acquisitive instinct as tangible evidence of Divine favor. Men of letters, from Petrarch through Salutati, had contributed manfully to this new assessment. Riches had been seen as no serious impediment to virtue, and the love of glory had certainly not been despised. The solicitude and tenderness with which many in civic circles regarded the trials of man's earthly pilgrimage were touching. Neither merchant nor politician went unappreciated, and loyalty to country loomed as a positive good. The radical voluntarism of Salutati and his circle placed a sizable premium upon the idea of work and the active life. So many traits associated with later conceptions of the Renaissance public world are explicit in the character and career of Franco Sacchetti. The process we have been observing was indeed gradual and therefore tight-woven. What then marks the difference between the early years of the transformation at mid-*trecento* and the late years when the final unfolding took place in the first third of the *quattrocento?*

Social, economic, and political forces co-operating over three-quarters of a century had given final shape to a new paradigm. The values of the public world were cemented together into a regular pattern. Now rhetoric with its emphasis upon "decorum" and "harmony" would serve as the new capstone of the civic paideia. One could seek release from private chaos in an *agora* made to conform to mathematical law by a Brunelleschi and never be intimidated by inhuman scale or transcendent space. At early *quattrocento* civic audience, state authority,

---

[68] E. Garin, *Italian Humanism*, p. 43. Cf. also Leonardo Bruni Aretino, *Humanistisch-Philosophische Schriften*, p. 32.
[69] E. Garin, *Italian Humanism*, p. 44.

pride of empire, imperatives of law, and needs of public finance coalesced to lend structure to this model.

IV

It would be pleasant to follow the lead of the charming Don Quixote who, while recuperating from illness, passed the time conversing with priest and barber on the noble theme of the "razon de estado." Better, though, to search out what illumination can be obtained from a final raising of the lantern of "the dismal science." Rather than deal with arguments of brilliant *quattrocento* publicists, so effectively treated by modern scholars, a final review of persistent economic forces that were operating to intensify awareness of "ratio reipublicae" might be in order.[70]

The exigencies of the *camera* were prompting the Arno republic to move away from a private economy where government intake and outlay were negligible causal forces toward formation of an economic system in which public spending and borrowing were the decisive elements. As we have observed, starting at mid-*trecento*, medieval immunities, privileges, and liberties tended to be undermined by the energetic quest for revenue by the signory. Tuscan church, the guilds, and the Court Merchant were stripped of many traditional privileges. By the 1380s this process had reduced the political influence of the *Parte Guelfa*, Court Merchant, guilds, and religious confraternities. The treasury's need for income was too vast to be appeased by minuscule subsidies from the clerics or modest loans from the Guelf party, or even direct imposts on the city's guilds. As citizen capital was siphoned off into the burgeoning public debt, so, too, did citizen claims for interest payment rise astronomically. No clique or set of merchant corporations could successfully underwrite these public obligations. Unlike the situation in the early fourteenth century when families like the Bardi, Peruzzi, and Strozzi could alleviate the fiscal bind by loaning 20,000 or 30,000 florins, no private fortune could tide over the hard-pressed *camera*. Almost every affluent Florentine had a substantial portion of his patrimony invested in government securities. Between 1345 and 1427 the number of shareholders had increased more than twentyfold, and in the majority of instances the sums involved were thirty and forty times greater than investments in the original *Monte*

---

[70] Particularly useful is F. Gilbert, "Florentine Political Assumptions in the Period of Savonarola and Soderini," *Journal of the Warburg and Courtauld Institutes*, 20 (1957), 187–214, and his very recent *Machiavelli and Guicciardini; Politics and History in Sixteenth-Century Florence* (Princeton, 1965).

of 1345. The *Catasto* of 1427 reveals that virtually every Florentine whose wealth exceeded 5,000 florins was a shareholder in the funded debt.[71] There were few at that time who could afford the luxury of being disinterested in the fate of the public economy. The nexus between individual and polis tightened as larger parts of the citizen patrimony were invested in the *Monte*.

By the 1380s the public debt was the pivot around which multiple treasury operations rotated. Merely to meet minimal interest obligations on the *Monte* would consume approximately half the commune's total tax income from customary sources. Amortization could be little more than a pious hope as the *Monte* became more inflated and unwieldy. In 1387 carrying charges on the debt topped 150,000 florins, and this was but a harbinger of things to come. By 1394 the total was approaching 190,000 florins, and ten years later, upon the outbreak of a new war with Pisa, it had escalated to approximately 250,000 florins. As an aftermath of the conflict this figure increased by an additional 25,000 florins; a special *Monte* was founded for the single purpose of underwriting costs for the conflict. During the next two decades *Monte* totals remained relatively constant, with new funded debts being created from *prestanzoni* (special forced loans) paying interest at rates of 7 or 8 per cent.[72]

The formation of new funded debts paralleled expanding operations of the *Monte* and its officials into new fields. They were responsible for funding special loans for merchants or consolidating the various *prestanze* levied on the *contado*. Since 1378 they had been charged with the task of paying interest to those clergy and pious foundations whose properties had been appropriated by the government during the War of the Eight Saints (1375–78). Sixteen years after the termination of hostilities, *Monte* officials were still delaying payment of 15,000 florins a year interest to Tuscan ecclesiastics so that additional mercenaries might be hired. Their other duties included negotiating with cartels of pawnbrokers in the city and *contado*, prosecuting manifest usurers, and even protecting patrimonies of Florentine orphans. Needless to say, the fortunes of the latter would promptly be invested in shares of *Monte* stock. They were also given the task by the communal councils to finance construction of a Florentine fleet, as well as to support the intellectual activities at the republic's center for higher studies (the *Studio*). When the chronicler Gregorio Dati wrote that these *Monte* officials held great power and authority ("grande balia e auctorita"), it was no exaggeration, for he was well aware of the situa-

---

[71] *PC*, 4, fols. 272–276r; *ibid.*, 10, fols. 245–265; *ibid.*, 19, fols. 256r–269.
[72] *Ibid.*, 10, f. 260.

tion and his comment "that almost all the income of the commune comes into their hands" is an exact description.⁷³

Commencing in 1390, forced loans were exacted at a frantic pace and totaled half a million florins. The following year they climbed to 673,937 florins, and the next year saw a return of a little over 600,000 florins. By 1393 the total soared above 1,200,000 florins, and this figure was reached again during the early years of the *quattrocento*. Additional *prestanzoni* were imposed on inhabitants of territories under the republic's rule. Many of these bore interest at rates of 7 or 8 per cent; in the year 1407 the treasury set aside approximately 85,000 florins for payment of just such obligations. In that same year the treasury was disbursing 11,584 florins interest to those who paid *prestanze* in the recent war against Pisa. Rate payers had an option: either they paid a smaller assessment, losing both interest and capital, or they paid a heavier assessment, receiving interest and eventually regaining their capital.⁷⁴

Precise estimate of these *prestanze* are not always possible since the communal system of treasury bookkeeping was exceedingly complex. Balances were not always struck, and on occasion the statistics are less than complete. Recalling this and making the most conservative estimate, the total for all *prestanze* during the decade of the 1390s would stand at approximately 5,000,000 florins. During the first five years of the *quattrocento* this total increased by 3,500,000 florins. Judging from the tax returns of 1427 (the *Catasto*), this commanding figure would be at least seven times the total of all commercial wealth in the city. Even if these latter-day tax returns were not an altogether candid presentation of an individual's patrimony, still, by any standard the amount of citizen capital now being absorbed by the state was tremendous. Nor was there any respite: in 1424 *prestanze* amounted to 560,912 florins; in 1426, 888,309 florins; in 1427, 439,590 florins; and finally, in 1431, almost 600,000 florins. The total of all *prestanze* exacted by the government from 1390 to 1427 equaled the total wealth of the entire citizen body as recorded in the *Catasto*. With the major portion of these *prestanze* soon incorporated in the *Monte*, the public debt became further inflated and the number of citizens who were state creditors augmented. Needless to say, the average size of individual holdings in the public debt increased substantially.⁷⁵

Beginning in 1388, with the first war against the Visconti, military expenses spiraled; in that year the outlay for hiring troops was just

---
⁷³ *L'Istoria di Firenze di Gregorio Dati dal 1380 al 1405*, ed. L. Pratesi (Norcia, 1904), p. 153.
⁷⁴ For the year 1390, see *PC*, 8; for 1391, *PC*, 7; for 1393, *PC*, 9; for 1407, *PC*, 21.
⁷⁵ *Ibid.*, Vols. 6–37.

under 300,000 florins. By 1391 it exceeded 750,000 florins. In 1400 it was almost 500,000 florins, and it sustained this peak over the next half decade. Chronic increments in public indebtedness caused by persistent war over the next third of a century made this burden awesome. For the war year 1424 the total exceeded 2,500,000 florins; expenditures for troops (only a single item in a military budget) between the early 1390s and the late 1420s reached the grand sum of 10,000,000 or so florins. Adding the *Entrata della Castelle*, the outlay for provisions and arms, and the subsidies to emperors and princes would increase the total by at least 1,000,000 florins. Again the amount is in excess of the total capital of all Florentines which, according to *Catasto* records, is fixed between 8,000,000 and 9,000,000 florins.[76] Certainly this stands as the most convincing instance of massive state intervention in communal life. Over an interval of only slightly more than a generation, government spending and public fiscal policy had conspired to precipitate an unprecedented acceleration in the flow of capital from private investment into the public sector of the economy.

This redeployment of capital into the hands of the state was further intensified in 1425 when the *Monte delle Doti* was founded. This credit institution served as a type of insurance bank in which deposits were made by families so that their daughters might be guaranteed a dowry and they might be assured a progeny. In an age when a girl without a dowry had little opportunity to marry, this ingenious plan appeared a boon to the unfortunate. Contracts with the officials of this *Monte* could be drawn up whereby a fixed sum was deposited over a specified number of years and a suitable dowry assured. The term of the normal contract ran from seven to fifteen years; if one selected the shorter term, a larger annual premium was paid. If a girl died or entered a convent before the term expired, part of the deposit reverted to the commune; however, should she have marriageable sisters, the capital was transferable and a new contract might be drawn up under less favorable conditions. This particular *Monte* added substantially to the obligations of the republic, for Florence was committed to pay $3\frac{3}{8}$ per cent on all deposits. By 1470 the liability of the republic for the *Monte delle Doti* was 198,000 florins yearly, and this figure was well over half the annual revenue of the city.[77] Now the republic was responsible not merely for defense of the Florentines but even for proper marriage of their children. As much as any single fiscal stratagem, the

---

[76] *Ibid.*, Vols. 5–29. P. J. Jones presents materials on the extent of Florentine wealth in his "Florentine Families and Florentine Diaries in the Fourteenth Century," *Papers of the British School at Rome*, 24 (1956), 197.

[77] L. Marks, "The Financial Oligarchy in Florence Under Lorenzo," in *Italian Renaissance Studies* (New York, 1960), 128–29.

foundation of this *Monte* induced the citizenry to look toward the state for its well-being. When Cosimo de' Medici postponed payments on the *Monte delle Doti*, the chronicler Giovanni Cavalcanti charged that he had broken the bond which tied "la grandezze della Repubblica colla libertà del Monte."[78] So tight was the nexus between the grandeur of the state and the integrity of the *Monte* that in the mind of this chronicler they had become inseparable.

The problem of finding fiscal support for this inflated credit structure was indeed the most pressing to confront Florentines who sat in the *balìe* over the years. That their efforts met with success is attested to by the fact that the value of shares in the public debt did not decline appreciably over the years between the 1380s and 1430s. They were traded on the market at a price that varied between 25 and 35 per cent of their face value, and this quotation differed little from that of the decade of the 1370s. For tax purposes they were assessed at from 50 to 60 per cent of their value.

As for the *Monte delle Doti*, it proved extremely popular despite abuse heaped on Cosimo when he deferred payment. Indications are that Florentine confidence in the fiscal reliability of the state diminished little over the sixty-year period 1370–1430. The alacrity with which citizens made short-term loans to the *camera* suggests that faith in the integrity of the public fisc was durable. Despite complaints, lampoons, and even invective, Florentines continued to underwrite the burgeoning expenses of war through numerous loans. Gregorio Dati enumerated the republic's outlays for warfare during the years 1375–1405, arriving at the sum 11,500,000 florins; he expressed naïve doubt that anyone would believe there was so much money in the world. Indeed, just how could Florentines have raised such a staggering amount? The answer for Dati was separable into two parts: first, much of the money loaned the republic was inscribed in the *Monte*, and, second, the wars proved a boon to the Florentine economy. Mercenaries spent much of their pay in the city, Florentine merchants imported provisions, and businessmen made all manner of profit on government contracts. Even more beneficial for the economy and public morale, however, were the sweet fruits of victories. Conquest of Pisa in the early *quattrocento* expanded investment opportunities for Florence's capitalists while increasing the republic's general revenue.[79]

The chronicler Giovanni Cavalcanti underscores comparable points in

---

[78] *Istorie fiorentine*, 2, 203. Much later, Francesco Guicciardini was to quote Bruni and say, ". . . el Monte disfare Firenze e Firenze disfara el Monte." Cf. *Le cose fiorentine*, ed. R. Ridolfi (Florence, 1945), p. 109. (I wish to thank Professor Anthony Molho for this reference.)
[79] *L'Istoria di Firenze*, pp. 138–39.

his account of an oration purported to have been delivered by the republic's leading politician, Renaldo degli Albizzi. After extolling Florence's ancient forebears, "our fathers the Romans," and eulogizing the citizenry's love for their republic, he says he intends to speak with candor: To tell you the truth, during periods of warfare our city is crowded and everyone profits from our successful martial undertakings.[80] Moreover, there was every reason for predicting victory; even in the darkest days of the conflict with the Visconti, when all seemed hopeless, Florentines could believe sincerely that the Duke of Milan "was only a *uomo mortale*." When he died, then, "finito lo stato suo," but as for Florence, she would endure and thrive again because "il Comune non puo morire...."[81]

General confidence in the reliability of officials over the *Monte* appears to have been well placed; treasury records show these public servants to have been scrupulous in performing their exacting duties. Although the state frequently was compelled to suspend interest payments to *Monte* shareholders, as soon as conditions improved the treasury resumed its accustomed disbursements. Every month a certain portion of the customs toll, the gabelle on wine, salt, contracts, the *estimo* on the *contado*, and a host of other levies were assigned to a special section of the *camera* for the purpose of restitution. Each *Monte* and many of the larger *prestanze* were supervised by a staff of accountants and financial rectors who kept meticulous accounts, setting aside monies regularly for the republic's creditors.

Ultimately, both the psychology and mechanics of this complex system of deficit financing was dependent on general business conditions for it was the state of the economy that determined the amount of revenue available to the treasury. Unless Florentine prosperity were sustained at a reasonable level, the intake of the *camera* would fall and the inflated credit structure collapse. At times the signory was forced to cut rates, but when crisis passed the old rate was restored. Florentines remained convinced the state would recover its vigor, and creditors be paid in full.

Such confidence was amply justified by the *camera*'s intake from traditional gabelles.[82] Returns from the customs toll sustained their

---

[80] *Istorie fiorentine*, 3, 2. When Florentine foreign policy met with success, the value of *Monte* shares rose. Cf. D. Boninsegni, *Storie della Città di Firenze dall'anno 1410 al 1460* (Florence, 1637), p. 93.
[81] *L'Istoria di Firenze*, p. 74.
[82] This statement has validity only if we recall that until 1427 the enormous forced loans collected by the treasury were used to underwrite the costs of war and diplomacy. Therefore it would be possible to use the yield from the gabelles to pay interest on *Monte* stock. After 1427 returns from direct taxes on property and capital would bring in sizable returns. In 1429 the yield from the *Catasto* was 168,502 florins, and in the following year it ascended to 414,758 florins. This type of levy did not increase the public

high plateau, with the treasury collecting even more revenue than in the prosperous years of the early *trecento*. Yields from this gabelle had never been higher than 90,100 florins. Commencing in 1384, however, the return was 119,133 florins, and it rose still higher in the following year when it registered 132,475 florins. Though it declined to 82,496 florins at the height of the Visconti war, it soon recovered and stood almost at the level it had attained in 1384. By 1394 it recorded a total of 115,667. Between 1410 and 1420 it rocketed to 127,421 florins. Over the following years there was a sizable decline, and in 1424 the figure was only 94,732 florins. It sustained this sum until 1427, when once again recovery set in and the customs toll climbed above the 100,000-florin mark.

Despite the hardships of war and the uncertainties of diplomatic maneuver, despite invasion and occupation of Florentine territories, despite plague and famine, this crucial indicator of the republic's well-being never experienced dramatic fluctuations, which suggests that foreign trade and communal customs receipts remained vigorous and thriving.[83] Certainly, rates of customs tolls must have been adjusted periodically, but the stability of this gabelle is attested to by a constant yield for almost half a century. Nor was this an isolated phenomenon; comparable patterns of behavior were registered by other economic indicators. The return from the salt levy was more erratic; it plunged precipitously in a single year but regained its value and finally surged upward. The general curve, however, was on the ascent during 1384 to 1427 (the year the *Catasto* was founded). In the earlier year it registered 63,870 florins, whereas in the latter it totaled 82,150 florins, with other returns differing little from the customs and salt gabelles.[84]

The republic was assured an income approximating that of the mid-

---

debt as did a *prestanza* which was interest-bearing and inscribed in the *Monte*. The *Catasto*, then, relieved much of the fiscal pressure on the treasury and served to inspire confidence in communal creditors. A preliminary investigation suggests that it was not until the 1470s that the value of *Monte* stock declined. Cf. L. Marks, "Financial Oligarchy," pp. 129-30. It may be that this decline was much accelerated in the eighties by the sharp decrease in gabelle returns. Cf. L. Marks, "La crisi finanziaria a Firenze del 1494 al 1502," *ASI*, 112 (1954), Disp. 1, 60-72.

[83] The statistics on the *gabella portarum* are virtually continuous for the period under consideration, and this may militate against the invalidation of the argument by citing increases in rates. My position is merely that the economy remained vigorous and that there was no sharp and sudden drop. Cf. *PC*, 34, fols. 56-59; *ibid.*, 35, fols. 69-74; *ibid.*, 36, f. 61r; *ibid.*, 38, f. 97, for returns of the gabelle in the early 1430s. Again the statistics demonstrate that it sustained its vigor.

[84] The contention made concerning the *gabella portarum* has validity for most of the other communal levies. Also there was little change in their yield immediately after 1427. Cf. *ibid.*, 30, fols. 76-112; *ibid.*, 32, fols. 74-112r; *ibid.*, 33, fols. 70-113.

dle years of the *trecento* or even during the apogee of Florentine prosperity, the biennium 1336–38. If the index of communal income is any measure, there was no more reason for men to doubt the fiscal potency of the state in 1430 than in 1360 or even in 1330. Returns from indirect taxes also proved steady; this was significant since they accounted for approximately 270,000 florins a year. Not until the late 1480s did they begin to tumble, after which public confidence in the fiscal reliability of the polis atrophied. Civic faith, as evinced in art and letters, was at lowest ebb. The exact nature of the psychological factors inspiring trust in the economic potential of the state remains elusive; but surely the steady decline of returns from indirect levies did little to shore up civic confidence. In 1487 income from these levies was only 160,000 florins, and by 1490 had dropped to 105,000 florins.[85]

The state was assured of a substantial income from gabelles and customs tolls so that in periods of peace returns could be pledged for payment of interest to communal creditors. Customs tolls and gabelles on wine and contracts, in addition to the *estimo* on the *contado*, were assigned to creditors of the *Monte Comune* (largest of all *Monti*, bearing 5 per cent interest). The gabelle on salt was pledged to those who made 7 and 8 per cent *prestanzoni*, while the tax on mills and fisheries went to those who made special loans for the Pisan war. Such a system did much to reassure creditors of the republic and sustain morale, but almost no monetary residue remained to underwrite the expenses of government and costs of war.

As we have seen, with the bulk of the republic's regular income committed for payment of interest to shareholders in the public debt, the signory resorted to numerous forced loans. Such action only added to the communal debt and made it necessary to seek more revenue to pay increased interest. The acceleration of a trend in progress since the middle years of the *trecento* was responsible for the development of specialized and imposing forms of state organization. Subject territories, rural parishes, and country villages continued to lose much of their fiscal autonomy during the middle years of the fourteenth century. Movement toward greater dependence on Florence resulted from pressing demands of the *camera* on these subject territories. Further, Florentine bureaucracy expanded and the city assumed the role of guardian and sometimes spoiler of rustic wealth. The *contado* of the later Middle Ages was little taxed, and because communal budgets were small, little reason existed for exploitation. The very citizens who staffed the signory were owners of extensive rural patrimonies. There

---

[85] Cf. footnote 82.

was always opposition to the levying of direct taxes on the countryside, and in the early *trecento* Florentine regimes were reluctant to incur the enmity of communal councils, even in times of budgetary crisis.[86]

To repeat, the shift to a sterner regimen over the *contado* began gradually in the middle years of the *trecento* and intensified until by the late 1380s it had achieved formidable dimensions. The contribution of the *contado*, rural districts (the outlying reaches), and subject cities bore perhaps one-fifth the brunt of all imposts. This was a substantial increase over the figure of a half century before, when the fraction was perhaps no more than one-tenth. Moreover, the levy on such commodities as meat and wine in the *contado* continued to rise.[87]

The *estimo* on rural wealth was a regular feature of Florence's tributary system, and where earlier there had been only a single direct levy in the course of a year, now there were sometimes two and often three. Beginning with the eighties the commune levied not only an *estimo* but what was euphemistically termed an "extraordinary impost" on the countryside. By 1388 this latter assessment was a regular feature of the Florentine system and continued to be collected throughout the early *quattrocento*. Starting in 1393 the republic imposed an "extraordinary *estimo*" on the rural regions, and this, too, became a regular feature of the Florentine tributary system. By 1395 the *estimo* yielded just over 17,500 florins to the *camera*, while the "extraordinary *estimo*" returned approximately 31,500 florins and the "extraordinary imposts" brought in almost 15,500 florins.

The tax on wine produced in the *contado* stood at 17,000 florins, so that the sum of all rural imposts reached the impressive figure of 85,000 florins at a time when intake from general taxation was slightly over 300,000 florins.[88] By 1402 the figure climbed until the *contado*'s contribution to the Florentine *camera* was almost 140,000 florins annually, a sum frequently exceeded during the next years. Soon fixed

---

[86] For evidence of hostility to the enactment of the *estimo* on the *contado*, see *CapP*, 12, f. 173 (February 1, 1337); *LF*, 14, fols. 41–45 (December 18, 1329); *ibid.*, 16, II, f. 77r (November 8, 1335); *ibid.*, 17, f. 90 (January 19, 1339).
[87] By 1388 the levy on *macello* in the *contado* had reached 6,979 florins, and this figure was over one-third higher than that cited by Giovanni Villani for the prosperous biennium, 1336–38. Cf. G. Villani, *Cronica*, 9, 92, and *PC*, 5, f. 238r (1388). For the 1380s the tax on wine in the *contado* averaged 15,000 florins, and this figure was at least one-third higher than that collected during peak years of the middle *trecento*. *CCE*, Vols. 80–86.
[88] For the "entrata del estimo ordinario del contado" in the year 1395, see *PC*, 11, f. 267. For the "entrata del estimo straordinario del contado" for the same year, see *ibid.*, 11, f. 205. The returns for the gabelles on wine and meat are reported in the same volume on folios 227 and 278, respectively.

payments were substituted for certain of the old levies, and the rate of "extraordinary imposts" was greatly augmented. Now the wealth of the countryside contributed almost one-half to the general revenues. Special taxes were placed on rural communes and country parishes, and Tuscany was required to pay forced loans. By 1431 approximately 80 per cent of all monies collected from rural locales was distributed to the treasurers of the various *Monti* in order that payments could be made to communal creditors. After 1427 the wealth of the environs and districts of Florence was inscribed in registers of the *Catasto*: each time direct levies were imposed (frequently several times a year) the contribution of the *contado* was fixed at 18,594 florins, while the city's stood at 25,341 florins. Considering the greater concentration of wealth in the city, the *contado*'s share does seem disproportionate.[89]

Over the late *trecento* and first quarter of the *quattrocento*, fixed payments were substituted for certain old levies while rates of the extraordinary imposts were raised, despite the fact that the countryside was suffering from the desolation of war and rural population was declining. Each year the signory enacted special legislation encouraging immigration into rural Tuscany, with the government promising immunity from seizure for debt and tax concessions to all who established residence and farmed in the countryside.[90]

Although no detailed portrayal can be drawn of economic conditions in the *contado*, it is certain this harsh regimen came at an unfortunate moment. Nor would it be a simple matter to determine the effects of the republic's stern program on long-range rural developments; but when we note that Florence's intake from the *contado* reached the grand sum of 150,000 florins in 1405, and in succeeding years new assessments were levied on the countryside with monotonous frequency, we understand that fiscal demands of the polis hardly promoted an energetic rural economy. Furthermore, in the 1420s numerous *prestanze* were collected from the environs and districts of the city. The bulk of this revenue from the *contado*, some 80 to 90 per cent of the total, was assigned to the treasurers of the various *Monti* for payment of interest to communal creditors.[91]

This Spartan regime in its search for money acted to integrate rural territories into a political complex that can perhaps be best described as a Renaissance state. So altered was this type of regime from its

---

[89] G. Canestrini, *La scienze*, 1, 122–25.
[90] For a model for such a type of provision, see *P*, 72, f. 161r; *LF*, 41, f. 116r (October 21, 1383); *P*, 80, f. 197; *LF*, 43, f. 232 (December 15, 1391). The reason given by the signory for the enactment of such measures is that the lands of the *contado* are not sufficiently cultivated. The greater incidence of such provisions occurred over the late *trecento* and early *quattrocento*.
[91] Cf. *PC*, 34, f. 154; *ibid.*, 35, f. 141.

medieval predecessor of the thirteenth and early fourteenth centuries that although terms like "republic" or "commune" might still be employed to describe the Florentine political landscape from the thirteenth through the fifteenth century, the terrain described in the later period differed markedly from that of the earlier time. The lax and easy government of the Middle Ages had receded, and in its stead emerged a strict, almost exploitive type of regime. By the fifteenth century the term "commune" no longer signified a government characterized by a relaxed rule over its rural domains. Instead the government was anxious to garner substantial tribute from the countryside so that in peacetime it could be disbursed to the republic's creditors and in time of war it could be deployed for mercenaries. The laissez-faire rule of a medieval commune was replaced by the strict rule of a Renaissance territorial state, a change dictated in part by economic exigencies of the world of the late *trecento* and early *quattrocento*.

We have seen stringent control of subject cities begin in the second half of the *trecento*, and this development paralleled the emergence of the republic's sterner policy for the *contado*, under which Florentine officials appointed by the signory supervised the collection of gabelles in certain districts. In the 1360s and 1370s taxes paid by subject cities into the Florentine treasury were utilized for hiring troops or paying interest to communal creditors.[92]

Florence won valuable territory during the second half of the *trecento* and early *quattrocento*, gaining such prizes as Volterra, Arezzo, Pisa, Cortona, and, finally, Livorno. Pisa is the city for which the most abundant treasury records survive and thus is most suitable as a test case. Florence conquered her neighbor in 1406 and occupied her territory; the Florentine signory established a special section of the *camera* expressly devoted to managing Pisan fiscal affairs. In 1407 an itemized statement of Pisa's income was drawn up by officials of the Florentine *camera*. All gabelles of the subject city were turned over to her conqueror, so that by 1408 Florentines were making a generous profit on the Pisan tax intake. The *Entrata* of the treasury exceeded the *Uscita* by approximately 200,000 lire, and though long-range assessments of the fiscal advantage won by Florentines through conquest are difficult to judge, the early years of domination were certainly not unprofitable.[93] Beginning in 1414, special military levies, averaging between 33,000 and 56,000 florins a year, were placed on Pisa. In addition, an *estimo* of thirty soldi per lira, high by Florentine standards, was levied on the Pisan *contado*, with a special tax placed on grain. Again the major part of all this revenue was diverted to the

[92] Cf. *CCE*, Vols. 135–53.
[93] *PC*, 22, fols. 181–96.

Monte for restitution to communal creditors. In 1428 Pisa, along with many other Florentine subject cities, was declared liable for the *Catasto*.[94]

A comparable but less amply documented history can be constructed for such prize Florentine acquisitions as Arezzo, Cortona, and Volterra. They also paid the customs toll and gabelles on wine, salt, meat, and contracts directly to Florentine treasury officials. The greater part of these revenues were employed for usual purposes: hire of mercenaries or paying interest on the *Monte*. Figures are scattered and records discontinuous, but it appears that the *Entrata* for these towns did exceed expenses of administration and defense, and, therefore, that Florence, at least during the early *quattrocento*, did realize a surplus. Additional levies were placed on the subject cities so that, as in the case of Cortona, such an assessment was in excess of that town's total *Entrata* for a given year. Prato was another special case, where as early as 1420 extraordinary taxes were imposed by officials of the *Monte*. Shortly, all income from gabelles collected by Livorno were placed at the disposition of these Florentine officials.[95] The numerous levies upon lesser places and more remote rural regions were augmented by some 70 per cent during the course of the 1380s, and the added intake was utilized for defense. Beginning in 1393 these imposts were boosted from approximately 18,000 florins to 28,000 florins; such communities were subject to heavy fines if they failed to comply with Florentine regulations.[96]

With the establishment of the *Catasto* in 1427, essentials of communal finance altered. Treasury records reveal that from the date of its establishment until 1431, this direct tax on real and personal property was exacted some thirty-three times. Though several of these exactions were not for the full value of individual assessments, the republic still realized in a single year, 1429, close to 170,000 florins income from its collection. The following year saw the intake climb above 400,000 florins, and in 1431 the total rose above 700,000 florins. Although the treasury could rely upon this substantial income, taxpayers were not relieved from the burden of *prestanze*, because the outlay for mercenaries remained high. In 1431 forced loans exceeded 550,000 florins, so that the public debt continued to mount despite added income from the *Catasto*.[97] Nor did the total indebtedness of

---

[94] G. Canestrini, *La scienza*, pp. 127 ff. On diversion of revenues from Pisa into the hands of the treasurers of the *Monte*, see *PC*, 38, fols. 168 ff.

[95] *Ibid.*, 27, f. 311r (1419); *ibid.*, 28, f. 375 (1420); *ibid.*, 29, fols. 332–413 (1424); *ibid.*, 30, f. 259 (1426).

[96] *Ibid.*, 8, fols. 374–78; *ibid.*, 9, fols. 375–89r.

[97] Cf. "Ritratto dei Catasti," *ibid.*, 34, fols. 303–66. Many of the *catasti* imposed were for a fraction of the total evaluation of citizen patrimonies. Cf. *ibid.*, 32, fols. 332–38

the polis diminish over the *quattrocento*; the signory regularly imposed special *prestanze* (short-term war loans) sometimes at 12 per cent interest. A telling difference between the credit structure of the early *quattrocento* and that of the latter part was largely a resultant of a precipitous fall in revenues from indirect taxation. For the first part of the century income from gabelles stood firm, and this served to encourage public confidence in the fiscal reliability of the polis. Discussions in the advisory councils to the signory in the late *quattrocento* reveal a decline in public trust at a time when revenue from gabelles reached their nadir and inflation of the *Monte* was all too evident.

V

The period of economic and political change treated in this chapter coincides with the era of flourishing civic humanism in Florence. There is discernible correlation between this intellectual movement and economic factors prompting the growth of empire, centralization of polis, increased control of city over *contado*, and, finally, acceleration of flow of citizen capital into the public fisc. The Florentine chancellor Leonardo Bruni Aretino asserted the familiar metaphor on the positive value of wealth, averring that wealth was to the city as blood to the individual. Shortly thereafter, another chancellor and an equally eminent humanist, Poggio Bracciolini, extolled trade and commerce, because he considered that only through these activities did cities gain that wealth which made possible their splendor, beauty, and art. Justifying the acquisitive instinct, he contended that the desire for wealth was good, since it was natural to all men. There were the hypocritical clerics who preached disrespect and even contempt for material possessions; if their message were heeded, the very fabric of society would be undone.[98]

Deeply civic-minded, these humanists responded generously to the needs of their times. Readily apparent to them was the nexus between private wealth and civic well-being. A new economy had emerged more dependent upon government spending and government credit. Under the hold of this new economic system, affluent citizens became major shareholders in a giant corporation that might be termed a "Renaissance state." This entity came into being in the early *quattrocento*,

---

for revenues from the *catasti* of 1429. For the year 1330, see *ibid.*, 33, fols. 332–78. For a summary of *prestanze* levied in the year 1431, see *ibid.*, 31, fols. 202–24.

[98] E. Garin, *L'umanesimo italiano* (Bari, 1952), pp. 59–60; H. Baron, "Franciscan Poverty and Civic Wealth as Factors in the Rise of Humanistic Thought," *Speculum*, 13 (1938), 16 ff.; R. Roedel, "Poggio Bracciolini nel quinto centenario della morte," *Rinascimento*, 11 (1960), 51–67.

and although it was not until 1470 that Florentine legislation referred to the *Monte* as "the heart of this our body, which we call city" and argued that "every member small and large contributes as suitably as it is able to the conservation of all the body: as the guard and most secure fortress and most certain establishment of the salvation of all the body and government of our state," this was but a delayed if florid acknowledgment of the most imposing of Florentine institutions responsible for this transformation.[99]

As we have seen, the metaphor of wealth and blood had become all too familiar by the early *quattrocento*. So had the panegyric of the beauty and grandeur of Florence. Bruni himself had been accused by a Milanese humanist of exaggerating the splendor of the polis. Such exaggeration was a proper rhetorical *topos* legitimized by the term "amplificatio," but to give it a Latin title is no license for dismissal.[100] From the vantage point of earlier developments we can see the gradual enmeshing of private lives with the well-being of the polis. Citizen wealth and civic pride conspired to foster stern mercantilism and lofty imperialism. Once this energetic polis was galvanized, there was continued need to affirm its reality, worth, and even grandeur. It served not only as a safe harbor for citizen patrimony but also as the *raison d'être* for such citizen emotions as the quest for honor and glory. Through the pages of its history alone could come the only immortality one man can bestow on another. Not surprisingly, Florentine technology and science were directed toward buttressing the illusion of the monumentality of just such a public world. If poetry and painting were the high arts of late medieval Florence, then architecture was reigning sovereign of early *quattrocento*. The lure and invitation proffered by a Brunelleschi or Alberti was to find one's humanity in the world of the polis.

The revival of the free-standing column *all'antica* was evident throughout north Italy in the late Middle Ages. The image of the patron saint in Venice or Ravenna or Vicenza or Verona was commonplace. In 1420, on a site where the ancient statue of *Abundantia* was believed to have stood, a column figure by Donatello bearing "emblems of prosperity" was erected. A representation of this figure along with three other statues standing on tall columns can be seen in the Walters Art Gallery in Baltimore.[101] On this panel we observe the geometric plan for an ideal city; three of the figures are meant to represent the

---

[99] Quoted by L. Marks in his "Financial Oligarchy," p. 127. In the above article, the passage is translated from the Italian into English.
[100] E. Gombrich, "The Early Medici as Patrons of Art: A Survey of Primary Sources," *Italian Renaissance Studies*, ed. E. Jacob (London, 1960), 279–311.
[101] Charles Seymour Jr., *Sculpture in Italy 1400 to 1500* (Baltimore, 1966), pp. 6–7.

cardinal virtues of Temperance, Justice, and Fortitude, but Prudence has been displaced by *Abundantia*, or Wealth.

For the artist of the panel, as well as for Brunelleschi and Alberti, mathematics conferred a quality of indestructibility and the eternal to theme and material. Like the rhetoricians and teachers of early *quattrocento* Florence, they presented no catalogue of the earth's beautiful minutiae. Instead, their confidence in geometry and proportion sustained them.[102] The virtues of the public orator and artist became almost interchangeable with the stress upon harmony and decorum. With Brunelleschi we move to a new mentality wherein perspective was mathematically controlled, and for Alberti knowledge was attainable only through measurement. Codes of personal conduct were replete with emphasis upon decorum, harmony, and *gravitas*. The ideal of beauty was expressed in terms of a congruity of the parts. The assumption was that an enduring correspondence exists between public and private worlds, with the former taking precedence over the latter. Alberti made this correspondence more attractive by emphasizing the architectural continuity of inside and outside.[103] In mural painting Domenico Veneziano, Piero della Francesca and Castagno lowered the line of the horizon in order to increase the monumentality of the figure.

Perspective was of course ocular, implying a fixed and measureable distance between observer and object, and no startling hypothesis will be offered here as to why it had its onset in Florence. Two facts acted to render this polis especially amenable to so revolutionary an alteration in perception. The first we have treated in this chapter—namely, the economic forces at work to create a Renaissance territorial state which produced an entity that itself became the subject of veneration. A desire to believe in its durability was ministered to by a great profusion of public art endowing the contemporary scene with dignity and splendor. Secondly, the territorial state was the work of *novi cives* and their adherents, who persistently asserted the sway of the public world over ancient sources of identity such as *consorteria, Parte Guelfa,* confraternity, and so forth. The effects of such a triumph were repressive, so that "the violent tenor of life" and "the high-strung personality" observed by J. Huizinga in his classic account of contemporary northern European life (*The Waning of the Middle Ages*) were no longer so evident in Florence. The general decline of lawlessness

---

[102] G. Fasoli, "La nuova spazialità," *Leonardo: saggi e richerche* (Rome, 1954), pp. 293–311. Cf. also E. Panofsky, *Renaissance and Renascences in Western Art* (Upsula, 1960), p. 20; G. Argan, *Brunelleschi* (Milan, 1955).
[103] R. Wittkower, *Architectural Principles in the Age of Humanism* (London, 1949); L. B. Alberti, *On Painting*, trans. J. R. Spencer (New Haven, 1956).

among Florentines is one of the most compelling developments to occur over the last half of the fourteenth century.[104] It was accompanied by the passage of laws of increasing severity as well as by the augmentation of agencies of enforcement. Private violence and the chivalric ethic receded, and, as they did, modifications in human perception ensued. In the north of Europe there was preference for vivid and contrasting colors, whereas olfactory, auditory, and tactile functions were more highly developed than the sense of sight.[105] Huizinga's style of inquiry was brilliantly continued by Lucien Febvre in his *Le Problème de l'Incroyance au XVIe Siècle: La Religion de Rabelais* (Paris, 1947), where he explicated upon the "visual backwardness" of sixteenth-century Frenchmen. A world that Florentines would have described primarily in visual terms is rendered by the French through touch, taste, and sound. Not that Frenchmen had faltering eyesight; rather, they adjusted to their environment differently from Florentines—this is the point at issue. Febvre goes on to describe the fluid qualities of the Northern world in which objects did not preserve their distinctness and the separation between object and subject was so blurred as to count for little.

In Florence the effects of repression compelled the individual to cultivate a more civic persona. The admonition "to live *civile*" was internalized dramatically and impressed by father on son. The public world had a fixed character, distanced and differentiated from the individual. Description of its qualities was not through senses of taste, touch, or smell, but visually. In 1410 the first colossal statue since antiquity was commissioned by the Florentines. Donatello was instructed to make of brick and plaster a Joshua, meant as a temporary figure soon to be replaced by one done in marble, to be installed on the north side of the Duomo.[106] This statue was to displace an Isaiah that had

---

[104] See the very useful account of this problem in Zevedei Barbu's *Problems of Historical Psychology* (London, 1960), pp. 21–26. I have followed his account closely and am convinced that psychological research into possible relationships between "ego-feelings" (the development of the "self") and the individual's perceptions of the external world would be valuable to the historian of the early Renaissance.

[105] See the suggestive statistics presented by U. Dorini, *Il diritto penale e la delinquenza in Firenze nel secolo XIV* (Lucca, 1916), pp. 28, 38, 64 ff. This theme will be treated in greater detail in Volume 3. Of particular relevance is the emotional quality of public oratory in the late thirteenth century. The speaker rolled his eyes, tore his clothing, and wept to move his listeners. How different was the sense of measure and decorum of the humanist speakers of the early *quattrocento*. Cf. E. Garin's "La giovinezza di Donato Acciaiuoli," *Rinascimento*, 1 (1950), 43–70. Likewise the quest for arcane meaning through intricate allegorizing came to be ridiculed by a Poggio whose scholarship was governed by rational and moderate expectations. E. Garin, "Noterelle sulla filosofia del Rinascimento," *Rinascimento*, 2 (1951), 320–21. For comments on earlier oratorical styles, see A. Galletti, *L'eloquenza (Dalle origini al XVI secolo)*, (Milan, 1938), pp. 511 ff.

[106] H. Janson, "The Image of Man in Renaissance Art: From Donatello to Michelangelo," *The Renaissance Image of Man and the World* (Columbus, 1966), 85–86.

been found much too small to be effective when placed at such a height. The new *Joshua*, eighteen feet high, was not inspired by a Roman forebear; instead, the human eye was the revolutionary agent at work. Because the distance between onlooker and statue was great, the scale had to be colossal. Unlike all the Gothic cathedrals to the north, whose statuary was created "to the greater glory of God," *Joshua* was designed to be appreciated by the human eye.

The two other disciplines flourishing in Florence at this time likewise emphasized the sense of distance. In rhetoric we observe clear distinctions between public and private worlds, with the orator disdaining traditional emotional appeals in favor of stratagems designed to harness imperatives of the super ego to the requirements of polis. From Bruni through Machiavelli we see the problem of the orator determined by the realization that human nature is after all basically selfish and incapable of *renovatio*. Oratory served as a bridge between public and private worlds to provide selfish men with the opportunity to transcend their basic nature by acting creatively in the public world. Separate from God, bereft of sacramental bonds, ceremonial identity, and ritual ties, men had to rely upon their own resources. Distanced from the virtuous heroes of Rome and Greece, these egoistic creatures had nonetheless to imitate their forebears. Rhetoric at this level was intertwined with history. Both were concerned with a community of experience—that is, politics. The search for arcane meaning receded; symbol and allegory fell by the way. Historian stood apart from subject, a relatively simple feat since problems of conscience and spiritual crisis remained uninvestigated. Enough to say that men are selfish or fragile; the limits of conventional wisdom defined them simplistically; the older Christian depth psychology was surrendered. Neither marked by grace nor stained by sin, men could be treated without attention to the motions of their souls. Enough to record their public acts using a simplistic, behavioral psychology. With Machiavelli there was a final emptying out of conscience and its problems, with state and public world determining the perspective.[107]

Rhetoric and history instructed men in rules of decorum. Biographies of *quattrocento* Florentines demonstrate the price of this new

---

[107] The theme of Renaissance perspective will be treated extensively in a subsequent volume where developments in Florentine historiography from Dante through Bruni shall be considered. In thinking of a fixed perspective it might be useful to recall the way in which a medieval writer shifts from time, as it is apprehended in the phenomenal world, to the timelessness of the transcendent and then back again.

On the tie between rhetoric, poetry, and history, see the decree of the signory of September, 1397, calling upon Giovanni Malpaghini to instruct Florentines in rhetoric "ac etiam ad legendem unum autorem hystoricum moralem, aut poetam quolibet anno," see A. Galletti, *L'eloquenza*, p. 553.

paideia: the loss of loved ones, personal suffering, and even exile were to be borne with equanimity and grace. Time came to be measured in terms of work and accomplishment. Competition between citizens had to be intellectual or esthetic rather than emotional or physical. Small wonder that defense of the interior world was conducted by excessive Neoplatonists. The autonomy of political thought was demanding and the price of ordering the "self" was harsh.[108]

Machiavelli, who understood so well that caring for country might put the citizen's soul in jeopardy, perhaps could not escape anguish in pondering why the ancient peoples were braver than his contemporaries:

> I conclude it [bravery] came from the same cause that makes men now less hardy. That I believe is the difference between our religion and the ancient. Ours, because it shows us the truth and the true way, makes us esteem less the honor of the world; whereas the pagans, greatly esteeming such honor and believing it their greatest good, were fiercer in their actions. This we infer from many of their institutions, beginning with the magnificence of their sacrifices, compared with the mildness of ours. There is in ours some pomp, more delicate than magnificent, but no action either fierce or vigorous. In theirs neither pomp nor magnificence was lacking in the ceremonies, and in addition there was the deed of sacrifice, full of blood and ferocity in the slaughter of a multitude of animals; this terrible sight made the men resemble it. Ancient religion, besides this, attributed blessedness only to men abounding in worldly glory, such as generals of armies and princes of states. Our religion has glorified humble and contemplative men rather than active ones. It has, then, set up as the greatest good humility, abjectness and contempt for human things; the other put it in grandeur of mind, in strength of body, and in all the other things apt to make men exceedingly vigorous. Though our religion asks that you have fortitude within you, it prefers that you be adapted to suffering rather than to doing something vigorous.[109]

---

[108] Books on Machiavelli are legion, but see L. Russo's *Machiavelli* (Rome, 1945), pp. 28–32. The Florentine presents experience not as a "res gesta," complete once and for all, but as a "rem genere," ongoing and never finished. Distanced from his subject, the men and events he depicts are transported "in cotesto clima d'arte, in un atmosfera di serena tragedia della tecnica politica." See also F. Chiappelli's careful appraisal of the political language of *The Prince* in his *Studi sul linguaggio del Machiavelli* (Florence, 1962), pp. 88 ff. My colleague Professor Hayden White has been most helpful in allowing me to read some of his materials on Machiavelli.

[109] Niccolò Machiavelli, *The Chief Works and Others*, trans. A. Gilbert (Duke University Press, 1965), 1, 330–31 (Discourses 2, 2).

EPILOGUE

In my next volume, I hope to consider that panoply of medieval commitments and imperatives which stocked the psyches of *trecento* Florentine citizens. That these values were in crisis and frequently in disarray does not imply they lacked durability. The present volume, however, has subsumed experience under the metaphor of *growth* and, therefore, treated them with less consideration than they deserve. The next will be concerned with the vexing problem of aging. Older beliefs were precisely those generating tension in the political sphere and anxiety in the social realm. The dialectic between past and present gave the times their dimension, if not their tragic import. The filter of the public world, as constructed in this volume, is hardly adequate for suggesting the intricate qualities of medieval culture. A brief survey of the ideas of prominent thinkers such as Petrarch or Salutati would demonstrate that the varied subtleties of their literary minds cannot be confined within the limits of a public forum, no matter how grand the architectural design.

There is also the fact of political and social loss that cannot be suggested in a volume devoted to emergence and triumph. Yet the tamed and sometimes defeated patriciate of *trecento* Florence should elicit the sympathy of the historically minded. Further, there were those who were all but excluded from the citizen world of the late *trecento*: the working class (*il popolo minuto*) were discriminated against in a brutal manner by the rule of guild law. If aristocrats rejected the claims of the state as an offense to honor as well as a contradiction of higher allegiance, *il popolo minuto* suffered the economic oppression of the disinherited. Their revolutionary activity was over after 1382 and their political vitality eradicated from historical memory. Justice and the territorial state of the greater guildsmen meant exploitation for a Florentine proletariat whose experience is little commented on in this volume. A tax system, crucial to the formation of the territorial state, was constructed to guarantee the affluent a substantial return on state bonds. It was hoped that interest payments would be met by levies falling on petty producers and consumers.

The subsequent extirpation of egalitarian religious ideas, widespread among *il popolo minuto*, must be delineated. To understand the consequences of the defeat of revolutionary medieval ideology is a formidable problem. From the vantage point of Italian *quattrocento* culture the frustration of medieval democratic ideas meant the undermining of the solid bridge between private and public worlds. Had medieval democracy intensified after 1382 instead of being aborted, a univalent political and moral code might have been achieved. The more extensive the popular participation in the signory, the greater the likelihood that a single standard would prevail. Florentine puritanism was a product of mid-*trecento* democratization and was manifest in a fervency in enforcement of sumptuary laws, in legislation against prostitution, statutes against sodomy, and implementation of court verdicts against delinquent magnates. The challenge to inadequate standards for judging the behavior of the *maiores et potentes* was linked to the admission of *novi cives* into the signory. Likewise, severe legislation against the Tuscan church necessarily weakened the hold of ritualistic and aristocratic Christianity. The growth of religious nonconformity, connected intimately with the diffusion of heresy, peaked in the year 1382. Again, had democratization continued, sacramental religion might well have receded further and popular religious conscience undergone more extensive habitation.

Without additional investigation such inferences can be formulated only in the pluperfect subjunctive. Much more vulnerable is the historical problem of the emergence of the Florentine burghers from the corporate world of the Middle Ages. Although Burckhardtian insights concerning their individuation are valuable, they still require modification. First, we must recognize that this individualism was not only a source of energy and pleasure, but also of anxiety. The burden of selfhood and the problem of alienation remain to be studied by the historian of the *trecento*. Clearly, the individual acted both to affirm and to subordinate his identity to the public world. He sought surcease from the erosion of traditional ritual ties, sacramental bonds, and ceremonial identities by legitimizing the quest for fame. Like the civic world that conferred renown upon the individual, so, too, the nuclear family served to repair his frayed ego. Second, liberation of the citizen from time-honored corporate restraints did not foster that unbridled egoism of which Burckhardt speaks with such exquisite concern. Indeed, the Florentine public world of late *trecento* and early *quattrocento* seldom allowed this egoism to operate as an effective social force. General histories of the earlier renaissance risk misunderstanding the texture of culture when they deny the Florentine penchant for strict enforcement of law and unyielding constitutionalism. The citizen was released from certain medieval restraints only to be contained posthaste within a demanding world of public discipline. Increasingly, the imperatives most likely to shape his persona were those of the polis. Not accidental is the fact that new humanist ideas of educating the young for service to polis were first formulated in early *quattrocento* Florence.

To affirm repression is not to suggest that the citizen role was quiescent or

EPILOGUE

that civic humanism lacked confidence in the vitality of human will. From Petrarch and Salutati through Bruni and Alberti the image of "man the maker" *(homo faber)* was elevated until it became that hallmark of his uniqueness and dignity. Even so ascetic a thinker as Marsiglio Ficino celebrated the earthly role of man the builder. Basic to this theme was the belief that civilization is a human construct. Later, Renaissance thinkers drew upon this faith when proclaiming the power of man to transform his world. The earlier intellectual movement contributed heroically to the sixteenth-century belief in the magical capabilities of human vitality. What we observe in the early *quattrocento* is a tension between extreme voluntarism on the one hand and the repressive mechanism of society on the other. If culture was in process of intensifying a feeling for community, with the polis as focus of man's political life and the Renaissance family as core of his moral expectation, there was still lively criticism of public values and social forms. Repression produced its antithesis in the free play of critical imagination that sometimes denied even the possibilities of the minimal co-operation necessary for human association. Witness the obsessive interest of Poggio and others with the motif of hypocrisy.

The individual emerged from the corporate and associative world of the late Middle Ages. His citizen ego was stripped of numerous props; he stood remote from many of the comforts of a hierarchical medieval cosmos just as he was alienated from older extended sociabilities. The emotional history of the Renaissance was characterized in part by the quest for new ego supports. The search for fame assumed ligitimacy only when collectivized concepts of honor were failing. If the individual became more liberated, he was also more vulnerable. If *homo faber* was celebrated, his dwelling lost many of the sociable qualities of communal life and assumed the burden of privacy. Just as the extended family business gave way to the impersonal holding company of the early Renaissance, so, too, did the world of the extended clan contract into that of the nuclear family. The amplitude of social constructions, wherein medieval ideals of pervasive love assisted the generalization of emotionality until they became increasingly lateral, was on the decline. The Renaissance family circumscribed and deepened affection by channeling it only to the immediate kin. Intensity of feeling was reserved for father, mother, and wife. The child became an object of veneration. The household was elevated to a religious ideal and *quattrocento* painting and literature served to make domesticity sublime. Renaissance naturalism in painting must not be explained in nineteenth-century terms, with its penchant for the sensual. Limited burgher society became a receptacle for sacred objects, and when Ghirlandaio depicted society with such fidelity in his fresco cycles at Sta. Trinita, the apotheosis of the bourgeoisie was achieved. Instead of longing after the subtle and illusive, one elevated the familiar and everyday.

In the early fifteenth century, when Bruni set out to write the life of Dante, he made obeisance to the earlier biography written by Boccaccio. Despite Boccaccio's concern with his subject's public career, Bruni thought this *Vita* to be too full of sighs, yearnings, and the other sweet ingredients of love: "... this most delightful and charming Boccaccio of ours wrote the life and manners of so sublime a poet just as though he were writing the *Filocolo*, or the *Fiametta*. For it is all full of love and sighs and burning tears; as though man were born into this world only that he might take his place in those ten amorous *Days* wherein enamoured ladies and gallant youths recounted the hundred Tales. And he grows so warm in these passages of love that he drops the weighty and substantial parts of Dante's life, passing them over in silence, while he records trivial matters and holds his peace concerning grave ones."

What became dominant was the externalization of perspective whereby character and action were viewed from the vantage point of the public world—"the weighty and substantial parts." Deeper psychological insights were sacrificed in order to portray the civic Dante of politics and warfare. Medieval strategies for gaining knowledge of the interior world, such as scholastic psychology, metaphysical poetry, and the introspective tactics of chivalric literature, receded. The pull of the public world intensified, and humanists were anxious to lend support to a beleaguered ego by justifying claims for civic identity and renown. A separation between the highly cultivated civic persona and the deepest recesses of interiority emerged.

What was in process of being colonized in the human mind was the rim of consciousness visible to society and the psychic center ministered to by the ceremonial and liturgical. The culture was all too anxious to furnish justification for the civic persona as well as consolation to the unquiet center. The obligation to make viable connections between rim and core was not encouraged by early humanism. Petrarchism, so popular among north Italians, established mobility of ego as an operational principle. The human condition was, then, precisely defined by its failure to sustain ideals and commitments. Further, the psyche was depicted as being circumscribed by its own laws, which rendered much of religious and ethical philosophy useless. The lyricism of the Renaissance became a noble stance in the face of inevitable loss. Renaissance poetry was constructed from such antitheses as love and hate, youth and old age, thus demonstrating the evanescence of all things human. A depth psychology could not readily be formulated to connect these polarities of human experience. Italian prose employed a behavioristic psychology whereby character was revealed through action and there was little temptation to probe the recesses of the human mind. Clearly, the comic view of antiquity provided the most entertainment and comfort, for it alone recounted man's fate and charted his knowable personality. Significantly, the tragic mode was alien to Renaissance dramatic art. Finally, in humanist historiography it was the phenomenological and limited that were championed against the transcendent and infinite. More thoroughly than any other intellectual activity, Renaissance historians rejected the grand quest for the noumenal.

A new taste for the gaudy in religious ceremony accompanied the accentuation

EPILOGUE

of styles and forms in civic life. What is suggested here is that the origins of the baroque were in the early Renaissance. In order to believe in the public world it became necessary to exaggerate its qualities. Intellectuals were perhaps too tender and solicitous in their desire to provide justification for the newly acquired ego props. Moreover, their fideism and contempt for metaphysics and theology encouraged a separation between the deep center of irrational yearning and the rim of cultivated ego.

In the north of Europe neither public world nor civic Christianity served to structure personality. Moreover, the extended sociability and chivalric ethos of medieval times still sustained the individual ego. Metaphysics, theology, and pietism readily acknowledged mystical alternatives; hence guilt and expiation were at the level of consciousness. The northern intellectual may have suffered more, but he continued to maintain his awareness of evil and sin. His world witnessed the gradual recession of medieval magic (sacramental bonds, ritual ties, and ceremonial identities); therefore the irrational was omnipresent, luring him to seek a deeper understanding of its equivalent in himself. His sensibilities became protestant: the colonization of the rim of the mind (public world) diminished and his energies served to clear new pathways between the outer and inner worlds.

BIBLIOGRAPHY

PRIMARY SOURCES

Alberti, L. B. *On Painting*. Translated by J. R. Spencer. New Haven: 1956.
Aquinas, St. Thomas. *Summa Theologiae*. 3 vols. (Edition of The American Dominicans) New York: 1947–48.
Augustine. *The City of God*. London: 1966.
———. *Confessions*. London: 1925.
Barberino, Francesco da. *Reggimento e costumi di donna*. Bologna 1875.
Battaglia, Salvatore. *Il Pecorone di Ser Giovanni Fiorentino, e due racconti anonimi del trecento*. Milan: 1944.
Benvenuto (da Imola). *Comentum super Dantis Aldigherii Comoediam*. 2 vols. Florence: 1887.
Bernardino, San. *Prediche volgare*. Edited by C. Cannarozzi. 3 vols. Pistoia: 1940.
Berti, P. "Nuovi documenti intorno al catasto fiorentino," *Giornale Storico degli Archivi Toscani*, 4 (1860), 32–62.
Bisticci, Vespasiano da. *Vite di uomini illustri del secolo XV*. Edited by P. D'Ancona and E. Aeschlimann. Milan: 1951.
Boccaccio, G. *Lettere volgari*. Florence: 1834.
———. *Genealogiae deorum gentilium libri*. Edited by V. Romano. 2 vols. Bari: 1951.
———. *The Fates of Illustrious Men*. Translated by L. Hall. New York: 1965.
———. *Le lettere edite e inedite*. Edited by F. Corazzini. Florence: 1877.
———. *Il commento alla Divina Commedia*. Edited by D. Guerri. 3 vols. Bari: 1918.
———. *Trattatello in laude di Dante*. Edited by P. Wicksteed. London: 1904.
Bonaini, F. "Statuto della parte guelfa di Firenze," *Archivio Storico Italiano*, 5 (1857), 1–41.
Boninsegni, D. *Storie della Città di Firenze dall'anno 1410 al 1460*. Florence: 1637.
Brucker, G. "Un documento fiorentino sulla guerra, sulla finanza e sulla amministrazione pubblica (1375)," *Archivio Storico Italiano*, 115 (1957), 165–76.
Bruni, Leonardo Aretino. *Istoria fiorentina*. Translated by Donato Acciaiuoli. Florence: 1861.
———. *Humanistisch-Philosophische Schriften*. Edited by H. Baron. Leipzig and Berlin: 1928.

BIBLIOGRAPHY

Cavalcanti, G. *Istorie fiorentine.* 2 vols. Florence: 1839.
Certaldo, Paolo da. *Libro di buoni costumi.* Edited by A. Schiaffini. Florence: 1945.
Compagni, D. *Cronica.* Edited by I. del Lungo. 3 vols. Florence: 1889.
Conti, P. *Il libro segreto della ragione di Piero Benini e compagni.* Florence: 1937.
Cronica fiorentina di Marchionne di Coppo Stefani. Edited by N. Rodolico in *Rerum Italicarum Scriptores.* New ed., Vol. 30, Part I (Città di Castello, 1903–1955).
Cronica volgare di anonimo fiorentino. Edited by E. Bellondi in *Rerum Italicarum Scriptores,* Vol. 27, 2 (Città di Castello, 1915, 1918).
Dante, Alighieri. *Opere* (Edition of the Società Dantesca). Florence: 1960.
———. *Epistolae.* Edited by P. Toynbee. Oxford: 1920.
Dati, G. *L'Istoria di Firenze dal 1380 al 1405.* Edited by L. Pratesi. Norcia: 1904.
Delizie degli eruditi toscani. Edited by Fr. I. di San Luigi. 24 vols. Florence: 1770–89.
Documenti di storia italiana pubblicati a cura della R. Deputazione toscana di storia patria. Edited by A. Gherardi. Florence: 1876.
Dominici, Giovanni. *Regola del governo di cura familiare.* Edited by D. Salvi. Florence: 1860.
Ellinwood, L. *The Works of Francesco Landini.* Cambridge, Mass.: 1939.
Gherardo, Giovanni da. *Rime di M. Cino da Pistoia e d'altri del secolo XIV.* Edited by G. Carducci. Florence: 1862.
———. *Il Paradiso degli Alberti.* Edited by A. Wesselofsky. Bologna: 1867.
Guicciardini, Francesco. *Storia fiorentina.* Edited by G. Canestrini. Florence: 1859.
———. *Le cose fiorentine.* Edited by R. Ridolfi. Florence: 1945.
I Capitoli del Comune. Vol. 2. Edited by C. Guasti. Florence: 1893.
I trattiti morali di Coluccio Salutati. Edited by E. Garin. Florence: 1943.
Lami, Giovanni. *Deliciae eurditorum.* Florence: 1743.
Leoni, L. "Breve di Clemente VI en favore di Gualtieri di Brienne Duca d'Atene," *Archivio Storico Italiano.* Vol. 22 (1875).
Machiavelli, Niccolò. *The Chief Works and Others.* Translated by A. Gilbert. Durham: 1965.
———. *History of Florence and of the Affairs of Italy.* Edited by F. Gilbert. New York: 1960.
Mazzei, Ser Lapo. *Lettere di un notaro a un mercante del secolo XIV.* Edited by C. Guasti. 2 vols. Florence: 1880.
Mehus, L. *Epistola o sia ragionamento di Messer Lapo da Castiglionchio.* Bologna: 1753.
Morelli, Giovanni di Pagolo. *Ricordi.* Edited by V. Branca. Florence: 1956.
Palmieri, M. *Della vita civile,* in *Prosatori volgari del Quattrocento.* Edited by C. Varese. Milan-Naples: n.d.
Petrarch, F. *Petrarch's Secret.* Translated by W. Draper. London: 1911.
———. *Lettere senili di Francesco Petrarch.* Florence: 1892.
———. *Invective contra medicum.* Edited by P. Ricci. Rome: 1950.

BIBLIOGRAPHY

———. *La vita di Scipione l'Africano.* Edited by G. Martellotti. Milan-Naples: 1954.
———. "De sui ipsius et multorum ignorantia," Translated by H. Nachod, in *The Renaissance Philosophy of Man.* Edited by E. Cassirer. Chicago: 1948. Pages 47–133.
———. *De viris illustribus.* Edited by G. Martellotti. Florence: 1964.
———. *Le Familiari.* Edited by V. Rossi. Florence: 1942.
———. *Rerum memorandum libri.* Edited by G. Billanovich. Florence: 1945.
Prosatori latini del Quattrocento. Edited by E. Garin. Milan-Naples: 1952.
Roover, R. de. "Il trattato di fra Santi Rucellai sul cambio, il monte comune e il monte delle doti," *Archivio Storico Italiano,* 111 (1953), 3–34.
Sacchetti, F. *Il libro delle rime.* Edited by A. Chiari. Bari: 1936.
———. *Il libro delle trecentonovelle.* Edited by V. Pernicone. Florence: 1946.
———. *Opere.* Edited by A. Chiari. 2 vols. Bari: 1938.
Salutati, C. *De saeculo et religione.* Edited by B. Ullman. Florence: 1957.
———. *De laboribus Herculis.* Edited by B. Ullman. 2 vols. Zurich: 1951.
———. *Epistolario di Coluccio Salutati.* Edited by F. Novati. 4 vols. Rome: 1891–1911.
———. *De nobilitate legum et medicinae.* Edited by E. Garin. Florence: 1947.
Santini, P. *Documenti dell'antica costituzione del comune del Firenze.* Florence: 1895.
Sercambi, Giovanni. *Le cronache.* Edited by S. Bongi in *Fonti per la storia d'Italia.* Vol. 22. Lucca: 1892.
Sereno, R. "The Ricordi of Gino di Neri Capponi," *American Political Science Review,* 52 (1958), 1118–22.
Sommario delle reforme leggi e ordini dell'ufitio conservatori del contado. Florence: 1553.
Sorio, B. *Le Lettere di Beato Don Giovanni dalle Celle monaco vallombrosano e d'altri.* Rome: 1845.
Statuti della Repubblica fiorentina. Edited by R. Caggese. 2 vols. Florence: 1910–21.
Statuta populi et communis Florentiae. 3 vols. Freiburg: 1778–83.
Testi fiorentini del dugento e dei primi del trecento. Edited by A. Schiaffini. Florence: 1926.
Velluti, D. *La Cronica domestica.* Edited by I. del Lungo. Florence: 1914.
Villani, F. *Liber de civitates florentiae famosis civibus.* Edited by G. Galletti. Florence: 1847.
Villani, G. *Cronica.* Edited by F. Dragomanni. 4 vols. Florence: 1844–45.
Villani, M. *Cronica.* Edited by F. Dragomanni. 2 vols. Florence: 1846.

SECONDARY SOURCES

Ancona, A. D. *Saggi di letteratura popolare.* Livorno: 1913.
Antal, F. *Florentine Painting and its Social Background.* London: 1948.
Antonelli, G. "La magistratura degli Otto di Guardia a Firenze," *Archivio Storico Italiano,* 112 (1954), 3–23.

BIBLIOGRAPHY

Argan, G. "The Architecture of Brunelleschi and the Origins of Perspective Theory in the Fifteenth Century," *Journal of the Warburg and Courtauld Institutes*, 9 (1946), 96–121.

———. *From Van Eyck to Botticelli*. New York: 1964.

———. *Brunelleschi*. Milan: 1955.

Auerbach, E. *Mimesis*. New York: 1957.

———. *Dante Poet of the Secular World*. Translated by R. Manheim. Chicago: 1961.

Aurigemma, M. *Saggio sul Passavanti*. Florence: 1957.

Barbadoro, B. "Finanza e demografia nei ruoli fiorentini d'imposta del 1352," *Atti del Congresso Internazionale per gli studi sulla populazione* (Rome, 1931), 13–34.

———. *Le finanze della Repubblica fiorentina imposta diretta e debito pubblico fino all'instituzione del Monte*. Florence: 1929.

Barbu, Zevedei. *Problems of Historical Psychology*. London: 1960.

Baron, H. *The Crisis of the Early Italian Renaissance*. 2 vols. Princeton: 1955.

———. "Franciscan Poverty and Civic Wealth as Factors in the Rise of Humanistic Thought," *Speculum*, 13 (1938), 1–37.

———. *Humanistic and Political Literature in Florence and Venice at the Beginning of the Quattrocento*. Cambridge, Mass.: 1955.

———. "The Social Background of Political Liberty in the Early Italian Renaissance," *Comparative Studies in Society and History*, 2 (1960), 440–51.

———. "Das Erwachen des Historischen Denkens in Humanismus des Quattrocento," *Historische Zeitschrift*, 147 (1952), 5–20.

Battara, P. "Le indagini congetturali sulla popolazione di Firenze fino al Trecento," *Archivio Storico Italiano*, 93 (1935), 217–32.

———. *La popolazione di Firenze alla metà dei 500*. Florence: 1935.

Bayley, C. C. *War and Society in Renaissance Florence*. Toronto: 1961.

Becker, M. "The Republican City State in Florence: An Inquiry into its Origin and Survival (1280–1434)," *Speculum*, 35 (1960), 39–50.

———. "Florentine Politics and the Diffusion of Heresy in the Trecento," *Speculum*, 34 (1959), 60–75.

———. "Economic Change and the Emerging Florentine Territorial State," *Studies in the Renaissance*, 13 (1966), 7–39.

———. "Un avvenimento riguardante il cronista Marchionne di Coppo Stefani," *Archivio Storico Italiano*, 117 (1959), 137–46.

———. "Problemi della finanza pubblica fiorentina della seconda metà del Trecento e dei primi del Quattrocento," *Archivio Storico Italiano*, 133 (1965), 434–66.

———. "Some Economic Implications of the Conflict between Church and State in Trecento Florence," *Mediaeval Studies*, 21 (1959), 1–16.

———. "Some Aspects of Oligarchical, Dictatorial and Popular Signorie in Florence, 1282–1382," *Comparative Studies in Society and History*, 2 (1960), 421–39.

———. "Florentine Popular Government (1343–1348)," *Proceedings of the American Philosophical Society*, 106 (1962), 360–82.

———. "La esecuzione della legislazione contro le pratiche monopolistiche delle

BIBLIOGRAPHY

arti fiorentine alla metà del secolo quattordicesimo," *Archivio Storico Italiano*, 117 (1959), 8–28.

———. "Dante and His Contemporaries as Political Men," *Speculum*, 41 (1966), 665–80.

———. "Three Cases Concerning the Restitution of Usury in Florence," *Journal of Economic History*, 17 (1957), 445–50.

———. "Nota dei processi riguardanti prestatori di denaro del 1343 al 1379," *Archivio Storico Italiano*, 114 (1956), 93–104.

———. "Notes from the Florentine Archives," *Renaissance News*, 17 (1964), 303–4.

———. "Florentine *Libertas*: Political Independents and *Novi Cives*, 1372–1378," *Traditio*, 18 (1962), 393–407.

———. *Florence in Transition*. Vol. I. Baltimore: 1967.

Beloch, K. J. *Bevölkerungsgeschichte Italiens*. Berlin and Leipzig: 1937.

Bernardo, A. *Petrarch, Scipio and the "Africa."* Baltimore: 1962.

Besta, E. *La famiglia nella storia del diritto italiano*. Padua: 1933.

Billanovich, G. *Restauri Boccacceschi*. Rome: 1945.

Blackmur, R. *The Lion and the Honeycomb*. New York: 1955.

Bonnell, R. "An Early Humanistic View of the Active and Contemplative Life," *Italica*, 43 (1966), 225–39.

Bonolis, G. *La giurisdizione della Mercanzia in Firenze nel secolo XIV*. Florence: 1901.

Borsook, E. *The Mural Painters of Tuscany from Cimabue to Andrea del Sarto*. London: 1960.

Bosco, Umberto. *Petrarca*. Turin: 1946.

Bowsky, W. "The Impact of the Black Death upon Sienese Government and Society," *Speculum*, 39 (1964), 1–34.

Branca, V. *Boccaccio medievale*. Florence: 1956.

Brown, J. Wood. *The Dominican Church of Santa Maria Novella*. Edinburgh: 1902.

Brucker, G. "The Ghibelline Trial of Matteo Villani (1362)," *Medievalia et Humanistica*, 13 (1960), 48–55.

———. *Florentine Politics and Society 1343–1378*. Princeton: 1962.

———. "The Medici in the Fourteenth Century," *Speculum*, 32 (1957), 1–26.

———. and Becker, M. "The *Arti Minori* in Florentine Politics, 1342–1378," *Mediaeval Studies*, 18 (1956), 93–104.

Buck, A. *Das Geschichtsdenken der Renaissance*. Cologne: 1957.

Burckhardt, Jacob. *The Civilization of the Renaissance in Italy*. Translated by S. G. C. Middlemore. 2 vols. New York: 1958.

Caggese, R. *Firenze delle decadenza di Roma al Risorgimento di Italia*. 3 vols. Florence: 1912–21.

Calasso, F. *Introduzione al diritto comune*. Milan: 1951.

Calcaterra, C. *Nella selva del Petrarca*. Bologna: 1942.

———. *I Trionfi*. Turin: 1927.

Cambridge Economic History of Europe. Vols. 2, 3. Cambridge: 1952–63.

Canestrini, G. *La scienza e l'arte di stato*. Florence: 1862.

Capponi, G. *Cronichette antiche di vari scrittori*. Florence: 1853.

BIBLIOGRAPHY

———. *Storia della repubblica di Firenze.* 2 vols. Florence: 1930.
Carpentier, E. *Une Ville devant la peste. Orvieto et la peste noire de 1348.* Paris: 1962.
Cassirer, E. *The Individual and the Cosmos in Renaissance Philosophy.* Translated by Mario Domandi. New York: 1964.
Cavallari, E. *La fortuna di Dante nel Trecento.* Florence: 1921.
Cessi, R. "Il problema bancaria a Venezia nel secolo XIV," *Atti della R. Accademia di Torino*, 52 (1917), 789–93.
Chabod, F. "La 'concezione del mondo' di Giovanni Villani," *Nuova Rivista Storica.* Vol. 13 (1929).
———. *Machiavelli and the Renaissance.* Translated by D. More. London: 1958.
———. *Scritti su Machiavelli.* Turin: 1964.
Chiappelli, F. *Studi sul linguaggio del Machiavelli.* Florence: 1962.
Chiappelli, L. "Formazione storica del Comune," *Archivio Storico Italiano*, 84 (1926), 3–24.
Chiari, A. "La fortuna del Boccaccio," *Questioni e correnti di storia letteraria.* Edited by A. Momigliano. Florence: 1949. Pages 275–348.
Cividali, P. "Il Beato Giovanni dalle Celle," *Atti della R. Accademia dei Lincei, Memorie*, 12 (1906), 354–477.
Cristiani, E. *Nobiltà e Popolo nel Comune di Pisa.* Naples: 1962.
Davidsohn, R. "Tre orazioni di Lapo da Castiglionchio," *Archivio Storico Italiano*, 20 (1897), 225–46.
———. "Blüte und Niedergang der florentinischen Tuchindustrie," *Zeitschrift für die gesamte Staatswissenschaft*, 85 (1928), 225–55.
Davis, C. T. *Dante and the Idea of Rome.* Oxford: 1957.
Davis, J. C. *The Decline of the Venetian Nobility as a Ruling Class.* Baltimore: 1962.
Doren, A. *Le arti fiorentine.* Translated by G. Klein. 2 vols. Florence: 1940.
———. *Die florentiner Wollentuchindustrie vom vierzehnten bis zum sechzehnten Jahrhundert.* Stuttgart: 1901.
Dorini, U. *Notizie storiche sull'Università di Parte Guelfa in Firenze.* Florence: 1902.
———. *Il diritto penale e la delinquenza in Firenze nel secolo XIV.* Lucca: 1916.
Douie, Decima. *The Nature and the Effect of the Heresy of the Fraticelli.* Manchester: 1932.
Duby, G. *La société aux XIe et XIIe siècles dans la region Mâconnaise.* Paris: 1953.
Emerton, E. *Humanism and Tyranny.* Cambridge, Mass.: 1925.
Ercole, F. *Da Bartolo all'Althusio.* Florence: 1938.
Fahy, C. "Early Renaissance Treatises on Women," *Italian Studies*, 11 (1956), 30–35.
Falletti-Fossati, C. *Il tumulto dei Ciompi.* Florence: 1882.
Fasoli, G. "La nuova spazialità," *Leonardo: saggi e richerche* (Rome, 1954), 293–311.
Ferri, Ferruccio. *La poesia populare in Antonio Pucci.* Bologna: 1909.
Fiumi, E. "La demografia fiorentina nelle pagine di Giovanni Villani," *Archivio Storico Italiano*, 108 (1950), 78–158.

BIBLIOGRAPHY

———. "Fioritura e decadenza dell'economia fiorentina," *Archivio Storico Italiano*, 116 (1958), 443–509.
———. "L'imposta diretta nei comuni medioevali della Toscana," *Studi in onore di Armando Sapori*, 1 (Milan, 1957), 329–39.
———. *Storia economica e sociale di San Gimignano.* Florence: 1961.
———. "Sui rapporti fra città e contado," *Archivio Storico Italiano*, 108 (1950), 18–68.
Flamini, F. *La lirica toscana del rinascimento.* Pisa: 1891.
Fusco, E. *La lirica.* Milan: 1950.
Galletti, A. *L'eloquenza (dalle origini al XVI secolo).* Milan: 1938.
Garavaggi, G. *Folgore da San Gimignano.* Milan: 1960.
Garin, E. *Italian Humanism, Philosophy and Civic Life in the Renaissance.* Translated by Peter Munz. Oxford: 1965.
———. *Dal medioevo al Rinascimento.* Florence: 1950.
———. *L'umanesimo italiano: Filosofia e vita civile nel rinascimento.* Bari: 1952.
———. "La giovinezza di Donato Acciaiuoli," *Rinascimento*, 1 (1950), 43–70.
———. "I cancellieri umanisti della repubblica fiorentina da Coluccio Salutati a Bartolomeo Scala," *Rivista Storica Italiana*, 71 (1959), 185–208.
———. *Der italienische Humanismus.* Bern: 1947.
———. *Filosofi italiani del Quattrocento.* Florence: 1942.
———. "Noterelle sulla filosofia del Rinascimento," *Rinascimento*, 2 (1951), 320–21.
Gasperetti, L. "Il 'De fato, fortuna et casu' di Coluccio Salutati," *La Rinascita*, 4 (1941), 355–82.
Gentile, M. "Le corporazione delle arti a Pisa nel secolo XV," *Annali della Scuola Normale*, 60 (1940), 197–200.
Getto, G. "La pesta del 'Decameron' e il problema della fonte lucreziana," *Giornale Storico della Letteratura Italiana*, 75 (1958), 507–23.
———. *Saggio letterario su S. Caterina da Siena.* Florence: 1939.
———. *Vita di forme di vita nel Decameron.* Turin: 1956.
Gilbert, F. *Machiavelli and Guicciardini: Politics and History in Sixteenth-Century Florence.* Princeton: 1965.
———. "Florentine Political Assumptions in the Period of Savonarola and Soderini," *Journal of the Warburg and Courtauld Institutes*, 20 (1957), 187–214.
Gombrich, E. "The Early Medici as Patrons of Art: A Survey of Primary Sources," *Italian Renaissance Studies.* Edited by E. Jacob (London, 1960). Pages 279–311.
Li Gotti, E. *Franco Sacchetti, uomo "discolo e grosso."* Florence: 1940.
———. "Storia e poesia del 'Pecorone'." *Belfagor*, 1 (1946), 103–10.
Gray, H. "Renaissance Humanism," *Journal of the History of Ideas*, 24 (1963), 497–514.
Grayson, C. "The Humanism of Alberti," *Italian Studies*, 12 (1957), 37–56.
Guasti, C. *La cupola di S. Maria del Fiore.* Florence: 1857.
———. *San Maria del Fiore, la construzione della chiesa.* Florence: 1887.
Guelluy, R. *Philosophie et théologie chez Guillaume di Ockham.* Paris: 1947.
Hankey, A. "Domenico di Bandino of Arezzo." *Italian Studies*, 12 (1957), 110–28.

BIBLIOGRAPHY

Hatfield, R. "Five Early Renaissance Portraits," *The Art Bulletin*, 47 (1965), 315–34.
Heers, J. *Gênes au XVe siècle. Activité économique et problèmes sociaux*. Paris: 1961.
Hegel, G. *Reason in History*. Translated by R. Hartman. Indianapolis: 1953.
Herde, Peter. "Politik und Rhetorik am Vorabend der Renaissance," *Archiv für Kulturgeschichte*, 47 (1965), 141–220.
Herlihy, D. "Direct and Indirect Taxation in Tuscan Urban Finance, ca. 1200–1400," in *Finances et comptabilité urbaines du XIIIe au XVIe siècle*, pp. 385–405.
———. *Pisa in the Early Renaissance*. New Haven: 1958.
———. *Medieval and Renaissance Pistoia*. New Haven: 1967.
Hyde, J. *Padua in the Age of Dante*. Manchester: 1966.
Janson, H. W. *The Sculpture of Donatello*. 2 vols. Princeton: 1957.
———. "The Image of Man in Renaissance Art: From Donatello to Michelangelo," *The Renaissance Image of Man and the World*. Columbus, Ohio: 1966. Pages 77–103.
Jones, P. J. "Communes and Despots: The City State in Late Medieval Italy," *Transactions of the Royal Historical Society*. Vol. 15 (1965).
———. "Per la storia agraria Italiana nel Medio Evo: lineamenti e problemi," *Rivista Storica Italiana*, 76 (1964), 287–348.
———. "Florentine Families and Florentine Diaries in the Fourteenth Century," *Papers of the British School at Rome*, 24 (1956), 183–205.
Karmin, O. *La legge del catasto fiorentino del 1427*. Florence: 1906.
Lane, F. "Family Partnerships and Joint Ventures in the Venetian Republic," *Journal of Economic History*, 4 (1944), 178–96.
Leff, G. *Gregory of Rimini*. Manchester: 1961.
Léonard, E. *Histoire de Jeanne Ire reine de Naples*. 3 vols. Paris: 1932–37.
Lisio, G. *La storiografia* in the series *Storia dei Generi Letterarii Italiani*. Milan: n.d.
Lopes Pegna, M. *L'origine di Firenze*. Poggibonsi: 1957.
Lopez, R., and Raymond, I. *Medieval Trade in the Mediterranean World*. New York: 1955.
Lukács, G. *Realism in Our Time*. New York: 1962.
Luzzatto, G. *Il debito della pubblico della Repubblica di Venezia*. Milan: 1963.
———. *An Economic History of Italy from the Fall of the Roman Empire until the Beginning of the Sixteenth Century*. Translated by P. J. Jones. New York: 1961.
Magri-Leone, F. "La Politica di Giovanni Boccaccio," *Giornale Storico della Letteratura Italiana*. Vol. 15 (1890).
Mariani, U. *Il Petrarca e gli Agostiniani*. Rome: 1946.
Marks, L. "La crisi finanzieria a Firenze dal 1494 al 1502," *Archivio Storico Italiano*, 112 (1954), 40–72.
———. "The Financial Oligarchy in Florence under Lorenzo," *Italian Renaissance Studies* (New York, 1960). Pages 123–45.
Martellotti, G. *Le redazioni delle Genealogie del Boccaccio*. Rome: 1951.

BIBLIOGRAPHY

Martines, L. "La famiglia Martelli e un documento," *Archivio Storico Italiano*, 117 (1959), 29–43.

―――. *The Social World of the Florentine Humanists, 1390–1460*. Princeton: 1963.

Marzi, D. *La cancelleria della repubblica fiorentina*. Rocca S. Casciano: 1910.

Masi, G. *Il sindacato delle magistrature comunali nel secolo XIV*. Rome: 1930.

McIlwain, Charles. *The Growth of Political Thought in the West*. New York: 1932.

Mehl, E. *Die Weltanschauung des Giovanni Villani*. Leipzig: 1927.

Meiss, M. *Painting in Florence and Siena after the Black Death*. Princeton: 1951.

Meller, P. "La Cappella Brancacci," *Acropoli: Riviste d'Arte*, 3 (1961), 186–227.

Minio-Paluello, L. "Remigio de' Girolami's De bonocommuni," *Italian Studies*, 11 (1956), 56–71.

Mommsen, T. "Petrarch and the Decoration of the Sala Virorum Illustrium in Padua," *Art Bulletin*, 34 (1952), 95–116.

―――. "Petrarch and the Story of the Choice of Hercules," *Journal of the Warburg and Courtauld Institutes*, 16 (1953), 178–92.

―――. "Petrarch's Conception of the Dark Ages," *Speculum*, 17 (1943), 226–49.

Monti, G. *Le confraternite medievali dell'Alta e Media Italia*. 2 vols. Venice: 1927.

Mousnier, R. *La renaissance en Italie au XVIe siècle*. Paris: n.d.

Musa, M. *The Poetry of Panuccio del Bagno*. Bloomington: 1965.

Novati, F. *La giovinezza di Coluccio Salutati*. Turin: 1898.

Nardi, B. *Studi di filosofia medievale*. Rome: 1950.

―――. *Saggi sull'aristotelismo padovano del secolo XIV al XVI*. Florence: 1958.

de' Negri, E. "The Legendary Style of the *Decameron*," *The Romanic Review*, 43 (1952), 166–89.

Oberman, H. A. *The Harvest of Medieval Theology*. Cambridge, Mass.: 1963.

―――. "Some Notes on the Theology of Nominalism with Attention to its Relation to the Renaissance," *Harvard Theological Review*, 53 (1960), 47–76.

Origo, I. *The Merchant of Prato*. New York: 1957.

Osgood, C. *Boccaccio on Poetry*. Princeton: 1930.

Ottokar, N. *Il Comune di Firenze alla fine del dugento*. Florence: 1926.

Padoan, Giorgio. "Sulla datazione del 'Corbaccio,'" *Lettere Italiane*, 15 (1963), 1–27.

―――. "Ancora sulla datazione e sul titolo del 'Corbaccio'," *Lettere Italiane*, 15 (1963), 199–201.

―――. *L'ultima opera di Giovanni Boccaccio*. Padua: 1959.

Palmarocchi, Roberto. *I Villani*. Turin: 1937.

Pampaloni, G. "Gli organi della repubblica fiorentina per le relazioni con l'estero," *Rivista di Studi Politici Internazionali*, 20 (1953), 261–91.

Panella, A. "Politica ecclesiastica del comune fiorentine," *Archivio Storico Italiano*, Vol. 2, Part IV (1913), 281–365.

―――. "Per la biografia del cronista Marchionne di Coppo Stefani," *Archivio Storico Italiano*, 88 (1930), 241–53.

―――. "La guerra degli Otto Santi e le vicende della legge contro i vescovi," *Archivio Storico Italiano*, 99 (1941), 36–49.

BIBLIOGRAPHY

Panofsky, E. *Idea*. Translated by E. Cione. Florence: 1952.

———. *Renaissance and Renascences in Western Art*. Upsala: 1960.

Paoli, C. *Della Signoria di Gualtieri Duca d'Atene*. Florence: 1862.

Partner, P. "Florence and the Papacy 1300–1375," *Europe in the Late Middle Ages*. Edited by J. Hale (London, 1965). Pages 76–121.

Pernicone, V. *Fra rime e novelle del Sacchetti*. Florence: 1942.

Perrens, F. *Histoire de Florence*. 4 vols. Paris: 1877–83.

Perrin, C. "L'histoire de l'église de 1378 à 1449," *Revue Historique*, 236 (1966), 317–46.

Pertile, A. *Storia del diritto italiano*, 2nd edition. 6 vols. Turin: 1892–98.

Peruzzi, S. *Storia del commercio e dei banchieri di Firenze*. Florence: 1868.

Piattoli, R. "Le leggi fiorentine sull'assicurazione nel medioevo," *Archivio Storico Italiano*, 90 (1932), 205–57.

Plesner, J. *L'émigration de la campagne à la ville libre de Florence au XIIIe siècle*. Copenhagen: 1934.

———. "Una rivoluzione stradale nel dugento," *Acta Jutlandica*. Vol. 10 (1938).

Pocock, J. " 'The Onely Politician': Machiavelli, Harrington and Felix Raab," *Historical Studies*, Vol. 12. Australia, New Zealand: 1966. Pages 265–99.

Pöhlmann, R. *Die Wirtschaftspolitik der florentiner Renaissance und das Prinzip der Verkehrsfreiheit*. Leipzig: 1878.

Pope-Hennessy, J. *Italian Renaissance Sculpture*. London and New York: 1958.

Post, G. *Studies in Medieval Legal Thought*. Princeton: 1964.

Rainaldi, L. "Di una fonte comune della 'Vita Civile' di Matteo Palmieri e del 'De educatione liberorum' di Maffeo Vegio," *Giornale Storico della Letteratura Italiana*, 130 (1953), 495–507.

Reeves, M. "Marsiglio of Padua and Dante Alighieri," *Trends in Medieval Political Thought*. Edited by B. Smalley. Oxford: 1965. Pages 86–104.

Renouard, Y. *Recherches sur les compagnies commerciales et bancaires utilisés par les papes d'Avignon avant le Grand Schisme*. Paris: 1942.

———. *Les relations des Papes d'Avignon et des compagnies commerciales et bancaires de 1316 à 1378*. Paris: 1941.

Ricci, P. "Studi sulle opere latine e volgari del Boccaccio," *Rinascimento*, 20 (1959), 3–32.

Ridolfi, R. *Vita di Francesco Guicciardini*. Rome: 1960.

Rodolico, N. *I Ciompi*. Florence: 1945.

———. *Il Popolo minuto (1343–1378)*. Bologna: 1899.

Roedel, R. "Poggio Bracciolini nel quinto centenario della morte," *Rinascimento*, 11 (1960), 51–67.

Roover, R. de. *The Rise and Decline of the Medici Bank 1397–1494*. Cambridge, Mass.: 1963.

Romano, G. "Niccolò Spinelli diplomatico del secolo XIV," *Archivio Storico per le Provincie Napoletane*, 26 (1901), 400–529.

Rossi, V. *Il Quattrocento*. Milan: 1933.

Rubinstein, N. "Some Ideas on Municipal Progress and Decline in the Italy of the Commune," in *Fritz Saxl 1890–1948* (London, 1957), 165–81.

———. "The Beginnings of Political Thought in Florence," *Journal of the Warburg and Courtauld Institutes*, 5 (1942), 198–225.

BIBLIOGRAPHY

──. "Il Poliziano e la questione delle origini di Firenze," in *Il Poliziano e il suo tempo*. Florence: 1957. Pages 101–10.

──. "Political Ideas in Sienese Art," *Journal of the Warburg and Courtauld Institutes*, 21 (1958), 179–207.

──. *The Government of Florence under the Medici (1434 to 1494)*. Oxford: 1966.

──. "Florence and the Despots: Some Aspects of Florentine Diplomacy in the Fourteenth Century," *Transactions of the Royal Historical Society*, 5th Series, 2 (1952), 21–45.

Russo, L. "La dissoluzione del mondo cavalleresco 'il Morgante' di Luigi Pulci," *Belfagor*, 7 (1952), 36–54.

──. *Machiavelli*. Rome: 1945.

──. "La poetica del Petrarca," *Belfagor*, 3 (1948), 541–68.

Salvini, R. "La Pala Strozzi in Santa Maria Novella," *L'arte*, 8 (1937), 37–41.

──. *L'arte di Agnolo Gaddi*. Florence: 1936.

Sapegno, N. *Il Trecento*. Milan: 1934.

Sapori, A. *Le crisi delle compagnie mercantili dei Bardi e dei Peruzzi*. Florence: 1926.

──. "Medioevo e Rinascimento, spunti per una diversa periodizzazione," *Archivio Storico Italiano*, 115 (1957), 135–64.

──. *Studi di storia economica (Secoli XIII–XIV–XV)*. 3rd ed. 2 vols. Florence: 1955.

──. *L'età della rinascità, secoli XIII–XVI*. Milan: 1958.

Schneider, F. *Die Entstehung von Burg und Landgemeinde in Italien*. Berlin: 1924.

Schneider, J. *La ville de Metz au XIIIe et XIVe siècles*. Nancy: 1950.

Seidlmayer, M. *Currents of Medieval Thought*. Translated by D. Barker. Oxford: 1960.

Sestan, E. "Il comune nel trecento," *Libera Cattedra di Storia della Civiltà Fiorentina: Il Trecento*. Florence: 1953.

Seymour, C. *Sculpture in Italy 1400 to 1500*. Baltimore: 1966.

Silva, P. "Intorno all'industria e al commercio della lana in Pisa," *Studi Storici*, 19 (1910), 329–400.

Smalley, B. *English Friars and Antiquity*. Oxford: 1960.

Soranzo, G. "Collegati, raccomandati aderenti negli stati italiani dei secoli XIV et XV," *Archivio Storico Italiano*, 119 (1941), 3–35.

Sorbelli, A. "I Teorici del Reggimento," *Bullettino dell'Istituto Storico Italiano*, 59 (1944), 30–136.

Stocchi, M. *Tradizione medievale e gusto umanistico nel "De montibus" del Boccaccio*. Padua: 1963.

Tenenti, A. *Il senso della morte e l'amore della vita nel rinascimento*. Turin: 1957.

Terracini, B. "L' 'aureo Trecento' e lo spirito della lingua italiana," *Giornale Storico della Letteratura Italiana*, 134 (1957), 1–36.

Theseider, E. "La duplice esperienza di S. Caterina da Siena," *Rivista Storica Italiana*, 62 (1950), 551–60.

BIBLIOGRAPHY

———. "L'attesa escatologiea durante il periodo avignonese," *L'attesa dell'età nuova nella spiritualitè della fine del medioevo*. Todi: 1962.

Tigri, G. *Canti popolari toscani*. Florence: 1869.

Tocco, F. "I Fraticelli," *Archivio Storico Italiano*, 35 (1905), 331–68.

Vasoli, C. "Le 'Dialectical Disputationes' del Valla e la critica umanistica della logica aristotelica," *Rivista Critica di Storia della Filosofia*, 12 (1957), 412–34.

Vignaux, P. *Nominalisme au XIVe siècle*. Paris: 1948.

Violante, C. *Il rinascimento significato e limiti* (Atti del III Convegno Internazionale sul Rinascimento). Florence: 1953.

Walser, E. *Poggio Florentinus Leben und Werke*. Berlin: 1914.

Weinstein, D. "Millenarianism in a Civic Setting: The Savonarola Movement in Florence," in *Millennial Dreams in Action: Comparative Studies in Society and History*. Edited by S. Thrupp. Supplement II. The Hague: 1962. Pages 187–203.

———. "Savonarola, Florence, and the Millenarian Tradition," *Church History*, 27 (1958), 3–17.

Welliver, W. *L'impero fiorentino*. Florence: 1957.

White, John. *Art and Architecture in Italy (1250–1400)*. Baltimore: 1966.

Whitfield, J. H. *Machiavelli*. Oxford: 1947.

Wilde, J. "The Hall of the Great Council of Florence," *Journal of the Warburg and Courtauld Institutes*, 7 (1944), 65–81.

Wilkins, E. *Studies in the Life and Works of Petrarch*. Cambridge, Mass.: 1955.

———. *Petrarch's Later Years*. Cambridge, Mass.: 1959.

Wittkower, R. *Architectural Principles in the Age of Humanism*. London: 1949.

Zaccagnini, G. "Jacopo da Montepulciano," *Giornale Storico della Letteratura*, 96 (1925), 225–88.

INDEX

Acciaiuoli (family), 31, 100, 156, 159, 173, 179
Accolti, Benedetto, 149
Adimari (family), 107, 125, 156
Agrarian policy, 113-14
Alberti (family), 89, 199; Benedetto, 133, 193, 194, 196, 197, 222; Caroccio, 127; Cipriano Duccio, 195; Jacopo, 176; Niccolò, 141, 171, 172
Alberti, Leon Battista, 4, 86, 90, 246, 247, 253
Albizzi faction, 68, 121, 122, 133-35, 136, 138, 139, 220
Albizzi (family), 60; Alessandro, 180-81; Franceschino, 53; Maso, 212-13, 219; Piero, 80-81, 82, 121, 131, 134
Alderotti, Francesco, 118; Matteo, 118
Aldobrandini, Luigi di Lippo, 135
Altoviti, Messer Tommaso, 170
Altoviti, Stoldo, 81
Amieri (family), 144
Amore, ideal of, 38, 54
Andrea da Firenze, 46
Andrea di Feo, 139
Aquinas, Saint Thomas, 9, 41, 62
Archival sources, list of, 23
Aretino, Leonardo Bruni: on the polis and culture, 17, 230; justification of wealth and emotions, 35, 230, 231, 245; evaluation of *novi cives*, 148-49; and primacy of the state, 159; on unity and leadership, 217; on education and the polis, 227, 228-29; and problem of the orator, 249; on "man the maker," 253; evaluation of Dante, 253-54
Arezzo, 244
Aristocracy. *See* Patriciate
Arrighi, Michele di Jacopo, 115
Arti maggiori, 113, 173-74. *See also* Guilds
Arti minori, 98-99, 136, 192. *See also* Guilds
Asini (family), 118

Auerbach, E., 40
Augustine, Saint, 9
Augustinians of S. Spirito, 76, 77
Avignon. *See* Papacy

Balìe, 100, 220
Bandini, Domenico, 17
Baptistry, 85
Barberino, Francesco da, 38
Barberino, Ser Albizo di Messer Filippo da, 118
Bardi (family), 31, 70, 100, 107, 111, 126, 144, 156, 159, 173, 179; Messer Bindo de', 180; Tommaso de', 58-59
Bargellini, 182
Baron, H., 17, 27
Baroncelli Chapel, 40
Bartolini, Bernardino Cini, 126
Bartolus, 62, 65
Bastari, Filippo di Cionetto, 123, 127, 133
Bastichi (family), 125
Becchi (family), 209
Bella, Giano della, 67, 130-31
Bello, Giovanni Geri del, 140, 141
Benini, Francesco, 125
Benini, Bindo, 118
Benvenuto da Imola, 54
Bertini, Simone, 118
Bianchi, 224-25
Bibbiena, 187
Bigliotti, Barnardo, 141
Black Death, 25-26, 167-68
Blackmur, R., 13-14, 22
Boccaccio, Giovanni: conception of poetry, 8-10; on chivalric and burgher cultures, 37-38, 40; on failure of medieval schema, 43, 44-45, 52-54; on primacy of the polis, 48; comments on Dante, 65; the polis and crisis, 74-77, 78; and evaluation of *novi cives*, 111-112; and evaluation of law, 227; and Bruni's comments, 253-54; works by: *Decameron*, 12, 36-38,

INDEX

40, 52, 53, 74; *Corbaccio*, 44, 53; *Filocolo*, 52; *De claris mulieribus*, 52; *De casibus virorum illustrium*, 52, 76; *Trattatello in laude di Dante*, 54, 75–76; *Genealogia*, 75; *Consolatorio*, 84
Bonaiuto, Francesco, 116, 124
Bonsi, Bianco di, 116–17
Bonsi, Ugolino di, 118
Bonus cives. See Political independents
Book of the Popes, 56
Bracciolini, Poggio, 35, 91, 148–49, 230, 231–32, 245
Branca, V., 37
Brancacci Chapel, 13, 87
Brunelleschi (family), 102
Brunelleschi, Filippo, 22, 85, 164, 232, 246, 247
Buondelmonti (family), 105, 126, 209
Buono, Niccolò di Bartolo del, 118
Burckhardt, J., 4–6, 25, 68–69, 252–53
Bureaucracy: numerical expansion of, 29, 31–32, 65, 213–16; and relationship to law, 34; and protection of the individual, 66; and rise of the state, 68 ff, 219, 225–26; and place of the *novi cives*, 100; and notaries and Ghibellines, 142–44; in the *contado*, 182–83; and praise of Salutati, 226–27

Caggese, R., 96, 181
Camera, 69, 71 ff, 159 ff, 173, 179–80, 189–90, 233
Camposanto, 39
Canigiani, Ristoro di Piero, 81, 82
Capital investment, 162–63
Capitalism, state. See State capitalism
Capitano del Custodia, 182–83
Caponsacchi (family), 101
Capsa conducte, 165, 168
Carità, 38, 47, 54, 226
Carletti, Puccio, 125
Casini, Frozzo, 117
Cassirer, E., 16
Castagno, 247
Castellani (family), 199
Castiglionchio (family), 144, 145, 146; Alberto da, 145; Lapo da, 121, 136–37, 144–46, 190, 203; Simone di Francesco da, 148
Catasto of 1427, 70, 71, 234, 235, 242, 244–45
Catherine of Siena, 45, 56, 59, 81–82
Cavalcanti (family), 100, 107, 111, 144; Giovanni, 72, 237–38; Guido, 53, 65
Cerchi (family), 31, 144
Chabod, F., 6
Chancellery of Florence, 212
Chivalry, 36–38
Church. See Papacy; Tuscan church

Ciari, Giovanni di, 117
Ciompi revolution, 191–92, 221–22
Circuli (family), 108
Civic humanism. See Humanism, civic
Civitas Florentiae. See State, territorial
Clement VII, 222–23
Cocchi, Augustino, 124, 125
Commission of Eight, 156
Communal debt. See *Monte*; Public debt
Communal theology, 55
Commune. See State, territorial
Compagni, Dino, 65, 149
Confraternities, religious, 32, 206–7
Consolatorio. See Boccaccio, Giovanni
Consorteria, 32, 89, 209
Consulte e Pratiche, 29, 70
Contado, 72–74, 95–96, 99, 127, 181–88, 189, 195, 209, 214–15
Contemplative life, 86
Coreggio, Donato, 59
Cortona, 244
Council of a Hundred and Ten, 221
Council of Eighty-one, 199
Councils, advisory, 68, 218
Court Merchant, 30, 98, 210–11
Court of the Grascia, 183
Curiani, Barna di Valorino, 141
Curiani (family), 197
Cursus honorum, 67, 98
Custom tolls. See Gabelle; Taxation

Daddi, Bernardo, 40
Dante Alighieri: and Thomism, 7; on social function of knowledge, 10–11; autobiography, 12; and medieval historiography, 35, 43, 58, 201; Aristotelianism, 62–63; the commune and exile, 65, 149; evaluation of new citizens, 111; mentioned, 34, 41, 51, 53, 72, 84; works by: *Convivio*, 10; *Vita Nuova*, 12; *Divine Comedy*, 43, 63, 84; *Monarchia*, 51, 63
Dante, Domenico, 123–24
Dati, Gregorio, 20–21, 229, 234–35, 237
Datini, Francesco, 6, 25, 224
Davidsohn, R., 96
Debt. See Public debt; *Monte*
Defender of the *Contado*, 182
Della Tosa (family), 101, 102, 105, 125, 126, 209
Delli, Niccolò, 115, 122
Deschamps, E., 6
Dieci della Libertà, 127
Dini, Giovanni, 118–19, 124, 139, 197
Dini, Tellino, 121
Divieto, 95, 137–39, 140, 217
Dolce stil nuovo ("Sweet New Style"), 38, 53
Dominici, Fra Giovanni, 62, 205–6, 223–24
Domenico da Certaldo, 170

INDEX

Donatello, 84, 85, 88, 164, 246–47, 248–49
Donati (family), 107, 111, 125, 209; Andrea, 122; Corso, 66–67
Duby, G., 90
Duns Scotus, 9

Economy, Florentine, 25–28, 162–64, 165
Education, 4, 229 ff
Eight Saints, 139
Elite, 219–20
Estimo: in the *contado*, 184–85, 186–87, 189, 241; implementation of, 193–94; conversion to *prestanze*, 194; mentioned, 169, 171–72, 176, 180, 191
Executor of the Ordinances of Justice, 183

Fabrini, Francesco, 122
Falconieri (family), 108
Fame, 17, 35–36, 230
Family partnerships. *See Fraterna*
Febvre, Lucien, 3, 248
Fei, Andrea, 126
Fei, Luca, 172
Ferreti, Ferreto de', 201
Ficino, 91
Fidati, Fra Simone, 39
Fideicommissum, 90
Fideism, 78
Fiorentino, Ser Giovanni, 39
Foraboschi (family), 108
Forced loans. *See Prestanze*
Foreign policy, 33, 119–22, 203–4
Forese, Stefano del, 140
Francesca, Piero della, 247
Francis of Assisi, Saint, 11–12
Fraterna, 90
Fraticelli, 30, 56, 57
Frescobaldi (family), 100, 107, 111, 159, 173; Messer Berto, 170, 171

Gabelles: as indicator of communal well-being, 25–26, 165–68, 168–70, 238–40; inadequacy of, 153–56, 226; and the public debt, 157–58; magistrates' discussion of, 170–73; *prestanze* and the *Monte*, 173–74, 175, 191–200, 240–43; in the *contado*, 184, 185–86, 189. *See also* Taxation
Gaddi, Agnolo, 13
Gaddi, Taddeo, 40
Garin, E., 16, 27
Genoa, 88
Geri, Francesco di, 139
Gherardi, Ser Jacobo, 125
Gherardini (family), 100, 125, 179, 195
Ghibellinism, 128 ff, 138, 145
Ghiberti, 85, 87, 164
Ghirlandaio, 253
Giandonati (family), 125

Giani, Giovanni, 170
Gianni, Gherardino di Niccolò Gherardino, 58–59, 60
Gilbert, F., 5
Giotto, 13, 39–40, 41, 42, 66
Giovanni da Milano, 42
Giovanni dalle Celle, 40, 55–56, 59, 61, 82–83, 205–6
Giovanni del Biondo, 42, 46
Goggio, Giovanni, 121
Grandi: effect of law on, 37–38; treatment of, by polis, 89, 106–11, 124–26, 208–10; power of, in early commune, 100–106; taxation of, 165
Guazza, Recco di Guido, 122–23, 125, 126, 139, 180, 197–98
Gucci, Giorgio di Guccio, 59
Gucci, Guccio di Dino, 139
Guccio, Ser Piero, 125
Guelf confederation, 119–22, 202, 207–8
Guelf Party: state's control of, 30, 135–37, 139, 207–8; evaluation of, by historians, 34; and attack on individuals, 65; conservatism of, 81; and scrutiny of new citizens, 97; as preserve of patricians, 98, 103; relationship with popular party and new citizens, 100, 128–34, 139–49; exclusiveness of, 112; and Guelf Confederation, 119–22; criticism of, by Salutati, 127–28; and Albizzi faction, 134–35; use of Ghibellinism, 138–39, 142–46; attack on bureaucrats, 142–44
Guicciardini, Francesco, 86, 221
Guicciardini, Piero, 178
Guidi, Counts, 30, 96, 127, 208
Guido del Palagio, 36, 55, 56, 59, 61, 67
Guidolotti (family), 108
Guilds: and public debt and law, 28; decline of autonomy of, 30; formation of painters' guild, 84; function of, in communal politics, 97–98; and *novi cives*, 112–13; political power and finances of, 161; effect of the state on, 210–11
Guittone d'Arezzo, 53

Hearth tax. *See Sega*
Hegel, F., 4, 7
History, medieval view of, 51–52, 249–50, 254
Holy Roman Emperor, 33
Huizinga, J., 3, 247–48
Humanism, civic: and law and virtue, 21; advent of, 25 ff; *Monte* creates audience for, 159; and formation of territorial state, 225–33, 245–50; and the ego and the public world, 253–55.

Identity, in medieval period, 87–92
Il popolo, 155–56

INDEX

Il popolo minuto, 83, 113, 222, 251–52
Immigration, 93–94, 96
Individualism, 252–55
Inquisitor, 57

James, H., 3, 6
Joachim of Flora, 11–12
Jones, P. J., 89

Knighthood, 36, 101–6, 119

Lanfredini, Giovanni, 140
Lapi, Silvestro, 172
Lapozzi, Niccolò, 139
Latini, Brunetto, 34, 65, 149
Law: as factor in rise of the state, 2–3, 68 ff; as basis of virtue, 21–22; and public finance, 28; support of *novi cives*, 30; and the bureaucracy, 34; and relationship to *libertas*, 60–61; extension of scope of, 66; and democratization, 67–68; and control of privileged class, 106; acceptance of, by late *trecento* elite, 219–22; humanists' affirmation of, 226–27
Lenzi (family), 85
Libertas, 60–61, 136, 202–4, 226
Livorno, 244
Loggia dei Lanzi, 205
Loschi, Antonio, 18, 19

Machiavelli, Filippo, 172
Machiavelli, Niccolò: on justice and order, 4; on separation of politics and conscience, 21–22, 91; and evaluation of law, 34, 37; on civic commitment, 86; on value of militia, 106; appraisal of *novi cives*, 119, 148–49; on primacy of the state, 159; and evaluation of bureaucrats, 219; on the polis and education, 228–29; on human emotions, 231; on conscience as determinant of perspective, 249–50
McIlwain, C., 64
Magalotti, Giovanni, 127, 135
Malaspina, Saba, 52
Manetti, Giannozzo, 6
Marsiglio of Padua, 55, 63–64
Marsili, Luigi, 15, 17, 55–56, 58, 59, 82, 205–6
Martino da Signa, 77
Marzuppini, Carlo, 149
Masaccio, 13, 85, 87, 88, 164
Maso di Nero, 139
Mazzei, Ser Lapo, 59, 224
Medici (family), 89, 199; Cosimo de', 31, 67, 68, 72, 203, 218; Lorenzo de', 218; Salvestro de', 78–79, 127, 133, 135, 141, 146–47, 177, 178, 196, 197
Mercantilism, 211–16

Mercanzia. See Merchants, High Court of the
Mercenaries, 105–6
Merchants, 34–35
Merchants, High Court of the, 136
Mezze, Jacobo, 125
Michele di Puccio, 143
Michele di Vanni di Ser Lotto, 134
Milan, 33, 120–21, 173
Modici cives, 132–33
Monachi, Niccolò di Ser Ventura, 143–44, 149
Monachi, Ser Ventura, 38, 53
Monte: and changes in Florentine economy, 28; expansion of, 69–70; founding and development of, 151–58, 164–70; and rise of territorial state, 158–64, 217–25, 234–45; magistrates' discussion of, 170–73, 191–97; and loans and taxation, 173–76, 176–81; and *contado* taxation, 181–88; and warfare, 188–91; and the Ciompi, 191; second consolidation of, 197–98. See also Public debt
Monte delle Doti, 71–72, 152, 236–37
Morelli, Giovanni di Pagolo, 227
Mozzi, Giovanni di Luigi, 135
Mussato, Albertino, 201

Nanni di Banco, 85
Naples, Kingdom of, 33, 119 ff, 202
Nardi, B., 16, 42
Nerio, 122
Nerli (family), 107
Niccoli, Antonio, 126
Niccolini, Andrea, 124
Nigio, Ser Giovanni Ser, 126
Nominalism, 7, 9
Notaries, 142–44
Novi cives: definition of, 28–29, 95; and support of law, 31, 69; evaluation of, by historians, 33, 35–36, 111–12, 127–28, 148; and role in democratization, 93 ff; and political power, 96–100, 113, 131–34, 135–38, 204, 217, 225–26; political and social background of, 98–99; economic policy of, 112–13, 114–15; leadership of, 115–19; foreign policy role of, 120–22, 134–35, 138–39; and relationship with conservative institutions, 122–27, 128–34, 139–48, 149–56, 159–65; and the *Monte*, 161–62, 173, 194–95; and the state, 247

Oratory. See Rhetoric
Orcagna, 39, 40, 42
Ordinances of Justice, 98, 101, 102, 103, 106, 107, 108, 109, 110, 125
Ottantuno, 220–21
Otto della Guardia, 195, 221

INDEX

Paideia, gentle: recession of, 11–13, 37; failure of, 100 ff; final defeat of, 106–11, 227–28; and personal qualities, 159–60; and conception of *libertas*, 203–5; persistent qualities of, 251–55

Paideia, stern: and the state and culture, 3; and affirmation of Sacchetti, 14–15; contemporaries' awareness of, 34. *See also* State, territorial

Painting: and relationship to civic consciousness, 3–6, 20, 21–22, 247; mid-trecento crisis in, 13, 39 ff, 46

Palazzo Vecchio, 88

Palmieri, Matteo, 228–29

Panciatichi (family), 199

Panuccio del Bagno, 53

Papacy, 55, 58 ff, 119 ff, 134–35, 202, 207

Parenti, Giovanni, 143

Parte Guelfa. *See* Guelf Party

Parte popolare, 131–49

Passavanti, Iacopo, 49

Patriciate: and stern government, 28–29, 132–38; and relationship with *novi cives*, 93 ff, 113–15, 122–28; and political power, 97–100, 135–38, 219; and fusion of social classes, 101; role of, in trecento crisis, 107–11; evaluation of, by writers, 127–28; and attack upon popular party, 138–42; and the *Monte*, 155–58; and casual government, 159–60; confidence in, 163–64; and the historian, 251

Paul the Deacon, 52

Pazzi (family), 96, 107, 111, 126, 209

Peruzzi (family), 31, 100, 144, 159, 173, 233; Simone di Rinieri, 170, 180

Petrarch, Francesco: and concept of the poet, 7–11; and secular models of virtue, 15; on human experience, 36, 231; on inadequacy of stoicism, 40–41; and empirical psychology, 41; and cultivation of feeling, 42–43; and attack on medieval philosophy, 49–52; and relations with Marsili, 55; and advice to Boccaccio, 74, 76–77; evaluation of *novi cives*, 148; on "man the maker," 253; work by: *Secretum*, 9, 41, 50–51; *De viris illustribus*, 50; *Vita Scipionis*, 50

Pisa, 243–44

Pisan War, 160, 176, 178

Pistoia, 187

Pitti, Buonaccorso, 61

Pizzini, Guido, 124

Plague. *See* Black Death

Polis. *See* State, territorial

Political independents, 65, 140, 147

Political moderates. *See* Political independents

Political theory, 18–22, 62–64

Popolani grassi, 101, 108–11

Popular party. *See Parte popolare*

Prato, 244

Prestanze: proliferation of, 69–70, 155, 179, 199; administration of, 172–73; and the *Monte*, 173–76, 176–78, 179–81, 234–35, 244–45; and War of the Eight Saints, 189–90; use of, by popular government, 191–93, 198; and conversion of *estimo*, 194. *See also Monte*; Taxation

Ptolemy of Lucca, 62

Public debt: factor in rise of the state, 22–23, 25, 28, 30 ff, 68 ff, 233 ff, 247–48. *See also Monte*

Pucci, Antonio, 44, 45–46, 57–58, 200, 202

Puccio, Jacopo Banco, 176

Pulci (family), 108

Regulatores, 183 ff, 214

Renaissance state. *See* State, territorial

Renovatio, 11–12, 83, 202–3

Rhetoric, 232–33, 249–50

Ricasoli (family), 102, 105, 144, 145, 146, 195, 209

Ricci (family), 60, 131–35, 136, 138, 139; Rosso, 197; Uguccione de', 75, 131–32, 133, 170–71, 172, 197; Uguccione Ricciardi, 194

Rinuccini (family), 199

Rinuccini, Cino, 18–20

Robert of Naples, 120

Roover, R. de, 89

Rossi (family), 100, 107, 125, 126; Pino de', 75

Rubinstein, N., 5

Rucellai (family), 108

Sacchetti, Franco: civic qualities of, 14–15; as witness for stern paideia, 38; and failure of medieval schema, 44; and coercive moralism, 45; and interiorized religious feeling, 46; and man's earthly role, 47, 53; on primacy of polis, 48, 202–5; attack on Aristotelianism, 49–50; on Florentine liberty, 57, 58; and democratization, 66; and crisis and polis, 77–80; evaluation of *novi cives*, 112; and dignity of the public world, 224; Renaissance qualities of, 232; and *Trecentonovelle*, 14

Sacchetti, Giannozzo, 80–81, 82

Sacraments, 46

Salutati, Coluccio: conception of poetry, 9–10; and dignity of the historical world, 15, 47, 53; on value of polis and Petrarch, 15–17; defense of merchants and tradesmen, 34–35; medieval concepts of, 38–40; and empirical psychology, 41; on interiorized religious feelings, 46; on primacy of polis, 48,

INDEX

59; on Florentine liberty, 57 ff; and emphasis on will, 80; evaluation of *novi cives*, 127–28, 148; praise of law and bureaucracy, 226–28; evaluation of emotions, 231; on "man the maker," 253; works by: *De saeculo et religione*, 14; *De nobilitate legum et medicinae*, 16; *Invectiva*, 17; *De laboribus Herculis*, 231

Salvemini, G., 181
Salvi, Filippo, 199
Salviati, Andrea Francesco, 127
San Bernardino, 62
San Gimignano, 187
San Miniato, 13, 72–73, 188
San Spirito, 55
Santa Croce, 39, 205
Santa Maria Novella, 85
Sapori, A., 5–6, 25, 27, 89
Sarzana: non-aggression treaty of, 33
Scali (family), 31; Giorgio, 133
Scholasticism, 49–50
Schiatta di Ricco, 122
Scolari (family), 195
Sega, 171
Sennuccio del Bene, 53
Sercambi, Giovanni, 38–39
Serragli (family), 145, 146; Bonaiuto de', 134
Siminetti, Bartolo di Giovanni, 134
Simone di Biagio, 115–16, 195, 196–97, 222
Social mobility, 22, 25, 225–26. See also *Novi cives*
Sodorini, Niccolò, 80–81, 82
Sovereignty, 60
Spanish Chapel, 41–42, 44, 46
Spini (family), 108
State capitalism, 28, 175–76
State, territorial: formation of values in, 3–6, 201–7, 216–25; evaluation of, by writers, 7–11, 48, 62, 228–33, 245–46; late medieval mistrust of, 11–13; linking of conceptions of order in, 13 ff, 21–22; public identity in, 22, 32, 248–49, 252–55; extension of authority of, 28, 207–16; civic humanism and rise of, 28 ff; and function of *novi cives*, 93 ff; fiscal policy and taxation in, 154–55, 158–64, 233–45; debt and fiscal responsibility of, 164–81; and *contado* taxation, 181–88; and formation of bureaucracy, 219; and protection of bureaucracy, 225–26; and humanists and law, 226–27; and transition from medieval commune, 227–33, 251–55
Stato, lo. See State, territorial
Stefani, Marchionne di Coppo: and acceptance of the world of the polis, 14, 48; critique of medieval institutions, 34, 44; evaluation of mid-*trecento* crisis, 110–11; evaluation of *novi cives*, 121–22, 123, 136; and the polis and patriciate, 127; evaluation of Ricci family, 134; and *novi cives* and Guelf Party, 141; and the public debt, 152–53, 195–96, 197
Strada, Zanobi da, 38
Strozzi (family), 70, 89, 137, 233; Carlo, 80–81, 121, 131, 134, 178; Tommaso di Marco, 133, 222
Studia humanitatis, 16, 77
Studio, 214
Subject cities, 187–88, 243–44
Sumptuary laws, 49
Superbia, 232
"Sweet New Style." See *Dolce stil nuova*

Talenti, F., 205
Taldi, Ricco, 121
Taxation: and mid-*trecento* economic vigor, 25–26; weightier burden of, 73–74; and citizen ambiguity, 86–87, 109; magistrates' discussion of, 170–73, 176–78, 188–200, 217–19; in the *contado*, 181–88, 195, 209, 240–43; and territorial state, 233 ff. See also Gabelles; *Estimo*; *Catasto* of 1427; *Prestanze*
Terii, Andrea, 122
Territorial state. See State, territorial
Tommaso di Mone, 139
Tournaments, 37–38, 104
Traini, Francesco, 39
Tuscan church: state's control of, 30, 64; hostility of *novi cives* toward, 122–23; taxation of, 169; loss of liberties and land of, 190, 206–7. See also Papacy

Ubaldini (family), 30, 96, 127, 168, 180, 195, 208
Uberti (family), 195; Fazio degli, 62
Urban VI, 222–23
Usury, 48
Uzzano, Niccolò da, 67, 84

Valdinievole, 187
Velluti, Donato: and consensus of *novi cives* and the patriciate, 114; criticism of Guelf Party and the Albizzi faction, 121–22; and Ghibellines and *novi cives*, 138; and conflict of *novi cives* and Guelf Party, 140, 141; and the *Monte*, 169; experience of the vendetta, 227
Vendetta, 207–8, 227
Veneziano, Domenico, 247
Venice, 88
Vespasiano da Bisticci, 218–19
Vigorosi, Francesco, 127
Villani, Filippo, 17, 227
Villani, Giovanni: evaluation of the

INDEX

public world, 12–13; and the Florentine economy, 26, 151; ambivalence toward law, 34; and medieval historiography, 43, vulnerability of, 65, comments on magnates, 102–3; and the mid-*trecento* crisis, 110; evaluation of *novi cives*, 111–12, 128–29; evaluation of Guelf Party, 128–29; criticism of bureaucrats, 218; criticism of *balie*, 220; and the medieval commune, 228

Villani, Matteo: on the polis and freedom, 14; evaluation of the polis and politics, 33 ff, 48, 64; evaluation of the emperor, 44; vulnerability of, 64–65; evaluation of *novi cives*, 111–12, 121–22; and the *divieto*, 137; evaluation of Guelf Party, 140; proscription of, 141, 143; and the public debt, 152, 169, 173–74, 174–75

Violante, C., 5–6

Visconti, 33, 160–61
Visdomini (family), 125
Volgare, 17–21
Volterra, 244

Walter of Brienne, 60, 65, 107–8, 119–20, 165, 166, 182
War chest. *See Capsa conducte*
War of the Eight Saints, 56, 71, 78–79, 160, 188 ff
Warfare: and crisis of magnates, 104–5; and the public debt, 156, 160–61, 165, 168, 235–36; Pisan War, 176, 178; War of the Eight Saints, 188–91; and Florentine unity, 223
Weber, M., 83
William of Ockham, 9
Wind, E., 4

Designed by Gerard A. Valerio
Composed in Baskerville by Monotype Composition Company.

www.ingramcontent.com/pod-product-compliance
Lightning Source LLC
Chambersburg PA
CBHW021120300426
44113CB00006B/223